THE TC AND TC MUSIC GUIDE

Cover Design; Baker Tamborini Creative Services
Book Design; Dave Crook

FANTAIL PUBLISHING
an imprint of Puffin Enterprises.

Published by the Penguin Group,
27 Wrights Lane,
London W8 5TZ,
England.
First published by T & C Publications Ltd., 1988.
Revised and updated edition published by Fantail, 1989.
Copyright © 1988 T & C Publications Ltd.

ACKNOWLEDGEMENTS

We would like to thank everyone who helped us to compile, write and illustrate this guide. Many people have given us their time, advice and encouragement. It would have been a far more difficult task without them, and a lesser book at the end of the day.

Particular thanks to Simon Long, our legal adviser, for his invaluable help and patience.
  The Simkins Partnership, 45–51 Whitfield Street, London W1P 5RJ.

A special thank you also to: Julian Able, Geoff Allen, Nick Angel, Mick Anthony, Keith Armstrong, Sharon Ashley, Nick Bigsby, Denis Campbell, Mark Chapman, Valerie Clark, Jona Cox, Brendan Croker, Mike Farmer, Martin Goebbels, Boss Goodman, Perry Haines, Martin Hammett, Dave Henderson, Paul Hutton, Phil Jones, Willie Kavanagh, Helene Kvale, Sarah Landeg, Judd Lander, Pete Lawrence, Steve Lazarus, John Lennard, John Leonard, Mark Little, Trevor Long, Les Malloy, Krista May Phelan, Wendy May, Mark Melton, George (Porky) Peckham, Andy Proudfoot, Guy Rippon, Alan Robinson, Nikki Rogerson, Nick Rowe, Terry Staunton, Ian Surrey, Dominic Walker and Paul Wilson.

See also: 'Copyright' – for PRS, MCPS, PPL and VPL.

See also: Publishing Contract – for PRS and MCPS royalty payments.

Nearly all professionals in the music business receive frequent unsolicited calls from inexperienced bands needing help and advice. Unfortunately, this help is rarely given to them and very often the caller has either been pointed in the wrong direction by someone else or is simply unclear as to the real role of the person they have contacted.

The Town & Country Club Office receives its fair share of such calls and, when we are not too busy, we try to be as constructive and as helpful as possible. Time, however, is not always on our side, so to provide some answers to the most commonly asked questions we started to put together a page or two of basic information which we could send out to the people who telephone us.

Once we started to do this we found that no matter what subject we wrote on, there was always more useful detail which we could include. The project began to mushroom and quite soon we made a decision to do the job properly and write this guide. The directory followed as a logical development. We hope that you will find it a useful tool of the trade – as opposed to the sort of reference work that you read once and leave on the shelf at home.

The book aims to provide concise and straightforward advice about the important areas of the business. We believe we are unique in trying to present recording, publishing and management contracts in an understandable form and we hope these provide a framework for your preliminary meetings with your lawyer. Technical detail, on the other hand, is not our forte, and where we know our limitations we bow down to superior sources of information. During our research we read almost all the available publications on every aspect of the music industry and whilst many were disappointing, we have happily listed those that we think do a better job than we do in certain areas. For instance, on copyright, studios and backline.

Some of the sections, nonetheless, are a bit stodgy and heavy going and this is unavoidable where the complex nature of the subject matter has these characteristics. Unfortunately, these particular sections are quite often the most important financially, and many are to do with your rights in law. We have tried to make these legal details as palatable as possible. Please don't take our advice as the last word on anything, because it is intended only as a guideline and introduction. Again and again we stress – get legal advice before you sign anything!

The 'motor cycle maintenance' style of our prose was a conscious decision to avoid seeming condescending and to enable us to put down some quite difficult concepts in a straightforward manner. This may make the guide itself seem a bit humourless, but the idea

is that playing music professionally is more enjoyable and less traumatic when you fully understand the business and have taken proper precautions against the pitfalls and dangers that will inevitably come your way. If you are playing music as a full-time job then a little knowledge is a highly desirable thing, especially given the vagaries of the music business.

The whole guide is noticeably weighted towards live music, and bands that will go on to have long term careers based upon their live performances. This is not surprising when you consider that our livelihood at the T&C depends upon live bands and this gives us a vested interest in encouraging their development! However, there are some sound reasons for perfecting your live ability, not least of them being the historical one that the biggest acts in the world with the longest careers, have always been those that have paid their dues on the live circuit, Springsteen, U2, Dire Straits, Tina Turner, Stevie Wonder and Michael Jackson have two qualities in common – they can cut it live, and have spent years perfecting their craft. Whilst we are not particular fans of stadium rock, the point that we are making is that live performance is what has been, and always will be, exciting about contemporary music and the better you are live, the bigger impression you'll make. By understanding who does what, where and when in the music business, and rehearsing and playing live at every opportunity, you stand the best chance of succeeding while getting the maximum enjoyment out of being a musician at the same time.

All being well, there will be a further edition of this guide, so please let us know if we have made any glaring errors or missed out any information that you might have found useful.

In the meantime, we look forward to seeing you headlining at the Town and Country Club soon, but don't call us – we'll call you!

Gook Luck.

OLLIE SMITH AND ANNA JENKINS.

Any live practice in front of a real audience is valuable – not only in helping you to perfect your stage presentation and persona – but also in trying out your material on new ears. A live performance will also test you in technical and practical ways. Guitar strings breaking in the middle of a song, hecklers, losing a drumstick and your amp blowing up are just a few of the myriad things which can, and do, happen in a live situation. Too many young bands fail to go through this learning process and seem to expect to be headlining large live events after one good show at the local disco. The most successful live and recording artists in rock history have been, and always will be, those who have learned their craft on the stage.

WHERE TO PLAY

Arts centres, community centres, village halls, wine bars, pubs and clubs are all potential 'venues' – although it does, of course, depend on how many people there are in the band, how much equipment you have and the kind of power supply you require. Also, if a pub does not have a music licence they will generally only allow soloists or a duo to play live.

A lot of bands seem to think that they are going to have to play the small London venues in order to make anything happen for them. In the majority of cases this simply is not true. Although nearly all the major record companies in the UK are based in London, you shouldn't really need to spend a fortune gigging in the capital in order to attract A&R interest. The A&R network in this country is well developed and if a band is creating a 'buzz' someone will be despatched from London to check them out. Another point to consider is that your most impressive gigs are probably those on your own home ground with a packed venue full of enthusiastic friends and fans. It can be very difficult to get a similar feel out of a sparse audience of strangers in unfamiliar surroundings, even if you are good.

CONTACTING BOOKERS AT PUB AND CLUB LEVEL

At pubs and small clubs you will most likely be dealing with the landlord or licensee. If the club or pub puts on a lot of live shows they may employ a resident promoter (for a more detailed description of the promoter's job see page 33). In either case a few simple questions should help you make sure you are talking to the right person. There is a skill to making telephone calls, and if you are a bit nervous it is best to be prepared. You are likely to be asked the following questions: 'What kind of music do you play?', 'Where have you played before?', 'How many people are you

worth?' – and it is a good idea to have some positive, confident answers ready.

Bookers will want to hear your sound, see some pictures, and ideally see you play live before they commit themselves to a booking. Your usual promotional package including your best demos, photographs and information on your band can be used – but bear in mind that you are trying to impress someone who is interested primarily in your ability to play live. To this end include as many live reviews or references as possible and, if you have one, send a live video showing the band in action. Most bookers will have access to a video machine and many clubs and even pubs have video screens installed but you may as well check before you send a video to them. The standard of the video quality is not crucial because all the booker wants to see is what your live act is like, so don't pay a fortune for a work of art. Enclose a stamped, addressed envelope if you want your video or cassette returned to you.

As with every other type of approach you make, follow up your promotional package several days later with a phone call. If you manage to get another gig nearby you could take the opportunity to invite the booker along to take a look at you. Put the booker plus a friend on your guest list and if they make the effort to come make them welcome with a drink or two when they arrive. Bookers have very few free evenings, so if one turns up at your gig it could be a sign that they have heard good things about you. Keep strictly to your stage times and don't hassle for a 'verdict' on the spot.

If you don't have any luck at first – be persistent. Bookers, like everyone else are more likely to pay attention to a recommendation from a friend or other respected source – so the more you do, the more chance there is of someone in this position getting to hear about you; re-contact the booker with news of any fresh developments or recent good shows – you never know when a last minute cancellation may make a space for you.

SUPPORT SLOTS

Inevitably you will have to accept poorly-paid support or opening slots at the beginning. You may have to play your set before the bulk of the audience has arrived and depending on the headlining act, you may get a mixed reception from their supporters, especially if your music is very different.

In the UK, possibly more than any other country in the world, support acts are given a very rough ride. They are rarely paid more than a nominal £50.00 fee, even at concert hall level, and they are frequently paid less. They are given minimal and sometimes non-existent hospitality in terms of food and drink, and are often expected to use the shabbiest dressing room available, if they get a dressing room at all. Soundchecks may be perfunctory and occasionally they will have to do without one. Combine all this with the general attitude of disdain with which support acts are generally treated – and you may have some idea of what you will have to put up with when you first start out!

SHOWCASE NIGHTS AND HOW YOU MAY BE PAID

Some venues have regular 'showcase nights' which are put together from recommendations and from the demos that venue bookers or promoters receive. For example, five acts might be chosen to each play a 20 minute set on a Sunday night. The deal under these circumstances may well be one where your band is paid nothing unless you attract a certain number of customers. You might be given 200 tickets for the show and be expected to earn your fee by selling them to your friends and supporters for, say, 50p or £1 each. A variation on this theme is a voucher system where all your customers pay a reduced entrance fee on the night by handing in a marked ticket which distinguishes them from all the other punters. At the end of the evening the vouchers are counted up and you are paid, say, £1 per voucher.

Another common alternative way of paying bands according to their pulling power, is to pay them on a percentage of the door sales only, after the costs of putting on the show have been covered. They might be given 200 hundred tickets and only if they draw, say, 50 people, would they begin to take a percentage of the business they generated on the door. The drawback of a percentage deal like this is that if you have a bad night you might not get paid anything at all. Ideally, however, you attract a lot of people, put on a great show and are invited back to play there again. Showcase nights like these are also often attended by A&R people.

As you build a live following and a better live profile you will be treated better and paid more. Not all club and pub promoters are ogres and some are genuinely helpful and interested in promoting new bands, if only to ensure a return visit from you should you become successful.

RETURN BOOKINGS

You will probably find that the managers and bookers of most venues in a given area will know each other. This can be an advantage if you have a successful night and can use that as a reference with another venue nearby when you are looking for a gig. However, it can be positively disadvantageous if you have a

The Frank Chickens supporting
Billy Bragg at the Victoria Palace,
London 1985.

Soho live at the Timebox – a now
defunct showcase gig in the back-
room of the Bull & Gate pub in
Kentish Town – 1988.

Hothouse Flowers make a personal appearance at the Virgin Megastore, London (see also back cover) to promote their first album in June 1988. These PAs can be enjoyable – although many artists dread them. It helps when a crowd actually turns up to greet you!

Fans at the Virgin Megastore for the Hothouse Flowers PA in June 1988.

disastrous night because bad news tends to travel fast. Even if venue managers are not on speaking terms, the word will get back to them. This also applies to bands that trash dressing rooms, turn up late, or are generally rude or unprofessional. Clubland is a small world, especially in the 1990's, so be warned!

POINTS TO DISCUSS WHEN YOU CONFIRM A BOOKING

Assuming you have obtained a booking, you should check out the following points well in advance of the gig.

(1) MONEY

Negotiate and confirm the way in which you are to be paid. The usual options are:

(**a**) A guaranteed or flat fee: this is usually the best (and most unlikely) option. It means you will be paid a guaranteed fee regardless of how much money is taken on the door.

(**b**) A guaranteed fee plus a percentage of the profits: usually a smaller guaranteed basic fee with the opportunity of increasing it by taking a previously agreed percentage of the profits from the ticket sales after all the promotional costs have been met. Percentages vary from a 50/50 split of profits up to 85% of profits in the band's favour. The deal has to be negotiated depending on the circumstances, (promotional costs include all legitimate expenses that the promoter has laid out putting together the show, including your own guarantee).

(**c**) A straight percentage split: this is the most likely option you will be offered. It means that in order for you to make any money at all, you will need to sell a significant number of tickets. Establish from the beginning exactly how the percentage is to be calculated. Most importantly, will your fee be a percentage of the gross door-take or will it be calculated after the promoters costs have been deducted? Percentage deals vary from a 50/50 split upwards. It is unusual to accept less than 50% of the gross door-take. Percentages of gross door-takes are obviously worth considerably more than percentages of door-takes net of costs.

(**d**) Establish that you will be paid in cash on the night and avoid, whenever possible, accepting cheques.

NOTE:
The Musicians' Union have a theoretical minimum fee that you can try insisting upon. In real life you will have to take what you can get.

(2) PROMOTIONAL COSTS

If you are being paid a flat fee the promoter's costs are not directly relevant to you unless you are expected to contribute to them. For instance, you may find you are expected to pay something towards the PA or lighting bill on the night.

Where you are being paid a percentage of the takings after costs have been covered, it is important to know what those costs include. Get the promoter to itemize the expenses and, without being pedantic, ask for receipts if you want proof of questionable or major outgoings. Try and ensure that the costs that you are taking into account are relevant to your particular show and that you are not paying the advertising, for example, on several other shows.

(3) PA and LIGHTS

It is often a bone of contention who is to supply and pay for the PA and engineer. Even where there is an in-house system someone will be expected to pay the PA operator. Agree in advance who is to do this. If there is an in-house PA system try and establish just how antiquated it is and see if you can talk to someone who has used it recently; it might be worth you bringing in your own gear for important gigs even if you have to pay to do so.

If there is no in-house system and the band are expected to supply a PA and pay for it out of their fee, then you may need to contact a local PA company to work for you on the night. If you are strangers to the area, then either the promoter or, possibly, a local record or music shop may be able to recommend somebody.

The PA company will need a letter of confirmation from you regarding the dates of the show and any equipment you require as well as confirmation of the agreed fee and method of payment. Most will want to be paid cash on the night – and you may be liable to pay them a cancellation fee if the show is pulled at short notice.

The above is also true of lights and lighting companies. Don't forget to check that there is enough three phase electrical power if you are ordering an outside lighting rig. Also check that there is enough stage to ceiling clearance to get any extra lighting into the venue. (See PA section, and Lights section.)

(4) GUESTLIST

Arguments can easily develop over guestlists. Promoters, not un-naturally, merely see guests as people who might have otherwise paid to come into the show. This is something which you should also bear in mind, particularly when you are on a percentage of the

door-take. It is reasonable for a small number of friends and relatives to be allowed in for free but especially at small venues, it isn't fair to present the promoter with a long list of complementary tickets unless an extensive guestlist is part of your deal. After all, both you and the promoter have got money at stake and would you be so happy giving away records or T-Shirts for free as you are giving away the promoters tickets?

(5) HOSPITALITY

Try and ensure that the promoter provides you with something to eat and drink, even if it is only a snack. You could send the promoter a 'hospitality rider' with your contract or letter of confirmation. Your rider can include quantities and types of drink that you require plus a list of the food that you would like. Unreasonable or silly requests are likely to be ignored until you are famous enough to get away with them.

A standard food and drink rider for a four piece band plus manager and roadie might read as follows:

    12 large cans lager
    6 large cans bitter
    6 tins Coca Cola
    4 litres orange juice
    2 litres mineral water
    Sandwiches and fruit or a hot meal for six
    All to be supplied after soundcheck.

You may get a lot less than this but it is worth trying, especially if you have travelled a long way to a gig and don't relish the prospect of searching a strange town for a cafe that is still open. Once you are signed to an agency they should help you to prepare and enforce your rider.

(6) ARRIVAL TIME

Establish the band's arrival time and when you will be expected to soundcheck. Find out who will be in charge on the day and make sure that they will be there to let you in. At the same time, double-check who else, if anyone, is on the bill with you. Find out if this means sharing equipment, particularly if the equipment in question is yours!

(7) PUBLICITY

Check how much publicity the promoter will be doing. Will it be worth sending the promoter any posters of your own? Will it help if you contact the local radio stations, especially if you have a playable record to send them?

(8) MERCHANDISE

If you have merchandise to sell check that this will be alright with the promoter and the venue manager, and arrange for the person who will be selling it for you to contact them before the gig. You may be expected to pay a facility fee at some venues (see Merchandise page 84).

(9) ACCOMMODATION

Can the promoter recommend a good local bed & breakfast or hotel, preferably one that is sympathetic to musicians? (See Touring in the UK).

(10) DIRECTIONS AND PARKING

Finally, don't forget to ask for directions to the venue and check whether there will be parking space available for you.

Once you have sorted out the details of the show to your satisfaction, it is useful to put them down immediately in a letter of confirmation to the promoter. Make sure that you have dated it, send it by registered post and either request a return letter from the promoter or, create a space at the bottom of your own letter which the promoter can sign and return. If you do the latter, keep one copy for yourself and send two copies to the promoter so that one can be kept as a reference when the signed copy is sent back.

Many clubs and pubs have their own standard contract which they send to you prior to the gig but if not, a letter of confirmation may suffice.

Whether or not contracts or signed agreements are ever exchanged, a letter followed by a phone call nearer the date of the gig means you at least have something on paper in the event of a dispute or argument. If nothing is ever written down by either party, you are leaving yourself wide open to misinterpretation or worse.

CANCELLATIONS

Shows are cancelled for any number of reasons – the most common being lack of ticket sales. From a promoter's point of view low ticket sales are usually a measure of the public's lack of interest in the act. This may well be true, and if the promoter has already paid out money to advertise and flypost the show and has the other costs of promotion to meet as well, one can sympathize with any attempt to minimize losses.

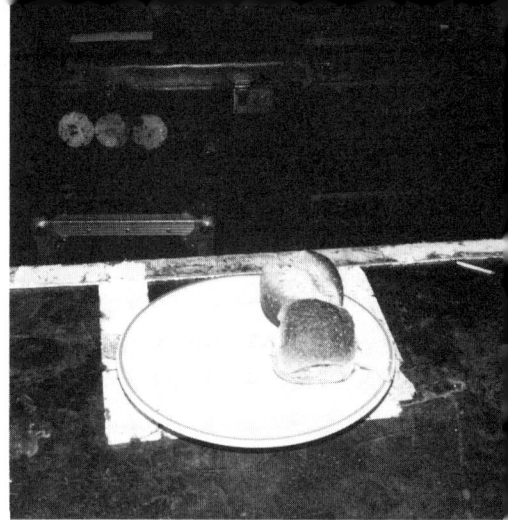

The best you can hope for

The band is more likely to feel that people did not come to their gig because the promoter failed to do any advertising, and so no-one knew it was happening!

Arguments are bound to ensue and if you feel that you are in the right, and can prove it, then you can try and get some sort of cancellation fee out of the promoter. It is very unlikely that you will get your full fee, however, and it is really much better to try and avoid such embarrassing and aggravating scenes occuring in the first place. Try ringing the promoter up from time to time to see how things are progressing in the weeks before the show. Better still, try and sound out local awareness of a forthcoming gig through an impartial contact in the area who can tell you whether posters have been put up and adverts run in the local press.

If, despite your combined efforts, the gig has still failed to generate any interest then it may be best for you to bow out gracefully and at least save your travel and hotel costs.

There are always gigs which are poorly attended for no obvious reason. This is one of the risks of promoting. Under these circumstances you should be as flexible as you can afford to be. Use your own judgement and, with future shows and your reputation in mind, treat each promoter as fairly as you can. There is little satisfaction in bankrupting a promoter who has done their best and may have failed to break even through some fault of yours.

When you are doing your first gigs, or even playing as a support act later on you will find that you are frequently treated more as a nuisance than a star attraction. Some promoters may turn out to be so objectionable and unreasonable that you may decide not to go ahead with the show. You may have plenty of valid legal reasons why you need not fulfil your performance contract but it is generally best to try and do so to avoid getting a reputation for failing to perform. Stand up for yourselves and always remember that the music business is a particularly small and incestuous one and that gossip spreads fast.

GIG CHECKLIST

Here are some points to bear in mind.

(1) Make every attempt to arrive on, or before the agreed time. Nothing will annoy a promoter more than late arrival. If you know you are going to be late, do your utmost to contact the venue and let them know.

(2) Once you have arrived to soundcheck, contact whoever is in charge of the show and introduce yourself to the stage manager and sound engineer. Do not mess around and if you are not the only band on the bill, try to be cooperative with the other acts. Some venues

have curfew restrictions so if you are supporting the headlining act and they are late you may not get a soundcheck.

(3) Backstage facilities vary widely but you cannot expect much from a small club or pub. Be prepared for spartan accommodation!

(4) Make sure your guest list has the approval of the promoter and then make sure it is given to the relevant person on the door.

(5) Adhere religiously to your stage time. If you have a couple of hours to kill after your soundcheck make sure that the whole band is back in plenty of time to go on stage.

(6) Don't leave the venue without making sure that you will be able to get back in later on. You may need a pass.

(7) If you are being paid on a percentage break and have any reason to doubt the promoter, use a clicker to count the paying customers coming in to the gig. This can seriously offend some promoters, so use a clicker carefully and, if necessary, secretly.

(8) After the show, if you have a minute or two, it is worthwhile thanking the promoter, having a chat and raising the prospect of a return booking.

THE TC AND
MUSIC
GUIDE

GIGS AT STUDENT UNIONS

In recent years, with the growth of the theme pub and the disco and a steady decline in privately owned live venues, the touring circuit around Britain has fallen into a pretty parlous state.

Correspondingly, the Student Union circuit has become increasingly important. It now forms the backbone for the live tours of many well established bands and increasing numbers of Student Unions have full-time Entertainments Officers who run their gigs for a profit. These two factors combined have possibly made it more difficult for unknown bands to get a gig. For a start, the full-time Entertainments Officers are likely to have developed their relationships with agents and be prepared to co-operate with them in putting on the support acts that the agent would like to see on the bill. Secondly, many big bands nowadays tour (see 'buy-on' page 31 and 174) complete with a support act who may have paid to be on the tour. Further, if the gigs are to be run at a profit, it gets more

Bono of U2 at the Smile Jamaica concert held at the Dominion Theatre in October 1988. Stories of U2's legendary treks around Britain's motorway system crammed in the back of an old transit van and playing to college audiences of less than two abound as the classic graft to riches rock and roll story.

difficult for student gigs to be a platform for unknown bands – who aren't generally profitable. However, they are still definitely worth aiming for! The range of facilities and venue size varies greatly from large universities with 1,000 plus capacity concert halls, to tiny bar gigs at Colleges of Further Education. The sort of entertainment presented at these places varies widely as a result, ranging from alternative cabaret to pop bands. Almost all colleges that stage events will feature a healthy proportion of live bands in their booking schedule.

STUDENT UNION ENTERTAINMENTS PERSONNEL

At Student Unions the person in charge of booking bands is variously known as the Entertainments Officer, Social Secretary, Ents. Sabbatical or Entertainments Manager. There are other variations on this theme but they broadly do the same job – sometimes as the head of an Entertainments Committee.

However, the amount of time that this person is able to devote to these responsibilities varies. For example, some universities and polytechnics employ full-time members of staff to book the entertainments programme. Some other colleges (and not just the smaller ones) have students who work on a part-time basis and look after entertainments when they are not studying. There is also a third kind of Ents. Officer who is elected at college student union level to be in charge of entertainments while taking a year off from his or her studies. This makes these 'sabbatical' personnel full-time but only for a fixed period.

The differences between staff and student entertainments personnel are subtle. A staff Entertainments Manager may imply a more professional approach by the colleges that employ one, but this approach need not necessarily be adopted by the person doing the job! Whilst sabbatical and part-time social secretaries can be very competent you should bear in mind that they are also, inevitably, amateurs. Perhaps the main difference is that the full-time staff will build up closer links with booking agents and outside promoters during their years in office. As a result they may be more inclined to take bookings from these sources and this inevitably includes the booking of support slots. A bit of persistent and friendly badgering over the phone should overcome this problem!

CONTACTING ENTS. OFFICERS

The most simple and effective method of approach to Student Unions is to obtain a list of Social Secretaries from the NUS head office in London. You are best served by selecting and concentrating

on a few venues, probably within easy travelling distance from your home. The list should contain the names, as well as the addresses, of the Ents. Officers and by finding out who the Social Secretary is, and using a personal approach you can often get a more positive reaction than by mailing a demo anonymously to 'The Social Secretary'. The receipt of a personally addressed package can do much to aid your chances of getting a gig.

You can use your basic demo package, (see page 89) but remember that you are trying to get a live gig so it is worth slanting your presentation in that direction. For instance, if you have a good live recording of your band then put that on the B-side of your demo. You could send invitations to any gigs you may be playing in their locality and include any recent rave reviews of your live performances elsewhere, particularly if these were at other colleges.

Leave at least a week to ten days after mailing your package before following it up with a telephone call. If and when you get through to an Ents. Officer, assuming that they are willing to give you a booking, the chances are that they will want to make out a contract for the gig. This will certainly be the case if the fee is over fifty pounds. If not, then a simple letter of confirmation should suffice.

NUS STANDARD CONTRACT

If you are booked for a gig then you will probably be sent a National Union of Students (NUS) Standard Contract. Read through this contract carefully because it is one of the very few live performance contracts which actually affords some measure of protection to the promoter of the event as well as to the artist. So, for example, if you have to cancel a show at short notice, you may be liable for some of the costs that the promoter has incurred. The NUS contract also includes 'exclusion clauses' which restrict your appearances in and around the vicinity of the venue. This could pose a problem if you are already doing a gig in the area near the college.

These details and other possible organizational problems should be dealt with before the day of the show.

BACKLINE AND PRODUCTION

Some colleges, for example Huddersfield Polytechnic, Portsmouth Polytechnic and others, have excellent in-house PA and lighting facilities. However, it is always advisable to check out what equipment is available at each individual college because the age, quality and efficiency of each piece of equipment can vary greatly!

Most colleges are likely to hire PA gear, in which case they may give you the PA company's telephone number so that you can ring through with your line-up and microphone requirements in advance. You must also find out whether the Entertainments Officer will be covering the cost of any extra equipment that needs to be hired or whether the cost will be deducted from your fee. The best thing to do to ensure that there are no ambiguities about this, is to put any agreements that you make on the phone in writing. Send all your letters by recorded delivery and keep a copy, so at the very least you have got proof of postage. This may seem ridiculously over cautious but it is worth it in terms of avoiding unnecessary arguments on the day of the gig. You may possibly need a DI box for a keyboard instrument; if you do then you owe it to yourself to find out in advance whether the college can supply it.

A lot of the guidelines on playing small venues are relevant to playing colleges (see Gigs, page 11). On the whole you will find Student Unions more pliable and easier to negotiate with than the more hard-nosed commercial venues, although as we have mentioned, they may also be less professional and less reliable.

SUPPORT SLOTS

A 'support slot' can either be regarded as a fob-off or it can be taken as an opportunity to prove your worth. Provided that the band you are due to support has a suitable and potentially sympathetic audience, then it is usually advisable to accept the offer as useful live experience, if nothing else. You can expect little or no money, no refreshments and perhaps no dressing room, but as support acts are notoriously badly treated in this country anyway you should be realistic in your expectations.

Occasionally a college will book a local act to support a major touring band. This happens infrequently and filling the slot brings problems of its own. Often a band that is touring with their own PA and lights will make anyone who needs to use their equipment pay a fee to their PA operatives. This can become more difficult should an act, or more likely the PA crew themselves, decide to get shirty over anyone else using their gear at all. You may find yourself caught in an argument between the Ents. Officer on the one hand and the band's tour manager or sound man on the other.

DOING THE GIG

Having persuaded a college to let you play and having clinched the deal, you should follow the general points outlined for doing gigs on page 16. There are, however, several points to make which are specific to Student Unions.

(1) Some colleges have curfew restrictions, and at some the actual venue space is used for other activities during the day, so if you

Low ceilings and ventilation pipes set the stage for World Domination Enterprises live at the London School of Economics Student Union in February 1988. A classic Student Union gig.

are supporting a headlining act and they are late, you may not get a soundcheck. This is tough but if it happens to you, then try to remember how annoyed you felt and don't do it yourselves when you are headlining! Most of the time an Ents. Officer will do his or her best to accommodate you, and you will need a modicum of patience and understanding to deal with the problem. Stroppiness and belligerence won't get you very far at all and are certainly unlikely to secure you a future booking.

(2) As pointed out in the introduction to this section, facilities at Student Unions vary greatly. Some colleges will have comparatively luxurious back-stage and catering facilities with air-conditioned dressing rooms and shower stalls. In others you are more likely to find yourself having to get ready for a gig in a lecture theatre or an office. If you have prepared yourselves properly before you arrived you should be aware of the sort of facilities to expect.

(3) As with point 2, you will find that refreshments will vary widely from college to college. You are fairly entitled to whatever you agreed as a contract rider but again, you need to be realistic.

(4) Guestlists can be a major bone of contention between a band and an Ents. Officer. Once again, you really need to have worked this out in advance so as to minimize problems on the night. You will have to be reasonable about it – most colleges will adopt a policy of 'two guests per band member'. Don't expect to be able to get upwards of twenty people into a gig for nothing, especially if you are only a support act. It helps if you refrain from making any wild or extravagant guarantees to your pals. This is particularly relevant to those colleges which operate a strict 'NUS members only' policy at their events.

(5) Given that there may be curfew restrictions in force, you should adhere strictly to your stage time.

(6) Make sure that you thank the Ents. person at the end of the show, even if the gig was poorly attended. If appropriate, you should also raise the prospect of a return booking.

All live work has its attendant organizational problems and gigs at Student Unions are not going to be an exception. They can, however, be particularly rewarding and useful in building your live career.

Agents are often a popular target for criticism. Perhaps because they are not seen to 'do' or 'make' anything, they appear to be living off their acts in a more blatant way than the other sections of the music business. This reputation is reinforced by the fact that agents are least likely to invest money in developing the acts they work with.

Record companies obviously incur huge costs in releasing and promoting records. Publishing companies may risk substantial amounts in advances. Concert promoters also have their own money at stake when they put on live shows – and even managers sometimes invest in their artist in real terms, perhaps paying personally for early demo time or instruments. Agents, however, don't put up any actual money of their own. Although many telephone calls may have been made, and many venue bookers hassled on the band's behalf, the general opinion of everyone else involved in the business is that they are a necessary evil, as opposed to a positive force within the industry. Whilst this is a common viewpoint – it is not necessarily a fair one.

WHAT AGENTS DO AND HOW YOU APPROACH THEM

In a similar way to record company A&R personnel, agents use what talent they have for finding and signing young bands whose live careers they hope they can expand and develop. Agencies come in all shapes and sizes – some working with a broad spectrum of music and musicians – whilst others specialize in particular kinds of acts. The most important agents in the pop world handle a wide variety of musicians – from reggae to heavy metal – and are based almost exclusively in London.

How they recruit artists to their rosters depends upon a number of factors. Broadly speaking the smaller agents have to work a lot harder than the bigger more corporate ones who tend to deal with the larger acts. All agents go to dozens of live gigs, mostly in London but also in the provinces, to see new acts that they have either read about, or been told about by their contacts in the business. It is possible to send an agent the same demo pack that you have sent to record or publishing companies, although agents are obviously primarily interested in your ability to play live. Record deals and hit singles certainly help the agent to book gigs and tours but some acts 'never tour' and this is a crucial consideration.

Before you send a demo you should ring your target agency and ask them to send you their latest 'representation list'. If they won't do this for any reason, then you will have to satisfy yourselves by asking them to tell you who they represent. As most of the agents

worth approaching work with all sorts of music, it is not as important to screen them as you might think. Nonetheless you should try and discover who else they represent, if only to get an idea of their musical preferences.

Find out who's job it is at each agency to listen to tapes. Most agencies have a 'listener' who will filter out the interesting material from the dozens of hopefuls which they receive every month. Address your information pack to this person and ring them a few days later for their reaction. If you are playing a live show – preferably in London – you can try and persuade them to make time to come and see you.

AGENT CONTRACTS

Agents make their money by taking a percentage of the fees that they negotiate on your behalf for live performances. (See below for an 'average' agency deal). In fact, depending on the structure of your deal, they can also expect a percentage of your earnings on any live work you do anywhere in the world – including radio and TV performances – unless you specify otherwise in your contract with them.

Unlike record and publishing contracts, agency contracts are relatively straightforward. Most of the important points of the contract are written on one foolscap page, although there may be several pages of small print attached. Because new acts may take between two to three years to earn any substantial money from live performances, you will find that agents will require a minimum of five years work from you. They are unlikely to consider contracts of less than five years unless you are a particularly desirable prospect.

The 'standard' accepted rate of commission that an agent will expect on your live fees is around 15%. Some agents will expect 15% of your live earnings, no matter how big the fees they manage to negotiate on your behalf. Others will concede a discount in their commission – say 10% only – on fees higher than £1,500. You must check this out before you sign, although in practice you should be able to renegotiate these points as you become a more valuable asset to them.

The agency contract will bind you not only for your UK work, but also for all the live work that you do throughout the world. Most UK agents insist on worldwide contracts and can effectively book and police European tours and usually handle Australian, Japanese and other tours themselves. However, they may well sub-contract your business to an American based agency for work in the States. This is because America constitutes such a huge market and plays to slightly different rules. Should your agent do this, you should not pay increased commission under any circumstances. The normal process when you have an American sub-agent is for the American agent to take 15% commission on your US tour dates and pass on around 5% of this to your UK agent. In this way you should pay a maximum of 15%.

Like all other contracts, agency contracts are enforceable by law. If you decide that you are unhappy working with a particular agent you can try to leave and work with another. The bigger agencies will have up to seven or eight agents/bookers, and if your dissatisfaction is a personal one with a particular booker, you can try working with alternative staff within the same agency. Where your dissatisfaction is with the company as a whole, you may have more of a problem. In theory, if you break your agency contract and go to another agent before you have been formally freed from your legal obligations, you can be injuncted by your old agent and prevented from playing live dates anywhere. In practice, most agents would agree that without the goodwill of both parties, continuing an unfruitful and unhappy relationship with a band makes the agency contract hard to enforce. What sometimes occurs in these situations is that your new and old agency negotiate between themselves an agreed percentage split on the commission on your live work along the lines of the US sub-agency deal outlined above. These sort of deals are rare and in most cases bands negotiate their own freedom with the help of lawyers.

Needless to say, this is only a very cursory outline of the agency contract and your contract lawyer should go through every aspect of your proposed deal before you sign anything.

WHAT YOU CAN EXPECT AN AGENT TO DO FOR YOU

Should you be successful in attracting an agency you can expect them to perform the following functions.

a) Agents can help and advise you on management should you need it. Most agents prefer to deal with a manager rather than all the members of a band.

b) They can help you get publishing or record deals by ringing their established contacts. It is in their interests that you become well-known, as the more you earn from live work, the more commission they will make.

c) They will put together individual live dates as well as booking tours and searching for appropriate support slots for your band.

Tanita Tikaram booked herself into the Mean Fiddler's Amateur Night in December 1987. While she sang and accompanied herself on the guitar in the Fiddler's tiny Acoustic room Paul Brady was playing in the main venue – and it just so happened that Paul Brady's agent and promoter wandered in to see what was going on. He was duly impressed and shortly afterwards became her manager. His ability to get her support slots with the other bands that he represents as an agent – particularly at gigs he himself promoted – gave her a lot of valuable exposure in some very impressive company. Three months later she was signed to WEA.

(**d**) Part of their work connected with live gigs involves 'policing' promoters and making sure that deals are adhered to and that you get paid.

To start with, the agent should discuss your future plans and career hopes with yourselves and your manager, if you have one. This discussion will be wide ranging and should include the latest information on your record release schedule, your record sales, the level of show which you are capable of doing, whether or not supporting a major act on tour is appropriate to your development, how much you need to earn to pay your costs on the road – and so on. Having decided between you on a live performance schedule the agent will then set about contacting venue bookers, promoters and colleges. It is the agent's job to negotiate the terms of your performance contract, and the fees that you will be paid by each promoter. As you will have discovered yourselves in trying to secure dates around the country, the UK club circuit is in a very sad state of decline. What clubs remain seem increasingly to relegate live music to midweek dates only (usually Thursdays, for some reason!) and the result is that club tours are very difficult to put together. They often end up as a series of bunches of dates as opposed to properly constructed tours.

THE CONTRACT THAT THE AGENCY DRAWS UP BETWEEN THE ARTIST AND THE PROMOTER

All agents have a standard contract which they will draw up between yourselves (or your representative), and the promoter, club manager or student Ents. Officer who will be responsible for promoting the show. Note that the contract is between the performer and the promoter and that the agent's name is rarely, if ever, mentioned. This is another reason why agents appear to wash their hands of responsibility – but it is nonetheless universal. The contract is normally appended with a 'rider' in which any special requirements of the band are listed. These requirements might include the size of the stage, the PA, lights and backline equipment and the refreshment and dressing room facilities that the promoter must provide on the day of the show. In theory, this rider constitutes an integral part of the performance contract, and you are within your rights to refuse to perform should the promoter fail to fulfil any part of it. In practice, especially in the early days, even an agent cannot fully enforce the performance contract in its entirety. You will have to use a combination of common sense and stoicism at those gigs where the promoter falls short of the agreement. It is rarely sensible to refuse to perform unless there is a gross breach of contract. In any case, you or your tour manager should have rung ahead several times to ensure that the basic necessities are provided for you.

THE AGENT AND THE PROMOTER

As we have mentioned above, successful records – chart hits and LP sales – make the agent's job a lot easier. Your higher profile, as a result of a hit record, will generate interest among promoters who may actively pursue your management and agency for the right to promote your tours. With any promotion, but particularly where one promoter is putting on a whole tour around the country, the agent's role is one not only of negotiating fees but also of policing the promoter. The promoter must send a detailed break-down of costs on each show to the agent well in advance of the gig or tour dates. The agent must check these figures very carefully for discrepancies or 'errors', looking particularly for unaccountable 'costs' and unfair or inappropriate expenses. This is particularly important where the artist's fee Is to be calculated on a guarantee plus a percentage of the profits net of costs.

'BUY-ONS' AND TOUR SUPPORT

Most tours, even at concert hall level, struggle to break even from the artist's point of view. The costs involved in putting a band and their crew on the road for a number of weeks are increasingly prohibitive and the fees that a young band can command are often insufficient to cover them. As a result, shortfalls on tours are a common problem, and it is part of the agent's job, in conjunction with the band's management, to try to (a) negotiate the highest possible fees for the artist, (b) keep the band's touring costs to a minimum, and (c) seek out alternative ways of raising money. Probably the commonest source of funding for a loss-making tour is record and publishing company 'tour support'. Tour support generally consists of a loan, or recoupable advance on the band's royalties, on their record or publishing deals. This is usually forth-coming where a tour is important to the promotion of an LP and fits in with record company plans for an LP release.

When you first start your live career with an agency you are more likely to be at the other end of the scale which may involve you supporting a major act on their tour. As the competition to get onto major tours has increased over the years, the unfortunate and expensive practice of 'buying-on' has developed. Basically, this entails a young band paying sometimes thousands of pounds to the

The Wonderstuff supporting All About Eve in Birmingham March 1988. The effectiveness of an established image – right down to an imposing backdrop – are both well illustrated here.

headline act for the right, and dubious pleasure, of supporting them around the country. Unless you, or your manager are particularly well-heeled, you will stand little chance of competing for tour support slots without a record or publishing company behind you. Your agency may be able to help you to secure good support slots by (a) persuading one of the acts on their roster to take you on tour with them for nothing, or for a reduced buy-on, and (b) persuading reluctant record companies that a tour is worthwhile and necessary to the development of your career. Note that the agent may expect to take 15% commission out of any buy-on or tour support thus negotiated. This is not really acceptable and should be discussed between yourself and your lawyer prior to signing with the agency.

MONEY ON TOUR AND PAYING AGENCY COMMISSION

The stage at which you and your agent get your money from live gigs and tour dates can vary. Some agents are happy to let you collect all your fees as you go along, and they then invoice you for their commission plus VAT as and when it becomes payable. Others deduct their commission at source from promoters' deposits and send you the balance at the end of the tour. Some promoters – especially on foreign tours – may have been required to send some of the money in advance to your agency. Whatever system is used, you should sort out an accounting procedure with the agent before you sign a contract, and get an accountant to check it if necessary.

AGENTS WHO ARE ALSO PROMOTERS

Some of the major agencies are multifunctional and not only act as agents, but also manage and promote their acts. This has the advantage of keeping all the functions of agency, management and promotion under the same roof and should mean that there is less room for the communication breakdowns which are the usual reason for mistakes and arguments in tour planning.

The major disadvantage is that the important policing role of the agent over the promoter is no longer there. The band's fee, and the promoter's costs are decided upon by the same people and there has to be an element of doubt as to who is keeping an eye on the band's interest. Having said this, there are some notably successful agent/promoters and you can always get legal advice if you suspect foul play. You can also get quotes on tours from other promoters from time to time to make sure that you are being paid what you are really worth – or simply insist that some of your tours are booked with outside promoters.

Promoters actually finance gigs and tours. Either by approaching bands direct, or by negotiating a band's fee via their agent or manager, it is promoters who organize and run live shows. Unlike agents or venue managers, promoters are the people whose money is at risk.

Promoters come in many shapes and sizes. Some have a genuine interest in music and some do not – but all are, of necessity, businessmen. They are often maligned, and sometimes rightly so, but it is important to understand their role and the pressures that they work under before damning them entirely.

If you have promoted a show yourselves, even at the lowest level, you will have some inkling of what the promoter's life can be like. Even a modest promotion can easily cost over a thousand pounds by the time artists have been guaranteed minimum fees, advertisements have been paid for, postering and handbilling accounted for – not to mention PA, lights, security and the hall hire. If the costs were exactly £1,000 and the ticket price was £4.00 then the promoter would have to sell 250 tickets just to break even (if VAT has to be accounted for the promoter would have to sell 287 tickets to break even). If the promotion has been done properly and the gig has been advertised imaginatively, the event might attract 500 ticket sales and the promoter would then make a tidy profit. However, as everyone will tell you, there is a large element of luck involved in putting on live music and a rainy Tuesday night in a dismal pub back room could easily achieve less than 100 ticket sales – especially if the gig coincided with a top rated TV show! It could also simply be that the band has not as yet built up a reliable following. In these circumstances it is sometimes difficult for artists to collect their fee at the end of the show, and promoters have been known to try tricks like leaving the hall while the band are still on stage! If you do end up arguing over your fee after a poorly attended gig, you might take some comfort from the fact that whatever the concert may have cost you, it has almost undoubtedly cost the promoter a lot more.

When you play larger and more prestigious venues, these problems and the element of luck do not go away. Say a promoter is putting on a festival and needs 60,000 paying customers at £10 per ticket to break even but, because it rains continuously, only 55,000 tickets are sold. Everyone at the event assumes that someone has made a huge profit and is drinking champagne in a luxury tour bus while the punters tramp through a morass of cold mud. In reality, the promoter is £50,000 out of pocket and may be desperately trying to avoid having to sell the family home in order to pay the security staff!

PROMOTERS

Having said all this, don't let promoters use the fact that they are risking their money on an event colour your attitude to them entirely. Presumably they have chosen to be promoters because they think they can make a living out of it. Don't for a minute think that they will voluntarily share out the substantial profits they can potentially make – and certainly don't feel that you should ever be expected to share the burden of the promoter's losses.

CLUB AND PUB BASED PROMOTERS

Some promoters are tied to a specific club or pub venue. They may be full-time bookers or managers employed by the licensee of the venue, or they may be independent individuals who have an arrangement with the landlord or the proprietor of a venue where they may promote frequently, but not exclusively. These are the promoters that you are most likely to come across in the early stages. Whether based in London or in the provinces, promoters at this level can be approached personally. They book the majority of their bands through a combination of personal taste and knowing which acts are up-and-coming. They are used to dealing directly with artists, although they will sometimes go through the London based agencies for their more ambitious promotions.

CONCERT AND TOUR PROMOTERS

Most of the major promoters are based, predictably, in London. There are some notable exceptions and you will find that Scotland and Ireland, in particular, have their own promotion companies (see Directory). At this level promoters deal almost exclusively through agents when putting together individual dates or tours. They hear about interesting new acts from the record companies (where they are likely to have contacts), and from a variety of other sources such as agents, journalists, lawyers and the managers of the concert halls that they regularly use. Bands with record deals and preferably with some record sales success are what they are searching for, although they may work with bands that require nurturing and building before being placed into the larger venues, offering them some appropriate support slots, for example.

MEGASTAR LEVEL

You will have long stopped reading publications like this one by the time you begin working with promoters at megastar level! There are some promoters who work virtually exclusively at stadia and festivals and rarely promote at a lower level. Others will promote at concert halls more frequently. Needless to say, these people are not interested in hearing from you.

If you cannot find anyone who will promote your band, why not have a go yourself? You may live in an area where there aren't any established clubs or promoters. Organizing and promoting your own show is useful experience and it can serve the dual purpose of giving you publicity and some practice in front of a live audience.

Try approaching the landlord of your biggest local pub. Check if there is a live music licence. If there isn't, this might not prevent you doing a one-off show, depending on the landlord's attitude. If you can, strike a deal with the landlord along the lines of you organizing and running the show and taking all the ticket sales, whilst he or she takes all the bar money. You may find the landlord unwilling to let you use the venue on a Friday or Saturday night, but you should be able to negotiate a midweek date or a Sunday lunchtime gig.

Schools, church halls, and other public buildings are usually good alternatives. You could also try your local Arts Centre or theatre.

WHAT DO YOU DO ONCE YOU HAVE FOUND SOMEWHERE TO PLAY?

How much money you have to invest in your live shows, and how important it is for you to recoup that money, will dictate how closely you follow the advice and checklists below.

It is a good idea to acquire the discipline of promoting properly and of keeping track of your out-goings and income, even on the smallest event. Later on, as you become more successful, even when the costs of a promotion are being met by a professional promoter, your knowledge of the economics and practical problems involved in promoting will give you a valuable insight.

PREPARING FOR A LIVE SHOW

1) *Plan your event*. Decide whether you are going to play a straight-forward gig as an individual band or whether you can usefully include any supporting acts. Two or three local bands together can generate more of an audience than one band alone. As live practice is all you are after at first, headlining the show is not that important. You can add a good local DJ (venue licence permitting), and run the show as a full evening's entertainment including your band. You could make it a special event, as a 'Battle of the Bands', for instance, or as a benefit show for a charitable cause (see Benefit gigs, page 57).

(2) *Prepare a budget*. Read through the list below and decide how you are going to spend your money. Ring around and get quotes on all the services and facilities you are intending to use.

NB. If you are registered with the VAT office you should either prepare your figures inclusive of VAT or exclusive of VAT. Try not to mix the two together. The VAT Office will want you to account for the VAT you collect through ticket sales. Unlike normal vatable purchases, where you are charged say £10 plus VAT @ 15% = £11.50, tickets are considered to have the VAT within the price.

For example, a £4.00 ticket includes 52p VAT, so the VAT Office is expecting you to declare 52p per ticket sold. You are actually only making £3.48 per ticket. If you add up your expenses on a gig net of VAT, then you should do your calculations of your income on a gig on a ticket price net of VAT. Conversely, if your costs include VAT then you must do all your figures inclusive of VAT (for more detailed information see page 208).

Early on you are probably not going to be VAT registered so you can merely add all the outgoing expenses together. Add a little extra for miscellaneous bits and pieces which you may not have thought of, such as telephone bills, petrol, postage and so on.

The total costs should then be divided by the ticket price you have decided on. This will give you the number of paying customers which you require to cover your costs. This figure is commonly called your 'break even' figure. The break even figure should be:

(a) realistically achievable
(b) lower than the official audience capacity of the venue you are using! Only tickets sold after you have met your break even figure will actually make you any money.

In other words, before you book or confirm anything, you should make certain that you will be able to run your show successfully without losing money. It is all too easy to be wildly optimistic about your band's ability to draw customers. Everyone thinks that their band will attract hundreds of interested people off the street from the start! Try and be objective about the audience that you will be able to pull, especially at the beginning.

You may be in a good financial position where losing a little money is not the end of the world, or you may be lucky and have a sponsor or some sort of tour support. Regardless of your financial status, someone from the band, whether it is the manager or a band member, should do a budget for every show. Apart from the good practice that this instils for the big events later on, it helps to save arguments and embarrassing moments, (when you realize that no one has brought the money to pay for petrol at the motorway station for instance, or that you need 250 customers to break even in a little pub that only holds eighty people!)

The following is a very comprehensive list of costs and would more typically be used by the promoter at a venue like the Town & Country Club. However, much of it is still applicable when budgeting a smaller gig and you may find it useful as a guideline.

ESTIMATED COSTS OF PROPOSED SHOW

Venue rental	£_____	
PA hire	£_____	
Lights	£_____	
Stage crew	£_____	____people at £_____ per person
Electrician	£_____	
Backline hire	£_____	
Drum risers	£_____	
Security	£_____	____people at £_____ per person
Box office staff	£_____	
Ticket printing	£_____	
Box office %	£_____	
Artwork/PMTs	£_____	
Poster printing	£_____	× ____posters
Handbill printing	£_____	× ____handbills
Flyposting	£_____	
Handbilling	£_____	
Advertising	£_____	NME ____ads at____cm × ____col = £_____
Headline band fee	£_____	MM ____ads at____cm × ____col = £_____
Support band fee	£_____	SOUNDS____ads at____cm × ____col = £_____
DJ	£_____	____ads at____cm × ____col = £_____
Hospitality	£_____	
Van hire/petrol	£_____	Sub Total: £_____
Driver	£_____	
Accommodation	£_____	
Other	£_____	
Total costs	£_____	Net of VAT

3) *Book and confirm the venue.* It is a good idea to check out a venue in person and, where possible, meet the manager or landlord to sort out financial and practical problems in advance. Never leave yourself less than 3 weeks to organize a show, and preferably give yourself 5 or 6 weeks to promote it properly. Always confirm a venue booking in writing and put any deal you may have agreed with the venue manager down on paper as soon as possible. If necessary deliver this letter by hand – having kept a copy for

Handbills is still the cheapest and most effect way of advertising a gig.

yourself or, alternatively, send it by registered post. The letter need only be a short, friendly note, but it is well worth doing to avoid arguments and disputes later on.

(4) *Prepare some artwork.* A simple bit of striking artwork including all the relevant information on the show will go a long way toward attracting an audience. It is worth doing this properly if you can, perhaps through an art student friend or even a graphic design company if you are unable to do the artwork yourselves. Where you can afford it, ask for PMTs (photo-mechanical transfers) of the finished artwork (a PMT will cost between £3 and £5). These are literally photographs of the complete artwork and can be given directly to poster and handbill printers and to newspapers and magazines. They ensure that no mistakes are made or inappropriate typefaces used by the art departments at the newspapers who neither know your music, nor your image. Using PMTs also means that you can have the same artwork for handbills, posters and press advertising, and by doing so the message that you are playing a show is reinforced and at the same time your image is established.

INFORMATION TO INCLUDE ON YOUR ARTWORK FOR POSTERS, TICKETS AND HANDBILLS ADVERTISING THE GIG

You would be surprised how even experienced top promoters still make fundamental mistakes in compiling their artwork – even to the extent of mis-spelling the headline artist's name! – so always check your artwork against the following simple list.

(a) Who is playing. This should be written in big letters – especially where you already have some sort of following. When you are just starting out maybe include a bit of information about the event itself. For instance 'Party night with a live Soul band and disco 'til midnight!'.

(b) Where the event is happening. Always give a full address where possible, and if the venue is not normally associated with live shows then you could possibly include a map or simple directions.

(c) When the event is happening. Put the day, the date and the month, to avoid confusion – and include a doors opening time and, where necessary, an on-stage time.

(d) How much the tickets are in advance and on the door. If you opt for advance ticket sales then include the ticket outlets and their telephone numbers in small print along the bottom of the artwork. (For more information on ticket printing see page 40).

5) *Order your handbills and posters*. Generally speaking, printing costs get lower per item the more items you have printed. With this in mind it is sensible to try and use your handbills as posters as well, so you only have one order. If your budget does not stretch to printing large posters, this makes good sense. Try ordering an initial print run of say, 2,000 A4 size handbills. Black and white handbills on cheap paper are usually very good value and really are a must, especially if you cannot afford any other form of advertising. (2,000 black on white, A4 handbills should cost around £25.00.)

These handbills can then be handed out at other gigs and local events in the weeks before your show, and you can use the rest of them to flypost the area, either individually, or in blocks of four to make a bigger impact. If you are clever you can design your artwork so that when the handbills are placed side by side, or above each other your design runs through them linking them together.

Find out if you can flypost in your town (some local councils are very strict about this). If you can do so without causing yourself too many legal problems and without treading on the toes of any local flyposting team, then it is a good idea to do it. However, it can be very ill-advised to cover up existing posters for events that are yet to occur. This can start feuds which have been known to be physically dangerous! Neither is it advisable to stick handbills or posters onto shop windows or on to official poster sites. You are very likely to be prosecuted, or the venue may be held to be responsible and prosecuted instead. Do your flyposting sensibly and, before you stick posters up, think who you may be upsetting.

6) *Press advertising and other publicity*. It may seem a bit obvious but if no-one knows your show is happening – then no-one is likely to come. Bearing this in mind it is a false economy to save money on advertising. You should try every method you can think of, or afford, to draw attention to the show. Word of mouth is a good and cheap start to promoting and you shouldn't miss any opportunity to tell people about the show. Tell all the people in the local pubs yourself and, if you can, get a DJ at your local radio station to play your record and announce the forthcoming gig on the air. In the two or three weeks building up to the show, never go anywhere without a fistful of handbills advertising your gig.

Decide whether or not you are going to pay for advertising in the press. Local papers are usually only too pleased to cover events in their area, and if your show is a benefit concert for a local charity, then it could be 'newsworthy' enough to merit some 'advertorial'. You should send information about your show to all the gig and tour news sections of the weekly national music papers as well. It costs nothing to be included in these sections, and if the gig has a newsworthy slant, and you include a decent photograph of the band, the editor might even decide to print the picture with a short caption. Check the deadlines and advertising rates in any publications you use well in advance. (See Press page 115).

(7) *Ticket printing and door price.* You should decide whether or not to print tickets for your show. If you sell advance tickets it is a good idea to use something sequentially numbered to keep an accurate account of your income. If you are only selling tickets on the door on the night, you can get away with using ordinary cloakroom tickets. It is a good idea to use a marker pen or a distinctive rubber stamp as well to 'brand' those customers that have paid. This is a must in the more open-plan venues or clubs with more than one entrance.

If you do a series of shows in your area it is also advisable to change the colour of the marker pen and the tickets on every show to try and prevent the more devious customers, or even touts, pulling a fast one on you and getting in for free.

It is especially important on advance tickets to ensure that you don't encourage forgeries or simple copies. Never get tickets printed in black ink on white paper. These can be easily photocopied. Even if you print in coloured ink on white paper there are photocopiers nowadays that can reproduce primary colours. The best option is to use coloured paper and black ink. Matching paper colour is difficult and if the tickets are numbered in sequence as well, this should put off most casual forgers. Even if a persistent forger succeeds in matching the paper for colour, it is virtually impossible to reproduce the typeface of the numbers. They are a good starting point to examine if you suspect anything.

It may seem ludicrous to go to these lengths but you would be surprised at what people will do to try and avoid paying, or to make some money. There is nothing worse than discovering forged tickets among your own genuine ones. Each forgery represents money that you should have earned.

Forgeries can also mean that you overfill the venues that you are playing, possibly to a dangerous level, without knowing it. This can lead to all sorts of problems, either from the landlord of the pub whose customers are uncomfortable and overcrowded, or from the local fire officer, who is empowered to stop your show and close down the venue if he thinks fit.

The information that you print on your tickets should obviously be the same as that on the advertisements and handbills for your

gig. If you intend to charge more money on the door for your tickets than you charge in advance, it is a legal requirement to print the word 'advance' next to the price on the front of the ticket, and on all other advertising for the show. You can then charge a higher price on the door if you wish. Note that not all printers can make tickets because they need a special machine to number tickets consecutively.

Where you are paying other artists on a percentage break it is useful to use a lap counter or 'clicker'. This is a mechanical hand-held counting machine which you can buy from most good sports equipment shops. Get someone that is above suspicion, or supervise someone impartial, to count in the customers. A clicker can be a good investment if you do shows later where you are being paid on a percentage break yourselves and need to keep an eye on the number of paying customers.

(8) *Selling tickets in advance.* Ask your local record shops if they will let you put up a poster in the window, or behind the sales counter, and sell your tickets for you. You can offer them some commission for doing this, either by letting them put a small mark-up on the ticket price, or by letting them take a small percentage of the value of the tickets that they sell. Other shops may sell tickets for you as well, such as local newsagents or musical equipment shops. Obviously, see if the venue itself can sell advance tickets, particularly if it is a busy pub or club.

Keep a careful record of who you have given tickets to, and exactly how many tickets you have at each outlet. Preferably get a small notebook or receipt book and ask someone at each outlet to sign for their ticket allocation. Make sure that someone trustworthy collects all the money and unsold tickets on the day of the show. You should do this in plenty of time so that you can calculate how many tickets you have sold in advance. This will tell you how many you have left to sell on the night. Knowing your costs should also enable you to decide whether you will need to charge more on the door to help you break even. Advance sales should give you some indication as to public interest in the gig.

If you haven't sold a single advance ticket by the day of the show then it may be worth cancelling the gig to cut your losses and avoid embarrassment. Having said this, however, never under-estimate the number of people who might just 'walk-up' on the night. With small local bands advance sales do not always accurately reflect eventual total sales, and some music is more prone to walk-up than others. Even at concert hall level there are many examples of promotions being saved at the last minute by a large walk-up audience.

(9) *PA and lights*. Having checked whether or not there is sufficient in-house equipment at the venue for you to use, you may need to hire PA and lights from an outside source (see sections on PA page 44 and lights page 52). If you need to hire any equipment, including backline, never leave it to the last minute to do so. Where you are using any in-house gear make sure you have agreed who is to pay for it and how much it is going to cost.

(10) *Accommodation, van hire and insurance.* (see Tours and Touring in the UK page 62.)

(11) *Prepare an itinerary*. Especially where your promotion includes other acts, make sure that everyone knows the schedule of events on the day. It is normal and sensible for bands to soundcheck in reverse order. In other words, the headlining act should soundcheck first and the opening act should soundcheck last. This gives the main act plenty of time to overcome any technical problems and means that opening acts can go straight on stage after their sound-check, should time be running short.

Crucially, other acts will need to know:

(a) their expected arrival time at the venue
(b) their soundcheck time
(c) their on-stage time
(d) the length of their set
(e) any other relevant information – such as whether or not equipment is to be shared
(f) directions to, and contact person at, the venue.

(12) *Gig security*. Depending on who is going to be selling tickets on the night, and depending on how secure the entrance to the venue is, you will need someone to keep an eye on the door for you. There are trouble-makers in every town that you may wish to exclude from the show, as well as needing someone to keep an eye on the door takings and to make sure that everyone pays. Check with the venue management as they may already have staff that can help you – if not then think of someone yourself and, if necessary, pay them.

(13) *The day before the show*. Do a quick ring round to make sure everyone that is essential to the gig is still able to take part, i.e. PA and lighting companies, headline bands, DJs and so on!

CHECKLIST FOR THE DAY OF THE SHOW

Make sure someone is collecting any advance tickets and money.

Get to the venue before anybody else to make sure that it is ready to be used and that the wedding party from the night before isn't still going on! Leave someone responsible behind, if necessary, should you need to go out.

Check that you have a float of change available to use on the door. The venue management may be able to supply this – alternatively go to the bank.

If you have the cash available, then prepare the payments you will have to make in advance. Put the amounts in clearly marked envelopes and put them somewhere safe – preferably not in the dressing room.

Make sure that soundchecks are running to time and that someone, maybe your roadie, is made stage manager for the day and makes sure everyone sticks to the schedule.

Open the doors on time, preferably a few minutes early. There is nothing worse, especially when your box office person is inexperienced with handling money, than being inundated with a queue of people because the doors opened late. Make sure you have given your box office person a carefully counted batch of tickets, preforably more than they require, and get them to check the float with you.

Run the show to time, especially where you have agreed a curfew with the venue. Some venue licences are dependent on sticking to curfews.

When your box office person has completed their sales get them to do their figures on the spot, checking both the float and their ticket income. Mistakes are always more difficult to trace later on.

Pay all the people that you are responsible for, and get them to sign a petty cash receipt when you give them the money. You will need the receipt to prove that you have paid them, in the event of a dispute, and to be able to accurately complete your figures. This is especially true if you are dealing with VAT registered people and where your own figures have to be legal and above board.

Thank everyone who helped you with the show and leave the venue as soon as possible after the gig. Don't outstay your welcome. Tidy up before you go and make sure that any equipment that you have to leave behind is safely locked away.

THE TC AND
MUSIC
GUIDE

PA, BACKLINE AND CREW

In a live public performance there are some obvious ingredients which can determine whether your show is a success or not. Ideally, you combine a brilliant performance, properly engineered through an adequate PA with an exciting stage and light display. When you can do this in front of a full house of enthusiastic fans at a popular venue then you probably have the basic recipe for a good gig.

If the lights go out, the venue is half empty, or the promoter decides to charge £10.00 per ticket then your gig need not necessarily be a disaster. BUT, if the sound is bad then you might as well have saved everyone's time and money and stayed at home. Unless you are the sort of band that wants to sound like a wall of white noise with howling feedback, then you should never underestimate the importance of either your own equipment or the sound system and engineer.

The first step in achieving the sort of sound you can control and be confident of is to get to know and understand the way your backline and PA work. After all, they are the tools of your trade.

WHAT IS PA?

As you progress up the live performance ladder you will rapidly reach a point where your on-stage equipment is no longer adequate, either because it isn't loud enough for larger audiences, or because you need to have more control over your sound.

Once you reach this stage and begin to play in established live music venues you will inevitably come across the 'PA system'. For the totally uninitiated, the PA would normally consist of a basic sound reinforcement system which serves two purposes:

(a) to further amplify the sound of vocals, drums and backline equipment
(b) to enable a sound engineer to effectively control and balance the sound both on-stage for the benefit of the band members, and out-front where the audience can hear it.

At the larger pubs and smaller clubs, depending on the exact size of the venue, you can expect to find a 16 to 24 channel sound desk, usually positioned somewhere in the middle or back of the hall. This desk will probably incorporate basic 'effects' such as reverb and echo. There is also likely to be a simple on-stage monitoring system which feeds a separate and different level of sound to the performers on stage than is heard by the audience out-front (at this level the on-stage monitoring system is likely to be controlled from the sound desk out front although at the larger venues separate on-stage monitor desks are provided. These serve the monitoring system alone, leaving the out front desk to deal with the out front sound).

Microphones are connected to individual 'channels' on the sound desk which are then used either for vocals or to 'mike-up' the drum kit, or various cabinets or combos on stage. Some instruments can be plugged directly into a channel on the sound desk and this is known as 'D.I.ing.' (via a 'direct injection' box instead of a micro-phone).

By 'mixing' the sound levels that come into the sound desk via the microphones, the sound engineer can achieve dramatically differing results. Vocals can be raised or lowered where necessary, drums or guitars given greater or lesser prominence and so on. As the sound passes via the mixing desk 'equalization' and any special effects required to improve the overall sound are added. Reverb can be added to the vocals or guitar, for instance.

The final sound then goes via large amplifiers to the speaker system which should be capable of producing bass, middle and treble sounds.

Even with the smaller sound desks, four to six piece bands will generally have no problem in sharing out channels unless they have particularly peculiar line-ups – such as 17 keyboards or a 10 piece drum kit! If your band's line-up is much bigger than the standard four-piece then expect to have to share microphones occasionally or make compromises elsewhere – for example on monitoring.

Some of the more frequently used venues, such as Dingwalls Dance Hall, London and The Leadmill, Sheffield have in-house PA systems installed. At other venues the organisers may hire one at their own expense or, more likely, the band may be expected to pay for it out of their fee. (For more detail on the various deals and financial agreements of gigs at this level see page 17.).

HIRING A PA

At current rates a small 1 to 2K PA will cost between £75 and £150 per night to hire. This price will include one, or possibly two, engineers but may not include other costs such as transport. If you are hiring the PA you should find out exactly what you are going to get for your money in advance and make sure there are no hidden costs. Ask the PA company to send you a 'PA spec' which is a full list of the components and effects they will be supplying.

A medium-sized 3K to 6K PA rig with a 24 or 32 channel desk and most of the popular effects will cost between £150 and £350 per night to hire. You should also expect a separate desk for on-stage sound at this level and two engineers. Again, there may be transport costs to add. Most PA companies, especially the small ones, will

T & C Crew

require some sort of deposit in advance and will almost certainly expect payment in cash on the night of the show. Rates of hire are always negotiable, especially on a series of dates or a tour.

SUPPORT SLOTS AND PAs

At the larger concert halls the PA will be costing the promoter between £350 and £1,000 per night – so bear that in mind when you use it! If you are the support band you will probably be expected to pay the PA engineer between £10 and £30 to be allowed to use the equipment set up for the headlining act. This may seem unfair, especially as you are not being paid very much, but it is uniformly accepted practice. Support bands get a notoriously bad deal in this country although some PA companies are fairer than others and may take pity on you. If you have a serious complaint your manager or agent should fight your corner for you. If you haven't got either, then it is up to you!

INSTRUMENTS, BACKLINE AND ON-STAGE EQUIPMENT

Live shows put on at smaller venues are likely to be run on a low budget and this is going to be reflected in the quality and sophistication of the PA supplied. The quality of your on-stage equipment will never be more important than it is at this level. In a nutshell – you will get out of a PA system only what you are prepared to put into it.

We could easily write a whole book on backline and equipment but there are already several excellent specialist publications in print and we refer you, for the most part, to them. However, no section on PAs would be complete without touching on the subject.

Sound engineers will be grumpy and unco-operative if you turn up to a gig with crummy gear and then expect them to work hard trying to conjure good sound out of your sub-standard equipment. So you owe it to yourself to invest in high quality backline and instruments if you are serious about your music. If this means selling your car or even your house – so be it! There is a good second-hand market for quality musical equipment, so if you buy wisely you can always sell at a later date if the worst comes to the worst.

The biggest mistake that young bands make, apart from skimping on their equipment budget, is to go into their local instrument shop and buy the first item that appeals to them. Whatever you do, take your time and shop around. Talk to anyone and everyone who you think has an idea about the sort of musical instruments and backline equipment you need. Take the three of four bands that you respect most, or whose sound you like the most, and find out what instru-

ments and backline they use. Then go to a good stockist and try them out. Always ask questions in music shops and don't let the assistants embarrass you or try to blind you with science.

Buying new is not always a good idea either and remember that there are plenty of under-used second hand instruments about. The ups and downs of the music business see to that! The back of Melody Maker is a good market place for both new and second-hand equipment and MM, International Musician, Music and Equipment Mart, and Making Music all do excellent write ups and reviews on the latest musical gear — as do many other specialist musical instrument magazines (beware, however, of 'advertorial' which is particularly prevalent in free publications that rely solely on advertising revenue for their income).

HIRING BACKLINE

If you are doing a gig a long way from home, or if your own backline is lost or damaged, you can hire nearly any piece of musical equipment you need. Most of the good, well stocked equipment hire companies are London based and they are not always eager to deal with the public — preferring to do business with established promoters, bands and venues they know. However, if you are polite and offer to leave a passport and credit card, they may let you hire their equipment. You may also have to leave a cash deposit.

Depending on the sort of gear you need, you will find most backline and instruments surprisingly cheap to hire considering their original value. You can hire £700 worth of guitar combo, for instance, for around £12.00 per night plus delivery and VAT — hence the hire companies' cautious attitude to strangers. The prices listed below are approximate and you may find companies that will hire equipment for less, but they give you some idea of what to expect. You can see that hiring a particular item and trying it out for a day or two could be a lot cheaper in the long run than buying that item new, and then discovering that it wasn't what you needed.

Guitar Combos	£10–£15 per night
Bass Combos	£20–£25 per night
DX7 or equivalent keyboard	£25–£30 per night
Basic four drum kit incl. cymbals and stands	£35–£45 per night

Delivery will cost approximately £5.00 each way in and around London, depending on where the gig is. If you expect a hire company to come out at three in the morning to Stoke Newington then it will cost a lot more, and this is true of any equipment hire company for obvious reasons. It is probably best to collect and deliver the equipment yourself if you can.

NB. There is no insurance policy available to instrument and equipment hire companies to cover their possessions after you have hired them. Once they hand equipment over to you, then you are responsible for it. In the event of theft or damage you will be expected to repair or replace it at your own cost. It is definitely worth insuring yourselves against disaster (see Insurance page 209).

SOUND ENGINEERS

Good instruments and equipment will need to be mixed and engineered effectively to get optimum results, so you will also need a good sound engineer. Usually, a house PA will have an in-house engineer. You may have a sound engineer of your own, but unless you know that he or she is good, it is more likely that the house engineer will be able to get the best sound out of the house PA system. By all means have your own sound person liaise closely with the house engineer – but bear in mind that the house technician has probably done hundreds of shows and will know the vagaries and problems of both the venue and the equipment inside out. Contrary to popular belief, this knowledge is far more important than knowing the 'sound' and songs of the band. So long as you have ensured that your own equipment is as good as it can be and so long as you do what is asked of you by the sound engineer when it is asked of you – you will have gone a long way towards sounding as good as possible.

Where the PA system is hired for the night and may be as new to the club as you are, then again, the person who owns the PA is still likely to produce better results than anyone else (unless your own engineer is a proven genius). If you have doubts as to a PA engineer's ability then bring in a sound engineer of your own from another club or PA company, at your own expense if necessary. If, for instance, you have been to see another band playing in the area and were particularly impressed by their sound then see if their engineer can do your sound for you.

Something that might be pointed out at this stage is that studio engineering is as different from live sound engineering as it can be. It is a myth that an engineer who has done a good demo for you can automatically reproduce those effects in a live situation. Very few studio engineers make good live engineers, although many will try!

THE TC AND MUSIC GUIDE

It is another myth that the friend of the band who owns the van, humps your gear and knows all your material is the best person to mix your sound. This friend may well be a faithful supporter of the band and has probably spent long, selfless hours driving you from town to town – but if you are taking the job at all seriously then you must put the professionalism of the band first. The point we have been labouring so far is that your live sound is only as good as your equipment, the PA and the sound engineer combined, so if the latter is not capable of getting the best out of your equipment and the PA you must make a hard decision. It may seem cruel and ungrateful to replace this kind of friend and supporter, but there is no point trying to protect their feelings by prolonging the decision to get rid of them. Besides, it will get harder to do the longer you leave it.

After serving your apprenticeship at pub and club level, you will hopefully progress onwards and upwards to larger and more prestigious venues. Any sound problems that you have failed to solve at the lower levels with bad equipment, incompetent crew or bad habits of your own will be magnified tenfold on a larger PA. Problems with sound do not simply go away as the PAs get larger and more sophisticated. On the contrary, that annoying background buzz that your guitar makes at pub level will be transformed into a sound like a swarm of killer bees when it is put through a 12 or 15K rig. By this stage you must have sorted out problems with both equipment and personnel.

CREW

Your manager should have been building a crew of dependable professionals around you over the months of playing live. As you build a reputation you will be approached by PA and lighting companies and various road crews looking for work. They will vary widely in their expertise and abilities although it is probably true to say that the higher you go up the ladder, the more professional and able they become.

Experienced rock 'n' roll stage crew can be invaluable. Knowing one end of a guitar lead from another, and which way up to stand the bass drum is not always enough. There will be plenty of occasions when a friend of the band, who humps your gear in and out of the van, doesn't have enough technical know-how to help out in an emergency. It is possible to learn the tricks of the trade through practical experience – indeed all professional roadies and stage crew started as novices – but it is useful to have someone on the road with you that knows the ropes already.

Knowledge, from the best way to pack a PA into a truck, to

re-stringing a guitar in mid-gig is crucial – not to mention acquired skills such as knowing how to get off Spaghetti Junction at the turning you actually want. An intelligent all-rounder, who takes little or preferably no drugs, knows a bit about PA, lights and the mechanics of a Ford Transit van is really necessary for a serious tour. This is particularly true if there are hotels to be booked, tour accounts to be kept, and a tour itinerary to be made up. Whilst they are not cheap, proper tour managers and roadies are worth the expense. Personal recommendations are the best way by far of acquiring crew and, if you can afford it, it is worth paying a retainer to a good tour manager to keep him or her 'on tap', especially if you do a lot of touring.

THE TC AND MUSIC GUIDE

LIGHTING

The lights and stage effects that you need will obviously depend on your image and the type of music you play. Clouds and thunder flashes just aren't appropriate for some acts – and for others a single spotlight with some colour washes is plainly inadequate. You will have to tailor your lighting effects to match your pocket, and remember that the lights and stage set you choose should complement, and not compete with, your music.

When you first start out you won't be able to afford more than the very modest lights that already exist in the pubs and clubs where you play. If, however, you are playing somewhere that does not have any stage lights, you should think about taking some of your own. Stage lighting is often overlooked as a mood creator, and even at the smallest venues the atmosphere could be destroyed if you are reduced to playing under plain white strip lighting. As you develop your live shows, it is worth considering what lights and simple stage effects you want to introduce on a regular basis. Many artists' live stage shows are made memorable by their lighting and staging, and it is not always the most extravagant displays which make the greatest impact. The next time you go to a gig yourself spend some time noting the detail that goes into making a visually exciting and appropriate stage design – and 'steal' the best ideas!

BASIC LIGHTING

A standard rock & roll lighting rig consists of 36K of lights usually backed by a small effects rack. A 'K' is 1,000 watts of light and 36K would usually comprise 36 × 1,000 watt par 64 can lanterns. These look like theatre lights, usually silver or black. The bulbs they contain emit bright, white light which can be coloured, as required, by placing coloured 'gels' in a frame, in front of them. Theatre gels are actually made of a special non-flammable gelatin which is able to withstand the extreme heat which the lights give off. You can get lighting gels from theatrical suppliers and you could take a selection of colours with you to stick safely over any existing lights in the smallest venues. If you are playing on a little stage in the corner of a pub, you could try colouring some of the more obtrusive white lights over the audience to create a different atmosphere and to help highlight the stage area. Make sure the gels do not actually touch the light bulbs. Do not be tempted to use anything other than fireproof theatrical gel to colour lights.

Hiring a lighting rig with an operator, and transport to and from the gig, will cost roughly £100–£120. Little one-man operations can sometimes offer the same service for less money (see the back of the Melody Maker) or can be persuaded to provide minimalist lighting (perhaps in venues where there is no room for a full rig), for as little as £50.00.

In theory, lighting rigs require a 3 phase 60 amp power supply. This is not always available in small venues so do check with the venue manager before you book the lights. However, if they don't have a 3 phase supply, this does not necessarily mean that you cannot have the lights you want. Any lighting company with experience of working at this level will be skilled at running their whole system off an ordinary 13 amp plug! Amperage can be calculated at roughly 5 amps per 1,000 watts of lights – so a 36K lighting rig ought to require 180 amps of electrical power. In practice, however, as you never turn all the lights on at once, the rig can be run on a 60 amp circuit with care. So long as your lighting operator doesn't turn on too many lights at once it shouldn't overload the system!

When you first contact a lighting company and order some lights, try to avoid ordering 'a 36K rig'. If you do order in this way you may end up with the same lights, lighting design and colours that the band up the road used the night before. From the very beginning see if you can build up a relationship with a lighting engineer who may also have some pretentions towards being a Lighting Designer (LD). Without being over ambitious try and introduce some ideas and enthusiasm into your initial discussions. A standard colour wash over the stage can be very boring, so ask if you can have some floor, side, or back lighting. Possibly, a strobe or even some pyrotechnics might be available. It is a good idea to get a backdrop, in either black or white, to drape over the back of the stage area. White will serve as good reflector of coloured light and can also be used as a surface for the projection of images or lighting effects. A black backdrop absorbs the light and can be used to create a feeling of depth to the stage. Backdrops can also serve to cover a multitude of sins at the back of the stage – anything from mock Tudor beams to the drum kit of the headlining act. You could have one made to your own specifications, possibly including the band's logo. Double-check, however, that any drapes or backdrops you use are properly fireproofed – especially if you are playing at one of the more professional venues. Apart from your own safety on stage, the stage manager probably lives in constant fear of fire inspections and will not let you use stage props which are not fireproofed. You can buy fireproofing chemicals from major fabric stockists but remember that most methods of fireproofing only last 3–4 months before you need to repeat the process.

Another way to make your set more interesting is to use risers – low platforms – to set the members of the band at different levels and angles to each other. If cleverly lit, the simple procedure of putting your drummer and keyboard player on a different level from the rest of the band can create a varied visual impact. Drum risers can be hired from staging hire companies. They normally cost between £15–£20 per night plus delivery and collection.

When you play at bigger venues you will need bigger lighting companies, and they will start to court you if they think you are going to be successful. They may even be pushy in their attempts to gain your business but, unless you are dissatisfied in some way with your own LD, it should not be necessary to change companies. By hiring the extra lights and equipment from a larger stockist you can benefit from the wider range that a big company can provide, without losing the LD that you know, and enjoy working with. Lighting designers, more often than sound engineers, seem to be able to 'grow' with the bands they work with, U2's LD, for example, has been with the band from the start and continues to do their lighting design even at the biggest venues.

PROBLEMS WITH LIGHT AND SOUND

A common problem which arises at live gigs is a loud insistent buzzing coming through the PA. It inevitably develops, apparently for no good reason, five minutes before the doors are due to open! You may have sound-checked without a hitch all afternoon when this occurs and it often leads to frayed tempers with everyone accusing everyone else of being at fault.

Where this interference can be directly linked to the lighting rig there are some practical things that can be done to try and alleviate it. If the buzzing increases as the lights are turned up, and decreases or stops completely as the lights are turned off, then it is probably a lighting fault. To try and avoid this problem in the first place, you can do the following:

(**a**) Never run sound and light cables in parallel or alongside each other around the stage. If they must cross, always keep light and sound cables at right angles to each other.

(**b**) If at all possible have totally separate power supplies and cable runs for sound and light systems. Sound problems associated with lights often occur when both systems are sharing the same phase. In small clubs this is difficult to avoid.

(**c**) Ensure that you have a proper neutral and earth on both sound and light equipment. Ideally, a 'clean' earth should be used in both cases – not one which is shared with other equipment – for example the beer cooling system at a pub.

(**d**) Do not make a messy job when 'tailing-in' or connecting up your PA and lights system to the mains supply. Where there is a bus-bar connection always ensure that it is screwed up as tightly as possible, otherwise heat can build up at the connection. Apart from creating possible interference problems, badly connected electrical points are obviously dangerous.

(**e**) Quite often gremlins and buzzing can be tracked down to the dimmer racks of the lights system. The better maintained and newer these are, the fewer problems you will have.

(**f**) It is not always the lighting man's fault when buzzing occurs. A badly screened and maintained PA cable can cause problems, as can your own instruments and backline – so make sure that all your equipment is properly maintained and repaired.

(**g**) Have a good look round the whole stage area and check for any possible physical links between lights and PA. On one occasion the interference at a major gig in London which was due to be televised live, turned out to be caused by a metal ladder hanging down from the front lighting truss and touching the back of one of the PA stacks. Someone moved the ladder while searching desperately for a more complicated technical explanation – only to find that the buzzing stopped the moment he did so!
Even having checked and satisfied yourselves that you have done all that is humanly and scientifically possible, you may find that the annoying interference has not gone away. Under these circumstances try and remain calm and get on with the job in hand. Arguments and recriminations do not help anybody and sometimes buzzing can go as easily as it came without any obvious explanation!

ARTS FESTIVALS, FESTIVALS AND BENEFIT GIGS

ARTS FESTIVALS

Local Councils and Arts organizations can be a good source of live work – especially if you are prepared to play for nothing. A book published by Rhinegold Publishing 'Arts Festivals in Britain and Ireland' profiles over 400 Arts Festivals indicating the type of acts they feature and giving dates and full contact information to would-be participants. However, not many of them promote pop. Some have tried, but, perhaps through pressure from local residents, have given up.

Unlike rock festivals, 'Arts Festivals', as run by Local Councils and other Arts organizations, can take place at many different venues. You should apply to the Arts Council Committee for permission to participate and, if you are successful, you may even be given a small grant. The venue which you will be playing, the date and the time, will all be allotted to you. Your name and details will be included in the Festival brochure, and tickets will be printed and sold for you at the official outlets. As you can imagine, if there are, say, five venues being used every lunch-time and evening for three weeks, this requires a lot of organization. For this reason you should get all applications in early, which will also give you a better chance of being awarded some money to cover your expenses.

In general, councils are worth approaching not only because they may be able to help you get live work, but also because they sometimes provide rehearsal facilities and other amenities. However, there is no Government directive from above telling our local councils to look after their pop musicians, despite the fact that pop music is a very valuable British export. All councils have a Leisure Services Committee, and if you want to start a festival, or perhaps you simply want to campaign for a live venue in your area, then lobby the councillors who are on this committee. Find out who they are and ask them what they are doing for young people in their area. You will find useful information on this kind of work from the Council Services book – ring your local council and ask them to send you a copy.

As a rule of thumb you will find that Labour and Liberal councils have more active Leisure Services Committees when it comes to young people. A lot will also depend on the history of live music in your area. Where there is an active promotion of youth-oriented events it is usually the result of hard work by a number of individuals and, as such, it can easily fall apart once those individuals stop campaigning. It may be worth checking with your councillor whether there ever were any useful facilities in the past, because if there were, it may be easier to revive them rather than starting again from scratch.

All Councils are under a lot more financial pressure nowadays, and this has meant that Arts budgets have been drastically cut. Correspondingly, Arts Festivals are now expected to run at break-even (or even at a profit) and facilities for any arts-based activities are suffering accordingly.

ROCK FESTIVALS

There are also a number of well established annual festivals – most of which you have probably heard of – notably Glastonbury (a CND fundraising event), WOMAD, Donnington, Reading, Nottinghill Carnival and the Cambridge Folk Festival. Depending on the sort of music you play you can try approaching the organizers of these events for an opening slot. Your chances will be slim, unless you have some sort of public profile and an agent to back you up. Perhaps your single biggest problem will be getting to the promoters early enough – most of the work on festivals is done many months in advance. However, whilst you may not get on to the main stage at your first attempt, there are sometimes smaller, peripheral stages at some of the concerts (notably Glastonbury and WOMAD) which you might get a chance to play on. If all else fails you can always go as a paying punter and just busk. There are thousands of people at these events and several bands have first brought attention to themselves by busking at major festivals. (For contact details see Directory: Promoters page 246.)

Sade at the Artists Against Apartheid concert, Clapham Common, 1986.

BENEFIT CONCERTS

Benefit concerts are another possible area to explore, whether you organize them yourselves, or try to get on the bill of a local one. As benefit shows are ostensibly put together to raise money for a cause, the promoters are usually primarily interested in acts that will pull a crowd. Even if you offer to play for nothing, or for 'expenses', this isn't necessarily helpful if you can't guarantee an audience (playing for expenses only, or a much reduced fee is normally expected at benefit shows). However, if you are worth a few hundred paying customers in your own area, you might have more luck if an event is planned nearby.

Greenpeace, CND, Red Wedge, Nicaragua Solidarity Campaign and Amnesty International are all obvious 'political' causes which are regularly associated with live benefit gigs and all can be approached if you wish to put on a show of your own. It is important that you get written permission to use the names of these associations before you go ahead with any event on their behalf.

Local charities and national charities such as Childline, Oxfam, The World Wildlife Fund and so on, will also need contacting before you use their logos in association with an event. It is definitely

easier to do concerts of any kind indoors rather than out, but if you have had lots of gig experience why not run your own small-scale 'festival'?

It may seem a little ambitious, but it is possible to plan a modest open-air event yourselves, in the absence of anyone else promoting one in your area. You will need a natural ability to organize people and things, as well as a lot of patience, plenty of spare time, and some source of financial help. You will also need a long run-up to the event itself, preferably at least three or four months.

Without the backing of your Local Council you have little hope of getting the event off the ground at all, so they should be your first line of enquiry. Councils work notoriously slowly so you have to be very patient and as persuasive as possible. If the event is going to cost the Council anything, or if they cannot be convinced that the event can be run safely, without upsetting local residents, you are unlikely to get the go-ahead. Do as much pre-planning as possible and enlist the help of as many local figures of authority as you can, such as local councillors, social workers, publicans, and journalists. Perhaps you could organize a petition among local youth asking for an annual festival to raise money for a youth centre, or some deserving local charity.

Once you have done your ground work go to your local Leisure Services Committee, with your ideas and the site you have in mind for the event. Having gained Council approval you will need to follow the basic guidelines for promoting any other gig – but note that there are some practical differences in the scale of an open-air event, which require some attention. Most of them are self-evident and include considerations such as those outlined below.

(**a**) Permission to use an open-air site, usually a Council owned park, where there are toilet facilities. Unless the event is being sponsored or is a 'free concert', you will need a secure, fenced area to keep out the non-payers.

(**b**) Very early in the proceedings you will need to contact and discuss your proposal with the local police, St John's Ambulance and possibly the local Fire Brigade.

(**c**) Your PA and lights systems will have to be considerably larger than the ones you would use for an indoor event, and the first problem to be solved will be that of a power supply. This may well entail you hiring generating equipment and qualified electricians and mechanics to operate it.

(**d**) Noise levels and public nuisance will also have to be discussed with local council, police and local residents' committees before you begin actually promoting the event.

(e) Unless you are lucky enough to have a site that has a covered stage area you are going to have to build one. It will have to conform to council safety standards, so get a reliable and professional scaffolding company to do the actual construction. The British weather also has to be kept at bay, and this means hiring tarpaulins and lots of plastic sheeting to protect the PA and other electrical gear.

(f) Whether or not you are trying to secure the whole event against non-ticket holders you are certainly going to need back-stage security to keep an eye on the equipment, as well as 'marshals' to make sure people know where to park, where the exits are, and so on. If you are securing the whole event you will definitely need to book a team of 'professional' security staff. You will also need a stage manager, as well as an overall event co-ordinator, to make sure everything runs smoothly. A compere of some sort will be needed to let the public know what is happening, make any necessary announcements, introduce the bands, and play records during the changeovers between acts. The event co-ordinator should liaise with the local authorities – such as the police and council officials.

Obviously, there is a lot of work involved in promoting a festival event of this kind, however small. If you can, find somebody with relevant experience and have a good talk with them before you start to do anything.

Prolific Jazz guitarist John Scofield at the Bracknell Festival, 1987.

Maxi Priest, Britain's best exponent of Lover's Rock, at the Artists Against Apartheid concert at Clapham Common, 1986.

Mick Jones of Big Audio Dynamite
at the Artists Against Apartheid
concert, Clapham Common,
summer 1986.

The Pogues allegedly practising for a cycle ride from London to Oxford organized by the Nicaragua Solidarity Campaign. As the lads only appear to have two bikes between them we suspect they didn't all make it!

An unlikely musical alliance but a shared political outlook unites Little Steven and Jerry Dammers at the Hammersmith Odeon, 1988.

Morrisey performing to huge crowds at the GLC 'Jobs For a Change' festival outside County Hall, London, 1984

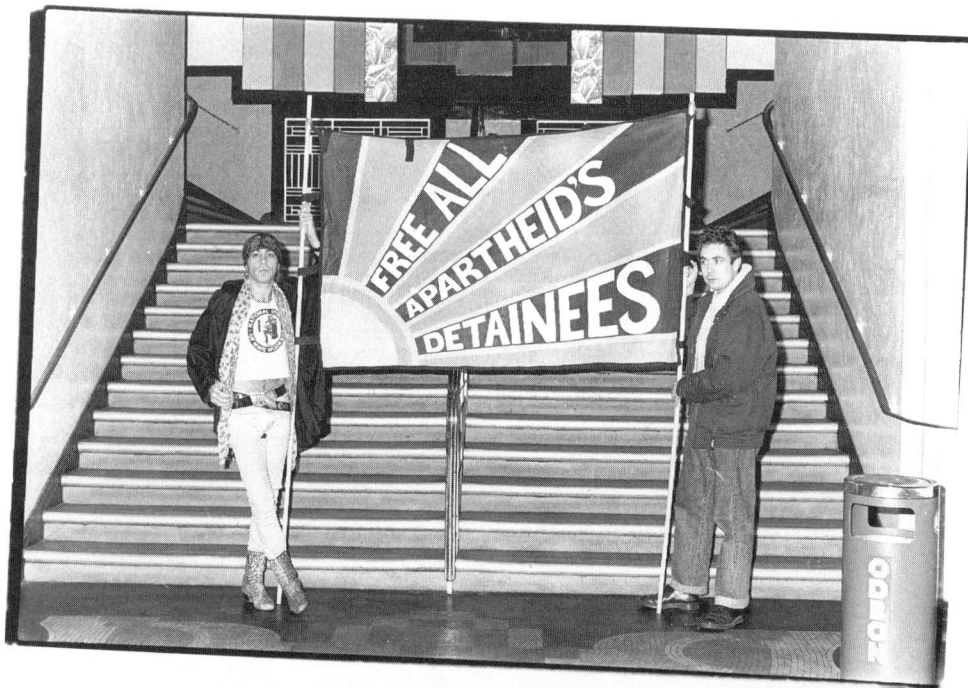

TOURS AND TOURING IN THE UK

An experienced booking agent can ring round promoters and venue managers to book tours relatively easily. For you it is likely to be a lot harder and, without a tour manager, you are also going to have to organize and co-ordinate the whole trip yourselves. Few people will have heard of you in the early days, and you are likely to be working on a shoe-string budget.

If you think touring the club circuit in the UK sounds glamorous, talk to someone who has recently been there. You will probably hear horrendous tales of plastic ham sandwiches and warm lager, filthy cubby holes masquerading as dressing rooms, promoters who don't pay, dingy hotels, decrepit PA systems, and audiences that don't turn up! You are unlikely to make any money on tours at this level, and even when you are getting reasonable fees, you may even end up travelling in the van with the equipment and sleeping rough at night. Good planning can help you to avoid disasters, but remember that you will be relying on a lot of other people and that 'other people' have a nasty habit of not doing their jobs properly. Short of making a complete nuisance of yourself by ringing them every twenty minutes, there is no real safeguard against this, so be prepared for some hiccups.

Tours can come together almost by accident – starting as a series of individual dates booked coincidentally around the same time in different places. If the gaps can be filled by finding gigs in the towns in between, or at other venues in the same area, then it may be practical and make financial sense to stay overnight after each gig, rather than travel home each night. You may, for example, have a support slot at a college, a couple of pub dates and be head-lining a showcase night for a London Club – all in the same week.

If you haven't already done so, it is worth reading through the section on Gigs, page 11), before you get to grips with touring.

TOUR BUDGET

The first thing you should do, once you have a series of dates, is prepare your budget.

Begin by adding together all the guaranteed fees that you expect to receive (see page 16). Try not to base your figures on earnings from percentage deals or on earnings from sources such as T-shirt sales and other merchandising which is not guaranteed income.

Then make a list of all the outgoings and costs that you are going to incur. This will entail finding out the price of accommodation, transport hire and fuel, possible backline equipment hire, PA & Lights hire, crew costs, band PDs (per diums – the term commonly used to mean the sum of money paid per day to each band member for their daily subsistence), and any other miscellaneous costs associated with the tour ('miscellaneous costs' can often be much larger than you expect and you should always budget a generous amount to cover contingencies from vehicle breakdown to guitar strings and drum skin replacements). In an ideal world you should already have enough money in the bank to pay all these costs. This is usually not the case and where you don't have either the guaranteed fees or the financial security to go on a tour – you will have to cut corners and take risks if you really want to go ahead. The checklist and advice below is an ideal which virtually no tour has ever attained: even at the top levels mistakes are made and money lost!

ACCOMMODATION

Avoid having to search for somewhere to stay on the day, or worse still, after the show. You may be lucky, and be offered hospitality by someone you meet at the gig but it is obviously foolish to rely upon this sort of windfall. Instead, try and get hold of the British Tourist Board's publications 'Hotels' and 'B&B/Farmhouses/Guesthouses' which, according to one tour manager we spoke to, 'will be the best tenner you'll spend'.

The Housemartins find a simple solution to the high cost of touring!

Photo courtesy of Go! Discs.

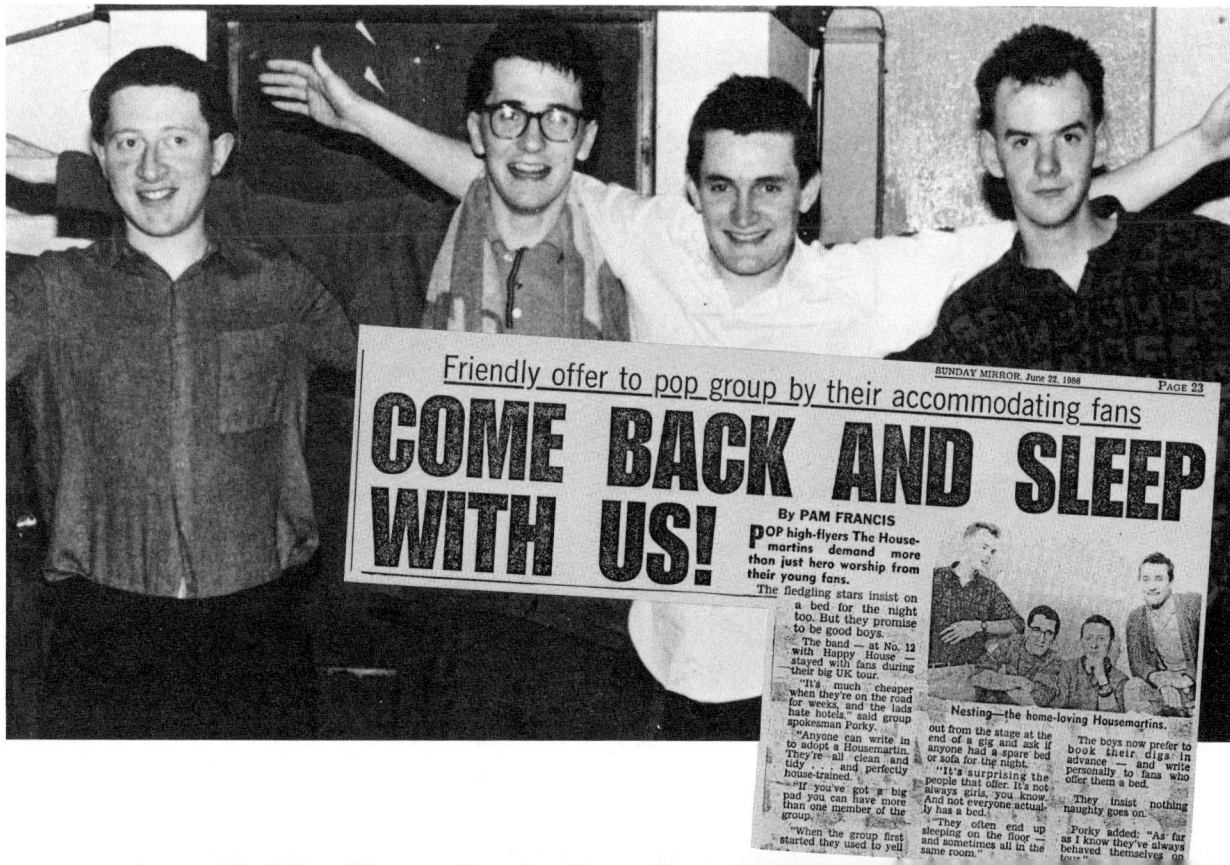

Friendly offer to pop group by their accommodating fans

SUNDAY MIRROR, June 22, 1986   PAGE 23

COME BACK AND SLEEP WITH US!

By PAM FRANCIS

POP high-flyers The House-martins demand more than just hero worship from their young fans.

The fledgling stars insist on a bed for the night too. But they promise to be good boys.

The band — at No. 12 with Happy House — stayed with fans during their big UK tour.

"It's much cheaper when they're on the road for weeks, and the lads hate hotels," said group spokesman Porky.

"Anyone can write in to adopt a Housemartin. They're all clean and tidy . . . and perfectly house-trained.

"If you've got a big pad you can have more than one member of the group.

"When the group first started they used to yell

out from the stage at the end of a gig and ask if anyone had a spare bed or sofa for the night.

"It's surprising the people that offer. It's not always girls, you know. And not everyone actually has a bed.

"They often end up sleeping on the floor — and sometimes all in the same room."

The boys now prefer to book their digs in advance — and write personally to fans who offer them a bed.

They insist nothing naughty goes on.

Porky added: "As far as I know they've always behaved themselves on tour."

Nesting—the home-loving Housemartins.

Billy Bragg at the Artists Against Apartheid concert, Clapham Common, summer 1986.

After a six month stint in the Army Billy Bragg bought himself out and began his distinctive solo career. Armed with just his guitar, his songs and his repartee he cut his teeth live in pubs and clubs around the country and built what is today an international and dedicated following.

Touring during the 1984 Miners Strike brought Billy into contact with people who were suffering from the effects of Thatcher's policies and in 1985 he joined forces with Junior Giscombe, D C Lee, The Style Council and the Communards to form Red Wedge – a group of performers committed to Socialist ideals and pledging their qualified support for the UK Labour Party. Through Red Wedge these musicians were able to step inside the political arena and their many benefit and solidarity gigs around the country did much to help raise funds and spirits.

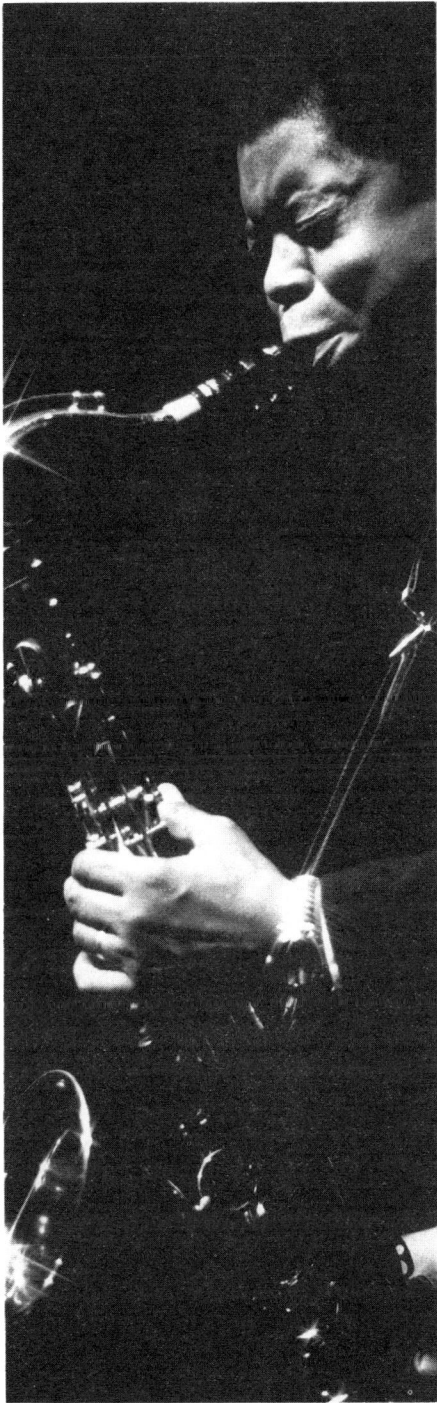

Courtney Pine at the Mean Fiddler, Harlesden, March 1989.

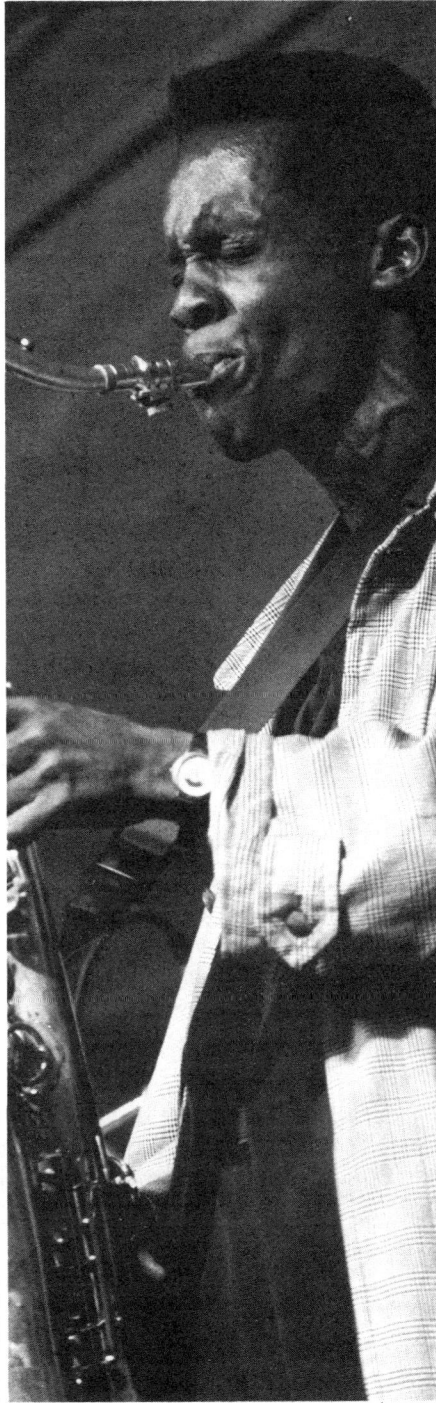

Steve Williamson, one of the most exciting saxophonists to emerge from the Jazz Warriors, at the Seen on the Green Festival, London 1988.

Andy Shepperd, winner of Wired Magazine's 'best instrumentalist of the year' award, at the Seen on the Green Festival, London 1988.

If you are playing in a city or a large town it is advisable to stay somewhere out of the centre. Accommodation is usually cheaper thirty miles or so outside a city, it is also generally quieter and, in terms of your van load of equipment, probably safer. Provincial hotels and guesthouses might be less amenable to riotous after-show parties but this can be offset against the fact that you can be thirty miles closer to your next show and clear of the traffic jams on the morning after.

Whether you stay in the town centre or not, you should ring and make your booking at least two weeks in advance. Speak to the manager, if possible, and introduce yourself. Whether you tell a hotel from the beginning that you are a pop band is up to you. Some hotels are very anti-performer and have a policy of refusing such bookings. By deceiving them over the phone you may face an embarrassing refusal when you actually arrive to check in. As management always 'reserves the right to refuse admission', honesty is probably the best policy. Having rung an hotel or guesthouse, check the following:

(**a**) The date and the time of arrival. If you are going to arrive in the morning make sure you will be able to put your luggage in your rooms. If not, can your bags be left somewhere safe and picked up later?

(**b**) Let the hotel know the approximate time of your return after the show. Will there be someone there to let you in – or will you need a key?

(**c**) How many of you will be staying and will you require single, double or twin rooms? (Twins are usually the best value but check with everyone before you ring to book the rooms.) Make the bookings under the surnames of everyone in the tour party. This way, if one of you returns later than the others to the hotel, he or she will still be able to get in.

(**d**) Check the cost of the rooms. Will you be getting breakfast within the price? Does it include VAT? Is there a discount for a party booking (particularly at weekends)?

(**e**) Most hotels will ask you to pay in the morning but you should check – especially at guesthouses, that payment is not expected at the time of the arrival. If you are to pay in the morning the hotel may request that one of the band leave a bank card with reception overnight.

Note that most hotels will require you to confirm the booking in writing and some may also require a deposit. Whilst you are writing to them it is worth confirming all the other points that you have agreed over the phone.

VAN HIRE

You are likely to come up against the problem that most van hire companies operate on an insurance disclaimer that excludes people connected with the entertainments business. There are some companies, however, who regularly deal with touring bands and have adjusted their insurance policies accordingly (see Directory, Information & Travel, page 236). If none of these are convenient for you then the best thing to do is ring round as many companies as you can find in your local Yellow Pages. The only statutory requirement is that your driver is over 21 and has a full clean driving licence. If you are approaching a company that you know does not deal with bands, bear in mind that you will be asked to state your occupation. You might be tempted to say 'driver' or 'unemployed' – but it could be an offence to do so under these circumstances and you would almost certainly be found out if there was an accident. Some van hire companies are satisfied if you use a driver or roadie to take the equipment whilst the band members travel separately, but this can be an expensive option.

The amount of equipment you are going to take with you and the room that the band requires, will dictate the size of the vehicle you need to hire. The classic touring vehicle is the Ford Transit. A popular van hire company that does deal with pop bands quoted us the following rates:

Ford Transit van: £38.95 per day (inc. VAT and third party insurance)
£158.70 per week (inc. VAT and third party insurance)

There is an optional £3.00 per day insurance supplement to cover 'goods in transit'.

If the band only has a small amount of equipment and would rather travel in a little more comfort then another option is to hire a mini-bus and remove some of the seats to make room for the equipment.

12 Seater Mini-bus: £48.00 per day (inc. VAT and third party insurance)
£245.00 per week (inc. VAT and third party insurance)

Ensure availability by getting your van organized at least two weeks in advance and be prepared to pay either a sizeable deposit up front or the full price plus a returnable deposit. A bit of research will be worthwhile and it pays dividends to spend a little extra for vans that are fully insured for your use, are in good condition, and have a back-up service should you need it.

THE TC AND MUSIC GUIDE

INSTRUMENT INSURANCE IN THE VAN

Make sure that all your equipment is insured prior to departure (see Insurance, page 213). It may be that your general instrument insurance policy only covers equipment left unattended in a van for half an hour after dark. This can be a greater or lesser problem depending on where you are staying overnight. Parking your van with the back doors close up against a wall is a worthwhile precaution, and you could also keep out prying eyes by covering the windows – but neither constitutes a safeguard against theft. The best method is probably to have someone actually sleep in the van and to keep particularly precious items with you.

ON THE ROAD

Get a good road atlas, preferably one which includes some town maps. It is also useful to ask the venue for specific directions, or better still to send you a map if they have one. At the same time check out any possible traffic problems or local diversions caused by roadworks or rush hour traffic. When estimating the time it will take you to get somewhere always give yourselves plenty of leeway and then add an hour!

ARRIVING AT THE GIG

It is probably best to either call round or ring the venue when you arrive in their area to make sure you have time to check in at your hotel before you go to the gig. Whatever happens, get there in plenty of time and make contact with the manager or whoever has been made responsible for running the show. If your contract has not been signed try to get this done as soon as possible. Don't be too officious about contracts but be friendly and insistent, if only to get the promoter to remember the important points. If you arrive early and something crucial has been left undone at least there may be time to put things right. If you have arrived late and things have been left undone, then you only have yourselves to blame. While you are checking that the major points have been covered also check the running order and sound-check times, whether there has been any change in the bill and so on.

PAY

At what point should you go and talk about money with the promoter? As we have already pointed out it is difficult to get guaranteed fees so you are likely to be on a percentage of the door takings. Whoever is actually running the door and taking the money, make sure that you keep a close eye on the proceedings. In this way you should have a pretty good idea of how much money to expect. As far as fees go, the promoter will give priority to the people who are used regularly by the club such as the PA or lighting company. If possible, get someone to see the promoter about payment as soon as the band have been on stage for 10 minutes or so.

On occasion, you may have to be prepared to play for nothing because in this country, contract or no contract, young bands are treated very poorly. If you have an agent you are better off under these circumstances, especially if your agent does regular business with the promoter in question. But even so, remember that agents make contracts between the artist and the promoter, and not between themselves and the promoter, so there is no way in which the agency is liable either for you not getting paid or for you not playing.

GIG OVER

Once the gig is over, start your load-out as soon as possible. Apart from keeping on the good side of the licensee of the premises, who is no doubt anxious to clear up and go home, you are also less likely to suffer lost or damaged equipment. Make yourselves responsible for leaving dressing rooms and the back-stage area clean and tidy and work on establishing a good professional attitude to your relationships with promoters. This way you are much more likely to be invited back. No-one enjoys working with slobs.

The following section assumes that all venue bookings have been made by a reputable booking agent: it would be fool-hardy for a band to attempt a full-blown tour outside the UK without one!

A foreign tour requires more preparation and you should by this stage have appointed a manager to take on the organizational responsibilities. Almost more important than a manager, is a good, well organized tour manager. We have outlined below the main items that should be on your checklist prior to departure and tried to anticipate some of the more typical problems which you might come up against.

PASSPORTS, VISAS AND WORK PERMITS

It goes without saying that passports must be up to date and in order for the countries you visit. Check this well in advance if you are going to non-EEC countries because you cannot get a visa on a Visitor's Passport. Application forms are available from main Post Offices and from Passport Offices.

British Visitor's Passports are obtainable over the counter at any main Post Office (unless you are in Northern Ireland where they are only issued from the Passport Office in Belfast) and they are acceptable for travel in Western Europe and West Berlin, but not for Yugoslavia. Note that this passport cannot be used for overland travel through the German Democratic Republic to West Berlin. A full 5 or 10 year passport issued by your local Passport Office can take up to six weeks to come through – especially during the summer period. Visas are not normally necessary for Western Europe if you are only visiting for a period of three months or less, but there are some exceptions, so it may be wise to check your position, especially if your UK passport was not issued in the UK, or if you hold a passport of any other nationality. Contact your local Passport Office for details.

(NB. Citizens of the USA must have a visa for France – even if they are resident in the UK.)

Work permits are not necessary for most EEC countries, (Spain and Portugal are exceptions). They are definitely required for non-EEC countries. Check the latest details with the Department of Employment.

There are companies that can organize work permits and visas for you. They are certainly worth considering, especially if you are going somewhere slightly problematic, such as an Eastern bloc country. The visa company we spoke to would process a whole band's visas and work permits for East Germany for around £100.00. They warned that it takes around five to six weeks to process Eastern bloc permits and visas, and that the promoter in the country where you are due to perform has to instigate proceedings at their end. For more information contact: Traffic Control, 211 Piccadilly, London W1. Tel: 01–548 9972.

DRIVING LICENCE

You should carry your national driving licence with you at all times – even if you have also obtained an IDP (see below). Make sure it is not going to expire while you are abroad and check whether the countries you visit require a translation of your licence to be made into their own language (this is the case in Algeria, Bulgaria, Turkey and also in Italy if you do not have the new 'pink' EEC format licence).

The AA and the RAC will both advise you to get an IDP or International Driving Permit. An IDP enables the holder to drive for a limited period in those countries where their national licence is not recognised. Check with either company for details.

VAN HIRE

A reputable van hire company that hires vehicles to be taken abroad will be able to equip you with all necessary legal and insurance documents for the countries you are going to visit. Do make sure you have adequate insurance.

MINIBUS

A minibus constructed and equipped to carry 10 or more persons (including the driver) and used outside the UK is subject to regulations which govern international bus and coach journeys. Generally, this means that the vehicle has to be fitted with a tachograph and that appropriate documentation in the form of a 'waybill' has to be obtained. This specifies the travel itinerary, the names of the passengers and of the driver, the registration number of the vehicle and how many seats it is registered for. If you hire a minibus from a reputable company all this will be provided for you.

For the tachograph (if the minibus is registered in Great Britain) contact the local Traffic Area Office of the Department of Transport (if the minibus is registered in N. Ireland contact the Department of Environment for Northern Ireland, Road Transport Department, Upper Galwally, Belfast BT8 4FY).

For the waybill contact Sardinia House, 52 Lincoln's Inn Fields, London WC2A 3LZ. Tel: 01–831 7546.

A minibus driver must be at least 21 and hold a full driving licence valid for group A or, if automatic transmission, group B.

VEHICLE REGISTRATION DOCUMENT

In order that you may use a vehicle abroad under its UK registra-

tion, the Vehicle Registration Document must be carried. If this is being replaced when you want to travel, you can apply to your local Vehicle Licensing Office for a Certificate of Registration. If the vehicle is not registered in your name you will have to get a letter of authority from the owner.

If you are hiring the vehicle you will need to obtain a Vehicle on Hire Certificate available from both the RAC and the AA.

TRANSIT INSURANCE

This is cover against damage in transit – such as on a Ferry or Motorail. Check this aspect with your insurer before you set off.

VEHICLE INSURANCE/GREEN CARD

Motor vehicle insurance is compulsory in all European countries so don't leave home without it. Although you will be covered by your existing insurance policy in most of Europe, the cover is only minimal. This means that even if you have a comprehensive policy you will get no compensation for damage, fire, theft or personal accident, and you will get third party cover only to the legal minimum laid down in the country concerned. It is therefore strongly recommended that you get an International Green Card of Insurance (available from your own insurance company) in order to secure the fullest cover available to you. If you hire, then this Green Card should be given to you by the hire company.

PLATE

It is a legal requirement in all European countries that visitor's vehicles display a distinctive nationality plate as near as possible to the back number plate. The AA and the RAC both issue these stickers.

EUROPEAN ACCIDENT 'STATEMENT OF FACTS' FORM

This is available from the AA and provides invaluable advice should you be involved in an accident.

CARNETS

Carnets are a kind of passport for equipment. They are required by the Customs and Excise department whenever you take any equipment out of the country. Carnets simplify the temporary importation and exportation procedures which are necessary to make sure that goods are not being illegally imported or exported, without the requisite duties being paid. Customs and Excise wish to prevent you from (a) selling any of your equipment while you are abroad, and (b) buying any new equipment while you are on your tour – without paying the appropriate duties and tax. Because the Carnet consists of a precise inventory of every piece of equipment you take with you, any missing or additional items will be revealed when your Carnet import/export documents are inspected as you pass through Customs control at a national border. You will then be charged duty on the value of any missing or new equipment by the customs officials in every country you visit, including the UK on your return. This makes the whole process of buying and selling equipment on tour problematic and expensive – so don't bother!

THE EEC CARNET

For temporary exportation/importation of your equipment within the EEC you will need a Carnet which is available free from your local Chamber of Commerce. There is a booklet of rules which apply to the EEC Carnet which is supplied free when you collect your Carnet forms. You will see that the EEC Carnet was specifically designed to help individuals such as professional photographers and sales reps, to travel more freely around Europe with small quantities of dutiable equipment. It is not intended for large scale movements of equipment and is certainly not appropriate for companies trading in equipment. Depending on the level at which you are touring, an EEC Carnet can save you time and money. It is particularly appropriate if you are all travelling in one van with small amounts of personally owned equipment. However, as soon as you progress to a level where you are hiring equipment owned by somebody else, it is advisable to use an ATA Carnet (see following page).

You are required to type detailed information about all the equipment you are taking with you on the back of the EEC Carnet forms and you will later have to submit these to the border officials whenever you move from one country to another. Often, however, a band using an EEC Carnet will have too much equipment to fit it all on the Carnet document. To get around this problem you can type the information on to a separate piece of paper – sometimes known as a 'load-in' sheet. You should then make photocopies of these load-in sheets and have them with you to hand over to the Custom officials.

Make sure that you will not be moving outside the EEC because, for tours that extend beyond the EEC member countries you will need a different Carnet (see following page). It is surprisingly easy to overlook the non-EEC countries when you are planning a European tour. Whilst you may only be playing gigs in, say, France and

Germany, you may find that your tour routing takes you through Luxembourg or Switzerland – neither of which are EEC countries.

The EEC members currently include: Great Britain, France, West Germany, Eire, Italy, Spain, Portugal, Greece, Holland, Belgium and Norway. (Turkey is currently seeking membership and note that neither Denmark nor Sweden are EEC members.)

THE ATA CARNET

If you are travelling beyond the EEC you will need an International Carnet, the ATA Carnet, which can only be issued by certain Chambers of Commerce (your nearest one will advise you). An ATA Carnet is a more expensive procedure all round. It will cost you £68.00 to have the Carnet processed and you will have to give them some money as a security against the payment of any duties you may incur. The money you leave as a security is known as a 'bond' and it is equal to the highest rate of Duty and Taxes applicable to your equipment in any of your destination countries.

For example, if you go to Hungary with £1,000 worth of equipment the 'security rate' is currently 300% of the value of that equipment. In other words, £3,000. If you go to France you would pay a French security rate of only 50% of the equipment's value – i.e. £500. If you did a tour of both countries you would have to pay the higher of the two rates. You can either deposit this money with the Chamber of Commerce yourself or, you can take out insurance to the value of £3,000 and pay the Insurance company the required premium.

When the tour is over and you have returned with all your equipment intact you will eventually get your security deposit back from the Chamber of Commerce – although it may take up to 31 months! The insurance company method can be more convenient and it doesn't require you to find a large lump sum, although you will have lost the money paid as a premium on the insurance policy.

HOW THE ATA CARNET WORKS

You will be issued with three different colours of document. The front and back pages of the Carnet are yellow. The front page constitutes an export of goods form to allow you to take your equipment out of the UK. The back page constitutes an import of goods form which allows you to bring that equipment back again without paying duty.

Sandwiched between the two yellow sheets will be a mixture of white and blue sheets. The white sheets have two sections. One forms the import of goods voucher and the other forms the export of goods voucher which you use coming into, and out of, foreign countries respectively. These have to be presented to the Customs Officers at the border posts with a photocopied list of your equipment attached, whenever you enter or leave a country where you play a concert. The blue document is for use whenever you traverse a country, but do not stop and play a gig there. Always ask for extra blue documents in case you need to cross more national boundaries than you first expected.

When your tour consists of confirmed dates, get a good map of Europe and plan your route carefully, noting the number of borders that you will be crossing, not only in and out of the countries you will be playing in, but also the borders of those countries which you may only need to travel through.

Submit the final tour itinerary on the completed Carnet to your Chamber of Commerce.

INFORMATION REQUIRED FOR A CARNET

Both types of Carnet require you to describe in a lot of detail the equipment that you will be taking with you. You will be asked to provide brand names, serial numbers, details of weight and condition and so on, the purpose of which is to try and verify that the equipment you travel with remains the same throughout your tour. For example:

Item 1:	Flight case containing:	(Valued at £50.00. Country of origin: UK)
Item 2:	1 × Mesa Boogie Combo Amplifier Serial No: 17337	(Valued at £650.00. Country of origin: USA)
Item 3:	Flight case containing:	(Valued at £50.00. Country of origin: UK)
Item 4:	Ampeg SVT Bass Power Amp 1987 series 95	(Valued at £..... and so on)

Make sure that the information you give is correct; NEVER attempt to defraud customs by missing items off the list and note that even flight cases count as 'equipment'. It really isn't worth trying to deceive them and you would be surprised how much Customs Officers know about guitars and other musical equipment! You must keep proof of purchase of any musical or other equipment – especially when you are using an EEC Carnet. The Customs and Excise are doing more random spot checks on Carnets, and will not hesitate to prosecute you if they find you have misinformed them in any way.

Your insurance company will probably charge you quite high

insurance premiums on your equipment, especially if you are travelling in 'risky' countries, and it is sometimes tempting to mark down the value of your equipment to reduce these and other related costs. If the Customs Officers then choose to check up on your declaration form and can prove (by demanding receipts) that you have under-declared the value of your equipment they will almost certainly prosecute.

Remember that the Carnet is a legal document and only authorised people can present it to Customs Officers. Always make lots of photocopies of the equipment list and the authorisation letters showing who is allowed to process the Carnet. Where you are dealing with your own equipment it is worth writing a letter of authorisation for yourself on your own headed paper. Where you are dealing with hired equipment you need a letter of authorisation from the hiring company.

Make sure that the Customs Officials properly process your forms by stamping and signing them at every border. If, for some reason, a border post is not manned – DO NOT PROCEED into the next country. If you do leave a country and enter another one without having your Carnet processed by both sets of Customs Officials you will render your Carnet imcomplete which will lead to more problems than we have got room to begin listing! In this situation either wait – or try another route.

When you arrive at a border post you will most likely be directed into the queue for HGV's and trade vans. No allowances are made for rock'n'roll and you will have to respect the formalities and comply with the rules – even if you are running late. Crossing a border will take time and you should make sure you allow for it. Normally you may expect a delay of about 10 to 40 minutes but if you are unlucky they might keep you for hours, especially if they decide to do a spot-check on you.

To avoid doing all the complicated preliminary paperwork involved in Carnets you can use a Carnet company to process your application. The company we spoke to charged £50 for doing an EEC Carnet, and approximately £200 for doing the work on an ATA Carnet (although the rates on an ATA Carnet vary according to the total value of the equipment you are taking with you). For further information you can contact John Henry Enterprises, 16–24 Brewery Road, London N7 9NH. Tel: 01-609 5161.

NOTE:
Do not try and take merchandise with you on a European tour because you will end up paying tax on it. All merchandising problems should be sorted out beforehand between yourselves or your agent and the foreign promoters.

There may well be changes in the laws relating to the import and export of goods after 1992; check if you are in any doubt.

FERRIES

Book well in advance and make sure that you have all the dimensions of your vehicle with you – including the height. Do not pretend your van is shorter or narrower than it is, in an attempt to get a cheaper ticket, because you will be found out when it gets squashed in some way.

You may find that your trucking or van hire company can organize ferry bookings for you – alternatively use a travel agent.

Arrive at the port in good time and make sure you join the right queue (most probably the HGV check-in).

DRIVING

Here are some pearls of wisdom from those that have travelled in peril on the European highways.

- Invest in a really good road atlas.

- In Italy you are required by law to carry a translation of your driving licence with you. Such translations are available free from the A A.

- Note that if you commit an offence other than parking in Europe you will find that virtually every police force has a system of on-the-spot fines.

- A common cause of accidents involving the British abroad is that traffic JOINING the roundabout has right of way.

- In Holland the bike is 'king' – so keep your distance!

- If you park illegally you are very likely to have your car towed away.

- West Berlin is inside East Germany even though it is a West German city.

- You may find that you have to pay road taxes or tolls. For example, the journey from the north to the south of France can cost you £50.00 in tolls if you use their motorway system!

- In Switzerland you will be charged a Road Tax of approximately £30 at the border.

- Sweden has a Road Tax on diesel vehicles which is calculated on a mileage basis.

- Leaving your engine running unattended is an offence in a lot of European countries.
- Keep to the speed limits on the transit road through East Germany to West Berlin – the East German cops are red-hot and will fine you an unspecified amount on the spot if you are caught.
- Note that Greek promoters are prevented by law from sending foreign currency out of Greece to pay gig advances. They normally lodge a 50% deposit with the Greek branch of your record or publishing company. They will then pay you 100% of your fee on the day of the gig, and get their money back from the record or publishing company later on.

HEALTH

You will need the DHSS form E101 which lasts for a year and provides varying degrees of medical cover in most countries. It is free and recommended. Otherwise, most banks and travel agencies will offer you health insurance. Seriously consider it.

ACCOMMODATION

Promoters abroad generally provide accommodation as part of their contract with you. If you have days off between gigs you could ask the promoter to recommend somewhere to stay. Otherwise look out for tourist offices at the border crossings and get a copy of the Michelin Guide to the Hotels of Europe.

THE GIG

The deal your agent will have negotiated for you should include accommodation, meal, PA and lights.

However, it is advisable to check on the plugs necessary for your equipment in the countries you will be playing. The electricity supply abroad is generally 20 volts less than ours and this can effect some equipment.

ALWAYS phone the promoter/venue that you are playing at least five days ahead of each show to double-check the technical specifications, riders, accommodation and anything else that is important to the gig.

FEE

The foreign promoter may well have sent 50% of your fee in advance to your agent. Your agent is required to hold that money 'In Escro'. This is a legal term which means that you are not allowed by law to have access to that money until the gigs you have been contracted for have been satisfactorily fulfilled. This is

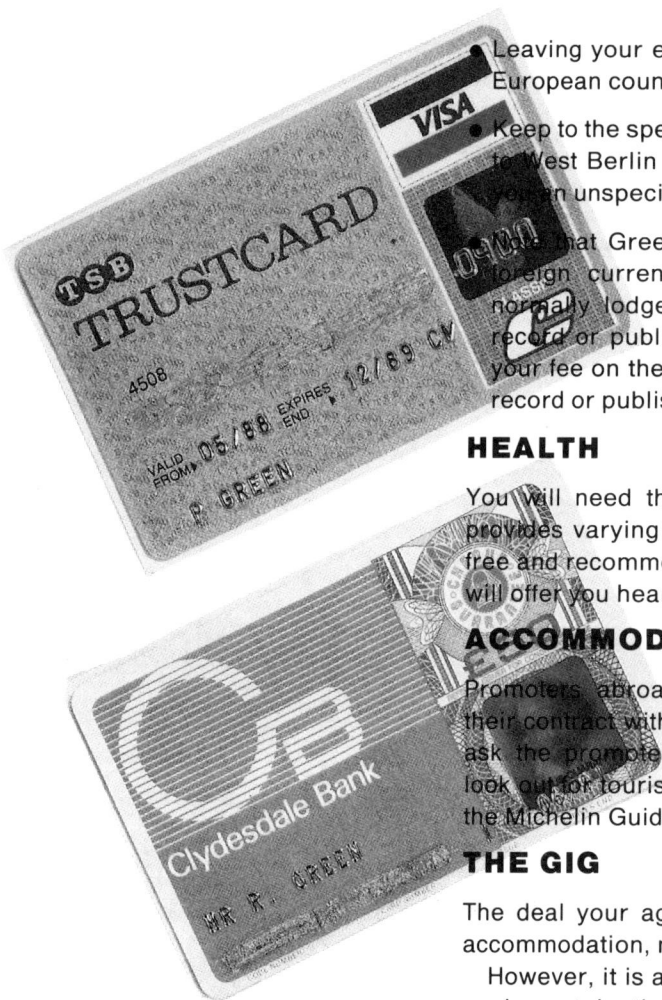

the theory, although in many cases it is what gets the tour on the road. The other half of your fee should be paid to you when you get to each gig. If all your fees have been agreed in sterling you can ask the promoter to pay you some of your fee in local currency.

BUDGET

If one member of the band has an international credit card with at least £500 credit facility on it – then you should be OK in case of emergency. However, you are going to have to budget for a number of possibilities whilst on the road. Make it a priority to always know when the banks and bureaux de change are open, and that you have enough currency on you to pay for petrol and a hotel.

CATASTROPHES

Ever optimistic – we have listed a number of possible catastrophes.

Lost Passport. Don't panic – losing your passport is not the end of the world. Ring your agent, the nearest British Consulate or Embassy and ring the Police. A tour manager once lost five passports and £4,000 by leaving his briefcase in a phone box in Germany. They were 60km away down the Autobahn before he realised and, of course, when they went back the whole lot had disappeared. However, the band did manage to play the next night in Holland. The Dutch and German promoters were able to explain the problem to the authorities and the British Consulate issued them with temporary passports.

A 10 year passport, crucial to enter certain countries such as East Germany and the USA.

Theft of equipment. This is going to be more of a threat in some places than others. You must report a theft, no matter how much of a rush you are in, because of the problems that will arise concerning your Carnet when you try to leave the country – the authorities will take some convincing that you have not sold the missing equipment. You may also have problems with your insurance claim when you return to the UK unless you have the police report.

Stolen/lost Carnet. This really will be a headache so don't lose it! Leave photocopies of all your important documents with your UK agent for reference. Notify Police and Customs and ring your UK agent immediately if you should lose it.

Member of the band gets arrested. Stay cool and be as cooperative as you can with the police. Let one person, preferably the tour manager, do all the talking. As soon as you can, contact the nearest British Consulate. Then ring the promoter and your agent.

DO NOT, UNDER ANY CIRCUMSTANCES, TRY TO TAKE ILLEGAL SUBSTANCES THROUGH BORDERS, AS A BAND YOU ARE A PRIME TARGET FOR A THOROUGH SEARCH BY FOREIGN POLICE.

MERCHANDISING: DOING IT YOURSELF

Once you have a regular and substantial following it may be worth considering selling promotional items at your gigs. It can be fun, it can earn you some extra money and, if it is done well, it is good advertising.

For successful bands merchandising can be an important source of income. At the top level merchandising companies can work on a basis similar to record companies, in that the artists are paid an advance for their merchandising rights and receive a royalty payment when this advance has been recouped. This involves substantial financial risk on the part of the merchandising company so they have to be very sure that your image is a saleable commodity.

For up-and-coming bands merchandising is predominantly about publicity and promotion and is unlikely to make much money. It is a way of getting yourself noticed which can make you a little extra money on the side.

There are merchandising companies around that can provide you with just about anything you might want – and a lot of rubbish too! Try to ensure that the companies you use are familiar with merchandising for the music business because you should then receive better advice on what kind of promotional item will sell and how many you should buy to test the market (see Tour Merchandising page 197). It is worth listening to them too, because they may be thinking about your merchandising programme in the long term. Although some of the smaller independent companies are only in the business of supplying merchandise, others would like to become involved in full-scale tour and retail merchandising but cannot afford to. They find it very difficult to get successful bands on their roster because they cannot afford to pay them large advances or provide the necessary point of sale services and backup. An alternative route for these companies is to look out for promising new bands and develop good business relationships with them. They could then reasonably expect to take on the band's tour merchandising if, and when, they become successful. Depending on your own interests, it might serve you well to ask some discreet questions regarding the nature of a merchandising company when you approach them.

The best recommendations are, as always, personal. Try to find a satisfied customer.

IS THERE A MARKET?

Filling a venue to capacity with enthusiastic fans is no guarantee of sales. A lot depends on the musical style of the band as well as the design, quality, nature and price of the merchandise. A lot of bands have been surprised to find that despite really good designs they have had difficulty in selling their products.

If you are about to go on tour supporting a well-known band and see it as a chance to launch your own merchandise, perhaps you should think again. According to the merchandising companies we interviewed, support bands usually sell very little. Nearly all the audience will have come to see the main band, many of them will not arrive until after you have played your set, and what money they do have spare is more likely to be spent on the merchandise of the headlining band. The same can apply to audiences in a pub or club. How many people are there as fans, and how many have just come in for a drink and a chat and only see you as an added bonus?

To a certain extent it is not how many fans you have, but their spending power which is important. It is up to you to offer them something worth buying but the only way you can really test your market is by trying out your ideas on a small scale.

WHAT TO SELL?

From T-shirts and badges to kites and cufflinks: whatever you want there will be someone out there who can make it for you.

But at what cost? It is not only your own pocket that you have to consider. Can you afford the capital outlay for 100 sweatshirts plus the wages of the person who will be selling them? Can your fans afford the retail price? The old style sweatshirt seems to have lost favour nowadays and most people prefer current fashion wear with a small logo and zip-top or roll neck. But these are quite expensive. While a printed sweatshirt will cost you around £5.50 + VAT, a fashion top will cost you upwards of £7.00 + VAT. Add on your mark-up and the retail price may become prohibitively expensive. So unless your audience looks particularly affluent, it would be unwise to sell expensive goods until you have proved that there is a demand.

Quality is another important consideration. It is not worth selling your fans shoddy goods. A poor quality T-shirt which develops a bell bottom and a greyish hue after the first wash is unlikely to become a favourite! And it won't do much in the way of good publicity for you either. Quality will cost more – but it is generally well worth it.

Depending on the band and the type and size of the crowd you might be able to sell some novelty items like boxer shorts, duffel bags and lighters, but they really should be 'relevant' in some way. The Boogie Brothers Blues Band are a good example of a band who have successfully sold their own special range of items from the very beginning. These include pork-pie hats and dark glasses à la Blues Brothers! – but if you go and see them play live you will realize why they sell such prodigious quantities.

T-SHIRTS

T-shirts are the traditional product to sell at gigs. Once you have a good design and the artwork prepared they are simple to produce and they can be very good publicity.

To reiterate, the quality of the shirt is going to be very important. Two of the best makes are American: 'Super Ts' and 'Screen Stars'. White ones will cost you £1.50–£2.00 each, but black and other colours will be more expensive. Indian T-shirts are recognized as 'middle range' and will cost about £1.50 each. Unfortunately British T-shirts can be relied upon to stretch or shrink and go grey, but they will cost considerably less. All prices will depend on the quantity ordered and you should be able to take samples home to wash and generally test for wear and tear.

If you have some idea of the design that you want to use and know someone who can put it on paper and do the artwork – you will save on designers' fees. The average fee for graphic designers is between £10 and £40 per hour. If you leave it up to the designers to come up with an idea it could easily take a week for them to produce something that you like.

'Artwork' means more than little sketches. The majority of shirts are silkscreen printed so the design has to be developed on to photographic paper (known as an acetate) and then on to a silk-screen. If you are having just one colour printed on your shirt then a simple design on paper (black and white) can easily be made into an acetate. If there are more colours, the design will have to be colour separated. You will need a different sheet for each colour, pinned together with the layout. If you have any clue about how to do this properly, or know someone who does, then do it yourselves because again it will save you time and money.

Using more than one colour is expensive. For a three-colour shirt the printer will have to make three separate screens from your colour separated artwork: one for each colour. The cost will be approximately £20 to £30 per screen and you will pay between 40p and 60p for each colour you have printed on a shirt. Your costs will thus include a minimum of £60 for the screens and the printing costs for each shirt will come to £1.20.

Taking into account the fee for the artwork, the price of the shirt, the screens, the printing and delivery, you may expect to pay approximately £5.50 for a three-colour shirt on a small order of 50 shirts! Of course, you may be able to trim these costs by doing your own artwork and making your own deliveries, but it is still going to make your break-even figure rather high. Alternatively, you can decide on a one-colour shirt which will require less artwork, fewer screens and incur lower printing costs. You may then anticipate paying around £3.00 per shirt on an order of 50. Ideally, you want to be able to sell your T-shirts at a reasonable price and still recoup all your outgoings. The way to economise is to reduce the number of colours you use, or even go with black on white (i.e. 1 colour).

It is always a good idea, whatever the merchandise in question, to test the market with a small run. This will make your costs higher but you really will lose money if you are left with stock that you cannot sell. Remember too that you will probably give away a certain amount free: one to each band member, their partners, your roadie, the venue manager, the security team – and so on. Thirty T-shirts @ £3.00 each will cost you £90.00. Allow for ten of these to be given away and for the remaining 20 to be sold for £5.00 each and you will make £10.00 profit. Give too many away, or fail to sell them all and you will soon be out of pocket.

Given the risks and expense of merchandising, it should come as no surprise that most suppliers will want to be paid a certain amount in advance.

POSTERS

You may need posters anyway if you are going on a tour of small clubs and pubs. Every bit of publicity helps and posters may come under your advertising budget. But if the design is good, you may also be able to sell them at your gigs. Printing is an expensive process but by sticking to simple colours it can be cost effective even for runs of less than 1,000. Again, your break-even will be pretty high so if you can produce a design which can be transferred onto other items you can save on artwork in the long run. A good idea is to leave a blank space on the poster for the venue, date, price and door-time to be filled in.

See also 'Promoting your own show' page 35.

BADGES

People have started buying badges again! Button badges are very cheap to make at around 10p, and you can put a good mark-up on them. Enamel badges can cost between 80p and £1.30 to produce, depending on the amount of colours used, but you can sell them for £2.00–£3.00 and with a good design they can look really classy. Again, all that will be required is some artwork or a good sketch for a designer to work from.

Whatever you wish to try selling, if you contact a good merchandising company they will be able to advise you on quality, quantity and what type of product you are likely to sell. Don't be afraid to ask for samples and remember that it is better to test a number of ideas on a small scale rather than jump straight into the deep end.

MERCHANDISING: SELLING IT YOURSELF

Taking into account the high break-even figures involved with small scale merchandising, it is unlikely that your supplier will agree to go on tour with you. By the time you have paid for their petrol, accommodation and labour there will be little, if anything left out of the profits, and if the stock has not sold, you could end up owing them a lot of money. It might be that your merchandiser thinks that you are going to be very successful, can already guarantee significant sales, and are worth taking on at an early stage. In this case the deal you are likely to be offered is one where you are paid an agreed percentage of the sales or profits only at the end of the tour. This does not happen often, so if a friend can take on the job, is willing to travel in the van with the rest of you, and can share a room with someone – you will be better off doing it yourselves.

Make sure, though, that whoever works the stall is not afraid to SELL. You want someone who is not afraid to shout above the crowd 'Get your T-shirts here!' It can be a lot of fun for someone with the right personality, but it is also very hard work. The T-shirt person has to set up before the gig and is often packing up the stall long after everyone else has finished. He or she may be stuck at the stall from 7 p.m. to 3 a.m. – and be working all that time.

PAYING FOR THE STOCK

You should pay for your stock out of your main merchandising account. The deal with your supplier will be an ordinary supply deal but, because they have probably learnt through experience that small scale tours don't always sell the goods, they might ask you for between 25% and 50% of the money up front. Set up a separate merchandising account at your bank and watch out that the band's other income doesn't subsidise it.

PLANNING AHEAD

Whoever is organizing the merchandising should look through the tour schedule checking all the relevant dates, venues and contact names and numbers. They should then ring all the places the band will be playing, speak to the venue manager, and check that it will be alright to sell merchandise at their venue. The response will vary. Some of the larger venues may ask for a facility fee of up to £100 (which they will expect you to pay whether you sell anything or not), or a percentage of your takings. You have to be very confident of sufficient sales to cover not only your costs, but also the facility fee, and still make some profit if working these venues is to be worth-while. At the other end of the scale, the smaller venues may say that there is no space to set up a stall, or that it will be contravening their fire regulations if they let you do so.

You should also find out when you will be allowed into the venue to set up your merchandise, and whether lights and a table will be provided.

TRANSPORT

Small quantities of merchandise can travel with the band which means you will cut down on costs and guarantee that you don't arrive late. You need something strong and sturdy that you can lock shut to put everything into. If you think a bin liner is adequate, you will soon realise it isn't when every member of the band has been in there to get a freebie for a friend! A flight case is a good idea – but check that it will fit in the van before you go.

SETTING UP AT THE GIG

Never just go into a place and set up without introducing yourself and clearing it first with the person in charge (who is not necessarily the caretaker!).

If there is no set place for your stall then you will need to find a spot. Beside the bar, close to the entrance or exit, or between them both, or even near the toilets – where everybody has to go at some point. Ask advice, because if you are in the way, you might be asked to move in the middle of everything. Whatever you do, don't set yourself up at the back of the hall: you need to be somewhere prominent where most people will see you at the end of the gig.

Venues usually have a table, and if not you can improvise with a flight case or two. Always have with you a good supply of chart pins, gaffer tape, scissors and Blu-Tack (always ask before you stick sellotape or gaffer tape to painted or papered walls unless you want an irate venue manager presenting you with a bill for redecoration at the end of the evening). You should consider taking some barriers with you if you think it is going to be busy, especially if the promoter might not be able to spare you any security person-nel.

Make sure you find out at the beginning of the evening what time the venue management are expecting you to be packed up and cleared away by. They will not thank you for keeping them waiting to lock up at the end of a long night. If you act professionally you can expect people to be helpful. If you don't, they will feel you owe them something and more more likely to try and blag some T-shirts!

DISPLAY

It is very important that you have a good, bold, well-lit display and not just a couple of T-shirts pinned up on a wall. If your stand

catches their eye people will stop, and then come closer to see what else you have got. If you take your own backdrop you can pin your display to it and just fold it up at the end of the night. Take your own spotlights and extension cable and, if you can, use them to illuminate the stall. No one will see you in the dark! You will also need a large, clearly written price list so that people can easily see what they are looking for (this could save you quite a lot of time).

THE FLOAT

At the start of the evening you should have a float of at least £20 in appropriate change. The venue may be able to provide the necessary change from behind the bar but it is a better idea to get your coins in counted bags from a bank earlier in the day.

SAFEGUARDING YOUR MONEY AND STOCK

It is difficult to protect yourself against theft when you are working on your own, but if you have a wall behind you and are within sight of a bouncer, you might have a certain peace of mind. It helps if there are two of you – so one can keep an eye on the stall whilst the other gets something to eat or goes to the toilet – but you can do it on your own. Sometimes there will be a rush period right after the show but at other gigs you may sell steadily all the way

through, so you shouldn't bank on there being a 'quiet period' and you should never leave your stall unattended.

It is not a good idea to have a cash box because it can be easily stolen. Merchandising at gigs is very similar to being a street trader and, like they do, you should always keep your money on you. Use a street trader's money apron which has zip pockets and two open pockets at the front for change. Above all, be discreet when you split your money up or count it at the end of the evening – there is less likelihood of someone stealing it if you don't make a song and dance about putting it somewhere 'safe' in the first place!

Pogues T-shirts bought at the Town and Country Club on St Patrick's night March 1988.

BANKING THE TAKINGS

It may be a good idea to open up a Post Office account, in addition to your main merchandising account, before you go on tour. The money you receive from sales needs to be banked as soon as possible and it can be useful to keep your tour accounts separate from your overall figures. Post Offices are a good idea because they are everywhere, have a longer working day than the banks, and are open on Saturday mornings too.

STOCK-TAKING

It is very difficult to keep track of your stock as you are selling it, so the best thing to do is wait until the end of the evening and count it then. Hopefully, you will have checked your stock before you set up and made a note of anything that has been given away. You can easily draw up a daily sheet listing all the different things you are selling. Put the individual items down the side and along the top put vertical columns headed: starting stock; extra stock (perhaps somebody Red Starred you some more shirts); stock given away and closing stock. This way you can keep track of the day's transactions.

You will have already budgeted for giving a certain amount of your merchandise away and, ideally you should stick to that quota. However, once you are on the road, one of your biggest problems will be 'blaggers' – people who try and get T-shirts for nothing. It is a good idea to have some replies ready to get rid of these people without offence. You can tell them that you are selling the T-shirts for 'the band' and that you will have to get their permission first. Alternatively, have an arrangement with the band so that a certain amount of product can be sold at cost price if necessary. Otherwise, practise saying NO!

A&R

A&R stands for 'Artistes & Repertoire' which is the rather archaic-sounding name for the record company department responsible for finding and signing new acts. A&R personnel also play a key role in developing the acts signed to the company. They are involved in choosing the studios and producers, they keep an eye on the recording process, decide which tracks are best released as singles, when they should be released on LPs, and so on.

Not all record companies have a special A&R department and the smaller companies may not even employ a specific A&R person. At a small indie label you may find yourself talking to one person who is company director, head of A&R, company accountant and secretary. When it comes to the major companies, however, there may be as many as seven or eight individuals whose specialist job is to search for and sign new acts to their label. A typical A&R department at this level will consist of a head of A&R, two or three fully-fledged A&R staff and two or three junior A&R people known as scouts. It is important, therefore, that you do some research on the A&R people you approach, getting the names if possible.

If you are approaching large record companies the scouts will be your first line of communication. They are the ones whose job it is to go to gigs and develop contacts at regional level in local studios, live venues and record shops. If you are creating a stir in your own area you should, in theory, come to their attention. Also, if you want to send introductory demo tapes, promo videos and press cuttings it is the scouts you need to target. There is little point in hounding the Head of A&R at a major record label because he or she will only pass your information down the line to one of the junior A&R personnel. Unless you have someone quite influential speaking up for you, it is unlikely that you will be able to take a short-cut through their system.

Once a scout likes you, he or she will raise your case at the weekly A&R meeting held at the record company's head offices in London, where the whole department get together to discuss the week's events and finds. Keep your contact primed with up-to-date information about what you are doing: some press, a radio session, or a marked improvement in your songwriting or playing might be just what it takes to get the rest of the A&R department interested in you. Your scout may then get permission to pay for demo time on your behalf. You could be given two or three days recording time in a 16 track studio (which will either be their own London studio or, more likely, one in your local area) and you will be expected to produce at least three decently recorded tracks for them to play back at head office.

At this stage a deal may be in the pipeline so you can expect them to want to see you play live and hear the rest of your material. Final decisions on signing will be made by the head of A&R although it is the A&R representative that first 'discovered' you, and spoke up for you, that will carry the can if you are not a success.

DEMOS AND PROMOTIONAL MATERIAL

The major record companies tend to operate on the theory that if an act is really good they will hear about it even if they aren't sent a tape. They also tend to think that if a band slips through their A&R net, it can be poached later on from a minor label, who will already have done most of the hard work. Quite often they are right – but this does not mean that you shouldn't go through the procedure of sending tapes and ringing A&R departments.

A&R people are more likely to listen closely to a tape that is referred to them by a 'well respected source'. This source could be a manager, solicitor, agent, promoter, other artist, producer, DJ, plugger, or in fact anyone they know connected with the music business, either socially or through work. Conversely, unsolicited demo tapes often don't get such a generous first listen and perhaps for this reason they are less likely to generate a positive response.

There will be a lot of competition from other bands who are also trying to attract A&R attention, but there are ways in which you can increase your chances of ultimate success when you send in a demo package, and some of these are listed below.

1) Find out the name of the person you need to target. Ring them up and tell them you are sending in a demo and 'do they mind'. Try to avoid sending your package to 'The A&R Department'.

2) Enclose one cassette tape with no more than three songs on it. Whatever you do, don't send your complete repertoire of songs. The idea at this stage is to get A&R interest rather than play them everything you've ever written!

3) Always make your best song the first track on the tape.

4) If you think you have a possible hit single include it on the tape. Your hit single may not be your best song, or even your favourite, and bear in mind that it shouldn't really be any longer than three minutes.

5) Never send out old, badly recorded or unfinished material. It is pointless sending outdated material, (possibly performed by individuals who are no longer band members), especially if it is no longer representative of what you are currently doing. The same is true of unfinished material. If you don't have three properly

recorded tracks – just send two rather than spoil the otherwise good tape by including a substandard track. (If you don't have three good songs in your repertoire then you shouldn't really be contacting A&R departments until you have written some more.) The quality of the recording should be as good as you can make it.

(6) Use the best quality blank cassettes that you can afford.

(7) List all three tracks in their correct order both on the cassette inlay card and on the cassette itself.

(8) Put the name of the band and a contact name, address and telephone number on both the cassette inlay card and the cassette itself. Cassettes and their enclosed cover letters often become separated.

(9) If you have a video of yourselves that is watchable and includes the current line-up, this can be helpful in encapsulating the band's image and presentation.

Videos can be made increasingly cheaply, especially if you borrow or hire the equipment to do it. (See section on Video page 132.)

(10) Enclose recent press cuttings, photographs, plus anything else that will help build up a picture of the band.

Don't send too much information and keep it to the point. A good live photograph can be more exciting and tell a lot more about you than posed studio shots. You will also probably make a stronger impact by preparing a one or two sheet collage of recent press cuttings and photographs rather than sending sheafs of paper through the post.

(11) Where you have the name of the person you are writing to always enclose a personal letter.

Keep the letter friendly but brief and indicate when the information you are sending was requested – remind your contact of the circumstances.

It is worth making copies of demos for yourself and sending them to your own address by registered post. You can, in this way, acquire a degree of copyright protection on your songs. It is important that you understand how copyright law operates with regard to the music industry (see Copyright, page 184). While this is not by any means a water-tight safeguard against plagiarism, it can give you a certain peace of mind!

Always enclose a sturdy stamped, self-addressed envelope if you want the contents of a demo package to be returned.

WHAT ARE A&R DEPARTMENTS LOOKING FOR?

This question has baffled many people for a long time! Major

Living Colour at the Marquee July 1988.

Heavy Metal up and comers – Horse!

Members of the Mutoid Waste Company – a band whose visual image is an integral part of their musical performance.

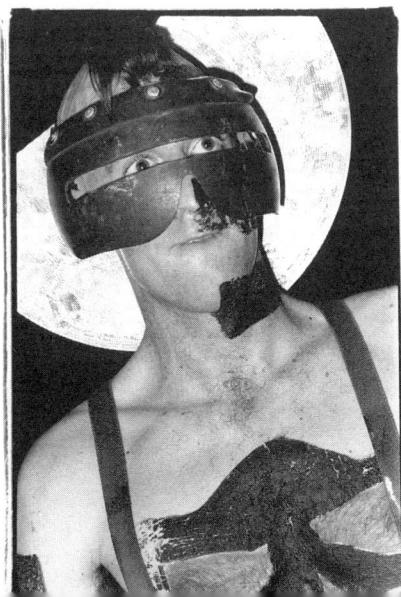

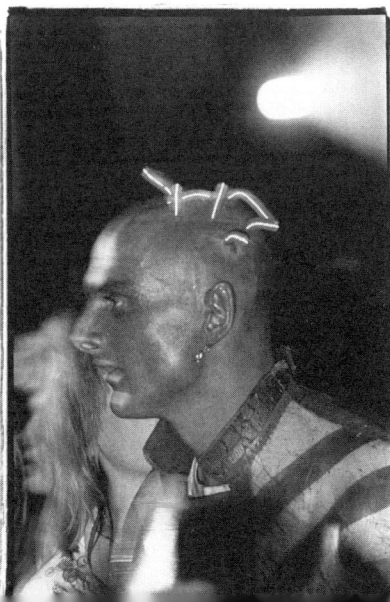

The La's at the Marquee, London, in April 1988. The La's are one of the few bands that can truly challenge the popular truism that 'no band has ever been signed from a demo'. Andy MacDonald, MD of Go! Discs, came across their tape when he was asked to review a pile of demos sent into Underground Magazine (no longer in existence). He was impressed enough by to go and see them play live soon after – and he signed them to his label a month after that!

record companies usually encompass a wide selection of music types covering the spectrum from chart-oriented pop to rock, reggae and country music. As new strains and directions in music occur they are usually initiated, or picked up and encouraged, by the independent and specialist labels. Later, if the 'new' music begins to attract general attention, then the major labels will move in, and either sign up the existing proponents of that music or even absorb the whole record label including the artists they want. The major labels rarely take risks on new types of music and, as a result, are not often responsible for introducing changes in musical taste. In an attempt to compete with some of the more adventurous independent record companies, some of the majors have set up subsidiary labels of their own, or structured a variety of deals with minor labels, to make sure that they don't miss out.

New types of music aside, all record company signings include an element of experiment and a large slice of timing and luck. For every successful band there are probably dozens of others who have been passed over despite the fact that they have been doing something very similar for years. Unfortunately, there are few prizes for being ahead of your time and whilst it is a difficult pill to swallow you must have a realistic and stoical attitude from the beginning if you are to avoid being too disappointed.

However talented you are, it is certain that you won't succeed if you lock yourself in your bedroom and sing to your goldfish! So if you think you stand a realistic chance of making a mark then have a go.

SONGS

The single most important element that record companies, publishers and management companies alike are searching for is songwriting ability. As the director of a major independent label put it, '. . . the only thing worth listening to is a decent song sung by a decent singer. If the demo package looks plain and sounds great then it may be worth following up, if it looks great and sounds crap then it will go in the bin.'

Time spent songwriting therefore, especially in the early stages of a band's development, is time well spent. Well written and original songs are more important than the band's image, instrumental ability, or looks.

It is also important that these songs are presented in an original fashion, highlighting the strong points of the material. For instance, if you have a lead singer with a distinctive voice, around which you are building your music, make sure it is heard. Vocals are often given the least time and attention in the recording studio, but if they

are your strong point you should make sure you spend an appropriate amount of time working on them. It is important that the band are agreed on the sound they are trying to achieve before they set out to record it. The resulting demo should also ideally represent the sound the band is actually capable of making in real life.

Try not to be derivative. This is very difficult but think hard about where you are getting your material from, and try not to sound like an existing successful band. It can be very discouraging if another group, who sound as if they are copying you, appear on the scene with a record deal. All you can do under these circumstances is press on regardless or make some changes.

IMAGE AND STYLE

The most elusive qualities of all – image and style – are, for better or worse, a central part of pop music. All pop music has an image, whether it be hip hop or heavy metal, and what every A&R department is looking for is 'originality' of style. It is very difficult to describe these qualities in words, but what everyone seems to agree upon is that your style should come from you and should complement your music.

Don't be a phoney because it always shows. A good test of your chosen image is whether or not you are prepared to walk down your local high street dressed in the same clothes that you wear on stage. This may seem a little unfair as there are plenty of acts that dress up for their stage show whilst keeping a low profile in normal life, but it will certainly serve as an introduction to the pressure and close scrutiny that you will be under should you attain any measure of success. Dramatic images are difficult to maintain unless you are happy and comfortable dressed flamboyantly. At the same time, bear in mind that once you have decided upon a style of presentation, the press and public are likely to expect you to live out your image for ever afterwards. Very few performers have successfully transcended images which they initially became associated with. David Bowie found his Ziggy Stardust persona a millstone round his neck for several years, even after he had changed his music and stage show dramatically.

It is perfectly possible to maintain an understated image as long as your own character and personality are best projected in that way. Your own personal style can become your image and as a result it will appear both unselfconscious and unmanufactured. In the words of one successful band manager that we spoke to, 'always try to create a fashion rather than follow one.'

Do not underestimate the importance of your visual style even if it is just jeans and a T-shirt. Robert Cray and Dire Straits both have

The Legendary Monster of Rock, Lemmy of Motorhead, at the Hammersmith Odeon, 1987.

their own individual images, even though they are not as obviously and carefully packaged as are many of the more ephemeral chart acts.

WHAT YOU CAN EXPECT FROM AN A&R DEPARTMENT AFTER SIGNING A RECORD DEAL

The A&R person who is responsible for bringing you into a record company will be your closest contact and ally. He or she will introduce you to all the other departments within the company and will help you and your manager to liaise with the company hierarchy (see Record Company Structure, page 181). Should you be less than successful, that person will also bear the responsibility of your failure.

You may reasonably expect that 'your' A&R person will want you to demo every bit of your material – including songs which you may have avoided putting on past demos. The reason for this is that quite often the embryos of good songs are hidden amongst your reject material. Once they have enough songs to work on they will start to discuss with you which producer they think would be appropriate, which tracks should be released as singles, and in what order. Normally LPs are constructed around successful singles. The idea is that you release three singles, and then release the LP containing them, with other carefully selected tracks.

'LP BANDS'

Whilst chart singles are obviously important to record companies and can dramatically accelerate the career and public profile of a band, this is not necessarily appropriate to all types of groups. Some artists are recognised from the start as being 'LP Bands' and although they will release singles, these will probably not be hits. Bands whose music is not instantly accessible quite often take longer to develop a market. Whereas it will take patience and hard work for notable record sales figures to be achieved, it is probably true that their careers will last longer than those of some of their more instantly marketable contemporaries. Some bands have successfully constructed long-term careers, spanning several LPs over a number of years, having begun in the business as singles chart artists. But, for every one that has succeeded in this way, there are a hundred more 'one-hit wonders'.

Producers help you locate and select your material, they choose the studio and engineer and they direct the session although they may not mix the final product. If you need session musicians, singers or arrangers for strings, the producer may hire them and negotiate their fees. All this will be done in conjunction with your manager or publisher, or with the A&R department of your record company.

It is unlikely that you will become involved with top producers unless you are recording master tapes in expensive studios. Generally you choose a producer you think will give you the sound you want. You probably also hope that their association with you will help sell your record. Established producers rarely get involved at demo level unless they have some form of stake in the career of the artist. Occasionally a producer may think that you stand a good chance of becoming successful and offer to sign you to their production company, hoping to sell you on to a record publishing company at a later date. Needless to say, get legal advice before you sign this sort of deal.

Many producers are linked to a specific studio where they are familiar with the equipment, in particular the mixing desk, and where they find the environment good to work in. They will also have developed a good working relationship with the sound engineer, who they can trust to be accurate and fast. Because of these factors the choice of a producer does, in many cases, determine the choice of studio.

The more well-known, fashionable and successful a producer is, the more likely it is that he or she will be dictating the terms. They will also be more expensive and you should keep this in mind, because their fee will come out of your advance or your royalties. Don't just go for a 'name' because it really is important that the producer you choose is enthusiastic about your music, gets on well with you, and does not intimidate you. You need to be very clear about why you want a particular person and how much money you are prepared to spend. You also need to decide whether or not you are prepared to let that person dictate the time, place, and possibly even the country where you are going to record! Make sure you and your manager approve the budget and are clear on all the above points before you sign anything. Don't let yourselves be hassled into recording your LP in Los Angeles at vast expense when a 'lesser' producer in the UK could have achieved just as good a result at half the price.

As a young band, paying for your own release, you may be lucky and attract someone well-known to work with you for less than their usual fee, or for a promise of royalty payments if the record sells.

From the established producers point of view, work they do for the large record companies can often subsidize work with smaller, Indie bands whose music they particularly like. The relationship is often mutual because while the band benefits from the producer's musical skill and A&R contacts, the producer benefits through royalty payments and is credited with 'finding' and 'making' the band. If you decide to let someone as yet unestablished work on your music, you have no guarantees, beyond your own ears, as to their ability to record your sound. You may well benefit from the skill of a good new producer, but make sure that they are not merely using your studio time to practice their technique.

RECORDING FOR YOUR RECORD COMPANY

The decision to record will be made between you, your manager and the A&R department of the record company. It is very likely, however, that the first thing the record company will require you to do is to go into a studio and demo nearly everything you have written. There will then be long discussions about the pros and cons of releasing particular songs as singles and the search for a producer will commence.

WHAT MAKES A GOOD PRODUCER?

Experience is very important – along with studio techniques, familiarity with the technical aspects of recording sound, and a good knowledge of music. It also helps if a producer can exercise criticism without intimidating the band. They need to be able to get the best out of an artist without going over budget – and to do this they need to be able to manage people and finances.

WORKING WITH YOUR PRODUCER

Once the decision has been made your record company should arrange a meeting between you and your prospective producer. At this stage it is easy to change your mind, so make sure you know how the producer feels about your songs, listen to any advice on arrangements and generally make sure you are talking along the same lines. There is usually a gap of at least a couple of months between the time when the producer is contracted and the date you actually start work in the studio. As you may have written new material over this period you should invite your producer to rehearsals so that you can discuss any changes in style or content. Any pre-production meetings you have will help minimise problems later on. You need to be able to communicate, and the producer has to be able to relate to your music. Personality clashes can cause serious problems in the studio, so it is quite important that you meet to play your most recent demos and talk about what you want to achieve.

An experienced producer should be able to handle the psychological and technical problems that arise from nerves and the general pressure of 'time being money' in the studio. Producers sort out certain routines which they know make it easier for them to get a finished master out of an inexperienced band. If people are not happy in the studio, it will reflect in the recording, so the first objective is make sure everyone is relaxed and knows what they are supposed to be doing. For example, if you are uncomfortable sitting with headphones on trying to hear what you have just recorded then the producer may suggest that you come back into the control room to listen. The main thing is to come to terms with the fact that you cannot do everything at once and to trust the producer to put you on the right track.

If, once you have started work in the studio, you find you have made a bad choice of producer, contact your manager or A&R person immediately.

HOW MUCH IS THE PRODUCER PAID?

The producer's tee is negotiable, but a lot will depend on what you agreed to in your recording contract. There is no average payment we can quote here: the fee a producer can command depends entirely upon their track record and whether or not they are 'flavour of the month'. Producers are usually paid an advance against a percentage of the royalties on the record (see Recording Contracts page 167).

WHO CHOOSES THE STUDIO

The producer will probably choose the studio in conjunction with your record company and yourselves. You should make sure that this choice is suitable and that it comes within the recording budget. The sound on a record has as much to do with the engineer who recorded it as the technology used in the process. The biggest studios are not necessarily the best, and you can't expect to achieve the same quality of sound that you heard on another record with a different engineer! In fact, the engineer is extremely important so make sure you get a professional and in this instance, you certainly will get what you pay for. Perhaps it is best to leave this choice to the producer once you have decided what you are going to need in terms of studio facilities.

STUDIOS

CHOOSING THE STUDIO

Before you go anywhere near an expensive 16 or 24 track studio, you should find somewhere cheaper and accustom yourself to working in the studio environment. If you can afford it, there are some excellent examples of home recording equipment available, on which you can practise the basics (see the back of Melody Maker and the other specialist press). Obviously, you want the best quality sound you can afford for your demos, but don't feel you have to pay a fortune. Most A&R people would say that the quality of the recording, as long as it is half-way decent, is secondary to the content. Put another way, a high quality recording cannot compensate for poor material, and good material will still be recognizable on a modestly recorded tape.

Look for a cheap, 8-track recording studio and get thoroughly comfortable in it. You really do need studio experience, and a 24-track costing £45 per hour is not the place to get it! £30–40 per day is a more reasonable price to pay at this stage. You may well find a good pre-production studio with an unintimidating engineer who will help you work things out. It is really important that you can relax in the studio, otherwise you might be panicked at a later stage and find yourself neglecting something elemental like tuning.

If you use a lot of MIDI equipment then you will probably need a well equipped 8-track with a programming suite. If you find a good studio and engineer, it is worth really trying to learn and understand the computerized aspects of studio recording and mixing. Soul, Jazz, Funk and 'house' music of any kind can effectively be recorded by one person using a computer system and a sampler. In a big studio the programming is taken out of your hands, and the array of technology can be both off-putting and baffling. At a small studio you are more likely to become involved, and you may make more of an effort to understand the equipment and use it as a tool to help you get what you want. It is easy to make mistakes if you are working with expensive technology you cannot handle.

CONTACTING THE STUDIO

If you can, try and meet the engineer and assure yourself that you will be able to communicate. Check that the equipment you need is available, what other facilities there are at the studio or nearby – shops, cafes, banks, equipment hire, and so on – and whether you will be able to get food and drink at the studio itself. If you are planning on spending a couple of days in the studio, check if you will be able to leave your equipment there overnight. Has the studio got the necessary insurance cover? Does your own insurance policy cover you to leave it there?

The studio is likely to want some, if not all of their money in advance so you should sort this out with them, and put any deal you make on the phone down in writing and keep copies.

PREPARING FOR THE STUDIO

Rehearsal

When you are paying for studio time, you should not be using it to rehearse. Preparation is the key to a good session and when it comes to practising your material, you probably cannot do enough. Even when you think you could do it in your sleep, you may find that once you are in the studio, with excellent speakers and mikes, lots of problems suddenly appear. The only way you can prepare yourself for this is to record your rehearsals and listen to them very critically. Try and think out how you are going to use your studio time and go over every aspect.

Annie Lennox and Dave Stewart in the studio back in 1982/3. Then they put up with flock wall paper and cramped conditions – now they have their own converted church!

If you have a producer, it is likely that you will work out together what instrumentation and backing vocals you may need.

Instruments

It is not a good idea to get new instruments to go into the studio with. If you have to borrow or hire any equipment do so in advance so that you can practise on it.

To take with you

Take spares of all the obvious bits of your equipment to avoid wasting time. Take a snack and something to drink where the studio doesn't have canteen facilities – especially if the session is going to be a long one. Take a ghetto blaster or equivalent so that you can play back in super grotty quality what your beautifully recorded tape sounds like. The advantage of this is that it will bring you back to earth a little. Neither DJs nor A&R people are likely to be listening to your tape through the kind of speakers you will have in the studio. If being creative makes you sweat, you might also want to take some fresh clothes and your wash kit.

ADVICE AND TIPS FOR THE STUDIO

Be prepared.

Get to know your engineer.

Start with an easy song that everyone likes and if you get into difficulties – move on to another.

Make sure you have a good headphone mix so that you can hear yourself play.

Michelle Shocked at the Kerrville Folk Festival in Texas, May 1986.

Michelle Shocked was busking at this festival in the hills of Texas when Pete Lawrence (MD of Cooking Vinyl) first heard her singing and playing guitar. He was soon convinced that she had totally unique qualities as a performer and he asked her to record a couple of songs on his Sony Walkman, Michelle obliged by filling a whole C90 cassette!

Back in the UK Pete Lawrence realised that the tape was very special – complete as it was with chirping crickets and the occasional passing truck. DJ Andy Kershaw was impressed enough to give it an airing on Radio One – and the response was overwhelming. It therefore seemed a good idea for Cooking Vinyl to release a record from the tape calling it simply 'The Texas Campfire Tapes'. Michelle agreed and the LP came out in late November 1986.

Within two months it was No 1 in the Independent LP charts!

The question to ask yourselves before you read any further into this section is 'Why are we releasing a record?'. The reasons most commonly given are:

a) You think record companies will take you more seriously if they receive a record instead of yet another cassette. This may sometimes be true, but are you sure that the considerable amount of money you will spend on record production couldn't be better spent on something else? Perhaps you could make a cheap video instead.

b) You want to try for some radio play and know that radio stations are much more likely to play records than tapes. This raises the further question: what do you want radio play for? If you want air-time to attract record company and publishing company interest, then a radio session will not only save you considerable time and expense –but you may actually get paid to do it! If you are hoping to get a 'hit', have you got the production budget and the sort of professional distribution around the country that you will need to be able to shift 100,000 singles? Can you afford the services of a plugger to get you the necessary Radio 1 airplay?

c) You have always wanted to see your name on a record and things are moving too slowly for you to wait for a record company to sign you and release one. This is probably the real reason behind an awful lot of record releases if the truth were known! Everyone has an ego, which sometimes needs boosting – the brutal question is 'can you afford a £1,500 ego boost?'.

Having said all this, if you have the resources and think you've got a couple of really good songs that merit a single release, then by all means have a go. At the very least, you will find the whole process interesting – if a little more complex than you thought – and at best, you could sell enough records to get your money back whilst attracting enough attention to yourselves to clinch that elusive deal.

Let's assume that you have spent some time in a studio recording your chosen songs on to a multitrack master tape. This needs to be reduced down to a two-channel master to be used when cutting the record. This has to be done with care, and you should make sure that you are there, because an error in the reduction of a multitrack to a two-channel master tape can result in real problems later on. For example, if, when you play your first record, you realize that the lead guitar solo is missing, the reason will be that it was originally recorded on a separate channel which was lost when the multitrack was reduced because you weren't around to remember it!

In summary, the process of making records from a master tape is

RELEASING YOUR OWN RECORD

THE TC AND
MUSIC
GUIDE

as follows. The master tape is taken to a cutting room where a master lacquer is literally cut from a wax disc. This lacquer is duplicated into nickel production plates and from these the master stampers are made which stamp out the records at the pressing plant. Before the pressing starts, however, artwork for the labels and sleeves should have been completed and sent to the printers, who then deliver them to the record pressing plant. Often the printers of the sleeves and labels will be separate companies as different materials and inks are used for each process. The artwork for the labels should incorporate the appropriate details (see below), and both the cutting studio and the pressing plant will want to know your catalogue number and contact details so that they can inform the MCPS when they actually manufacture your record. Obviously, there is quite a lot of work involved in making sure that this process runs smoothly so you may decide to employ a production and manufacturing service to organize and co-ordinate it for you (see below).

If you decide to do the whole thing yourself you should do some homework and allow yourself plenty of time. First of all decide which companies you are going to use. If possible seek personal recommendations and make sure you use a good cutting engineer. You can ask your engineer to recommend a pressing plant and you can ask them to recommend a printer for the sleeves and for the labels. If the companies you talk to have worked together before they will probably be able to get each other organized to a certain extent, and save you the trouble. You will need to confirm production times so that you know how long the printer is going to need, and can make sure labels and sleeves are delivered to the pressing plant the day before, and not the day after, pressing is supposed to start!

ORGANIZING PRODUCTION YOURSELF
Cutting
The cutting stage is very important and the skill of your engineer will have a lot to do with the quality of your finished product. Often, the cutting house is marked on a record on the 'run out' near the label along with the catalogue number. The studio time will cost you approximately £75 + VAT per hour (it will take approximately one hour to cut a 7″ single) and you will also have to pay for the master lacquers which should cost about £22 + VAT per side. The final charge is then related to the type of tape you supply the cutting house with ($\frac{1}{4}$″ Analogue is standard), and the time it actually takes to do the cut (you are likely to spend between $1\frac{1}{2}$ and 2 hours cutting an LP). It may also depend on whether or not you attend the cut and ask for playbacks and extra studio time. Some cutting

studios charge a flat rate to cut a record not involving an hourly charge. Mayking Records, for instance, charge £70 per side for a 7″ single, and £85 per side for a 12″ single or £110 per side for an LP. Prices do seem to vary, so it is worth shopping around.

The engineer will first play your master tape through a simple mixing desk. If there are any last minute alterations to be made to the basic sounds on the record, such as boosting or cutting bass and treble, it is possible to do them now. More importantly, the engineer is looking out for sound patterns that may cause distortion when the master lacquer is cut. Quite often, it seems, the engineers in recording studios do not realize how the sound which is recorded on tape will turn out when cut on to vinyl: boomy bass or sharp vocals are not easy to reproduce mechanically and a burst of very high frequency after a long passage of bass frequency can cause problems. The cutting engineer may be able to effect a solution by levelling out the high and low peaks. The danger of too much smoothing-out of the sound is that the final result can sound a bit muddy, even though the original sound was hard and bright. The actual speed at which the tape is finally cut on to the lacquer can make a difference to the sound or 'feel' of a record as well, and the engineer can either increase the 'beats per minute' (BPM) or slow them down in a final series of adjustments. Obviously the best cuts come from well-recorded master tapes, but it is important that you are present at the cut and are consulted about any changes suggested. One pressing company we spoke to said that half of the problems they dealt with stemmed from an unattended cut where decisions concerning the sound were made by the engineer alone.

(Note that if you take a digital master to a cutting room that requires additional editing this can prove a long, expensive process – so if you are mastering on Betamax in the studio make sure that any 'count-ins' or other unwanted sounds are taken out before the final master stage.)

When the cutting engineer has finished the preparation stage and is confident that there will be no problems, the master lacquer is cut. Sound frequencies will be converted into grooves and cut by a fine lathe on to what looks like a blank waxy record. The master lacquer is a 'positive' – in other words it can be played just like a record but it is very soft and would wear out after only seven or eight plays. For testing purposes an 'acetate' can be cut which can also be played and then kept for reference. The master lacquer is sent on to the pressing plant to be used to make the metal masters or 'negatives' of your records. On a long record pressing run the metal masters will gradually wear out and fresh ones are made from the master lacquer when replacements are required.

Mary Coughlan at the Mean Fiddler, Harlesden, December 1988.

In 1983 Mary Coughlan was encouraged by her friends to enter a local talent competition in Galway. She came second and later joined forces with Dutch composer/producer Eric Visser to record her first album 'Tired in Emotional' in a small studio on a shoestring budget. An initially unsatisfactory deal with a minor Irish record company nonetheless brought enough attention to her for her new manager to get her a deal with WEA Records for her second album – 'Under the Influence'.

LABELS

As the labels are actually heat welded to the record when it is pressed, they are an integral part of the manufacturing process and you cannot give your pressing plant the go-ahead until the labels are ready. Also, the labels must be made by a specialist printer using paper and ink designed to withstand extremely high temperatures and pressure. If you supply labels printed on ordinary paper the results can be disastrous – leading to them sticking to the hot presses and even bursting into flame! Find out exactly when the record pressing company require the labels because they will want to make sure they are properly dry before pressing begins and they may even bake them before they use them.

Most printers will do the design and typesetting for you if you have not sorted anything out for yourselves although this will, of course, be added on to the bill. It might be a good idea to find out if they are sub-contracting this work because, if they are, you might be able to get it done more cheaply somewhere else. The cost will vary according to the number of colours used and the complexity of the overall design: black and white is the cheapest.

Most labels carry the following information:

- the letter 'P' in a circle followed by the name of the copyright owner and date of first publication. Also, the letter 'C' in a circle followed by the name of the owner of the copyright on the sleeve or packaging. You should also make sure that you include the usual copyright blurb round the edge of the label. (All rights of the Manufacturers and of the Owners of the recorded work reserved. Unauthorized copying, public performance and broadcasting of this work prohibited.)

- the title and the names of the tracks (including their timings if you want to be particularly kind to DJs and producers)

- the publisher or copyright owner should also be clearly written under the title. This is so that if the record is sold or played on the radio the relevant bodies know where to send the royalties. If you do not have a publisher then you should put a contact address on the label. See page 189 and 190 for details concerning MCPS and PRS membership

- you can also include the name of the producer under the song title

- an indication which is the A or B side of the record

- the catalogue number. If you are not with a record company you can make up your own catalogue number. For example, ours could be TC001.

SLEEVES

When the records come off the press the sleeves should be ready and waiting for them at the pressing plant. You should be thinking about your sleeve design and production well in advance of the pressing date. Go to the printers and look at the different types of paper, card and board available, and the different finishes they can offer you: matt (machine finished), glossy (UV finish) or grain, for example. The quality you choose will be reflected in the price, but the major cost consideration will still be whether or not you need full colour separation of your artwork. If you use black and white as your colours, the film and plates used for the printing will only cost you between £40 and £75. If you use colour, colour separation on a scanner could cost you between £300 and £400!

It will cost you between £30 and £60 to get a graphic designer to put the artwork for your album sleeve together if you provide them with a design and the information you want typesetting.

Otherwise, plain white sleeves can be bought very cheaply and you can easily stamp your own details or design on them.

PRESSING

The record pressing company is likely to charge you a nominal fee for the 'metalwork', or the manufacture of the metal stampers which will be approximately £43 + VAT per side for a 7″ single plus 75p for test pressings (test pressings are the first few records to actually come off the production line). The metalwork on 12″ singles and standard LPs will cost more – around £60 + VAT per side plus 95p per test pressing.

When the record pressing company has made up the metal masters of your record you should ask for a few test pressings. This is your last chance to do some quality control, so take them home and give them a good listen. A lot of people find their first record a little disappointing because they think it is going to sound like the master tape did in the studio – through £10,000 worth of monitoring equipment! So be prepared for less, and look out for problems which may have arisen at the cutting stage such as 'ghosting' (being able to hear the next track before it actually plays) which is caused by the grooves being cut too close together.

If you do have any problems of this kind – either the master lacquer will have to be taken back to the cutting room and the grooves opened up – or the problem may be located in the actual production process. Today's modern equipment has really reduced the likelihood of something like this happening to your record, but you should ideally allow yourself the time to deal with these snags.

If everything is as it should be then you can give the pressing plant the go-ahead for mass production. Quality control should be maintained by the pressing plant throughout the production process and you should not find at the end of it all that the labels are torn or the hole in the record is not centred. The records will be placed in an inner sleeve and put inside your own outer sleeve, should you want them to do this for you. LPs, once they are in their outer sleeves, are usually boxed in 25s – so if you have ordered a thousand records there will be 40 boxes, packed four to a carton into ten cartons. If the records are in simple white inner sleeves then they will be packed 40 to a box. Seven inch singles are packed 50 to a box, and twelve inch singles are packed in boxes of 30 or 40 depending on the quality of the sleeve.

Usually, 1,000 LPs should take about 3 weeks to produce from receipt of the lacquer masters. If you are in a big hurry, however, it may be possible to turn out a record in 3 to 4 days – and we have heard of records being made in 48 hours – but don't you count on it! If you are thinking of pressing a record between October and December then you should really give the pressing plant at least four weeks to allow for the Christmas rush. At particularly busy times of the year pressing plants may well turn down short production runs as they are less profitable than bulk orders for many thousands of records.

PRODUCTION AND MANUFACTURING DEALS

Obviously, there is quite a lot of work involved in ensuring that the process of making a record runs smoothly and many people choose to hand the whole job over to a production or manufacturing service.

Some of these companies are purely sub-contractors, or middlemen, who will take your master tape and transform it into the required number of records or tapes you want, complete with the necessary packaging (designed to your specifications). They do regular business with all the requisite suppliers and can perhaps pull weight if there is a rush to release your record, or if there is a problem that needs dealing with.

It is more likely, however, that your cutting studio offers to arrange the pressing for you, or that your pressing plant asks you if you would like them to look after the labels and sleeves. The best thing to do is make a few phone calls and work out how much is being charged for the separate aspects of the job and see how they compare. If the 'package deal' is competitive then it might be a good idea to go for it because it could save you the time and expense of making all the initial approaches, chasing up your suppliers and paying separate bills.

The following is
For 1,000 7" singles:

Cutting from ¼" master tape @ £70 per side:	£140.00
Processing acetate into master stamper @ £43 per side	£ 86.00
Two test pressing @ 75p each	£ 1.50
Labels in one colour	
Origination from camera-ready artwork	£ 35.00
Plates £19.00 each	£ 38.00
Labels printing @ 2.5p per pair	£ 25.00
Record pressing @ 19.8p per single	£198.00
Sleeves in one colour on 170gsm card	
Origination from camera-ready artwork	£ 78.00
Plate £35.00	£ 35.00
Printing @ 14.8p each	£148.00
	£784.50
VAT @ 15%	£117.67
TOTAL	£902.17

Cost per 7" single, not including transport and distribution, is 90p.

The company also added a 10% surcharge to cover their liability to their suppliers in case they over-pressed the short record run. Any overpayment was refundable as they assured us that we would only pay for the actual quantity of completed product.

For 12" singles and LPs the costs are higher and the equivalent to the job outlined above will cost between £1.25 and £1.30 per record plus 95p per test pressing. Add to this amount the cost of putting the records in boxes and transporting the finished product around, and you can see how an order of a thousand 12" singles or LPs could easily cost over £1,300.

Given that the origination costs make up a large proportion of your outgoings on a small run of records, it makes sense that your costs per record go down the more you have made.

THE MCPS

If you release your own record and use somebody else's song you should fill in a form for the MCPS at least 15 days before the actual release date. Anyone who issues a record for sale should notify the Mechanical Copyright Protection Society (see Copyright: MCPS, page 190) in order to ensure that they comply with the requirements to pay mechanical copyright royalties on songs to which they do not hold the copyright. The form asks you to give full details of the titles of the music used on each side of your recording, the name of the composer, author and arranger, and the publisher/copyright owner. You will also be required to give the release date, the format (whether tape, CD or record), the retail selling price (excluding VAT) and the name of the persons or company who are issuing the record to the public. If you are releasing your own record, this is you! If you have a record company the form will be completed by them. The purpose of the form is to make sure that you are not covering anybody else's songs. As we describe in the section on Publishing Contracts (page 158), if you make a cover version of somebody else's song and put it on one side of a two-track 7" single, you have to pay them a mechanical royalty of half $6\frac{1}{4}\%$ of the notional retail selling price of the product (excluding VAT). Also, if you plan to change the lyrics or melody of a copyright song then you need the permission of the copyright owner in advance.

No permission is necessary, and no mechanical royalties are payable if you record:

(a) your own music (unless you have assigned your rights to someone else, for example, a music publisher)

(b) non-copyright music, i.e. traditional songs, or songs which have gone out of copyright.

Note, however, that there is copyright in an arrangement of a song and that if you record someone else's arrangement you will have to pay a royalty.

Under these circumstances it is not a legal requirement for you to notify the MCPS. It can be worth doing, however, because it can provide a safeguard against possible copyright disputes if the MCPS have got you on their computer, although this will not afford you any actual copyright protection.

Another important point to note is that unless you are a major record company the MCPS royalties on copyright material are calculated on the number of records you PRESS – regardless of whether you sell them or not.

An information sheet which goes into greater detail about mechanical copyright is available free from the MCPS CUSTOMER SERVICES ADVISER.

MCPS Ltd., Elgar House, 41 Streatham High Road, London SW16 1ER. Telephone enquiries: Customer Services Adviser, 01–769 4400.

For important information on PPL and PRS royalties which arise from the public performance of records see Copyright, (page 184). Your record may be the best thing ever put on vinyl, but it won't

sell unless you make an effort to put it in the public eye. There are a whole combination of ways of doing this, some of which we go into below. If you play a specific, specialist type of music, there may be a market for your product in outlets and areas which we do not cover.

You should do all the following things simultaneously as there is little point in bringing everyone's attention to a record that they then cannot find. Reviews can be obtained from your local paper, fanzines, and even the national music press if you send out a reasonably professional press release and enclose a copy of the record. As we have mentioned elsewhere in the book, you are most likely to get some attention if you release your record in the quieter months of the year. Certainly don't expect record reviews in October, November or December.

Sending copies of the record to appropriate DJs and producers might also get you a free plug (see Plugging and Promotion page 120), and airplay can make a lot of difference to record sales. How many 'freebies' you can afford to give away is something you will have to calculate carefully based upon your break even costs. As with merchandising it is all too easy to give your profits away, and whilst records may be regarded more as a promotional item, they have still cost you money and are arguably more valuable to people if they have had to pay for them. One independent band manager who released his artists' records himself in the early days had a policy of sending no free records out whatsoever. This meant that anyone who was interested had to go out and buy a copy – even the music papers – and it didn't do his bands any harm!

In the meantime, you can start by approaching your local record shops to see if they will stock your record. If you can afford a small A2 poster run, possibly advertising a series of live dates as well as the record, then see if you can't get the shops to put them up – preferably in the shop window. Another obvious outlet is to sell your LPs at your gigs. Again, putting posters up around the venue can help your merchandising person as well as drawing attention to any other gigs you might be doing in the area.

Depending on the sort of music you play, you may find that fanzines, particularly foreign ones, may be able to sell a few copies by mail order. Write to the individual editors and see if they are interested.

DISTRIBUTION COMPANIES

Once your record begins to sell in any kind of quantity you may want wider distribution and more efficient coverage than you can cope with yourself. There are many commercial distribution companies – most of which we list in our Directory (see page 233). We have restricted ourselves to a brief examination of the Cartel group of companies which will give you a yardstick, if nothing else, to measure the others against.

THE CARTEL

The Cartel is a group of independent record companies based throughout the country. The major partner is Rough Trade Records based in Collier Street in London. The individual members of the Cartel are each responsible for a different area within the UK and were all in existence separately before the Cartel was set up in the late seventies. They originally united to provide a nationwide distribution service in competition with the major commercial distribution and record companies, when they saw that they could never effectively compete with them as individual outfits. All can still independently sign bands and manufacture and distribute records as they wish.

Up until relatively recently all the Cartel companies, including Rough Trade, signed bands largely on a sometimes dubious artistic merit basis. This led to them stocking small quantities of records by literally thousands of artists. The paperwork and general administration involved in distributing many tiny quantities of records and accounting to hundreds of disorganised individuals for every record sold, almost bankrupted Rough Trade and defeated the reason for the Cartel's existence.

As a result of this experience, Rough Trade, and to a lesser extent the other members have changed their policy towards new bands. They are now much more selective and prefer to deal with record labels where they know there is an established company structure with a plan for some sort of future. In the last two or three years they have rationalized the distribution centre to their base in Collier Street where they have a National Accounts Manager who deals with the large shop chains such as HMV and Virgin. To cover the provinces they have two wholesalers in each area to distribute around all the remaining independent record shops. They now also have Press and Promotions departments and a Sales Force available. In these respects they are now very similar to any other major record company, although they still claim to be different in that everyone working for them has a genuine enthusiasm and love of music.

Despite this change in policy, it is still worth approaching Cartel members both for record deals and for distribution deals. Rough Trade receive 30–40 tapes per week and although virtually none

are accepted this is true of the other record companies as well. However, if they are interested in you, they can offer you a more flexible deal than any of the majors would do. For instance, they may agree to manufacture and release a relatively small quantity of a three or four track 12″ single without expecting you to sign a five-year deal with them. (Seven inch singles are 'a waste of time', apparently!) If you can persuade them to do something like this for you, or to distribute the records you have already made yourselves, then the deal goes as follows:

For every 12″ single or LP they sell, they will take approximately 30% of the 'dealer price'. That is to say that they will take 30% of the amount that the record retailer pays for your record before the retail mark-up is added. At current rates that is £1.99 for a 12″ single and £3.65 for an LP. The minimum quantity they will distribute is 1,000 records and after you have sold 5,000 copies the percentage that they require drops according to negotiation.

In the Directory we list the Cartel members that you can send your tapes or distribution proposal to. The regional companies are more approachable and are smaller organizations with whom you can do deals that Rough Trade would probably reject out of hand. However, even they prefer to deal with small established record labels rather than individuals.

Getting mentioned in the press, for whatever reason, is one of the few ways that you can draw attention to yourselves for free. It is a crucial part of any promotion campaign. Good reviews and articles can be used not only in approaching record and publishing companies, but also in arousing further press and media interest. Once the media have had their attention drawn to you, there is a tendancy for that attention to snowball and for a while you may even be 'flavour of the month'. Learning to harness media interest is not easy and some would say it was a full-time job in itself.

Press reviews are likely to affect your image more than they will affect your actual record sales. The general public forms their opinions on a band from reviews and interviews, but will usually only buy a band's records once they have heard them on the radio. Very few people will rush out and buy an album that they haven't heard just because they have read a rave review in a music paper. Those that do buy on press recommendation alone – the 'taste-makers' – are likely to comprise your first hardcore fans and are therefore very important.

Ironically, you are more likely to get good press when you are an up and coming band. In general music journalists seem to save their more vitriolic criticisms for successful bands that they were singing the praises of last year! Bear in mind too, that even bad reviews are not always bad news. There is some truth in the axiom that 'any publicity is good publicity' and a really stinking review can sometimes attract more attention than a wishy-washy one!

WHO TO APPROACH

The three main music papers, NME, Sounds and Melody Maker, are obvious first targets. Depending on the sort of music that you play, you may find one of these three more sympathetic than the others. For instance, the NME led the way in promoting Hip Hop and House music. However, these papers are by no means the be all and end all. There are literally dozens of other large circulation pop papers and magazines, not to mention scores of specialist music papers. There are at least half a dozen magazines which deal exclusively with Blues music and this is true also of Heavy Metal, Folk, Country and R&B.

Don't overlook your local paper and 'What's On' magazines, especially if you are playing live gigs. If you play elsewhere, try and find their equivalents in the towns you are playing. These papers often have quite high circulations and nearly all have pop music sections (usually at weekends), which need to be filled. This is also true of the local and national student papers. Most colleges and universities have campus-based publications and, where the colleges are also venues, they will have a live music section.

There are still quite a number of fanzines in the UK, although there are far fewer than there were in the mid to late seventies. They might be worth considering when you send out singles or press releases, depending on the music you play. On the whole, their circulations are only small and they tend to come and go on a regular basis.

On the continent, depending on the country, there are lots of so-called 'fanzines' which are worth contacting – especially if you are considering doing a European tour. British acts are still highly regarded and many of the editors of these magazines are only too pleased to receive a press pack and record from new bands. You shouldn't be deceived by the label 'fanzine', either. Many of them are glossy, full colour magazines with circulations exceeding those of the British music papers, and their editors and contributors are extremely knowledgeable and tend to be less cynical than their London counterparts. (See Directory, page 252 for a concise list of foreign fanzines which wrote to us saying that they welcomed information about new UK bands.)

APPROACHING UK JOURNALISTS

The thing not to do, which a lot of bands still do, is to turn up at the offices of a music paper and ask for a particular journalist or, worse still, for 'somebody' to come downstairs and see them. These bands seem to labour under the illusion that the music press are just sitting around waiting for them to turn up. Apart from the fact many journalists are not based at the head office of the paper they write for, those that are there are likely to be busy trying to meet their deadlines.

Before you actually contact a journalist you should get to know the paper they write for and read their contributions carefully. If in doubt about the author of a particular article, ring the newspaper concerned and ask for the editor, or the assistant editor, who should be able to help you. They will need to know the date and issue number of the publication as well as the page number and the subject of the article. Once you have identified journalists who seem either to share your musical outlook, or to enjoy reviewing bands whose music is not dissimilar to your own, then it is worth writing to them or to their editor.

Terrence Trent D'Arby at the Brixton Academy. An expatriate American who has his base in the UK.

Send them your usual promo package with a covering letter, mentioning the particular article or news item you read that prompted you to contact them in the first place. If you have already appeared in the gig guide or tour news section of their paper, mention this and add any other useful information such as whether or not you have had any radio sessions, released any records, and so on. Try to keep all this concise but informative. Where you enclose photographs, they need to be of decent quality if they are to stand any chance of being published. Polaroid photographs will not do.

As usual, follow your initial letter with a phone call a few days later. It is worth finding out when the paper's press deadlines are, so that you don't bother your contacts on their busiest day (see end of section). If you have selected journalists whose opinion you respect, then any criticisms or comments they make can be very useful. Remember that in all likelihood they receive a large number of unsolicited tapes, and that talking to new bands is only part of their job. If a journalist does not like your music, or does not think it is appropriate for the paper in question, then look for someone else. Continuously harrassing a journalist who is not interested may well colour the opinions of the other writers in the office, especially if they hear constant complaints about you.

Where a journalist is not on the staff of a paper they will probably be working freelance. You can ask either the editor, or one of the full-time staff reporters, to tell you who your nearest freelance journalist might be. Many of the live music reviews, for instance, are written by freelance journalists who work mainly in their local area. The pop and arts pages of the national and other daily newspapers will also be compiled by a combination of staff and freelance reporters. These papers have far larger circulations than most of the specialist music press and are well worth approaching. However, whilst journalists may be freelance, this does not mean that they can contribute to any paper they like. A freelance music journalist is unlikely to be able to get their article about you published in the Guardian, for example. Most of the national daily papers only use a small number of journalists that they already know, so check each paper individually for the relevant contact names.

You can even try reviewing your own live shows – but be careful! It is not wise to try and deceive the editor of a music paper by failing to point out that you are the lead singer of the band whose gig you have just reviewed. In any event, papers are unlikely to publish a review of an unknown band by an untested writer. However, if they like the way you write they may ask you to cover a gig by another band. Apart from earning you a little pocket money, this could also help you to get to know the other journalists working on the paper. Send your gig and album reviews to the assistant editors of the relevant publications. Unless you are particularly good at writing you are unlikely to get them published, but it might help to draw attention to the band.

There are some unwritten rules that operate as well. For instance, if a journalist writes a feature on a band, that journalist may not be allowed to review the same band's LP. The idea behind this is to achieve a spread of opinion within a publication. As a result, it is advisable to approach more than one journalist at each paper. The more journalists you know, the better, because you can easily risk over-using a contact if you only have one.

Press reviews and articles should be part of an overall promotional process, so try and time your approaches to the press to fit in with your other activities. Even full-colour articles on your band are of limited use if there is very little else happening in terms of live shows or record releases. Bear in mind too, that unless your career really does take off in a big way, there is only so much that can be usefully said about you within a given period of time. Otherwise, at a later date, when you really do need publicity you could find that the music press feel that they have done enough on your act for the time being. Tours and record releases may then not be newsworthy enough in their own right to justify giving you more press coverage.

PRESS DEADLINES AND PUBLICATION DATES

All newspapers are run to a strict timetable, so it is important that you know their copy deadlines if you aim to get articles printed and your press releases timed correctly. For example, if your tour starts on a Monday, there is little point in sending any information which arrives the preceding Friday, because you will have missed the copy date. You may also find that the publication date of the paper is not until the following Wednesday. (The publication date is the date when the paper actually appears on the streets not the day the paper is printed.) Also, it is worth considering that the day of the copy deadline is usually the busiest day of the week which means that journalists are unlikely to be in a receptive mood with regard to unsolicited phone calls. If, when you ring, a journalist sounds busy and asks you to call back at 5.00 p.m., hang up straight away and call back later.

Below are some of the copy deadlines for both advertising and editorial for some of the well-known music papers. Note the surprisingly long lead times, which may be even longer on commissioned articles.

Melody Maker   Published Wednesday. Dated following Saturday. All copy to arrive eight days preceding publication.

NME   Published Wednesday. Dated following Saturday. All copy to arrive one week preceding publication.

Sounds	Published Wednesday. Dated following Saturday. All copy to arrive ten days preceding publication.
Blues and Soul	Published fortnightly Tuesdays. All copy to arrive twelve days preceding publication.
Echoes	Published Wednesday. Dated following Saturday. All copy to arrive nine days preceding publication.
Kerrang!	Published Tuesday. All copy to arrive eleven days preceding publication.
Record Mirror	Published Wednesday/Thursday. Dated following Saturday. All copy to arrive ten days preceding publication.
No. 1	Published Wednesday. Dated following Saturday. All copy to arrive nine days preceding publication
Q	Published 10th day of month. Dated following month. All copy to arrive 23rd of previous month.
Guardian	For Friday publication all copy required previous Wednesday a.m.
Independent	For Friday publication all copy required previous Wednesday a.m.

All these dates and times were correct when we went to press. Always ring and check before you send advertising or editorial copy. Deadlines were made to be broken but don't depend on too much leeway, especially at busy times of the year.

PLUGGING AND PROMOTION

'Promotion' means advertising, radio airplay, TV appearances, live performances, newspaper articles, interviews and publicity stunts – anything, in fact, that draws the attention of the public to a band and their records. 'Plugging' refers specifically to the promotion of your music to radio producers and DJs, club DJs, record shop buyers, and the producers of music TV programmes. Whereas self-promotion is an integral part of working as a performer, plugging only becomes necessary when you have a product (usually a record) which you want to have played on the radio and/or sold in the shops. The professional plugger is a salesperson and this what you will have to be, to a certain extent, if you want this kind of exposure. Plugging and the attention seeking promotional activities outlined above should complement and reinforce each other. If you do a tour and simultaneously release a single, then the posters for the gigs should include information about the record and vice-versa. If, while you are seeking radio play, you get a support slot at a major venue, this is news that you can ring the radio producer about. Whatever you do, try to avoid treating each element of promotion in isolation.

What if you do get a good reception from a radio station? The fact is, that it is unlikely to make a substantial difference to your career unless it is part of some form of sustained marketing campaign. Even airplay on Radio 1 will be of limited value unless you use it and capitalize on it. If you do get airplay like this – tell everyone! You need to keep your contacts at radio stations, venues, record companies and the press, aware of a constant flow of information about you, without appearing pushy, rude or arrogant. If you do a series of gigs let all your contacts know and send journalists and A&R people some tickets. As soon as you have some success with one radio station, call back all your other target stations and tell them. This is what promotion is all about – the idea being to keep people aware of your existence and how exciting and interesting you are. If one member of the band is good at this kind of thing, let them do the talking so that they stand a chance of being recognized or remembered next time. And if you have got what it takes to carry off a gimmick or publicity stunt – go for it!

DOING YOUR OWN RADIO PLUGGING

Airplay is the single most important factor influencing the record-buying public, so when people talk about 'plugging' what they generally mean is plugging for radio play or a broadcast on TV. Each week an overwhelming number of records are released in the UK and they all have to compete for the attention of the key radio producers, presenters and playlist selectors who compile the play-lists for the most listened to and influential radio programmes. Essentially this means Radio 1 closely followed by the big regional and pirate stations. Less influential, but still important in building a following, are the local BBC and Independent Radio stations. The pirate stations can be of prime importance for particular kinds of music, namely club dance music.

Doing your own plugging will require a telephone, discipline, organization, personality, and enough spare cash to cover packaging and stamps. It is not an easy job, especially if you do not have any contacts to help you, so make sure you have considered the following:

a) How are you going to describe your record? You may hate being labelled, but people will always ask you this question.

b) Who is likely to play your music? Be as objective as possible so that you do not waste your time targetting inappropriate people.

c) Is your energy and time best spent plugging your record immediately? Might it be more useful in a month or two when the gigs you are due to play supporting a well-known band make you more 'newsworthy'?

d) How will you follow up a positive response to your record? Do you have adequate record distribution to fulfil public demand? Are you ready to discuss a deal with record or publishing companies?

Remember also that time is particularly pressing at the busy times of the year: September to December. In fact, it is the policy of some record companies to release no new material at all after September the 1st. If your single or LP is not ready for release until October or November it is highly advisable to postpone your release date to the New Year. Selling enough records to make any impact on the charts in the build-up to Christmas will require a major sales and promotion initiative and your release will almost certainly be lost amongst the huge TV and press advertising campaigns run by the major record companies.

While you need to sell large quantities of records to get any sort of chart placing in the teeth of the pre-Christmas competition, you will require far fewer record sales to make the charts in the period immediately after Christmas. For some reason, the major record companies delay most of their post-Christmas releases until the beginning of February. This is probably to give their executives an opportunity to get over the prolonged Christmas binge! You can

take advantage of this to sneak your record out onto the market in the first or second week of January. As many DJs will tell you, there is usually nothing new to play or to talk about in these two weeks. The Christmassy, party-time records become inappropriate after January 1st and they usually leave a yawning gap in the playlists when they disappear.

LOCAL AND REGIONAL RADIO

There are things in common when approaching any professional radio station, so start with local radio and press and use what you achieve there when you later approach the bigger stations. This will give you the opportunity to learn from your mistakes with producers at stations which aren't crucial to your career!

Begin by finding out who produces the most appropriate programmes for your type of music. Be as realistic as you can and try not to waste your time, or anyone else's, by contacting just anybody. Phone the producer or DJ you have selected to tell them that you are sending them some material and 'do they mind?'. Keep this initial call short and polite and don't do obviously stupid things like calling when they are actually on the air. Get their correct contact details, and send them your mailout package. It really will help if you are business-like and to the point. Use stiff envelopes to send records – ideally the ones designed for the job (see Directory: Envelopes, page 233) – and send one record per envelope with all the information you want to include and a brief introductory note. Avoid sending cassettes in those bags that are padded with the contents of someone's vacuum cleaner! Use the self-sealing bags which are available from your local Post Office and are padded with little pastic bubbles. Wait a few days – then call them back.

INTERVIEWS

Independent Local Radio stations (ILR) might well be interested in your story along the lines of 'local band makes good' or they may even want to interview you if you have something interesting to say. Unless you are naturally entertaining there will have to be a newsworthy 'peg' to hang the interview on. You might be doing a charity gig or be campaigning to keep a local venue open, for example. If you do get an interview, take the opportunity to meet as many people as you can at the station and, it goes without saying, be as professional and friendly as possible. Even at local radio level producers and DJs talk to record company and A&R scouts regularly and could easily put in a good word for you if you make the right impression.

Morrisey of the Smiths performing and signing autographs at the 'Jobs for a Change' festival run by the GLC at County Hall 1986.

THE
TC
AND
MUSIC
GUIDE

RADIO 1: DAYTIME

For an 'unknown' band unable to afford professional plugging services, and without contacts in the business, airplay on day-time Radio 1 is going to be well nigh impossible to attain.

The power that Radio 1 has to affect record sales makes it a totally different ball game to regional and local radio. The only really important pop chart in the UK is the Gallup Chart which is based on a measurement of national record sales across the country — and Radio 1 is the only truly national radio station. Consequently, every record company in the UK is pushing for Radio 1 airtime and this, in turn, puts the playlist compilers under pressure.

At Radio 1 the day-time radio playlists are compiled by the producers of the programmes and the DJs actually have very little control over the selection of records that they play. This means that national day-time radio is essentially in the hands of the key day-time producers based at BBC Broadcasting House, London. (Their names are printed in the Radio Times underneath the programme details.) Each day these producers and, to a lesser extent the DJs, face a constant barrage of new material from pluggers, record companies, band managers, agents, and hopeful young bands. This can amount to literally hundreds of new singles per week.

The ultimate goal for this army of people plugging various releases is a place on the revered 'Radio 1 Playlist'. This is a carefully prepared list that lays down the basic core of records which will be played on air each week. Other records may be played as well, but playlisted ones will get a 'guaranteed' minimum number of plays — particularly during the peak listening hours of the day. So, if your single is on the playlist, you have the best advertising available — for free — for a week! This playlist is compiled each week by a caucus of only seven day-time producers. Every Monday morning they get together to discuss the merits of the new releases and decide which ones should be added to the playlist and which records should be dropped from it. Given the power of Radio 1 airplay it is easy to appreciate that while the playlist is not the be all and end all, it is very important if you want to sell quantities of records and is extremely difficult to get on to.

It should therefore come as no surprise that it is very difficult to get through the front doors of Broadcasting House. The day-time producers and DJs work to tight schedules and cannot be easily persuaded to meet everyone who would like to see them. Try and get an interview and you will come across an effective barrier of assistants, secretaries and commissionaires who protect them from uninvited and unwelcome guests. This is why, as far as the day-time programmes are concerned, approaching Radio 1 is really a job for a professional plugger (see below).

RADIO 1: EVENING

The sort of music you will hear on Radio 1 in the evenings is markedly different to the highly chart-oriented day-time selection. There is more time given over to new bands and to types of music not normally played on air during the day. Unlike the day-time DJs, John Peel and the other specialist DJs have much more say in compiling their programmes, but even they have to plan the content of their shows in conjunction with a producer. Evening DJs receive a lot of demo tapes from hopeful young bands and most are conscientious and try to listen to as many as they can. All will play records that arrive through the post, if they and their producers like them, and most are able to invite bands in to record sessions if they are sufficiently impressed (see below). Whether or not you risk trying to approach the day-time DJs and producers, it is certainly worth having a go at the night-time programmes. Again, your music must be appropriate to the shows that you approach, but you will find that the evening shows have a more relaxed and open-minded attitude to new music.

CLUB PROMOTIONS

One sort of music that is far from dependent on Radio 1 airplay is club and dance music. In fact, immediate mass airplay on a dance record can actually spoil its prospects for success, so a special approach is used for 'club' records. This approach is very much a marketing exercise and entails feeding the new records, very selectively and possibly even on an unmarked 'white label', to the 'taste-makers' on the dance music scene. The first recipients of a 'hot' dance record will probably be the specialist record shops, the trendy club DJs and a handful of the most respected radio DJs – including those on pirate stations. Most of the early promotion strategy starts in London, although as the word spreads on a new record, the trendiest of the provincial club DJs soon get to hear of it, and will hopefully do their best to be first in their area to play it.

The initial market for dance records is very small and, in the early stages, very volatile – so it is important to give away as few free copies as possible. The idea is to create an urgent sales demand for a record among those people who are anxious not to be the last to own a copy of the latest dance hit. Once this initial wave of enthusiasm has been sated the tastemakers will rapidly lose interest and move on to the next 'big thing'. In the meantime

their concentrated burst of record buying will probably have been enough to put the record into the top levels of the Dance Charts, and may even have done enough to chart it in the national Top Fifty. Also, by playing the record in hundreds of discos across the country to thousands of young record buyers, the DJs create a further wave of demand which could well be sufficient to put the record inside the national Top Forty. These two overlapping surges of sales mean that you must have excellent, nationwide distribution organized before you release your record.

At this point, almost whether they like it or not, Radio 1 has to recognize the public interest in the record and include it on their playlist. By this time all the radio stations across the country will be giving the record some airtime and, if it can capture the mass imagination and 'cross over' into the mainstream pop market, the record could go 'all the way'. Where a record fails to make this final, but crucial, leap it will probably disappear from the charts as quickly as it came.

This simplistic sketch only outlines the theory of club and dance music promotion and many thousands of identical sounding, sub-standard dance tracks never make it beyond the white label stage.

TV PROMOTION

This is one of the most difficult media to approach yourself with any success. Part of the reason for this is that most of the programmes you see on television (aside from the purely chart-based programmes) have mainly been researched, filmed and edited several weeks – if not months – in advance of the broadcast. Most of them will have the ability to include newsworthy or particularly 'important' items at very short notice at the discretion of the director and producer – but these items usually involve established superstars or major pop events and you are unlikely to fulfil these criteria without record company backing and a professional plugger.

PROFESSIONAL PLUGGERS

Professional pluggers and promotion companies, whether or not they work independently or for record labels, specialize in using their contacts in TV, Radio and the club circuit to get your records and videos played.

If you are signed to a major record company, or one of the larger independent record companies, then the task of getting your record national and regional airplay will be handled by in-house pluggers. A lot of publishers have their own pluggers as well, and if you have signed a publishing deal it may include someone plugging and promoting your records. However, if you release your own record you will either have to do this work yourselves, or consider using the services of an independent plugger or promotions company. This can be quite expensive so it is important that you are aware of what a professional plugger is realistically going to achieve for you at this stage in your career.

You also have to be clear about what you are setting out to achieve through having your record plugged, and whether it is worth paying for. If you are hoping for a chart position then it is crucial that you have sorted out adequate distribution of your record to shops throughout the UK. It is no use getting ten day-time plays on Radio 1 in a week if the public cannot find your record anywhere. The cost of pressing enough singles to distribute in this way may be prohibitive unless someone else is paying for them, for instance, the distributor or the record company. If, on the other hand, your priority is just to gain media attention with a view to getting a record or publishing deal, then you will not need to worry about pressing or distribution because it is just the airplay that matters.

For a fee, independent pluggers visit radio and TV stations with your record – play it if possible, and try to get the radio and TV producers to include it on their playlists. In a nutshell, they make sure that the 'right people' take some notice of you. If appropriate, they will also target influential club DJs. The advantage of using a plugger is that their contacts are ready-made. The main disadvantage, especially if you are still a small band on a minor label, is that you are likely to be low on their list of priorities and may well get lost in the system.

Pluggers make their rounds with several records at a time, and may be inclined to concentrate their efforts on regular clients including, perhaps, some of the major record labels. Good pluggers will only work a maximum of three or four records at any one time. If they try and take on more then be suspicious of the job that they are doing for you. Bearing in mind the amount of time that producers and DJs will have to talk to them, a plugger is unlikely to be able to hold their attention for longer than a few moments. Three or four seven inch singles, each with their own publicity material, is really the most that a plugger should be presenting at one time.

On the whole, the influential pluggers almost exclusively deal with record company releases and are only likely to take on an unsigned band in return for some kind of stake in their future career. You will tend to be caught in this classic Catch 22 situation in the early stages. If a plugger is offering to plug your record for considerably less than the going rate, it is questionable that you will receive a worthwhile service and you could spend the money

more effectively doing the job yourself. When you contact a plugging company ask what artists they are currently working with. This will give you an idea of how suitable they are for your music and also show how many other products they might be working alongside yours. The good news is that very occasionally a reputable promotion company will be so enthused by a record that they will offer to plug it for a much reduced fee.

Normally, to cover Radio 1, Capital Radio, Radio Luxembourg, and all the important regional radio stations and relevant TV programmes, a promotion company will charge around £1,500. They will also need 300–500 free sample records to give out. You may pay less for a 'regions only' deal and you will need to give the plugger fewer free records, but this kind of deal is only of limited value, and you could probably do a reasonable job of the regions yourselves.

All plugging deals are for 'the life of a record' – that is the period during which the plugging company is actually working a record. If, after three weeks or so, there is still no sign of success, then the plugging company will quite quickly leave your record to concentrate on something more profitable. Conversely, if the record becomes a hit and its 'life' is extended to eight or ten weeks, then the basic fee will remain the same. No plugging company can give you a guarantee of chart placings and it would be unfair to expect them to.

Watch out for performance-related 'chart bonuses'. Chart bonuses are extra, pre-agreed sums of money which the plugging company will charge you as your record rises up the official UK charts. These bonuses are usually justifiable, especially if they are related to the higher chart placings. However, some plugging companies build in an extra charge for getting your record to number 75 in the charts. This is a relatively easy target to achieve as you will not sell significant quantities of records until you have reached a chart position inside the top 50. Bear in mind too, that sales vary depending on the time of year and the standard of the competition. The build-up to Christmas is the busiest sales period and the competition is greatest then.

If a plugging company is particularly enthusiastic about your record they may offer you the option of a reduced fee plus a percentage of the profits from the record sales or music publishing. This gives the pluggers a real incentive to work on your record as they get paid more money each time the record is played. Use your own judgement and take independent advice whenever you are offered a 'points' deal like this. While it may seem to save you money in the short-term, it could lead to you paying considerably more in the long-term and may be applied to all the records you go on to release. Another possibility is that a plugging company may offer to work for you on condition that they can recoup their fee if, and when, you get a record deal and are paid an advance. As with most of these situations, get independent legal advice before you sign anything.

SESSIONS

Radio stations have to negotiate with the PPL and PRS for permission to play records for a specific period of time. What this basically means is that they pay the PPL a blanket fee towards the royalties owed to the copyright owners of the records which are played on the radio over a given period and they pay a blanket fee to the PRS for the permission to broadcast copyright songs over a given period. The PPL fee is translated into so many hours of 'needletime' which should not be exceeded. One way in which a station can continue to play music without having to pay needletime is if they record it themselves in a 'session'. (See Copyright. PPL and PRS, pages 192 and 189 for a more detailed explanation.)

LOCAL AND INDEPENDENT RADIO

Sessions for local BBC and Independent radio are restricted by their budgets and also by their recording facilities which may not be too good. For example, if the programme's MU fees allowance for sessions is less than £6,000 a year they are more likely to do an 'in concert' type programme with some big names than spend this recording small local bands which nobody has ever heard of. Sessions can also be broadcast live from the studio or be recorded elsewhere. If this is the case, the band may have to pay their own recording costs but be paid session fees by the station. Alternatively, you may be asked to record music for them without being paid anything for it. The MU are obviously very much against this but with some local stations the situation is that if they had to pay the musicians, they wouldn't be able to do the sessions. One potentially positive aspect of increased airtime on Radio 1 and the other stations is that if the needletime is not increased correspondingly, it could mean more session time for young bands.

RADIO 1

It is not easy for new bands to get a session on Radio 1 while there are bands around who have got a deal, released a record which is at number 75 and have the requisite backup to influence the producer or DJ concerned. For the early evening show it is probably only worth approaching the producer for a session if you already

Billy Bragg signing albums as part of the promotion of his LP 'Reading Poetry to the Taxman' at HMV, Oxford Street, 1988.

are at this stage. Peel and Kershaw are more likely to make their choices on personal grounds: perhaps they saw the band play live, perhaps they were tipped off by someone they know or perhaps they were sent the tape through the post. They would then approach their producer for the studio time and clearance.

You need to be well prepared beforehand for a BBC session because you will be required to put down four tracks and be mixed and finished in six hours! If you do not have much experience in recording studios you should (a) only use material that you are very familiar with, (b) make sure all your equipment is working and tuned and, (c) be ready to start when the session is ready to start.

The producer for a Radio 1 session cannot really 'produce' – that is change things and make suggestions because there isn't enough time and the job at hand is to be the first listener, make sure everyone is happy, and help out at the mixing stage. BBC engineers usually have a lot of experience and are good at their job.

The BBC owns the finished tape but you can buy a cassette – a 'listening copy' – from the BBC Sound Archives for around £17.25. You will be required to sign an agreement saying that the tape is to be used for promotional purposes only. If you want to release the tape as a record, then you have to contact BBC Enterprises and inform them exactly how many records, tapes or CDs you will be making, and the selling price. If you are releasing the record yourself then you may be offered a 'buy-out' deal – so long as the number of pressings is limited. For example, if you were to press 1,000 copies of a 12" which you propose to sell for £3.70 – the BBC would currently charge you around £250.00 for the tape. However, if a record company tries to buy the tape with a view to pressing a larger number of records, they have to negotiate a royalty rate with the BBC which, again, will be calculated according to the format of the proposed release, the selling price and the quantity.

You will be paid MU rates for the BBC session, and you will normally be expected to be a member of the MU. You will also be paid as if you had done two sessions. This is because an MU session is $3\frac{1}{2}$ hours and you will actually do two sessions of three hours. Rates are currently £40 per session per band member so you should get £80 each – plus you will also be paid for one repeat which should be half your original session fee – making £120.00 per band member.

VIDEOS

MUSIC VIDEO FOR YOUNG BANDS

'I've always thought it was a great shame that many of the potentially most rewarding bands to work with in video production are the very ones least able to afford it. With the absence of any real promotion budget, most unsigned bands and small Indie record companies are reluctant to invest what little money they have in a quality promo, or live video'.

Mark Chapman, *Dramatic Video*

How much you spend on making a video will depend on a number of factors which we examine below, but perhaps the first one to consider is why you want a video – what is it for? Is it going to be aimed at bookers at clubs, A&R personnel or TV producers? Quality videos that can be broadcast on TV can cost a lot of money, but not necessarily as much as you might be led to believe. This brief, general introduction to low-budget video for bands will hopefully point out some of the ways in which you can trim your video production budget whilst retaining a level of professional quality which may, or may not, be 'broadcast quality'.

Video has the ability to encapsulate your image and music at the same time and this can make it an excellent promotional tool. Before you commit yourself to anything, however, you should have thought the whole process through and made sure that you are accounting for every cost you will come across. A common mistake is to be over-ambitious, trying to emulate videos seen on TV – but without the budget or skill to make it work. An inaudible, badly edited or pretentious video is a waste of money that could have been spent on pressing 1,000 singles or recording a decent demo.

The consensus of opinion appears to be that the best sort of video for a band starting out is either a multi-camera recording of a live show, or a video promo which includes at least some footage of the band miming a live performance. In other words, simple, straightforward videos are easier and cheaper to make and are often more effective. Lots of special effects are more likely to draw attention to the director than the band.

PROMO VIDEOS AND TELEVISION

With the imminent advent of cable and satellite television it will be easier than ever before to get good quality videos actually played on air. This is because there will soon be dozens of TV channels, all searching for cheap, new material to fill their airtime. 'Pop music' and related 'magazine' programmes seem to be enjoying a new-found popularity – and there are more in the pipeline. With this in mind, it is worth considering the pros and cons of making a video of 'broadcast quality'.

WHAT IS 'BROADCAST QUALITY'?

All professional film and video formats, except low band U-matic, are viewed as potentially 'broadcast quality' by the record and TV industry. As we hope to show, it is possible to break from this tradition.

When established record companies spend large sums of money on the production of a video (the average cost of which has now gone down to a mere £28,000), they are paying for three important things:

a) A Director

A record company will usually choose a director who has worked on other successful pop videos, although this makes the director's fee expensive. High fees tend to give the record company the false impression that they are guaranteed value for money, and also appeals to their natural propensity to follow an established formula. Using new directors involves an element of risk which most record companies are unwilling to take, whereas established directors give the record company confidence that their ideas on the image of the band will be carried out according to their expectations. (Any ideas the band may have are rarely an important consideration!)

b) The Crew

Either the director, or a video production company will rapidly assemble a suitable crew including an art director, a lighting operator, camera operators, and post-production personnel. All these are key roles and paying for the best professionals helps to assure delivery of a quality finished video, sometimes within tight deadlines. Videos are often produced within a week of commissioning.

c) The Equipment

To ensure picture quality and variety in the technically sophisticated field of broadcast video production, good quality cameras, expensive film stock and trucks full of lighting equipment are usually felt to be essential – along with the technical crew to rig and operate it all.

The resulting video is of broadcast quality but the expense puts it beyond the reach of an unsigned band. It is possible, however, to make a broadcastable video without going to these lengths. Concentrating on the three areas above, there is room for compromise.

One problem 'successful' video directors have is that they end up making far too many promos. Thinking up new approaches and techniques is creatively exhausting, as is evident in the cliché-

ridden imitations seen so regularly nowadays. Directors who may have made far fewer promos are often able to give their work a fresher more innovative edge, drawing upon influences not derived from work on other music videos. A 'new' director could be more exciting to work with, as well as costing you less.

It is possible to cut down considerably on crew. For example, shooting with a hand-held camera will convey energy and also means that only one person is needed to operate the camera. Fixed camera positions mean several cameras and several camera operators. Similarly, shooting in available daylight alone may result in the loss of some facial details, but it will certainly cut down on lighting costs!

The equipment factor is more complex and requires a more detailed explanation.

CHOOSING YOUR EQUIPMENT

In professional video there are several different tape formats, all utilizing fast-moving tape and advanced electronic circuitry. In order of quality, these are:

SP High-band U-matic	One-inch (open reel)
High-band U-matic	SP Betacam
Low-band U-matic	Betacam

Much music video is originally shot on 16mm film, or 35mm film if the budget is generous enough. This is because celluloid is, among other things, able to show more detail and subtleties of tone. It is widely preferred for shooting, though it will usually be transferred to video for post-production and it is very expensive.

The only way of really saving money – without losing quality altogether – is to work on Low-band U-matic. Officially, this is unacceptable on TV because the amount of copying and transferring involved in the post-production process can cause 'breakdown' (fuzziness) of the final image. One way of getting around this problem is make the video look as if it is supposed to look the way it does! You could, possibly, originate some of the footage on Super 8 if you want slow-motion, stop-frame or grainy film effects. This will cost about £2 per minute of film plus the cost of transferring the results onto video.

A quick comparison of shooting and post-production equipment hire will illustrate this point. Prices are for one day's hire of camera, recorder and tripod only, and for 1 hour's tape or film. (All the figures given are approximations.)

		Equipment	Tape/film & Processing
Shooting (per day)	Low-band U-matic	c £150	c £35
	SP Betacam	c £300	c £25
	16mm	c £170	c £600 (incl. processing)
	35mm	c £260	c £1600 (incl. processing)
Post production (per day)	Low-band U-matic	(basic edit suite)	c £100
		(effects edit suite)	c £400
	SP Betacam-One inch	(basic edit suite)	c £1000
		(effects edit suite)	c £1800

The video maker we spoke to made his first video by hiring a Low-band shooting kit for one day and a basic Low-band edit suite for two days. It was a video of 'I'm a Teapot' by the Geisha Girls which attracted a lot of attention when Jools Holland introduced it on 'The Tube' as having been made for £300. The following week a viewer's poll indicated that 8 out of 10 viewers had preferred it to Queen's 'Radio Gaga' video which was previewed on the same show.

That there are not more low-budget videos made is largely due to the fact that it is difficult to make any money in producing them although a few Indie video producers have found that they can subsidize their production costs by distributing both their own and other productions.

LIVE SHOOTS

As far as multi-camera live shoots are concerned, bands on their own are rarely in a position to fund say, a 3-camera shoot of a well-lit gig with 16-track audio. This would cost at least £1,500 if filmed on Low-band U-matic. If, however, three bands playing the same bill decide to share the costs, each could end up with a professional-looking video with a 16-track audio-recording for a little over £500 each!

HOW DO YOUNG BANDS FIND GOOD LOW-BUDGET FACILITIES?

Once again, word of mouth is probably the best guideline. There are many budding directors around who would love to use your money to gain experience for themselves, and some of these will be hopeless although they will try to persuade you otherwise! You really need to talk to people who work in this field to find out who might be worth approaching. Bear in mind, though, that some producer/directors may be quite choosey about the type of bands they work with. If you're on a really low budget, you could try approaching your local College of Art & Design, or Polytechnic and find out if they run film and video courses. Students will often have

easy access to quite good equipment, though they may have more ideas than expertise and experience.

Finally, if you simply want to have a go at doing it yourself, you could enrol on a music video workshop course and learn the basic skills and techniques. You will be at an advantage because you will know how to dissect your tracks into separate components. Add to this a good cinematographic eye and some professional help in pre and post production, and you can achieve quite pleasing results. If you're going to have a crack at music video this way, one last word – allow much more time and money than you think you will need!

NOTE

(1) In order for your video to be broadcast on the TV you will have to be members of the Musicians' Union and the video itself will have to be cleared by the Union. This will involve a certain amount of paperwork and cost – although the money will be paid back later. If you think there is any possibility of you getting a video you have made yourselves broadcast on the TV you should investigate this properly with the MU.

(2) In order for your video to be 'broadcastable' it will also need to come within the IBA guidelines concerning 'Offence to Good Taste and Decency, Portrayal of Violence, etc.' Basically this means no drinking, smoking, nudity, motorcycle driving without crash helmets, driving of cars without seat-belts or dangerous driving – especially if the video is to be shown during the day. Contact the IBA for further information.

The Independent Broadcasting Authority, 70 Brompton Road, London SW3 1EY. Tel: 01-584 7011.

We have not included video production companies in our Directory because all of the ones that were readily contactable turned out to be more interested in high-budget video making than in helping struggling young acts. There didn't seem to be any source of information on good value studios either – please contact us if you know any different. We spoke to Mark Chapman of Dramatic Video, 17 Shenstone Road, Reading, Berks, RG2 0DT. Tel: (0374) 311 625.

The British Film Institute Film and TV Year Book contains information on workshops, courses and facilities for film and video around the country. It is available from BFI Publications, 21 Stephen Street, London W1P 1PL. Price: £11.95 incl. p & p. Tel: 01-255 1444.

The BFI also publish 'Directions' which lists training courses in film and video in the UK. It is updated three times a year and costs £1.80 incl. p & p. Available from the above address.

The contractual and legal aspects of the music business have become increasingly more complex and sophisticated. It is, however, only relatively recently that it has become the 'norm' for managers, record companies, publishers and so on, to insist that the artists whom they wish to contract, should have the benefit of independent specialist professional legal advice before signing.

This is at least in part due to the fact that over recent years there have been numerous examples of court cases where contracts have been set aside for being 'harsh and unconscionable'; where one side has taken unfair advantage of the other's lack of bargaining power. In fact, artists' lack of bargaining power at the time of negotiating their first contract is one of the most common causes for subsequent dissatisfaction with their management, recording, or publishing company. Several years on, and perhaps having had some degree of success, they may find themselves held to terms that were only agreed to under pressure, and in order to get their career underway.

Another common cause of problems which arises between band members and between a band and their management is, quite simply, lack of business experience. Newcomers to the music industry seldom have much idea of how business in general works, and mistakes are easily made. Often, too, matters which should have been taken care of at the outset, such as opening band bank accounts, registering as self-employed, registering for VAT, deciding who has written what part of which song, and so on – are left until it is too late.

Many of these problems can be avoided if professional advice is sought right from the beginning. Any 'harsh and unconscionable' deals that you may be offered can be improved by an expert lawyer adding weight to your bargaining position. Your lawyer should also be able to tell you in advance if you are likely to be taken for a ride. Disasters need not occur if you, or your manager, will acknowledge your lack of experience and seek advice.

AT WHAT POINT SHOULD YOU START THINKING OF FINDING YOURSELF A LAWYER?

The vast majority of artists first become aware of the need for professional advice when they are presented with their first long term contract and are advised to consult a solicitor over its terms.

However, the earlier you can involve a lawyer the better. Professional advice will help you to negotiate many of the commercial points (as opposed to strictly legal issues) yourself and if you can resolve the major commercial aspects before the first draft contract

is prepared, this should reduce the time that your lawyer has to spend in getting the contract agreed for signature – and consequently reduce your costs. Also from the point of negotiation, many matters are better discussed before they are committed to paper as once they have been committed to paper it is harder to get the other party to make concessions.

Artists will get the most out of their professional advisers if they can develop a good relationship with them. It is therefore worthwhile getting to know your lawyer as soon as you have something constructive to discuss. This way, when he comes to reviewing your contracts he or she will have more of an understanding of your situation and aspirations.

It should be noted that the Musicians Union run a free contracts advisory scheme open to fully paid MU members. Contact them for further details (see Directory for address). However, you will not get as comprehensive a service from the MU as you will get from a specialised music lawyer and the MU service should not be your first choice.

HOW DO YOU GO ABOUT CHOOSING A GOOD LAWYER – WHAT ARE THE NECESSARY CREDENTIALS?

It is probably best to choose a lawyer recommended by friends and acquaintances in the music business, and not necessarily one of those you read about in the music papers. Aggressive deal making is not always the same thing as career building, and you need to know that your lawyer is not just thinking about his own pocket. If you don't know anyone already established in the music business, ask the person giving you the contract to supply you with a list of 3 or 4 firms of solicitors, or look in our Directory for some useful numbers. You may well think of asking to see more than one lawyer before asking one to represent you. You shouldn't have to pay for such an audition.

Bear in mind, however, that it is not always a good idea to simply use the lawyer suggested by the manager, record company or publishing company offering you the deal, because that lawyer might be rather more friendly towards the company to which you are signing than is good for you. This is not to say that such a lawyer will do anything unprofessional, but perhaps they might not push the deal as far as they should ... On the other hand, it does have to be said that there may be some advantages if your lawyer has had frequent dealings with the manager, record company or publishing company, as they will then be familiar with the structure of the contracts, and know the parameters for negotiation.

It is an important decision and you must be satisfied that the lawyer you choose will be sympathetic to your aspirations and will conscientiously represent your best interests.

DOES YOUR LAWYER NEED TO BE AN EXPERIENCED MUSIC BUSINESS LAWYER?

Lawyers in general practice or lawyers who specialise in other areas are not really qualified to deal in music industry contracts, so you should enquire just how much experience those who might be professing to be qualified to act for you have really gained in the music business.

Familiarity with the sort of contracts involved is crucial since only someone who knows what ought to be found in such a contract will be able to recognize if anything is missing.

A good lawyer should be a vital part of your team – anticipating problems and drawing your attention to them in advance – rather than merely reacting to problems which you bring to the office. He or she should be able to give you advice concerning your choice of accountant, business structure, insurance adviser, agent, bank manager, and also in many instances on the reputations – good or otherwise – of the various companies and individuals involved in the business with whom you may have dealings.

YOUR FIRST MEETING WITH A LAWYER

If you are seeking advice on a contract which has already been issued, be sure to let your lawyer have a copy in advance of the meeting, so that he or she has an opportunity to give the task ahead some consideration before you meet.

You should work out what it is that you actually want from the meeting. Do you want the lawyer to handle the negotiations from the start, or do you want advice to enable you to do this?

You should try and give your lawyer a full breakdown of your circumstances. They will want to know what sort of music you play as this may help in evaluating the importance of different parts of the contract. If you have a definite career plan tell your lawyer and ask him or her to explain how making one particular contract as against another may affect these plans.

HOW DO LAWYERS WORK OUT THEIR FEES?

Most reputable firms will probably give you an initial interview at no charge, but if contracts follow they will expect to add this on to the total charge, later on when the matter is completed. Generally speaking, lawyers charge on a time basis, that is to say that the charges would be worked out on an hourly rate. The present

'going rate' is between £75 and £120 per hour, depending on the experience of the person dealing with the matter. The Law Society lays down the criteria for assessing legal charges and in essence, these permit solicitors to take into account a number of factors, such as the complexity of the matter, the importance of the matter to the client, the urgency with which the matter is dealt with and so on. This means that the solicitor will be able to take into account the value of the deal to his client and as a result uplift, or in some cases reduce, the charge based on an hourly rate.

Whilst some firms have been known to charge on an agreed percentage basis, (that is to say where the charge is worked out by reference to a pre-agreed percentage of your initial advance or advances), or to take 'points' (i.e. part of your royalty) this is not a general practice and seldom suits the circumstances.

You will usually be asked for money 'on account' (that is where money is placed into the lawyer's client account pending submission of an invoice) or, in some cases, for an authority addressed to the record company or publishing company for the initial advance to be paid to the lawyer's client account so that the legal fees can be deducted and the balance paid out in accordance with your instructions.

For an average management, recording or publishing contract you should expect to be asked for £250 – £500 by way of an initial 'on account' payment.

The best advice is to be honest with your legal advisers, let them know how much you can afford to pay and how you intend to pay.

WHEN DO YOU NEED A MANAGER

Many groups and artists have successfully brought out their own records, booked and advertised their tours and negotiated distribution and agency deals – without ever having a manager. Some have even been major success stories and still continued to manage themselves. What you have to ask yourself is whether you, or anyone in your band, really has the knowledge, experience and self-discipline to do the manager's job effectively.

Another important consideration is whether you have enough time to manage yourselves. This may not be a problem in the beginning, but as you begin to generate interest among promoters, agents and record companies, you may find life getting a little bit hectic. Apart from the logistical and practical problems you will come across, there will be little time to spare for the real business of writing, recording or playing live.

Employing a manager can be a career move on your part, or it may be a necessary response to the mounting pressures that success brings. To some extent it will depend on the personalities and music involved, your ability to handle your own affairs effectively and whether or not you meet and inspire the right person. Whilst good management can really 'make' your career, bad management can also 'break' it. Think carefully about what employing a manager involves and what you hope to achieve from the relationship.

WHAT MANAGERS DO

Managers normally handle the business side of an artist's career; from booking gigs and supervising the nitty gritty of live shows to negotiating royalty settlements with record company executives and publishers. From the start, the role of manager combines hustler with administrator, horse-sense with business acumen – and the often thankless task of 'looking after' the band. He or she will liaise with lawyers, accountants, journalists, record company A&R departments, roadies and tour managers taking full responsibility for running the practical side of events and guiding your career forward in the right direction.

All this can be very hard work and involve long hours, and unless you have signed to a management company with their own staff and office resources all these responsibilities could be on the shoulders on one person.

CHOOSING A MANAGER

Management commission is currently about 20% of their artists' income. You should consider carefully the cost of employing a

manager and weigh it against the potential you think there is for that particular person to make a difference to your future. Are they going to achieve things for you that you alone could not? Will they be able to do it faster? Make sure that they really earn their money – not only by relieving you of administrative burdens – but also by using their contacts in the business to actively promote the band. At the very least your manager should have a good understanding of the current music scene and have an idea of where you fit into it.

Unfortunately, however, a lot of bands tend to seek out management too early in their careers which means they are likely to fall victim to the more unscrupulous and untalented managers who circle around the edges of the business. Whilst good management is a sound investment, inadequate management can be a real problem, so you should take your time when considering a management deal and get professional legal advice.

THE 'FRIEND OF THE BAND'

In the early stages you may do perfectly well by yourself, or with the help of a competent friend who is genuinely interested in the band and who can assist in a practical way, booking gigs, organising the poster printing, booking PAs and so on. Perhaps this person is particularly good at getting you press coverage and hustling for A&R interest, so you decide to let them manage you properly. Many of the managers of successful bands started their careers in this way.

This type of manager, who starts as a friend of the band, can turn out to be an excellent choice, especially if they have a good basic grasp of finance. One point in their favour is that they are real fans of your music – something which can be all too easily overlooked in discussions with the more commercially-minded professional managers. However, you also have to be prepared for the fact that even if they develop with the band and know what the band want, they are less likely to have sufficient knowledge of the 'business' to avoid some of the pitfalls. This needn't be an insurmountable drawback, as long as they learn quickly, take good advice, and can adapt to the new demands of their role as you become successful. If you are not 100% sure that your friend will be the right person to work for you full-time, then make it clear from the start that you will be seeking professional management at a later stage.

PROFESSIONAL MANAGERS AND MANAGEMENT COMPANIES

We have not included managers or management companies in our Directory. This is because management is much more a question of personalities and individual opinion than any other aspect of the business.

Someone with a ready-made network of contacts can be very useful and with friends in the right places they can use their influence to move your career forward. Management companies can be good at this but may be less inclined to listen to your ideas and are more likely to try and package you like a commercial product rather than let you develop naturally. This is not to say that they are always inflexible, but more that they are likely to try and make you fit the mould of their previous experience. Of course, if you are a commercially-minded band then this approach could be just what you are looking for, and you will certainly benefit by association if your manager is already handling other successful acts.

Effective and experienced managers are really only going to be interested in you after you have some good material, a good live stage show and live following or real record company interest. The major management companies rarely 'discover' acts unaided and they survive largely by picking up acts from record companies where they have contacts or by poaching independent acts from less influential managers. Well known managers are also likely to have equally good connections with agents and promoters and their reputations will help open the doors even to those people and companies with whom they haven't actually worked before.

OTHER SOURCES OF MANAGEMENT HELP

Your lawyer or accountant can be an invaluable source of help and advice concerning your career and some are good band managers already. However, bear in mind that managing a band is a full-time job and that successful accountants and lawyers will probably be too busy to fulfil a management role effectively. There are also many examples of record company executives, agents and pro-moters taking on the management of bands. As with lawyers and accountants, their jobs may have brought them into contact with an artist or band that they are interested in managing. In some cases they are serious enough about the prospects to give up their current job in order to become full time managers. Record company employees, in particular, will be expected to resign their position under their employment contract. Attempting to combine band management with an existing career can lead to clashes of interest and neither job being done well.

The Godfathers are a good example of how management can successfully advance a band's career. In 1986 Peter and Chris Coyne formed the Godfathers and recorded a three song 12″ single called 'Capo Di Tutti Capi' on their own label, Corporate Image. They signed a production and distribution deal with Red Rhino and, with only three weeks to the release date they approached Roland Hyams to enlist his services as a publicist. Hyams would normally require at least six weeks to publicize a record properly but he decided to take them on because he saw their potential and their need for management. He went to see them play live: they had no sound monitor and no lights and they were, he said, 'diabolical but incredibly powerful'.

In 1987 the Godfathers released their single 'Love is Dead' with Hyams as their manager. The release date was February 14th 1987 and the single was launched with a special Valentine's Day gig in the London Dungeon. In the meantime, since the major record companies in the UK had failed to take an interest in the band Hyams successfully signed them to Epic (CBS) New York. Just one year later – on February 14th 1988 to be precise – The Godfathers were headlining a sold out show at the Town and Country Club. And on Valentine's Day 1989 they sold out the even larger capacity Kilburn International.

There is no such thing as a standard management contract – but here are some general guidelines and points to consider. Seek specialist professional legal advice before you sign anything.

THE CONTRACTING PARTIES

Is the manager contracting in a personal capacity or is he or she contracting through a limited company? If the latter, you should try to ensure that the company undertakes to provide your particular manager's services and that, in turn, your manager personally guarantees the performance of the contract by the company. If the company is no longer able to provide the services of this person then you should have the right to terminate the contract.

THE MANAGER'S RESPONSIBILITIES

It is hard to pin down in specific terms the obligations your management should undertake towards you, but your agreement should at least incorporate a provision for them to use their best endeavours to advance and promote your career, and to ensure that all monies payable to you are collected and properly accounted for.

Generally speaking, a manager will wish to be appointed as your sole and exclusive manager throughout the world in respect of all your activities in all branches of the entertainment and literary industries. If you are already established with a career in a related area (perhaps as a model or session musician), or wish for any particular reason to exclude certain activities from the *ambit* of the management contract, you should make this clear from the beginning.

THE ARTIST'S RESPONSIBILITIES

A management contract is a two-way agreement and your management will want assurance that you will endeavour to fulfil your contractual obligations towards them. They are likely to require the following:

- that there are no impediments to your entering into the management agreement (such as already being contracted to someone else)
- that your management deal with them is exclusive
- that you, the artist, will perform contracts entered into on your behalf to the best of your ability
- that you will refer all enquiries for live engagements to the management
- that you will not attempt to negotiate contracts on your own behalf

MANAGEMENT CONTRACTS

THE LENGTH OF THE CONTRACT

A management contract with an initial term of three years seems to be becoming 'the norm' provided that there is an 'escape route' in the event that the band is not successful. Success can be qualified by reference to various points such as procuring a recording contract within a specified time, selling a certain number of albums, a level of chart success, or earning a certain level of income.

If the manager has not achieved the level of success required within a period of say, twelve months, then you should have the option to terminate the contract.

It can take longer than three years to develop a band, so a manager may well want to extend the term of the agreement beyond this period to be able to reap the rewards of the success that follows. Whether or not you renew the contract is open to negotiation and will depend on how effective you feel your manager has been in developing your career. Even if you have been successful within the agreed period, but for one reason or another, you do not wish to stay with your manager, there is no onus on you to renew your contract. However, where a manager is justifiably aggrieved, it may be propitious to pay him or her a reduced percentage of your future income. The manager will probably claim it – and may well deserve it!

Needless to say you should get legal advice well in advance of the contract expiry date.

COLLECTING YOUR MONEY

How much control your manager has over your money is something you will have to decide between you.

Some managers will try to gain as much control over an artist's earnings as possible. They might even insist on collecting all their artists' earnings and paying them into a bank account for which they (the management) are the sole signatory. Under this arrangement a manager usually accounts to the artist after the deduction of management expenses and commission on a quarterly or monthly basis. If this is the deal you are offered make sure you have good legal advice because you should have some control over your own earnings! At the very least, you should make sure that your manager cannot use your earnings to finance other bands or business projects.

At the other end of the scale the artist's earnings are paid direct to their accountant who then works out the commission and expenses due and pays the manager on receipt of an invoice. The only problem to sort out then, is how the manager gets hold of urgently needed cash if he or she is not a signatory to the account.

A common 'halfway house' is for the artist and manager to set up a joint bank account which operates on the basis that the signature of the manager and one of the artists, or a specified signatory such as a lawyer, will be required before sums can be withdrawn. If this is the alternative you are offered, bear in mind again the practicalities involved in having every cheque agreed and signed by two people and make sure that the person you specify will be readily available whenever their signature is required. Another possibility is to run two accounts, the first account being a joint account or even the artist's sole signature account, which receives the artist's income and from which funds are, on an agreed basis, put into a second account which is used by the manager for paying the band's expenses.

Above all, make sure you get a lawyer or an accountant to check these financial details; they will be very important if you start making money. Your intended manager may propose any number of different arrangements; there is no set practice. As with most of the commercial points in any music business contract, this issue is entirely open to negotiation.

You will probably need the advice of an accountant to help you organise financial arrangements with your manager, particularly with regard to his or her own commission and when and how it is to be paid.

MANAGEMENT COMMISSION

Although this is open to negotiation, management commission tends to be between 15–25% with the average rate being 20%.

Exactly what income is deemed as 'commissionable income' depends on the specific terms of your contract. The way contracts are written means that they usually start off with the premise that the manager is entitled to commission on all the earnings from the artist's activities during the Term and on earnings from agreements entered into during the Term. The artist and lawyer then negotiate back from this point imposing limitations and restrictions. For example, with respect to recording contracts, you may want to stipulate that the manager can claim commission only on records recorded during the term of the management contract, or, for a limited period afterwards. Similarly, with respect to your publishing contract, you might wish to stipulate that only songs written during the term of the management contract are commissionable and not ones written after the agreement is over. There are also items that you can specifically exclude from being 'artists earnings' such as

advances to cover recording costs, video production costs, or money from tour buy-ons, for example. All of this is negotiable, which is why you need an experienced music business lawyer.

It is also important that you look very carefully to see what the manager's percentage is based on.

First of all, you should make sure that you will be paying commission only on 'receipts' (money you actually receive) and not on 'monies payable' (money promised or owed to you). You do not want to end up paying commission on money that you do not receive. For example, your manager may have negotiated a fee of £1000 for you to play a live gig – but on the night you only receive £100. Your manager should take 20% of the actual fee received (which is £20) and not 20% of the fee promised in the contract (which would be £200!).

Generally, the manager's percentage is on the artist's gross income but in respect of income from live work there is a strong argument that this should be calculated on earnings net of costs.

In the simple example below management commission has been calculated at 20% of earnings from a live show. The dramatic difference between the manager's commission when calculated on gross income, as compared to that calculated on net income illustrates the point.

The following figures are based on a four piece band on tour with a manager and tour manager. The tour has been booked by an agent. For simplicity's sake we have assumed that the band are VAT registered. (For a full explanation of VAT see Tax and Financial Planning page 201.)

It would therefore seem to be reasonable to ask for management commission to be calculated on net earnings on live work.

Alternatively, you might agree to a reduced rate of management commission on the gross income from live work. A reduction to 10% or 12% commission might be agreed but try to ensure that the management share does not exceed 50% of the net profits on any given show.

Whatever you do, it is important that you pay attention to this provision because it can become one of the most contentious points in a management agreement. This is particularly true if your manager has been invoicing you for commission but not actually taking it at the time. You may then find, when you do get a measure of success, that the money you eventually earn is already earmarked to pay management commission on past gigs which may now be only a distant memory.

A manager should not normally be entitled to commission on tour support, buy-ons or those record company or publishing company advances which are required to cover recording costs, video production costs, remuneration to record producers or the purchase of equipment.

MANAGEMENT EXPENSES

Attention to detail is important here. You should ensure that the manager does not have the right to charge all the office overheads to the band's account. Only expenses reasonably and necessarily incurred on behalf of the band should be reimbursable by the band.

TERMINATING THE CONTRACT

You should have the right to terminate the agreement if:

- the manager becomes bankrupt or if your management company goes into liquidation

- the company or the individual manager to whom you are signed is unable, for any reason, to attend to your affairs for a period that lasts longer than two months

- the company or individual manager to whom you are signed should be guilty of any serious breach of the contract

In cases where you are alleging a breach of contract it is common for there to be a 'cure period'. This is a period of say, 30 days, starting from when you inform the manager of the breach during which he or she is given the opportunity to make amends. If the manager fails to do so within this time you then have the right to terminate your contract.

Any verbal agreement made between yourself and your manager, or any complaint or requests you may have, should be put in writing and copies kept. This may be awkward for you and appear to be a little unnecessary at the time, but it is a very good habit to get into, and may well make all the difference should you fall out seriously. Managers may begin to neglect their contractual responsibilities towards you in a number of small and apparently insignificant ways. Over a period of months these failures may accumulate to the extent that you are keen to cease your management contract. This process of degeneration can then be usefully illustrated by a file of letters you have written to your manager in which you have spelt out your worries and reasons for complaint.

MANAGEMENT COMMISSION AFTER THE CONTRACT IS OVER

How much of a clean break you can get from a management deal will depend on your bargaining position. A manager is not auto-

EXAMPLE A: NET EARNINGS

The manager's commission calculated on earnings after costs have been deducted:

Fee for live performance:	£850.00	net of VAT

Less costs (net of VAT):

Booking agent's commission at 15%	£127.50
PA hire and transport	£220.00
Lights	£100.00
Tour manager	£50.00
Hotels (B&B for 6 people)	£93.00
Van hire	£39.50
Fuel, Guitar Strings, Miscellaneous Meals etc	£100.00

Total Costs (net of VAT):	£730.00

Fee:	£850.00
Less costs:	£730.00

Balance:	£120.00

Management Commission at 20%	£24.00	plus VAT
Band Income:	£96.00	plus VAT

Earnings per band member:	£24.00	each

EXAMPLE B: GROSS EARNINGS

The manager's earnings calculated before costs have been deducted:

Fee for live performance:	£850.00	plus VAT
Management commission at 20%:	£170.00	plus VAT

Balance:	£680.00

Balance:	£680.00
Less all other production costs (as above):	£730.00

Deficit:	£50.00

In this second example whilst the manager earns £170.00, it actually costs the band members £12.50 each to do the show!

matically entitled to commission in respect of your earnings from songs written or recorded after the management contract has expired, even if he or she had negotiated the deals under which the records are released or songs published. If your manager refuses to forgo claims to commission on such income, or if you feel the manager deserves some commission, then you may be able to negotiate a reduced rate as a compromise. Apart from the fact that your old management may have had nothing to do with your success after your agreement with them expired, you may find it difficult from a financial point of view, if you are having to pay old and new management full commission on all your earnings!

ON BEHALF OF MANAGERS...

Most of the advice given above is weighted heavily in favour of the artist and represents an ideal which is not often attained. You must be prepared to be flexible and to make concessions from time to time using any advice you are given more as a guideline rather than treating it as the law.

Many managers are extremely hardworking and genuinely have the interests of the band at heart. For every heartbreaking story of unscrupulous and evil management there is probably another one about an intractable, unreasonable and unprofessional band. There are plenty of managers who have worked for next to nothing for months only to see their band break up over 'musical differences'. No one flies a flag for them or worries about how they continue to make ends meet. Good management will more than pay for itself and whilst 20% of £1,000,000 may seem a lot of commission to pay, you have to ask yourself whether you would have earned your £800,000 without management help. And remember, too, that 20% of no income is nothing at all!

PUBLISHERS

WHAT DO MUSIC PUBLISHERS DO?

Publishers earn their money by retaining a share of the royalties earned by the songs on which they hold the copyright. In the past, music publishers used to print and sell sheet music in much the same way as other publishers deal with books. They would buy the world rights to songs for a fixed, and usually small fee and would then derive their income from the sales of the sheet music as well as the royalties paid when their songs were performed on stage or screen. Nowadays, however, it is the royalties earned from radio and TV broadcasts, 'live' performances and the sales of recordings of their songs that form the bulk of the music publisher's income. As a result, many publishers actively search for and develop songwriters whose material they think will be commercially successful. In order to fully exploit their copyright songs publishers may go to great lengths – possibly making a demo at their own cost and personally taking it round to the heads of A&R departments – in order to get their new writers a recording contract or a 'cover' on a song. They will also try to get their artists' songs used on the soundtracks to films or advertisements. Other duties include 'policing' the copyright interests on their artists' songs and registering them correctly with the PRS and other societies which collect and administrate copyright royalties.

WHERE DO THEY MAKE THEIR MONEY?

Songs can generate income in several ways but the most obvious ways in which royalties become payable by law are when:

(**a**) a song is performed in public, or broadcast on TV or radio anywhere in the world. (Collection of these 'performing royalties' is, generally speaking, the responsibility of the Performing Rights Society, PRS see page 189.)

(**b**) a song is mechanically reproduced in any way, for instance, on a record, cassette, CD or video. (Collection of these 'mechanical royalties' is the responsibility of the copyright owner although, frequently, the Mechanical Copyright Protection Society, MCPS is authorized to do this on behalf of the rights owner. See page 190.)

Basically, when you sign a contract with a publisher you are assigning the copyright of your songs over to them for a given amount of time in exchange for a percentage of income from the songs' exploitation (see Copyright page 184). Should one of your songs be successfully recorded – leading to radio play, TV performance, record sales and possible cover versions – it will be your publisher's job to administrate, and redistribute the royalties due. The 'split' of royalties between writer and publisher is determined by the assignment contract.

DO YOU REALLY NEED A PUBLISHER?

It is possible to collect your royalties yourself without the services of a publisher.

In the UK, at present at least, it is fairly easy to collect 'mechanical royalties' (the royalties payable by record companies for mechanically reproducing copyright songs) direct from the record company. Alternatively, you can ask the Mechanical Copyright Protection Society to administrate your 'mechanicals' for you.

Once you have had three songs commercially recorded or broadcast within the past two years (or had one song in the Top Fifty of a recognized chart), you will be eligible for membership of the Performing Rights Society and able to collect your public performance income directly from them.

The obvious advantage of this is that you don't have to pay a percentage of your income to a publisher (although you will still pay a small administration commission to the PRS – and to the MCPS as well if you choose to let them administrate your mechanical royalties).

However, collecting your own royalties has some disadvantages:

(a) Ensuring correct registration of your interest in your songs with the appropriate organizations can be time consuming, complex and costly.

(b) If you don't get paid you may not have the 'muscle' to resolve the problem.

(c) If you don't have a publishing company there will be no third party contribution to the promotion of your songs. Whilst the PRS and MCPS can collect and administrate your royalties for you, neither body will promote your work or spend any time or money helping you to build your career. It is not their job.

(d) You will probably lack the ability to police and administer the copyright on your songs overseas. As a full member of the PRS and MCPS your foreign royalties will be collected for you but, once again, neither of these bodies, nor their affiliated societies in foreign climes, will promote your work. You could employ a good lawyer and sign separate deals with publishers in each individual country, but think carefully about this because a lawyer's fees for this kind of detailed and protracted work could be very expensive.

If you are seriously interested in setting up your own publishing company then you should contact the Music Publishers' Association for further information. A good music business lawyer or accountant should be able to answer your questions and help you decide whether or not collecting your own royalties is a good idea in your particular case. There is also a company which specializes in this field called

Westbury Music Consultants Ltd, who offer independent advice on the alternatives to signing your publishing to a major company. They can also give expert technical advice on direct society collection for your overseas royalties and provide the necessary administrative back-up. Their address is: 56 Wigmore Street, London W1. Tel: 01 935 5133.

WHAT CAN A PUBLISHER DO FOR YOU?

Good music publishers are more than just royalty collecting houses. They can, in fact, be a useful source of financial assistance, advice and backup. However, the size of the advance they offer and the extent to which they will put themselves out to help you will depend upon a number of related factors: (a) the stage you have reached in your career, (b) how much material you have, (c) how much work they actually need to do to ensure that your songs earn worthwhile royalties (for example, will they have to find you a record deal?), and (d) how successful they think you are going to be in the long term.

Many publishers like to see themselves as a breeding ground for new acts, spotting young songwriting talent and 'breaking it' using their experience and influence within the music business. If you haven't got a record deal they will pay for studio time and help you put together a package which they can then present to record companies. By using a network of established contacts a reputable publisher can, in this way, help your career. This may be especially useful if you do not have a manager working for you. If you write songs but do not perform them yourself, a publisher will help you make a demo of them, and take them round to record companies whose artists might be interested.

A publisher can advance money to produce a record or even, in some circumstances, a full-blown LP prior to a recording deal being signed. Prefab Sprout did their first LP in this way and they benefitted by being able to approach record companies with a completed album ready for release. CBS records were impressed enough to pay the band an advance on a long term recording contract. The band were then able to repay the publisher the relatively low recording costs of the LP. In this instance the publisher's foresight and investment successfully advanced and accelerated Prefab Sprout's career and, at the same time, enabled the publisher to enjoy some earnings from the copyright on their songs.

At the other end of the scale, if your career is already established, a publisher can provide further financial assistance by advancing large sums of money and contributing to touring expenses, video costs and so on.

WHEN AND HOW TO APPROACH A PUBLISHER

It is worth contacting the Music Publishers' Association if you have any miscellaneous queries regarding publishing. They will help you if they can, although they are not able to advise you on which particular publishing company to approach. (A list of MPA members is available on request at a cost of £2.50 inc. p&p.)

When deciding on a prospective publisher you can start by looking at the sleeves or label copy on records of the bands and artists whose music you like, or feel is similar to your own. The publisher or copyright owner is normally shown after the title of the works on the label. If in doubt, ring the record company to find the name of the publisher. It is important that you do some research of this kind because you will get nowhere by sending your Heavy Metal material to a publisher who specializes in Country music! Having decided on a particular publisher you should then be sure that you can fulfil the following criteria:

a) You should have written at least three songs and you should have spent some time and effort presenting them. To this end you can follow the basic guidelines for sending demos and information to A&R departments given on page 88, but in addition you should include a clearly typed or handwritten copy of the lyrics.

b) Publishers are not merely interested in the content and standard of your songs. They are also looking out for character – something that makes your music different or memorable. It is important therefore, that you should have some ideas of your own about how you would like to present your material. If you are a band this is something to be discussed amongst yourselves before a representative of the group contacts a publisher.

c) Publishers are obviously interested in any proof of your sales potential. If you already have a record released and can show proof of record sales, or if you have built up a reasonable live following around the country, then these figures can be useful in gaining a publisher's interest.

Both record companies and publishing companies are looking for similar attributes in their potential signings. It is important to remember that they keep in constant contact with one another and that no section of the music business works in a vacuum. A publisher may well have heard of you via a record company colleague before you make contact with them yourself.

'HOLDING OUT FOR PUBLISHING'

It is accepted wisdom in band management circles that you should wait until you have had a hit record before you sell your publishing rights. The theory behind this point of view is that a publishing company will pay far more money for the rights to your songs once there is a definite indication that your copyrights will earn them money. Chart success will make you more attractive to publishers and put you in a stronger bargaining position. The argument is therefore, that with a record company behind you, you can succeed in gaining a better publishing deal.

PUBLISHING AS A 'BACK DOOR TO A RECORD DEAL'

This is, as it were, the other side of the argument! If you are not yet in a position where you can command major record company interest, and especially if you don't yet have good management, you could consider signing a publishing deal before looking for your record deal.

A publishing deal can provide you with financial stability so that you don't have to sign the first record deal that comes your way. It can also provide you with someone professional and respected in the business who can take your material into record companies at a more senior level than you would be able to achieve yourselves without the benefit of heavy-weight management.

As in the example of Prefab Sprout (above), this approach can be successful in the long run – but it depends greatly on the personalities involved. You must be sure that the person who signs your publishing deal is unlikely to leave the publishing company in

Martin Stephenson and the Daintees promoting their LP 'Boat to Bolivia' on their 'Busking Tour of HMV Shops', 1987.

The band first met Keith Armstrong and Phil Mitchell of Kitchenware records when they busked outside the Newcastle HMV shop which Keith then managed. Keith and Phil liked the music so much they invited them in! It just so happened that Kitchenware's only other signing, Hurrah! were due to record their first single in the studio the next day and it was suggested that the Daintees come too and record a demo if there was time. Sure enough, Hurrah! went off to the pub for lunch and the Daintees took their chance to record a song called 'Roll on Summertime' which was later released as their first single! Off the back of this Kitchenware secured them a publishing deal and a record deal with a major soon followed.

the near future. If this person does leave, and is replaced by someone unsympathetic to your music, it could be very unfortunate for you.

In summary, if you have a record deal that is bringing in enough money for you to afford to wait to sell your publishing rights, then waiting can be a good idea. However, while you are without either a publishing or recording deal, 'holding out' can be very expensive and may result in you getting no deal at all. If you are in desperate financial straits then 'holding out for publishing' can become somewhat academic. So long as your songs are good enough, a publishing company may be more prepared to advance you money than a record company and this can provide you with the cash-flow and support you need to keep going. A good music business lawyer will be able to advise you on both the choice of publisher and the nature of the contractual details. Never sign anything without one!

(NB. It is always important to remember that whilst advances of money from either record companies or publishers can be very useful, they are almost always recoupable. In other words, provided you are successful, the money is recoupable In full. The larger the advance that you receive, the longer it will be before you see any income from your sales of records or from your publishing royalties.)

PUBLISHING CONTRACTS

THERE IS NO SUCH THING AS A STANDARD PUBLISHING CONTRACT – BUT HERE ARE SOME GENERAL GUIDELINES AND POINTS TO CONSIDER. SEEK SPECIALIST PROFESSIONAL LEGAL ADVICE BEFORE YOU SIGN ANYTHING

Music publishing and royalty collection is a very technical and complex area. It can take many years to acquire a full grasp of how it works at an international level. This section is only intended as a 'rough guide'.

Firstly, it is important that you are aware of the difference between the 'term of the contract' and the 'retention period'.

THE 'TERM', OR LENGTH OF THE CONTRACT

The period during which you are signed to your publishing company is normally referred to as 'the Term'. This is the period during which you will be required to render your song-writing services exclusively to the publishing company.

The Term is generally established by reference to a number of contract periods. There will normally be an 'initial period' of say, 12 months and then several 'option periods', usually of 12 months each. The 'option periods' provide the opportunity for the publishing company to terminate the contract should they decide that it is not worthwhile continuing. In a nutshell – if the publishers do not see themselves making any money out of the relationship – they can legitimately end it by refusing to 'pick up' the next option.

On the whole, song-writing agreements tend not to have such long Terms as recording contracts.

THE 'RETENTION PERIOD'

The author or creator of a musical work is the 'first owner' of the copyright. When you sign a publishing agreement you are signing over the copyright in your songs to the publisher for a specified period of time. This period, during which the publisher is the owner of the copyright and therefore entitled to collect the income from your songs, is variously called the 'Exploitation Period', the 'Rights Period' or the 'Retention Period'. It can be for as long as the 'Life of Copyright', (that is to say, until fifty years after the writers death), or for a fixed period of time if the publishers are prepared to do a deal on less than 'Life of Copyright'. This would normally be the Term plus, perhaps, 20 years, but in exceptional cases, it has been as short as the Term plus 3 years. It may well depend on whether or not your advance has been recouped.

YOUR COMMITMENT TO THE PUBLISHER

There are various forms of commitment and these depend on your contractual negotiations. The simplest form of commitment requires the songwriter to write and deliver a specific number of songs each year. However, the greater the level of advance from the publisher, the more onerous the commitment will be. For example, emphasis may be placed on the actual release of a minimum number of songs in each year – not just their delivery. Alternatively, the commitment may be expressed as a percentage of an album. The contract would then stipulate that between 75% and 100% of the songs on your LP are written by you.

If the commitment is not satisfied within the relevant option period then the period will normally be extended by three months or more to give the writer time to fulfil the contract. This will delay the start of the next option period and ultimately extend the overall term. For this reason you should try to put some limit on the possible length of any extension period.

The commitment is often referred to as the 'minimum commitment'.

YOUR PUBLISHING RIGHTS AND YOUR RECORD COMPANY OR THEIR ASSOCIATED PUBLISHING COMPANY

Apart from the fact that it is simply not wise to put all of your eggs in the same basket, signing your publishing rights to your record company can sometimes be problematic. This is particularly so if the songwriting commitment is linked to record releases. If, through no fault of your own, the record company fails to release a sufficient number of songs to fulfil your publishing contract, then the publishing company would be able to extend their contract period even though the 'fault' lies with the publisher's associated record company. The same scenario can occur in reverse and in this way they can both work together to keep hold of you.

ASSIGNMENT OF YOUR SONGS

When you sign a publishing agreement you will probably be required to assign (a) all the songs you had written prior to the agreement, (b) all the songs which you started to write before the agreement but only complete during the agreement, (c) and all the songs you write during the Term of agreement itself. Make sure that there is no room for doubt as to the extent of the assignment.

Collaboration in the writing of songs can cause problems if both parties are not signed to the same publishing company. The publisher will certainly want you to try and get your collaborator to

assign his or her share of the copyright over to them, and will provide in your contract that they should do so. If your minimum commitment is expressed as a percentage of an album, then you should be aware of the effect this may have on your ability to fulfil it. You may be able to get the publisher to agree to accept that your collaborator's share counts towards your commitment, so long as your collaborator assigns his or her share to your publisher tor no extra advance payment. In the absence of an agreement to the contrary, those parties contributing to the creation of a copyright will be deemed to own the copyright in equal shares. If you are unclear on your rights in this complex area – then get legal advice.

GROUP AGREEMENTS AND THE QUESTION OF RECOUPMENT

On the whole, publishers are not interested in band politics, so the question of who gets what from the publishing royalties is something you will have to decide between yourselves, and with your lawyer and/or accountant. Friction commonly occurs when the hit single which recoups the advance that everyone has had a share of, was written by only one band member. In this instance, the songwriter may be due royalties which exceed the shares of the advance that he or she was paid, but will not have received those royalties because they have been put towards recouping the total advance paid to the whole band. If your band writes songs in this way arguments and disputes can be avoided if you can come to some agreement about what you would do in these circumstances at the time of signing.

THE WARRANTIES THE PUBLISHER WILL REQUIRE YOU TO GIVE

The usual warranties are as follows:

● that the works will be your original works and will not infringe the copyright of anyone else

● that you have not previously granted rights in the works to any one else and will not do so in the future

● that you will not write songs for any other publisher during the term of the agreement

● that you have the full right to enter into the agreement

● that you have disclosed all songs written prior to the agreement which are to be included or excluded

● that none of the works will be obscene or defamatory

THE PUBLISHER'S OBLIGATIONS

The publishing company should be contracted to pay you an advance (and further advances are subject to you fulfilling your commitment), and royalties. They will also be responsible for collecting royalties due to you from the copyright in your songs in those foreign territories where you have given them the rights.

You should make sure that the publisher promises to exploit your songs and that this is clearly stated in the contract. If the publisher sits back and does nothing with your compositions, you may be entitled to treat this lack of exploitation as a breach and thereby terminate the agreement.

For this reason most agreements provide for a reversion of rights if, after a period of time – say 2 years from delivery of the song or from the end of the agreement – your songs have not been exploited in at least one of a number of ways. That is to say, unless your songs have been recorded, publicly performed, or included on a film soundtrack for example, you will be entitled to give notice to the publishers that you require them to exploit the songs. If they do not do so within a further period of, say, three months the rights will revert to you.

THE PUBLISHER'S RIGHTS TO TRANSLATE, EDIT, ADAPT, ARRANGE OR ALTER YOUR WORK

It should be written into your contract that 'no English language changes are allowed without (your) written consent' – but you may have to concede that such consent will not be 'unreasonably withheld'. Once you sign a publishing contract you have effectively assigned the copyright. This means that legally, the song is the publisher's property and that any use of the song is at their discretion. However, if the publisher wants to pay someone else royalties for partly re-writing one of your songs, they should do so out of their own share.

Whether or not your publisher can change the musical content of your songs, or let other people release cover-versions of your songs before your own versions have been released, depends upon what you have managed to negotiate in your contract. At present, a publisher cannot prevent a cover-version being made if the song has already been released or imported into the UK, so long as the party releasing the record pays the mechanical royalty.

WHAT YOU WILL BE PAID

1. ADVANCES

Advances are negotiated sums of money paid in advance. They may be paid on signing, on 'pick up' of each option, or on completion of the specified contractual obligations. Most 'advances' are what they say; an advance of money set against income which is to be generated by the writer. Needless to say, the advance must be fully recouped by the publisher before there can be any payment of royalties.

2. ROYALTIES

Royalty payments to you are based upon a percentage of the royalties which your publisher makes on the songs in question. Royalty rates are usually categorized under the following headings:

(a) Print royalties on sheet music and manuscript folios
(b) Mechanical reproduction royalties ('mechanicals')
(c) Synchronization rights
(d) Public performance and broadcasting royalties (PRS royalties)
(e) Any other

Royalty rates are negotiated with your publisher and are sometimes called 'royalty splits'. For example, a deal which provides for the writer to receive 60% and the publisher 40% is called a 60/40 split. Nowadays normal royalty splits are 60/40, rising to 80/20, depending on your negotiating power. (The 50/50 split is probably now extinct).

WHEN YOU WILL BE PAID

Advances will be paid at the time specified in the agreement. Usually this means at the start of each contract period and upon satisfaction of the commitment. Quite often advances may be triggered by releases – for example, an advance might be payable upon the UK or USA release of an album. Advances may be also triggered by achievement of certain chart positions, depending on your deal.

Royalties will normally be accounted semi-annually and paid 60–90 days after each accounting period.

PUBLIC PERFORMANCE INCOME (PRS ROYALTIES)

The Performing Rights Society is responsible for collecting income from public performance, such as radio broadcasts, on behalf of both its writer and publisher members. In the case of writer members the PRS will usually divide this income equally, sending half direct to the publisher and the other half direct to the writers of the songs – in this case we will assume the songwriters are a band.

The band should ensure that the share of performance income received by their publisher is divided in such a way that they eventually receive the correct agreed proportion of the total PRS payments in the same ratio that their other publishing royalties are divided. For example, if the band were entitled to a 75% royalty rate then their publishers should account to them for 50% of the half share that the PRS had automatically sent to them. This will leave the publisher holding 25% of the gross PRS royalties and the band in possession of their rightful 75%.

If you are not a writer member of the PRS they will pay all the fees collected for you to your publisher (assuming they are publisher members). Before they do so, however, they will require a notification card from your publisher which is signed by you and indicates the percentages you are both going to receive. The PRS stipulate that the composers and authors between them should not receive less than 50% or 6/12ths of UK earnings, and that the writers should receive 8/12ths unless they have signed a notification card supplied by the publisher which arranges for them to receive less.

Arguably Britain's best ever reggae band, Aswad, at the Mandela concert at Wembley 1988.

If the PRS account to your publisher for the entire performance income payable this may also mean, unless you have provided for this in the contract, that the publisher will be entitled to use the entire payment for the purpose of recoupment of advances. For further information on how, when and what the PRS pay out, you should consult the Performing Right Yearbook – available free from the PRS, 29–33 Berners Street, London W1P 4AA. Tel: 01-580 5544. (See also Copyright: PRS page 189.)

ROYALTIES FROM PUBLISHING ABROAD

In territories outside the UK your publishing royalties are the responsibility of sub-publishers appointed by your UK publisher. Quite what your royalties amount to from foreign publishing depends on whether your deal with your publisher is a 'net receipts' or an 'at source' deal.

A 'receipts' deal is one whereby your royalty is calculated as a percentage of the money that your British publisher actually receives in the UK (after the sub-publishers in the foreign territories have taken their percentage). An 'at source' deal is one whereby you royalty is calculated as a percentage of the total sum of money that is made (before any sub-publishers have taken their percentage). The following examples are based on a 75/25 royalty split in the artists' favour.

'RECEIPTS' DEAL

The publishing royalties generated are £100. The relevant foreign copyright collection society deduct their administration fee of 10% (i.e. £10) and pay the balance (£90) on to the sub-publisher. The sub-publishing company will then take their share, or retention, of the royalties usually 25% (i.e. 25% of £90 equals £22.50). The balance of £67.50 is then paid to your UK publisher. And you will be owed 75% of this sum (i.e. 75% of £67.50 equals £50.62$\frac{1}{2}$).

In other words you are receiving about half of the money actually earned at source.

'AT SOURCE' DEAL

Assuming the same figures as for the 'receipts' deal example above, with an 'at source' deal your royalty would be calculated on the amount received by the foreign sub-publisher – regardless of the amount your UK publisher received. In other words, you would receive 75% of £90 which equals £67.50. This is an improvement of £16.87$\frac{1}{2}$ on the 'receipts' deal.

MECHANICAL ROYALTIES – 'MECHANICALS'

As the writer of a song you are entitled to a royalty payment whenever your song is mechanically reproduced – whether on a cassette or record, a compact disc or music video. These royalties are often known as 'mechanicals'.

The rate of the mechanical royalty is currently under review (see the section on Copyright: MCPS and the 1988 Copyright Act, page 191). Regulations under the 1956 Copyright Act stipulated that the mechanical royalty rate was to be 6.25% calculated by reference to the retail price of a record. As the 1988 Copyright Act has abolished the statutory rate, the 6.25% royalty will only apply until such time as the MCPS and the BPI agree on a new rate of mechanical royalty or, in the absence of any such agreement, until the matter is determined by a government established Copyright Tribunal. For further information contact the MCPS.

Whatever the mechanical royalty rate is to be in the future, the basis of calculation of the actual mechanical royalty will be as follows:

The mechanical royalty rate (6.25%) is applied not to the actual retail price of the record, but to the 'notional retail price equivalent'. The 'notional retail price equivalent' was introduced when record companies ceased to determine the retail price of records. To get the 'notional retail price equivalent' you take the wholesale price of a record and apply an agreed 'uplift'. The 'uplift' in the UK is determined by an agreement between the BPI and the MCPS. It is currently, roughly speaking, 25% on a single and 31% on an LP, with 29% on CDs. Assuming the average wholesale price of a black vinyl LP is £3.65, when the agreed 'uplift' is added this gives a 'notional retail price equivalent' of £4.78 – considerably less, you will note, than the actual average retail price of full-price albums! If the royalty rate is 6.25% and this is applied to the notional retail price equivalent (£4.78) – the mechanical royalty will be approximately 30p. (£2.65 + 30% × 6.25% = 29.8p). This 30p has then to be divided amongst the copyright holders of the material on the LP.

How you decide to collect your 'mechanicals' will affect how much you receive. For example, if you do not have a publisher as yet, but you do have a record deal, you can arrange to have your mechanical royalties paid directly to you from your record company (see (a) below). Alternatively, you can arrange for the MCPS to collect your mechanical royalties and send them on to you (see (b) below). Where you have signed a publishing deal your publishers will send you your agreed percentage of mechanical royalties – having already deducted their share.

The examples below are based upon the assumption that you have a recording deal, and that any records released contain only material which you have written yourself.

When you will get your money and from whom	proportion of mechanicals that you will receive.
(a) Quarterly payment direct from record company	100% of mechanical royalty earned.
(b) Quarterly payment from MCPS	95% of mechanical royalty earned (less 5% MCPS admin. costs)
(c) Half yearly payment from publisher	60% – 80% of mechanical royalty earned depending on your contract. (See also 'at source' or 'receipts'.)

Note that the mechanicals are paid per song on a record. This means that if there is more than one track the mechanical royalty will be divided by the number of tracks on the record.

Elvis Costello, a prolific and excellent songwriter and performer is still writing some of the best songs to come out of the UK in the last decade. There is no sign of this ability waning and his political and personal convictions remain as strong as ever – as here at the Artists Against Apartheid concert at Clapham Common, 1986.

THERE IS NO SUCH THING AS A STANDARD RECORDING CONTRACT – BUT HERE ARE SOME GENERAL GUIDELINES AND POINTS TO CONSIDER. SEEK SPECIALIST PROFESSIONAL LEGAL ADVICE BEFORE YOU SIGN ANYTHING.

THE TERM

The period during which you are signed to your record company is normally referred to as 'The Term'. During this time you will be required to render your recording services exclusively to the recording company.

The Term is generally established by reference to a number of 'contract periods'. There will usually be an 'initial period' of perhaps 12 months and then several 'option periods' which could be for the same amount of time each. Put very simply, the Term is divided up into, say, five option periods of twelve months. At the end of each period the record company, not you, has the 'option' to continue the contract or not. If they decide to pick up the option then they usually have to pay you the next instalment of your advance. If they fail to pick up the option within the specified time limit – then you are no longer bound by the contract, and you no longer have a record deal. Some American-style agreements establish the Term simply by reference to the dates of delivery of the product, and time limits which are triggered off by the delivery dates.

The major record companies can insist on deals with a potentially longer Term than the smaller companies. The majors generally open negotiations on the basis that they will not agree a deal unless it gives them options on at least another seven contract periods after the initial period (or, if the deal is structured instead by reference to product, at least seven more albums after the first). A smaller 'Indie' company is more likely to be satisfied with a couple of option periods, but may well need more if it wishes to license your product to a major record company.

The more bargaining power you have when you sign, the better your chance of reducing the potential length of the Term.

This is important not just for the obvious reason of reducing the length of time that you will be tied to the record company, but also for the rather more subtle reason that it will help you to renegotiate the deal if you are lucky enough to enjoy some success. What usually happens then is that you agree to additional contract periods with your record company in return for improved commercial terms – such as better advances and royalty provisions. The success of the negotiation will depend on the remoteness of

RECORDING CONTRACTS

the extra option periods you are offering. If you still have another five contract periods to go, you cannot reasonably expect the record company to agree to your terms – but if you are close to the end of your deal, they may be anxious to keep hold of you and be willing to renegotiate your terms in order to do so.

WARRANTIES A RECORD COMPANY WILL REQUIRE FROM AN ARTIST

All record companies will expect you to be able to agree to the following:

- that you will not record for anyone else
- that you will not re-record the songs recorded under the record deal for a period of 5 years from the end of the deal
- that the songs recorded shall not be obscene, defamatory nor infringe nor violate the rights of anyone
- that you are a member of the Musicians' Union or Equity
- that you are entitled to use the name of your group
- that you will sign any further documents necessary to give effect to the record deal
- that there are no previously unissued recordings which could be released by third parties other than those of which they may already be aware – and if there are they will probably require at least control, and at most, ownership
- that they will be able to use your biographical material in connection with the sale and promotion of the recordings

HOW 'OPTIONS' WORK

Options to extend the Term are invariably on the side of the record company only. They should always be exercisable by service of written notice upon you.

Record companies will usually want to have until the last possible moment before they have to make a decision about picking up an option to enter into the next contract period (and pay any advances due as a result). However, you may be able to negotiate:

- that the record company shall give you notice of its decision, say, 30 days before the date on which the contract period would otherwise expire
- that the record company shall only be able to exercise its option if certain criteria have been achieved, for example, the release of the current contract period recordings, sales of previous releases or chart positions.

THE RECORDING COMMITMENT

Every record deal will stipulate a mimimum number of recordings which you must make for the company in each Contract Period. This is called the Recording Commitment or sometimes the Minimum Commitment.

The record company may not want to commit to pay for the cost of recording an entire album in the initial period and so may prefer to release a couple of singles first, but reserve the option to call for further tracks to make up an album if the singles are successful. This is what people sometimes refer to as a 'singles deal'.

In the subsequent contract periods the recording commitment will generally consist of sufficient tracks to provide an album. This is usually defined as being between 8–12 tracks. The less tracks on your LP the better, not just because it makes it easier to satisfy the Recording Commitment, but also because it will help to keep your recording costs down.

The more heavy-weight record deals sometimes make provision for the company to call for an 'overcall album'. This is an extra album 'called for' by a record company over and above the minimum commitment, i.e. in the same contract period. As far as record companies are concerned an overcall album is a way of obtaining 'the next' album at the same advance and royalty rates as 'the current' album. They are likely to call for it if they believe in the artist but think that previous record sales have not been sufficient to justify the heavier financial commitments that may have been negotiated for the next contract period (such as increased advance or improved royalty rates).

This option for an overcall album essentially means that a record company can ask an artist to make an extra album without extra payment! In practice the exercise of this option is rare, but you should still try to limit the number of overcall albums available to the company to perhaps no more than a couple over the entire term.

TIME SCHEDULES FOR RECORDING

You should also pay particular attention to the time schedules within which you are expected, under the agreement, to complete the recording of your minimum commitment.

The contract will normally provide for an automatic extension of the contract period, if you are unable to complete the recording commitment within the specified time limit, so that it continues until, say, 3 months after delivery of the minimum commitment.

Tracy Chapman tunes her guitar at the Amnesty International gig at Wembley Stadium 1988.

Most people first became aware of Tracy Chapman's talent as a singer songwriter when she appeared on stage at Wembley Stadium for the Nelson Mandela Birthday Party. Prior to this she had only played a handful of dates in the UK! The massive exposure this highly televized event gave her meant that she became a 'world' act almost overnight. The following Monday she sold 60,000 albums and her LP soared to the top of the charts.

Personal political motivations not withstanding, many careers have benefited from a benefit!

Mark E. Smith of The Fall recently signed to major label Phongram, lending his support at the GLC Festival at Brockwell Park, 1984.

This device may substantially extend the overall Term of your deal. So make any period of extension subject to a maximum of, for example, 12 months.

It is sensible to try and ensure that the record company cannot extend the contract period for non-delivery if this is due to their own delay in making recording facilties available, or because you have had touring commitments which have made it impossible.

WHO CHOOSES THE MATERIAL YOU RECORD?

A new artist will often be required to give the record company absolute approval over this. If there should be an impasse it could well destroy your relationship with the company so you would do well to discuss the issue with the A&R people signing you before the deal is negotiated. Beware of record companies insisting that you record certain songs if their motive is due to their own commercial interest in them, such as their publishing arm controlling the music copyright.

DECISIONS CONCERNING ARTWORK AND PROMOTIONAL MATERIAL

You should have a right of approval over publicity photos and so on in your contract, but the record company may only be willing to grant you consultation in respect of record sleeve artwork. If you can, get this changed to an absolute right of approval because your public profile is very important.

HOW EXCLUSIVE IS THE DEAL?

Whilst most agreements will require you to record exclusively for the record company, there may be exceptions.

It is not unusual for a record company to agree for you to be free to do 'sessions' provided you are not 'featured' and your participation will not be publicized. If your participation is to be rewarded with a credit your record company will probably require the usual courtesy credit.

The recording contract will normally prohibit you from recording the same material for another record company for a period of, say, 5 years. Make sure that this 're-recording restriction' is applicable only to songs which your record company has actually released within or during a reasonable period of time after the Term. It would be unfair if you could not re-record material that your record company was not prepared to release.

WHO PAYS FOR RECORDING COSTS?

Recording costs are treated by record companies as advances to the artist, in that the record company will want to recover the recording costs from artist royalties.

Attention should be paid to keeping recording costs down to a reasonable minimum – the lower your recording costs, the fewer records you have to sell to break even.

Where possible you should try to gain control or at least approval over the recording budget. This should include control over matters such as the choice of producer, recording studio and backing musicians, the length of time allowed for mixing and the number of remixes chargeable against your royalty account.

A few record companies make their deals 'recording cost inclusive' – that is to say that the overall advance payable to the artist includes an element for recording costs. The advance will then be a 'recording fund' and if the actual recording costs are less than the advance, then any balance left over will be paid to the artist as the 'cash advance'.

WHO PAYS THE RECORD PRODUCER?

The record producer's advance is normally paid by the record company and is treated as recording costs, that is, an additional advance to you, the artist. The royalty payable to the record producer is then deducted from your royalty so that, for example, if the producer is due to receive 2% and you are due to be paid 12%, you will actually only receive 10% after the producer has been taken into consideration.

If the producer's royalty is to be paid out of your own royalty in this way, you should ensure that you have a sufficient degree of control over the commercial terms of the appointment to prevent the record company from distributing too many royalty points to the producer. Some record companies will agree to bear all, or a proportion, of the producer's royalty to the extent that it may exceed, say, 3%. Where a producer is being paid a percentage on the A-side of a single, that producer may be entitled to a royalty on the B-side of the same single (it is customary for successful producers to negotiate something to this effect). If this is the case try to ensure that the record company agrees to accept responsibility for the payment of your producer's royalty in respect of the B-side – better still – produce your own B-sides.

It is not unknown for record companies to propose deals where the royalty is exclusive of the producer royalty and you should certainly ensure that this is the case where the company wishes to use an 'in-house' production team.

WHO PAYS FOR THE COST OF PROMOTING YOUR RECORD?

The record company will pay for advertising and marketing expenses.

Only in exceptional cases should you agree that an element of 'promotional expenses' be treated as an advance recoupable from your royalties.

With regard to the provision of your services in promoting the records, such as interviews and personal appearances, most contracts will provide that the record company will pay your reasonable costs so long as there had been some agreement in principle as to what will be involved. Try to ensure that these expenses do not have to be reimbursed or recouped out of your royalties as if they were further advances.

Concert tours are often considered the best way for a band to promote its records. As a consequence, most record companies will see the sense in providing financial support to enable you to do this. Generally speaking, such 'tour support' as it is usually called, is paid as a further advance, but it may be possible to get the record company to agree that only a proportion of it, say 50%, is recoupable.

'BUY-ONS'

Touring as the support act on a big tour is likewise regarded – sometimes wrongly – as being an important way to bring attention to a new act. Competition to get into large-scale tours is often very stiff, and the right to be the support act on a major tour is something bought at high cost. This is called a 'buy-on', and the money is usually paid by the support act's record or publishing company direct to the headline artist. It is then often used to defray the headline act's tour costs. Where you are put in the invidious, but unfortunately all too common, position of being 'bought-on' to tour, you should restrict, as far as is possible, the percentage of the buy-on that is recoupable by the record company (or publishing company), that paid it.

HOW YOU WILL BE PAID

ADVANCES

Advances are agreed sums of money – sometimes large – that record companies pay you literally 'in advance' of record sales. A common mistake is to think that you get all your agreed advance up front. You often hear of £100,000 record deals and may imagine a cheque for the full amount being handed over to the band by

smiling record company executives. Unfortunately, life is not quite so rosy! Inevitably, the overall sum is paid in instalments over a period of years — usually triggered by option periods or recordings that you have successfully completed.

These advances are actually pre-payments of royalties (see next section) which should be non-returnable. If the royalties you earn do not recoup the advance paid to you by the record company they should not be able to ask you to pay it back in any other way.

Certain other payments made by the record company on your behalf such as recording costs, video production costs, payments for equipment purchase and touring shortfall may also be considered as advances under the terms of your agreement.

These all have to be recouped from your royalties before the company will make any actual royalty payments to you.

Look carefully to see what may be used to recoup your advances. If you are also entering into a songwriting contract or a merchandising agreement with the same company, or a related company, ensure that the royalties payable under the songwriting or merchandising contract cannot be set off against the advance paid under the recording deal.

The amount of money you receive as an advance will depend on the record company you are signing to, whether or not they are bidding in competition with other labels, how many records they anticipate you will be able to sell, and how soon. Advances are a high risk investment which the company will only get back if you sell enough records, and for you the risk is that if you sign too soon, you will get a less favourable deal. So the main points to consider are:

- are you in demand?

- how high are the other companies prepared to bid to acquire your services?

- can you afford to hold out for a better offer?

- do you need a guaranteed minimum wage on which to survive, or are you prepared to speculate?

- does the band need to purchase its own equipment and at what cost?

ROYALTIES

The record company will pay you, or credit your account, with a royalty on each record sold. Only when you have earned sufficient royalties for the company to recoup the advances already paid to you, will you begin to receive a through-payment.

This is subject, of course, to the exclusions and qualifications which will be negotiated and set out in the royalty calculation provisions of your deal.

A good average royalty for a new band is probably between 10% and 12% based on 100% of sales (inclusive of record producer royalty). This should escalate as the deal progresses, and reflect successful sales figures (such as an extra 1% for records sold in excess of 'gold status' and/or 'platinum status' in the major world markets).

HOW THE ROYALTY IS CALCULATED

The payment and calculation of the royalty is a complex matter. Again, very careful attention must be paid to the detail of the provisions which govern this.

For a start, some companies will only pay a royalty on 90% of the records sold instead of 100%. The original reason for this is historical, in that it was intended as a breakages allowance for brittle 78 rpm records. However, this has not prevented several companies that did not even exist in the days of the 78 rpm records from offering deals based on 90%. So, if your royalty is calculated on 90% of sales, ensure that there is a compensatory mark up on the basic royalty rate. For example, a 9% royalty payable by a company which only accounts on 90% of sales should be marked up to 9.99% to give you the equivalent of what you would be paid if it were to be calculated on 100% of sales.

The royalty percentage is applied to a 'base price' for each record sold. It is then subjected to the various royalty calculation formulae set out in your deal. At present in the UK the base price is a national retail price (i.e. a retail price equivalent) arrived at by applying an agreed percentage mark-up to the wholesale price (excluding VAT). The appropriate percentage mark-up is taken from the agreement between the music publishers' industry organization (MCPS) and the record companies' industry organization (BPI) which relates to the method of calculation of the mechanical copyright royalty and varies according to the format of the record. It is currently 25% for a single and 30% for an album. By way of illustration using an LP this works as follows:

	whole-sale price	retail mark-up	base price	packaging deduction	
LP	£3.65	30%	£4.75	(− 20%)	= £3.80

Assuming (1) no other qualifications are set out in the royalty calculation provisions and, (2) an artist royalty of 10% on 100% of sales, then the artist will receive £0.38 for each LP sold.

Liam O'Moinlai of Hothouse Flowers in Limerick 1987.

WHAT IS THE 'PACKAGING DEDUCTION'?

The 'packaging deduction' relates to packaging costs and sleeve design. Generally, it seems that record companies pay for artwork and printing but feel – particularly where special artwork has been used – that a proportion of the retail price should be deducted to compensate them for this. These packaging deductions vary greatly from company to company, and will also vary according to the product: 12″ single, LP, cassette or CD. Records sold in 'house bags' or plain black sleeves should not be subject to a packaging deduction.

FURTHER REDUCTIONS TO THE ROYALTY

At this point the royalty calculation provision may specify further reductions to the royalty. Set out below are some of the more usual ones:

- records given away free of charge for review or sold at substantial discount – no royalty at all

- non-standard shape or coloured vinyl – 50% royalty rate

- TV advertised LPs – 50% royalty rate. (The MU warn against clauses like this. They point out that TV advertising is now a common form of promotion and that by paying the artist only half-rate royalties the record company is effectively subsidising its marketing costs.)

- compact discs – treated as if black vinyl records (record companies are beginning to make improvements to this one)

- 12″ singles – agreed quota royalty fee or three quarters rate (varies widely).

Also, watch out for the 'Reserves Allowances'. These are a percentage of the royalties due to an artist which are held back against faulty product, returned product and so on. They will be particularly high when records are sold on a 'sale or return' basis. In the UK it is not general practice to sell records in this way (unless they are advertised on television as part of a special campaign), so reserves allowances should be small. In the US however, the situation is very different and several companies are known to operate a 50% reserves policy. Be careful to ensure that the reserves are liquidated i.e. paid out within a couple of accounting periods.

These provisions are invariably complex but should not cause problems if your lawyer is familiar with the particular record company's standard provisions.

WHEN YOU GET PAID

It is 'normal' for record agreements to provide for the submission of royalty accounting on a semi-annual basis dividing the year into two accounting periods from January 1st to June 30th and from July 1st to December 31st with statements being issued within 60 to 90 days thereafter. However, if you are in a good bargaining position (and if your record company are not subject to semi-annual accounting themselves), it may be possible to negotiate quarterly accounting and for statements to be sent within 60 days instead. If you are signing to a small label who license their product to a major record company you may be able to negotiate for them to process the accounts and pay you within a much shorter period, say 28 days from their receipt of an accounting from the major record company.

If your royalties have recouped the advances previously paid then you should receive a royalty payment at the same time that the accounting is submitted. If you haven't yet recouped, you should still receive an accounting statement.

With regard to records sold overseas it will take longer for the royalties to work their way through the system, as the overseas royalties will be paid to your UK record company probably 90 days after the accounting period in which they were sold overseas, and your UK record company will then process them in the accounting period in which they received payment and pay you 90 days after that accounting period. For every extra sub-licensing arrangement entered into by your record company you can add another 6 to 9 months delay.

YOUR RIGHTS TO TERMINATE THE AGREEMENT

You should have the right to terminate if:

● the record company should become insolvent

● the record company is guilty of any serious breach of contract. This right to terminate is usually limited to a 'cure period' within which the company shall have, say 30 days to remedy the breach before you can terminate for failure to do so.

● a specified person leaves the company. If you sign to a small label you can sometimes insist on a 'Key Man clause' which means that if, for example, one of the directors should leave the company you may have the right to terminate the contract.

● your records are not released in the UK within a certain time limit.

RECORD DEAL PROPOSAL CHECK LIST

TERM

Length of contract periods?
Option period period?
How and when is option picked up?

MINIMUM COMMITMENT

In the initial period?
In each option?
When is Minimum Commitment to be delivered?

VIDEOS

When to be made?
Treatment of recording costs?

CREATIVE CONTROL

Material	Yes/No
Recording Budget	Yes/No
Approval/control of Producer	Yes/No
Artwork	Yes/No
Video Director	Yes/No
Video Budget	Yes/No

MISCELLANEOUS

Merchandising provisions	Yes/No

ADVANCES

Inclusive or exclusive of recording costs in years

1	2	3	4	5

Date when advance is payable?

ROYALTIES

(NB: 90/100% dealer/'retail')
Inclusive/exclusive of record producer?
Other points to consider:

> UK: Major Territories: Rest of World: Escalation provisions: 12" single provisions: packaging charges: 7" singles: 12" singles: Albums: Cassettes: CDs.

ACCOUNTING PROVISIONS

Accounting periods 60/90/120 days
Rights of inspection
Time limit for challenge of accounts
Reimbursement of audit costs
Interest on late payments/underpayments

Without going into exhaustive detail, it is useful to be aware of the role of the different departments within a record company. It can be very confusing and a bit overwhelming when you first enter a record company building, so an understanding of the various functions of the internal departments that you will come across can be helpful.

The A&R people are initially responsible for introducing you to the other departments within the company structure. Good A&R people will always keep an eye on the acts they sign and take an interest in their progress. However, the pressure of their work, which involves signing new bands as well as helping to develop existing acts that they have previously signed, usually means that in practice you are frequently left in the hands of other personnel.

The most important departments, once your career has begun, are the various divisions of the Marketing department, followed closely by the Sales department. Record company structures vary, depending on the size of the company, and upon the slightly differing ways in which they organize themselves. Broadly speaking, the Marketing and Sales departments are both set up as separate entities, each under a director who represents them at boardroom level.

THE MARKETING DEPARTMENT

The Marketing department usually consists of a MARKETING DIRECTOR who has several sections reporting to him or her, each with different responsibilities.

Under the Marketing director there is likely to be a MARKETING MANAGER who oversees and works together with three or four PRODUCT MANAGERS. They are responsible for the design and marketing of LP and singles sleeves, as well as the design and timing of the advertising in the press, and elsewhere, of the record product. This work entails devising, and keeping to, agreed budgets and liaising with the band's management and the relevant A&R personnel once the tracks for the record releases have been agreed. The individual product managers also have to work simultaneously on several other projects, keeping to release schedules. This may involve work on dozens of records by the other acts on the record company's roster. Their job must be done in time to coincide with each record's release date. PRODUCT MANAGERS are allocated specific acts to work upon, and it is then part of their job to speak up for their acts at marketing, production and sales meetings, along with the A&R person responsible for the act. Both the PRODUCT MANAGER and the A&R person are responsible for building enthusiasm and awareness of their band in all the staff, but particularly in the sales and promotion teams.

RECORD COMPANY STRUCTURE

The plugging and active promotion of a band's records is done by the PROMOTIONS DEPARTMENT, which is run by a PROMOTIONS MANAGER in charge of three or four PLUGGERS. The PLUGGERS specialize in TV, radio and club promotion. They actually go out to discos, and TV and radio stations, where they talk to the producers and DJs. Whenever possible, they will play the record in an attempt to get airplay and raise general public interest. It is a good idea to make friends with your promotions department because if they know and like you, it is likely that they will put a bit more effort into promoting your records.

There will probably be a PRESS MANAGER as well, working with a couple of PRESS OFFICERS. Together they prepare press releases and other forms of contact with the written media – from the specialist music press and magazines to the national daily papers.

These three departments are all answerable to the MARKETING DIRECTOR who has to have an overview of all the different projects going on at one time, and needs to keep an eye on more corporate problems such as the 'image and direction of the company'. Ultimately, the MARKETING DIRECTOR is responsible, along with the other directors, to the COMPANY CHAIRMAN and the COMPANY SHAREHOLDERS.

THE SALES DEPARTMENT

The SALES DIRECTOR is also a senior director on the board of the Company. Under the SALES DIRECTOR are a number of SALES MANAGERS who, in turn, have a total SALES FORCE of up to thirty or forty personnel working for them. In the large companies this SALES FORCE covers the whole country. The sales teams are based in the regions, each individual salesperson with their own sales area in which they sell records directly to record shops. Some companies have a SALES FORCE especially for pushing and selling singles and this is usually called a 'strike force'. They work to a weekly schedule based around 'chart day' when their efforts are measured against the chart position of the singles that they are selling. There is a less hectic and glamorous group of sales people who sell LPs, cassettes and compact discs. Their sales targets are usually set on a monthly LP release schedule. Like the singles sales team, they are also based around the country and deal with the buyers of the record shops within their designated areas. Major retail outlets and record shop chains will probably buy their records direct from the record company after negotiating with a senior sales executive at head office in London.

Both the Marketing and Sales divisions have structured weekly meetings with each other and within their own departments. The

Alistair McErlaine and Sharleen Spiteri of Texas backstage during their first UK tour in spring 1989.

idea is to keep track of developments and to exchange views and ideas. Some of these meetings are more constructive than others and you may find that there is some rivalry between the sales and marketing departments. This is less so than it used to be, but there is still a tendency for each department to claim sole responsibility for a band's success – and they tend to blame each other in the event of failure. In reality, neither department can do its job effectively in isolation, and at the end of the day, their success is really dependent on the quality of the acts they represent. That is where you come in!

COPYRIGHT

A basic knowledge of copyright, and how it relates to the music industry, is important for any artist because it is mainly through being a songwriter and/or composer that artists can earn a decent living. You could sell thousands of albums – but if you didn't write any of the songs you will earn comparatively little. We have outlined some of the important points below, but for a well-written and more detailed book which explains in clear and jargon-free terms what copyright is, and includes a section on the application of copyright in the music business – see 'A Users Guide to Copyright' by Michael F. Flint. (This was first published in 1979 by Butterworths, but an updated edition incorporating recent statutory changes in the copyright law was published in 1989: ISBN 0 409 20075 0.)

WHAT IS COPYRIGHT?

'Copyright is a right given to or derived from works, and is not a right in novelty of ideas. It is based on the right of an author, artist or composer to prevent another person copying an original work, whether this be a book, tune or picture, which he, himself has created. There is nothing in the notion of copyright to prevent a second person from producing an identical result (and himself enjoying copyright in that work) provided it is arrived at by an independent process.'

(This quotation is taken from the Report of the 1952 Gregory Committee on Copyright Law, whose recommendation formed the basis of the Copyright Act 1956, which was the predecessor of the 1988 Copyright Designs and Patents Act (the 1988 Copyright Act).)

'Copyright' means, quite literally, a right to prevent other people copying an original work (there is no copyright in ideas). As far as musical compositions are concerned, the author is the person who first created them. This person is known as the 'first owner' of the copyright and is automatically able to control and collect the royalties arising from certain uses of the work. There is also a quite distinct copyright in the sound recording made of the work. This copyright is, generally speaking, owned by the party who pays for the recording – i.e. the record company. Copyright can be very confusing for people working within the music business if they don't grasp this distinction. Unauthorised use of copyright material – such as copying, publishing, performing the work in public, broadcasting it on TV or radio, or adapting it in any way – is known as infringement of copyright.

Justified Ancients of Mu Mu 1988.

In March 1987 The Justified Ancients of Mu (The Jams) produced their single 'All you need is love'. It was hailed by some to be 'the first single to capture realistically the musical and social climate of Britain in 1987' – sampling as it did huge chunks of material from the Beatles, MC5, Hall & Oates, Samantha Fox and the Government AIDS adverts! The Jams hadn't played a note themselves but had stolen all the various beats and sounds they wanted from other people and stuck it all together. It was to be an interesting test case to see how the establishment would react. Predictably enough, the threat of copyright injunctions from a trio of majors meant that none of the independent distributors would handle it and the Ancients were obliged to 'doctor' the tapes themselves and plan a re-release.

Undeterred The Jams later released a track on their 1987 album called 'The Queen and I' which sampled in a wholesale fashion 'Dancing Queen' by Abba. The Mechanical Copyright Protection Society immediately instructed the Jams to withdraw '1987' from sale and at the same time to destroy all existing copies and masters. It was a clear warning that the MCPS will act to prevent unauthorized sampling. Even if the sound is re-recorded but virtually indistinguishable from the original (as The Jams snippets of Samantha Fox's 'Touch Me' were on their 'All You Need is Love' single), it can still be in breach of copyright.

Nevertheless, The Jams have had a huge hit single with their song 'Edelweiss' which obviously is based on another Abba song 'S.O.S.'. Presumably they are paying the appropriate royalties!

DO YOU HAVE TO REGISTER COPYRIGHT IN YOUR SONGS?

The short answer to this question is 'No' Under UK copyright legislation you don't have to do anything to 'copyright' a song because copyright protection automatically comes into existence as soon as an original musical work has been created – provided

THE
TC
AND
MUSIC
GUIDE

that it is written down or otherwise recorded in some way. (If you are sending tapes abroad you should check if the same conditions apply – see International Copyright Treaties page 188.)

However, you do need to be able to provide some evidence of the date when your songs came into existence. As it says above in the quote from the 1952 Gregory Committee on copyright law – there is nothing in the notion of copyright to stop someone else writing a very similar song and having copyright in it, providing they arrived at it by an independent process. In the event of a very similar work to your own appearing, which someone else claims to have originated, the time when both works were created becomes very important. If you can prove that your song existed before theirs, it will help your case should you decide to take them to court and pursue an infringement action. Conversely, if their song was written before yours, they could turn round and accuse you in the same way! This is, of course, a very simplistic example and any legal procedure involving copyright law will be a lot more complicated. Suffice to say that it is always important when you are sending other people tapes and manuscripts, to take the simple precaution of establishing, in one of the following ways, the existence of your work on a particular date.

One long-established method is to register the work at the Stationer's Hall Registry. A fee of around £23.00 together with the manuscript (mechanical recordings such as records and tapes are not accepted) – and an application form (supplied free of charge) should be sent to the Registrar, Stationer's Hall, Ave Maria Lane, Ludgate Hill, London EC4M 7DD. Tel: 01-248 2934. To save expense you can register a group of songs as an album, under one title.

Since, however, all you are trying to do is establish the date upon which the work came into existence, it is cheaper and simpler to do so by sending a copy of the work to yourself in a printed official registered envelope. (An ordinary envelope will not do). Write the title of the work on the outside of the envelope, seal the tape or manuscript inside, and when you post it, keep the Post Office receipt. A couple of days later, when you receive your package in the post DO NOT open it, but attach the receipt to the envelope and put them both in a safe place. You could use a safety deposit box if you think it is not safe at home. If, at a later date, you are challenged as to when your work was created, the receipt and the postmark will provide indisputable evidence – so long as the envelope is kept sealed and only opened in court to prove the nature of the contents. This is a sound method, although the envelopes may well pile up!

Another method can be to deposit your tape with a solicitor, bank manager or other 'reputable' person, obtaining a dated receipt from them.

NOTE:

Any of the above actions will do no more than show that your work was in existence on a particular date. This is important, but it does not afford a guarantee that the copyright in the work is yours. However, in order to give yourself as much protection as possible, you should take one of the above precautions – and if you ever have any problems get appropriate professional legal advice.

HOW LONG DOES COPYRIGHT IN MUSICAL COMPOSITIONS LAST?

Under normal circumstances, musical works enjoy copyright protection in the UK until fifty years after the end of the calendar year in which the author died – and after that the copyright expires and goes into the 'Public Domain'.

COPYRIGHT IN THE TITLES OF SONGS

In general, titles – whether they be of songs or books, are not entitled to copyright protection, unless they are so long or complicated that they can be said to be the result of the application of labour, skill AND originality. It is thus usually safe to assume that titles do not have copyright protection – although it is probably wise to steer clear of well-known titles to avoid any chance of confusion when your royalties are collected.

ASSIGNMENT OF COPYRIGHT

Ownership of copyright cannot be transferred by assignment or exclusive licence to anyone else until a written agreement has been signed by both parties – and this, of course, is what happens when you sign a Publishing Contract.

NON-COPYRIGHT SONGS

Normally, once the copyright in a musical work has expired it passes into the public domain which means that anyone can make a recording of it or perform it in public without having to pay the copyright owner. However, where a song – perhaps a traditonal song or classical work – is arranged and recorded in such a way as to make it distinct and different from the original, a new and separate copyright can be enjoyed by the arranger. If you make a recording of a traditional song which is a new arrangement – even if only slightly so – you will be entitled to receive the MCPS royalties due on the recording of it. If anyone does a cover-version

THE TC AND MUSIC GUIDE

of your arrangement then they will have to pay you copyright royalties in the usual way.

The PRS operate in a different way in these circumstances. They have a system whereby a 'musical classification committee' decides just how different from the original your arrangement is, and award a royalty percentage accordingly. If your version is very similar to the original, you could receive as little as 3/12ths of the standard royalty payment. If it is very different, you could receive as much as 9/12ths.

If you are in doubt about whether or not a song is no longer in copyright – check with the 'Repertoire' department of the PRS. They will need the title and the name of the composer. The name is important because there are often many songs with the same title.

Above all, do make sure that you are using the original music and not a more recent arrangement of it – which could still be in copyright.

INTERNATIONAL COPYRIGHT TREATIES

There are two major International Copyright treaties, and nearly all the countries which recognize the copyright concept belong to either one, or both of them. The UK belongs to both. The most salient feature of these treaties is that each member state is required to give the same protection to works of nationals, from all the other member states, as it does to its own nationals. Effectively, then, the works of British nationals are protected in most countries of the world and vice versa.

However, it is important to know that whilst under UK copyright law and, indeed, the copyright law of many other countries no formal registration is necessary to secure copyright protection. In countries which belong only to the Universal Copyright Convention, a condition of protection in the case of published works is that they carry the symbol followed by the name of the copyright owner and the year of the first publication. This is required practice if you want to send demos to the States, for example, because the registration of copyright is a fundamental factor in determining the ownership of copyright there.

In the UK there are four organizations, the PRS, MCPS, PPL and VPL which collect, administrate, and redistribute copyright royalties. Here is a brief, general introduction to the way they work, and how they are relevant to you. For more detail contact them yourself and ask for their free information packs – see Directory: Industry Organizations for contact details.

PRS

The Performing Rights Society Ltd, (PRS) is a non-profit making body which was founded early this century by composers, song-writers and publishers to protect the performing and broadcasting rights in their works. The PRS ensures that the appropriate royalties are paid for public broadcasts and performances.

Obviously, it would be very difficult for all copyright owners to individually monitor and collect the royalties due whenever someone else performed their work or played it on the radio. Similarly, it would be very difficult for every venue, disco, radio station, shop or pub to make a note of every record performed or broadcast.

The PRS solved these problems by acting as a collecting agency for its copyright owner members and charging a fee to every place in the country that has music publicly performed on its premises. They further assume that these places will be playing the usual standards mixed in with newer material and current chart entries. Theoretically all live music venues also pay a percentage (currently 3% of the total gross ticket sales) to the PRS for the right to pub-licly perform copyright songs. Even where the artist is performing their own material this levy is supposed to be paid by the venue, or the promoter, to be redistributed to the copyright owners later on.

In addition to this, they charge large sums of money to the BBC and IBA for blanket licences which permit them to broadcast copyright music for a specified amount of time. National radio and TV are able to be more precise about the actual works used than the smaller stations, and they submit their playlists to the PRS.

The PRS then has the job of sharing out all the money thus collected between the owners of the copyright on the individual songs performed. The amount of money you get is directly related to the number of public performances and broadcasts of your works. The most lucrative earners are television and radio broad-casts. Local radio airplay earns a lot less per broadcast than national radio, and a networked TV performance will earn you considerably more again.

If your song is broadcast on Radio 1 you can definitely expect to receive some payment sooner or later. Local BBC and Independent radio stations are a bit more difficult to monitor. Both the PRS and the stations themselves, find it almost impossible to keep track of every record played and they – like the discos and shops – have their payments based on a sampling system. Unfortunately, this means that if your record is played on a local radio station several times – but was not included in the sample sent to the PRS – you might not receive any money.

Performance income from overseas is generally collected by the local society equivalent to the PRS, and PRS members will receive their share of royalties by virtue of the affiliation between the PRS and the other international societies.

If you are not a member of the PRS, then the PRS will pay all the fees that they collect on your songs to your publisher, who will then pay you your agreed percentage. (See Publishing Contracts: Public performance income page 162.) If you are not a member of the PRS and do not have a publisher, then you will receive no performance royalties at all.

How do you join the PRS?

As a writer you can join the PRS once you have had three songs commercially recorded or broadcast in the past two years, or had one song in the Top Fifty of a recognized chart. For an explanation of the way PRS payments operate whether or not you have a publisher see Publishing Contracts, page 158, and Publishers: Do you really need a publisher? Page 153.

MCPS

The Mechanical Copyright Protection Society was formed to collect and distribute the royalties due to its songwriter, composer and music publisher members from the mechanical reproduction of their works. It has been owned by the Music Publishers Association since 1976.

Like the PRS, the MCPS is a non-profit making organization and is part of an international network of copyright societies whose function is to ensure that, wherever possible, all recordings of music copyrights are properly licensed and that the royalties are properly collected and paid to the copyright owner or controller.

The Mechanical Copyright Protection Society collects mechanical royalties on behalf of its copyright owner members. The Copyright Act decrees that a copyright owner is entitled to a royalty whenever his or her work is 'mechanically reproduced' in any way. Examples of mechanical reproduction include, records, cassettes, CDs, film sound-tracks, videos, reel to reel tapes for radio broadcast and so on.

Once a song has been recorded and released in the UK – provided you notify the copyright owner and pay the mechanical royalty – you can make a cover version of that song without the permission of the copyright owner. If, however, the song in question has never been recorded before, or you wish to change the lyrics of the song in any way, you will need the written permission of the copyright owner. Of course, if you are releasing your own record and the songs are written by you, it would be a waste of time for

the MCPS to take a royalty from you and then pay it back – less their commission – so under these circumstances you don't have to pay anything. However, if a record company mechanically re-produces your song they owe you – the copyright owner – a royalty for the right to do so. If they release a record by you but which contains none of your songs, you will receive no mechanical roy-alties at all. The record company will pay them to the copyright owner instead. Many bands fail to realize that 'mechanicals' – as these royalties are usually known – are paid to the songwriter and are properly seen as publishing income.

Most of the money the MCPS collects comes from mechanical royalties paid by record companies. The larger companies account to the MCPS on record sales whilst the smaller ones are invoiced on the actual quantity of records pressed – regardless of whether they are sold or not. They have agreements with pressing plants and duplicating companies who return pressing notices on a monthly basis (see Releasing Your Own Record: MCPS, page 110) indicating the companies they have been working for, the songs they have reproduced, and the number of copies made. Some of the larger record companies actually make their mechanical royalty payments direct to the copyright owner, usually a publisher, who then awards the songwriter their agreed percentage.

The MCPS has blanket agreements with the BBC and the In-dependent Television Companies Association who pay agreed roy-alty sums on an annual basis to the MCPS in return for the relatively unrestricted recording of its members' works. Video com-panies also pay royalties to the MCPS as do Film Companies, Advertising Agencies, Background Music Operators, Record Im-porters and anyone else who records MCPS members' works.

HOW DO YOU JOIN THE MCPS?

As a writer, once you have three or four works recorded which are earning royalties you can become a member of the MCPS. Member-ship is free – contact the Membership Division of the MCPS.

For a more detailed explanation of the way in which 'mechanicals' are calculated, collected and distributed see section on Publishing Contracts: Mechanical royalties, page 165.

MCPS AND THE COPYRIGHT ACT

The MCPS has differed from other (non-UK) mechanical royalty collection societies in that many UK publishers have traditionally chosen to collect their mechanical income from record companies themselves, seeing no reason to use MCPS for this purpose. There was, after all, a statutory royalty rate under the old Copyright Act

and apart from the first recording of the work there was no need for a record company to apply specifically for a licence. The MCPS therefore concentrated on collections from smaller record companies.

With the introduction of the 1988 Copyright Act and the arrival of the single European market in 1992 the MCPS has been trying to establish its mandate as the music publishers negotiating body. It would then be able to use its authority to become involved in major areas such as the issue of central European licensing of international products by record companies such as Polygram and BMG and also the negotiation of a new industry wide agreement on the level of mechanical royalty rate payable.

The 1988 Copyright Act abolishes Section 8 of the 1956 Act which had stipulated that the mechanical royalty was to be 6.25% of the notional retail price equivalent of a record. The new Act therefore provides for a free for all in that no royalty rate will be stipulated by statute.

There is concern that such a free for all, with the might of the major record companies set against the copyright owners, may lead to a reduction of the mechanical royalty rate.

At time of publication, the MCPS is therefore seeking to negotiate for the copyright owners/music publishers with the record companies' association, the BPI, to try and resolve what the mechanical royalty rate should be in the future.

If these negotiations are successful, it is likely that the UK will ultimately have a royalty rate higher than the one at present and possibly even on a par with the European rate (currently 17% higher than that of the UK). If these negotiations are unsuccessful the matter will have to be referred to a government established Copyright Tribunal who will determine the issue.

Until the issue has been resolved the old 6.25% mechanical royalty rate will continue to apply.

However, if you are putting your own record out or want any further information you should contact the MCPS directly to see what the latest position is.

PHONOGRAPHIC PERFORMANCE LIMITED (PPL)

Phonographic Performance Ltd (PPL), and Video Performance Ltd, (VPL), are both non-profit making companies which primarily represent the record companies. The owner of the copyright in a sound recording (as opposed to the musical composition) is also entitled to phonographic performance income in respect of any public performance of that sound recording.

The PPL maintain that a recording of a piece of music, for example on a record, is a performance 'captured' in vinyl. Every time the record is played in public that performance is recreated and the creators of the original performance should be paid. In current UK law the creators of recorded performances are considered to be the record companies who manufacture the records. This may seem a little unfair to the artists who sang and played on the records and who, strictly speaking, actually created the original 'performances'. This anomaly is partially recognized and, unlike either the PRS or the MCPS, the PPL does make sure that the artists involved, (and not just the copyright owners) get some money each time their performance is recreated in public. However, as the PPL are primarily a record company organization, it will come as no surprise that the largest proportion by far of the money they collect goes to their record company members.

Wendy James of Transvision Vamp playing what, for the careers of many British rock bands, is a virtually compulsory 'sold out' Marquee gig at the old Wardour Street address in July 1988.

THE TC AND MUSIC GUIDE

The PPL collects money on behalf of its members from any public premises where music is played, and from the BBC and the various commercial radio and TV companies. They issue 'phonographic performance licences' to discotheques, pubs, football grounds, shopping precincts – in fact anywhere you can hear recorded music being played. They don't have any jurisdiction in your home, you'll be pleased to know, where you are free to play your own records without paying a PPL levy. But as soon as you play those records in a public place – say in a local pub before one of your gigs – you come up against the warning which is printed on the label of every record. 'All rights of the manufacturer and of the owner of the recorded work reserved. Unauthorised public performance, broadcasting and copying of this record prohibited.'

Apart from the licences that the PPL grant to the places mentioned above they also make all radio and television companies pay them for permission to play recorded music on the air. The time when radio and TV companies are allowed to play records is known as 'needletime' and both the BBC and the commercial companies pay a very large sum of money every year to the PPL for their right to play recorded music. The total revenue that the PPL collects per year from all its licencees exceeds £7 million.

In brief this is distributed as follows:

20% goes to the artists whose performances are captured on the recordings.

$12\frac{1}{2}$% goes to the Musicians Union, who use the money 'for the benefit of the music profession generally'.

8% goes to the MCPS who pass it on to the composers

$67\frac{1}{2}$% goes to the record companies which are members of the PPL (currently there are about 700 such members).

How do you join the PPL?

Any record company, no matter how small, can join the PPL – so if you release and distribute your own record for sale (promotional copies don't count), you should register with them in order to receive your share of 'airtime' money.

All the addresses and contact details relating to the organizations mentioned above are listed in the Directory under Industry Organization, page 234.

VPL

Video Performance Limited represents the owners of copyright in videos and operate in a similar way to the PPL, in that it collects public performance royalties on their behalf whenever videos are performed in public.

Bands that tour the arena circuit can now expect to make more money out of their merchandising than they will make from ticket sales or even from the sale of an album! If you think about the fact that Whitesnake took £70,000 from official merchandise at just one of their shows last year, it becomes easier to understand why merchandising rights are so potentially valuable (six figure deals are not uncommon for the big acts). Even rising stars can expect to be offered larger advances by merchandising companies than those given by their record companies or publishers. For from the narrow profit margins associated with selling a few T-shirts and badges at your own gigs, large scale merchandising can be an international money spinner.

At this level, merchandising can work in a variety of ways. The deal can be very similar to a recording deal: the group signs with the company giving them sole rights to market paraphernalia carrying their official design. They then receive a cash advance against a royalty rate of each item sold (30% is a likely figure). Alternatively, the band might wish to retain control of the selling themselves, but retain the support services of an experienced supplier. Large venues like Wembley Arena demand a facility fee of 25%, so it can be more economical for merchandising companies to act just as suppliers and let the band pay the extra 25%. In this case the band would have to employ someone to manage their merchandising campaign on a contract basis, yet might still benefit financially. They will also have more control over their own products.

GUIDELINES FOR MERCHANDISING AGREEMENTS

There is no such thing as a standard merchandising agreement, although they all have similar ingredients. You will need professional legal advice, but this kind of agreement is not very complicated, and should not involve you in excessive costs. The strength of your bargaining position (your popularity, the type of merchandise you are likely to sell, and the quantity) – will determine the terms you are offered. These factors can change within a very short space of time so you should check that:

(1) Any contract you sign should cover the shortest possible period of time that you are able to negotiate. That way, if you have a hit single and expect to significantly increase your merchandise sales you will soon be able to re-negotiate the deal so that it reflects your improved sales potential.

(2) You do not jump at the first offer that is made to you. Timing is important. If you think you will get a better deal in a couple of months – then wait.

Further points to consider:

● Sign the agreement yourselves – do not let your manager sign for you. The right to sign your own deals should have been negotiated when you signed your management contract.

● Tacky, cheap products can affect your public profile, so you really should try to get as much quality control as you can, without inhibiting the ability of the merchandiser to perform. Normally, this takes the form of approval over samples.

● Initially, your merchandising company may stipulate an 'exclusive deal' – that they are the only ones to issue T-shirts of a specific design. When you have some degree of success you may be able to do non-exclusive deals.

● The band will have to come to a decision amongst themselves concerning how the money is to be split and should discuss what should happen if one of them leaves.

● Your manager will usually be entitled to commission on your merchandising income. If, however, your manager sets up a merchandising company to do your merchandising make sure that he or she does not take a 'double commission' – i.e. take a cut of both the company's profits and your own share. Also, try and ensure that the manager's interest in the merchandising company cannot continue beyond the term of the management agreement.

● Merchandising deals in the UK actually fall into three main categories: tour merchandising, retail merchandising, and mail order. You should really make separate deals for each.

YOUR MERCHANDISING RIGHTS AND YOUR RECORD COMPANY

If you are aware of the money to be made from merchandising then you should appreciate that if you become successful all sorts of people will become interested in your merchandising programme. Not least of these will be your record company who may have attempted to acquire your merchandising rights when they signed you up as a recording artist. You should resist signing your merchandising rights to your record company for the following reasons.

(1) The skills required to successfully merchandise an artist may not be genuinely possessed 'in house' by the record company. Supervision of your merchandising is probably best undertaken on your behalf by your manager, if you have one, because he or she is more likely to have an overview of your career.

(2) Independent control over this important source of income may be important later on. The last thing you want is your record company recouping recording costs from your T-shirt sales, but many record companies do see the acquisition of your merchandising rights as a way of spreading their financial risk. Also, if you should fall out with your record company you may have to look to touring activities to keep you solvent until the problem is worked out – but if your record company controls your merchandising income this may not be possible.

TOUR MERCHANDISING

This is where you can expect an advance against a royalty of between 20% and 35% of the price of each item sold during a period referrable to your touring activities. To give an idea of the size of the UK market, a successful artist would anticipate the total gross receipts of the merchandiser to be between £1 and £2 per head on a UK tour. This would mean that if the aggregate audience during a tour were fifty thousand then royalties of around £10,000 to £35,000 can be generated for the band.

You must make sure that the merchandising company undertakes to provide adequate staff and merchandise at every venue – and establish also that accounts will be made up within at least 14 days of the end of the tour.

The tour merchandising companies like to be able to extend the Term beyond the tour if they have not yet recouped their investment. This should be limited as far as possible.

If you cancel or postpone a tour for which a merchandising company have been contracted then you will probably have to re-pay the advance. You should really have an allowance for postponement in your contract which states that if the tour does not take place within, say, 6 months of the date for which it was originally scheduled, then the advance becomes repayable. The availability of insurance cover may also deal with this problem (see Insurance, page 213).

RETAIL MERCHANDISING

Retail merchandising is really dominated by a few big companies, although a number of smaller, independent ones survive. This is where you license your rights generally, or perhaps on an item by item basis (e.g. a licence for an individual T-shirt design).

The royalty should be in the range of 8% to 12% of the wholesale price and the group would be doing well to sell thirty to fifty thousand individual shirts through retail outlets. A successful band in the UK might expect to earn a little over £10,000 a year in this way.

MAIL ORDER

The bulk of this business used to take the form of orders from press advertisements but now the most significant level of mail order sales are generated through inserts in albums, advertising specific T-shirt or sweatshirt material. Merchandisers expect a two percent response for every insert in an album with an average order of around £8.00. Sales of one hundred thousand albums would therefore be expected to translate into earnings of approximately £16,000.

YOUR RIGHTS TO TERMINATE THE AGREEMENT

You should be able to terminate the agreement for: breach of contract, failure to account for money taken or merchandise sold, liquidation of the company and, if you can negotiate it, for failure to have your merchandise available for sale.

PROTECTING YOUR MERCHANDISING PROGRAMME

The three areas of law that are relevant to UK merchandising are the laws relating to copyright, trade mark and 'passing off'.

COPYRIGHT

There is no copyright protection afforded to an artist except by reference to photographs, designs and drawings of him or her – all of which will qualify as artistic work. Copyright does not exist in an artist's name or reputation as such.

Provided that you can establish that you own the copyright in particular designs, drawings or photographs then you can stop other people from reproducing them without your permission. The drawback here is that the merchandising company may well commission their own artwork or photographs for your designs – and would therefore own the copyright which your merchandiser commissions on your behalf.

It can be an extremely good idea to try to establish a logo and ensure that you own the copyright in that logo, so that the public only value your merchandise if it bears your official design. A good example is the ABBA logo where the first B is turned backwards. There is no copyright in the name ABBA, but there is when it is printed with a backward B. This form of protection has the advantage of being comparatively cheap since no registration formalities are necessary in the UK. (Registration is advisable for some overseas countries – for example, the USA.)

It is essential to have proper documentation evidencing the

rights of ownership in any logos, artwork or photographs. Note that in the case of a drawing the owner of the copyright would be the artist, unless the drawing is created during the course of an employment or in a case of a commission where it is a portrait that is commissioned.

The mere commissioning of a design (as opposed to a portrait) does not always vest copyright in the person placing the commission. In the case of photographs it is the person who owns the negative that owns the copyright. It is up to you to make sure that you have agreements with your photographers and designers so that they effectively assign their copyright interest to you. This has to be done in writing and be signed by both parties so that it becomes a contract of assignment of copyright. As merchandising is such an international operation, it is also a good idea to make sure that the assignment covers the requirements of the US copyright legislation. You do this by saying that the work is – and is expressed to be – 'a work made for hire' in the contract.

TRADE MARK

Another basis on which to try and claim some protection of merchandise is through the establishment of a Registered Trade Mark.

Since 1987 trade marks have been available not only for goods – but also for services. The basis of a trade mark action is that once the 'TM' is properly registered, the person owning it has the exclusive right to use it in the particular class of goods or services for which it is registered. Anyone seeking to use the 'TM' without authority would be liable as an infringer and could be injuncted or sued for damages. The trade mark itself is a symbol which is applied or attached to goods which distinguishes those goods from similar goods and identifies them with a particular trader – or in this context, artist. A good example of this is the tongue and lip logo developed for the Rolling Stones.

Artists in the music industry are normally advised to register in a minimum of four classes covering records, photographs, posters and other printed material, clothing and badges.

'PASSING OFF'

The third basis for protecting your merchandising rights is 'Passing Off'. This legal doctrine came into existence to protect the goodwill of a trader against the misuse of his or her business mark, name or more general 'get up'; it is a form of unfair competition law which allows one trader to stop another trader from misusing the original trader's reputation.

Lawyers take the view that it has considerable potential in form-

ing the basis for an action relating to unauthorized commercial exploitation of an artist's reputation. For an artist to succeed in a cause of action 'for passing off' there must be:

- a misrepresentation made by the unauthorized trader in the course of business to prospective customers or ultimate consumers of goods or services supplied by him

- the misrepresentation must be calculated to damage the business or goodwill of another trader in the sense that this was a reasonably forseeable consequence.

- it must also be shown to have actually caused damage to the business of the artist e.g. detracted from the artist's own merchandising sales.

Protection of another sort can also be achieved by having high quality products available at reasonable prices and which are effectively distributed and supported by successful advertising. This will help to deter the bootleggers.

SPONSORSHIP

Sponsorship in the UK is not yet fully developed, but there is, it seems, a growing awareness of the financial value of sponsorship – both to potential sponsors and for artists as a valuable source of income.

Sponsorship involves financial support being given by a company to fund an artist's tour or generally to his or her career over a specified period of time. There is generally a cash payment and a performance requirement – such as to undertake a major UK tour. Sometimes the sponsor will only be involved in providing equipment or 'bartering' an endorsement for goods by making a payment in-kind in the form of a new car, for instance. In return for its support the company is generally allowed to publicize its sponsorship of that artist in its public relations and advertising. It is often part of the arrangement that the artist agrees to appear in the company's TV and other advertising.

At the top end of the scale, corporate sponsorship involves vast sums of money and, some believe, a loss of credibility on the part of the artist. At grass roots level it could simply involve a graphic design company doing your posters and T-shirts in return for a name-check on the products.

Although this section is aimed generally at musicians, it is also relevant in many respects for songwriters, producers, DJs and anyone else who, on a full or part-time basis, is working in the entertainments industry.

If your ultimate aim is to make your livelihood through profits from live appearances and record sales, some knowledge of accountancy and the fundamentals of taxation is needed. Any money that you generate brings you within the scope of taxation and the Inland Revenue will demand that you make a tax return on all your income and expenditure.

It is no use burying your head in the sand and hoping the tax man won't see you, because sooner or later he will! And when he does eventually catch up with you, you will probably be charged interest and be liable to penalties on the tax which you did not pay.

SELF-EMPLOYMENT, LIMITED COMPANIES AND PARTNERSHIPS

You have the choice of operating as a self employed person, either as an individual or within a Partnership, or you can set up a Limited Company.

SELF EMPLOYED

The newly-started, and those that haven't as yet seriously considered declaring their income from their musical activities, would be best to start off as self employed under Income Tax Schedule D. You will then, quite simply, pay Income Tax on your profits. This will not mean that you have to give up any full or part-time job you already have. Going self employed, as far as your musical activities are concerned, is appropriate whether or not you already have a job. Once you hit the big time you can get professional advice on transferring your activities to a Limited Company, or, in the case of a band, you can even form separate companies for each member.

You might wonder if it is really necessary to own up to the Inland Revenue that you are a professional musician, especially if this is a part-time activity. Apart from the peace of mind, there are some good financial reasons for declaring your musical income. For instance, if you are already an employed person, taxed under Schedule E, your part-time activities as a self employed musician may well result in losses being made once you have taken into account the many expenses that you incur playing live. These losses can then be set against your employment income and a refund of tax can sometimes be obtained. (There is a checklist of general allowable expenses at the end of this section.)

Losses are a common experience in the early years of many

professions and particularly in this one. Many musicians never do achieve sufficient success to live off their earnings from music. Should you release your own record it is still a good idea to trade under Income Tax Schedule D. This way, you can offset any losses on your record sales against your other income thereby reducing the income tax you will pay. Any expenses that you incur fulfilling your work as a musician can be put against your earnings via music, but you will need to keep the receipts and appropriate books if your claims are to be taken seriously. (See below for book-keeping.) If you run at a loss as a musician, you can set that loss against your income from other activities and thereby reduce your tax bill on that income. Ask your accountant for details as this will not automatically occur.

NATIONAL INSURANCE

Another aspect of being self employed is that you have to buy Class 2 National Insurance Stamps (currently £4.25 a week). There is a small earnings exemption if your profits are less than £2,350 a year. There may also be an exemption if you are already employed and paying the maximum contribution for all earners of £29.25 per week, which means you would be earning at least £325.00 per week. (Limited companies also have N.I. responsibilities. See below.)

PARTNERSHIP

If you are a band, as opposed to an individual artist, you can set up a Partnership agreement via a solicitor as a way of organising your affairs. Loosely speaking, a Partnership is an association of self employed individuals with liabilities towards each other and, as a body, towards the local tax office. Your trading address will probably be your home address and your local tax office will be the one closest to your home.

Where an individual artist is clearly the lynch pin of a band (which may consist of hired session musicians), then that person is obviously solely responsible for all the costs associated with the band – and will be held responsible by the tax offices for any profits or losses that the band makes as an enterprise. However, where a group of musicians is equally involved, and the expenses connected with their band are not so easily divisible between them as individuals, then it would be practical for the band to form a Partnership. For instance, if a six piece band hire a van to travel to a gig, then it is really not sensible, or practical, to split the cost of the van hire six ways. As this is true of most of the other costs associated with the band, a Partnership may be a practical solution.

For tax purposes the individuals within a Partnership are assessed as if they were self employed under tax schedule D. However, all the separate individuals within a Partnership are each liable for their partner's taxes in the event of any member of their Partnership defaulting on tax payments. Likewise, all the individuals in the Partnership are liable for any debts that the Partnership itself might incur. This is an essential difference between Partnerships and Limited Companies, where the liability of the individual is limited in law. The joint and several liability of the individuals within a Partnership is a very potent reason for ensuring that every individual keeps their figures and dealings with the tax offices in order, and that someone keeps the Partnership's books properly.

There is an alternative to going into the minefield of Limited Companies, in the shape of Limited Partnerships – but this isn't the publication to instruct you. If you are interested, seek independent professional financial advice.

LIMITED COMPANY

If you form a Limited Company, the company will be liable to Corporation Tax on its profits. A company is a separate legal entity to its Directors. The Directors have legal responsibilities towards the company and its shareholders. Any money taken out of the company for your personal needs is treated as wages and taxed under Income Tax Schedule E (PAYE). Alternatively, as you will be a shareholder of the company, you can receive a dividend or share of the company profits on which Advance Corporation Tax is payable. Advance Corporation Tax can be set off against the company's mainstream Corporation Tax liability on its agreed trading profits. If you decide to pay yourself wages, an important additional cost to bear in mind is that of National Insurance contributions (N.I.). As an employer you have to pay Employer's N.I. contributions on any wages, including your own. As this figure is up to 10.45% of an employee's salary, your N.I. contributions could well amount to thousands of pounds a year.

As you can see, the Limited Company route is complicated! It can be expensive too, because you must have your accounts audited by a Certified or Chartered Accountant and file accounts and annual returns each year at Companies House.

There is also unlikely to be any tax saving in forming a Limited Company unless the band's profits are at least £30,000 per annum. Before leaping into a Limited Company agreement you should discuss your tax position with your accountant. At the moment an individual can earn up to £20,700 in any tax year before paying more than the basic 25% tax rate. The next tax bracket is at a rate

of 40%. However, you are taxed only after your personal and other allowances have been deducted from your income (see below) so, in fact, you can earn considerably more than £20,700 per year before you actually have to pay the 40% rate. For example, a married man on £29,000 per annum with a £30,000 mortgage will have a total of around £8,500 tax deductions (made up of the married man's allowance of £4,375 and estimated mortgage interest of £4,000). This will mean that he pays only 25% tax after his allowable expenses have been accounted for, £20,700 may seem a very high figure to you now, but you could achieve it at a stroke if you signed a publishing or record company deal involving a reasonable advance.

Whatever structure you adopt it should be workable for you in more ways than just tax savings. It is more than likely that a group of you will form a band, in which case it will probably be far simpler to start off as a Partnership in the first instance. This will allow you more flexibility to change to a different structure in the future should you want to.

WHAT HAPPENS IF YOU FAIL TO INFORM THE INLAND REVENUE THAT YOU ARE A MUSICIAN?

If the Inland Revenue inform you that they have reason to believe that not all your income has been declared, this will be swiftly followed by estimated tax assessments for the year they think these activities commenced, and for all the tax years after this. Their estimates of your profits will, in all likelihood, be far greater than the amount you actually earned and you may indeed have made losses. The problem you may be faced with now, however, is that you have not kept proper accounting records and thus find it difficult to challenge the Inland Revenue's estimate of your profits. The tax man will want to review all your personal finances and any figures you do put forward will be viewed with some doubt because you had not voluntarily reported your income in the first place. It is important that you are aware that the Inland Revenue are paying particular attention to PAYE audits, and that during their investigations they are following up on any payments they uncover to persons not employed directly by the company that they are investigating. If it is your local promoter or pub landlord whose books they are going through, they may discover payments made to entertainers such as yourselves. If this leads the tax man to your front door – it is best to be prepared for him.

If you do receive a tax assessment you must appeal against that assessment within 30 days of the date of issue. At the same time you must request in writing that the tax be postponed. Seek professional help immediately as the problem will not go away.

So, the message is: register as self employed with your local tax office and keep your books up to date!

WHEN YOU NEED AN ACCOUNTANT

A sympathetic Certified or Chartered Accountant can help you set up a beneficial working relationship with the tax office. A list of entertainment oriented accountants can be found in our directory, but any qualified accountant should be able to help. They should be a member of either the Institute of Chartered Accountants (ACA or FCA after their names, or just CA if they are Scottish), or the Association of Certified Accountants (ACCA or FCCA after their names). (Irish accountants have their own organisation.) Accountants with any of these qualifications have been properly trained and they have a disciplinary body to assist you if you have any complaints. Should they have the additional letters ATII after their name it means that they have specialized in tax related accounting.

It is difficult to say how much your accountant should cost because it will really depend on how much work they have to do, and it can be weighed against how much money they can save you in tax. You should probably be paying between £30–£60 per hour, depending on the level of work required, and your yearly accounts will cost about £400.

You will need a certified or chartered accountant when your turnover nears VAT limits to ensure that you know how to keep appropriate records. Life can start to become hazardous once the VAT office takes an interest in your accounts!

Before signing to a record company you will have sought legal advice on the recording contract and at this stage should also make contact with a firm of accountants who have knowledge of the music business. You will need to know about the treatment of record company advances and royalties. For instance, the quarterly limit on earnings before you have to register for VAT is currently only £8,000. This will mean that the group may need to register for VAT if the advance you receive exceeds £8,000 (see VAT section below).

At this stage, you may well have management, and if not, the record company or solicitors representing you may introduce you to suitable management companies. Whatever the situation, do not expect your manager to look after your personal finances and tax liabilities. Ignorance is no defence in the law, and totally relying on others to take an interest in your personal financial affairs is foolhardy. Remember that responsibility for paying tax rests with

you, as any income that is generated is assumed to be your income. Even if you entrust someone else with the management of that income, you should have your own accountant keeping a watchful eye out for your interests.

SOME BASIC GUIDELINES FOR MANAGING YOUR FINANCIAL AFFAIRS

When you start out you may not be able to afford to pay a professional accountant and there may not be enough work to justify employing an accountant anyway. In these circumstances you will have to handle your own financial affairs. In any case, taking an interest in your finances from day one will hold you in good stead for the rest of your career – even if you always remain a pub band. Financial difficulties are a common reason for group breakups, so the more you know, and the more confident you are in talking about your financial affairs, the better. Determined DIY enthusiasts can handle their own finances to a reasonable degree by following the advice we give in this section. There are also good beginners' guides on basic book-keeping and taxation which we would strongly advise you to consult.

INCOME TAX AND THE INLAND REVENUE

One of the basic tenets of tax law is that if income is taxable, then expenses are deductible. Your early gigs will almost certainly cost you more to do than the fee that you earn. The Income Tax office will be very quick off the mark to tax your fees regardless of the expenses you may have incurred in obtaining them. In order to be able to work out where you stand, and how much tax you owe, you need to keep an accurate record of both income and expenditure. This means: (a) issuing invoices for all the fees you receive, giving them a reference number, and keeping duplicates for your records, and, (b) attempting to get receipts and invoices for all business expenses incurred and giving them a reference number. A receipt should state who it is from, what it is for, the date, the amount and the VAT number (where applicable).

Each year all the individuals in the band will have to send in a tax return and the band itself will have to submit a set of accounts.

Whatever your tax status you need to register with the Inland Revenue. Your business address will normally be your home address so you should contact your nearest Inspector of Taxes office. Inform them of the nature of your business, when you commenced and the date you are making your accounts up to on your first year of trading. Your local Inland Revenue Tax office will issue your Schedule D number and it is to them that you should submit your accounts. The favoured year end date for accounts is the 30th April. This means that if you commenced business on 1/5/89 you would have a first year-end date of 30/4/90.

Once you have registered for income tax the Inspector of Taxes of your local tax district will raise an assessment of your income on your first year before receiving any figures from you. These assessments are thus totally arbitrary estimates and, as a result, they can be either too low or, more frequently, too high. As soon as you receive your tax assessment for your first year you must appeal against it within 30 days. Your appeal must then be backed by properly completed accounts soon afterwards. Provided that the tax office accepts your accounts, they will revise their original assessment and base their tax demand upon these figures. They will then base their future tax demands for the next two years on the same profit or loss figures. The collection of your taxes is the responsibility of the local Collector of Taxes.

If, in your first trading year, you made a loss then there would be no tax to pay in the first tax year (which always ends on the 5th of April). If you then went on to make a profit in the next two trading years, you would still pay tax at the first year's rate. That is, in this instance, no tax at all. But, see below for the consequences of failing to save money during this period.

Example:

First year trading accounts: 1.5.89–30.4.90.

These accounts are assessed by the Inland Revenue on the profit (or loss) in the tax year 1989–90. Any tax payable is paid in two equal installments as per revised tax assessment. It is payable in January and July 1990.

Your first year of trading in this example runs from 1.5.89–30.4.90. You therefore started trading in a Tax Year which began on the 6th April 1989 and ended on 5th April 1990. As you will notice about four weeks of your first trading year falls into the next Tax Year – which runs from the 6th April 1990 to 5th April 1991 and is known as Tax Year 90/91. This is very confusing! But the rules state that as your trading year falls across two Tax Years the Inland Revenue will assess you on a 'prior year basis' which, put very simply, means that you effectively pay your tax almost two years in arrears (see below).

During those two years you will have been presenting your actual accounts showing what you really earned during the years ending April 30th 1991 and April 30th 1992. Accounts for your second year's trading ending April 30th 1991 will be assessed by the tax office in the Tax Year 1992/93. You will only pay your first

tax instalment on these figures in January 1993 and later in July 1993, nearly two years after you actually earned the money!

The big danger of this system (taxation on a 'prior year basis') is that you will probably earn very little money in your first year. Should you then go on to earn large amounts of money in your second and third years of trading, you will still only be paying tax at the low rates on which you were initially assessed. By the time your tax returns for the second and third years have been processed and the tax demand duly despatched, you may have been tempted to spend the extra money. This situation can only be avoided if: (a) you have carefully saved money with which to pay tax bills two years ahead, (b) if your initial run of success has continued so that you have enough money in the bank to meet the tax bill regardless, or, (c) you elect to have your second and third years figures assessed on an 'actual basis'.

Actual basis taxation is an option which you can request for the second and third income tax years' trading only. Actual basis taxation means that you will be taxed on the profit that you actually earned during these income tax years, although you will be forced to return to the prior year system from the fourth year onwards. As with most things in life, you will end up paying tax on your earnings at some point, so don't treat the prior year system, should you opt for it, as tax-free living.

It is also important to remember that everything that you spend in forwarding your career must be accounted for, otherwise the tax office will assume that you have spent your money on yourself and tax you accordingly. You must keep receipts from day one for everything – from guitar strings and rehearsal time to van hire and poster printing. These will be invaluable when your accountant eventually gets to grips with your annual accounts.

VAT: CUSTOMS AND EXCISE

Currently, you should register for VAT (Value Added Tax) if you have 'reason to believe' that your turnover may exceed £23,600 per year, or £8,000 in any one quarter. Registration is not optional if your gross earnings (before you deduct your expenses) even approach this amount. You should keep a close eye on whether you are likely to exceed the limits in any one quarter because late registration may result in severe penalties. The penalty consists of up to a 30% surcharge on the amount of VAT that the Customs and Excise decide that you owe them. For instance, if you had earned £10,000 in a given quarter the VAT office will say that you should have charged VAT at 15% and will expect you to pay them £1,500.

Not only that, but they will also charge you a penalty of up to 30% of the £1,500!

To register contact your local HM Customs and Excise VAT Office who will send you an application form which is fairly straight-forward to fill in. You will receive a VAT number which you should write on your invoices and you should add 15% VAT to all your fees.

Once you are VAT registered you will be expected to charge Value Added Tax at 15% on all your fees. Promoters and other customers will expect a VAT invoice from you before they will pay VAT on a bill. They need a properly numbered VAT receipt for their own records.

Don't forget that VAT is a tax on top of your fee and that you are basically collecting the tax for the Customs and Excise depart-ment. It is a common mistake to believe that VAT is money which should be yours. You wouldn't be charging 15% in addition to your fee unless the VAT office required you to do so. With this in mind, it is sensible to start a separate bank account for your VAT. As you collect VAT you should immediately bank it, preferably in an account which will pay you some interest. This will mean that large VAT bills never come as a nasty shock and you will not only earn a little interest, but may well be left with some money in your VAT account after you have done your figures (see attributable VAT below). The VAT office will require you to account for all the VAT that you have collected during each quarter and send it on to them on time. If you do not do this there are costly penalties of up to 30% of the tax due but not paid by the end of the month following the end of your VAT quarter.

On the form that they send you to fill in every three months you will be able to take the opportunity to reduce your VAT bill by countering your collected VAT with any VAT you may have paid out yourselves. Rather confusingly, any VAT you collect on 'Sales' is known by the VAT office as 'output tax'. Net output is your sales figure before VAT is added. Conversely, whenever you pay VAT on a purchase, this is known by the VAT office is 'input tax'. Net input tax is the value of purchases before VAT is added.

For instance, you may have paid VAT on expenses connected directly with your business. Where this outgoing VAT (input tax) can be directly linked with your collection of incoming VAT (output tax) it is known as 'attributable VAT'. An example of directly attributable VAT would be VAT paid on the hire of a van which you used to get to and from a gig. Without the van the show would not have happened and you would not have earned a fee on which to charge VAT in the first place. Where there are expenses that

include VAT, which are not so obviously attributable, you may still be able to claw some of the VAT back where these expenses are 'partially allowable'. An example of partially allowable VAT might be the VAT on your telephone bill where your phone is your business, as well as your private, telephone. While you could claim that you needed the telephone to book your gigs, the VAT office would point out that only a proportion of your phone calls were business calls, and it would ultimately be a matter for negotiation and persuasion as to how much VAT the VAT office agreed was attributable.

Attributable and partially attributable VAT is added together and put against the VAT you have collected each quarter. The balance is then payable to the Customs and Excise department. Occasionally you may find that you have paid out more on attributable VAT than you have collected on your fees in any given quarter. Under these circumstances the VAT man may actually owe you money! Once this has happened you are highly likely to receive a VAT inspection, so be prepared.

Possibly the most worrying aspect of the Customs and Excise is that, unlike the Inland Revenue, the VAT people are not interested in whether you make a profit or a loss. If, for example, you had collected £1,000 VAT in a given quarter, but had made an overall loss on your business, you would still owe the £1,000 VAT. (The Inland Revenue would not require you to pay tax in this situation.) Don't forget that the Duty Men wield some of the most all-encompassing laws in the land. They have powers of inspection which mean they can come and look at your books without a search warrant, and take your property away as security against any money that they think you owe them.

VAT can be a minefield for the unitiated and ignorance is not accepted as a defence in law so get some professional accounting advice.

BOOKKEEPING

Sales Day Book:	a list of your fees giving the date, reference number, the payers name and the amount.
Purchase Day Book:	a list of expenses invoiced to you giving the date, the reference number, the suppliers name and the amount.
Cash Book:	an analysis of your business bank account giving the date and amount of your bankings and details of your payments.
Petty Cash Book:	an analysis of your petty cash expenditure.

It is always important that you keep a Sales Day book and when you start out it may be sufficient for you to keep just that and a Petty Cash book. Ideally, you should open a business bank account and keep cash books. It is worth noting that banks always charge for business accounts, even when they are kept in credit, but look out for special offers. One of the major banks was recently offering free banking for one year for new businesses.

ALLOWABLE EXPENSES

For expenses to be allowable they must be wholly and exclusively incurred for the purpose of the business. It follows, therefore, that normal business expenses such as travel, motor vehicle expenses, telephone, postage and accountancy fees are allowable. The nature of your activities are such that you will be able to claim many expenses peculiar to your profession including records, videos, concert tickets and trade papers.

Problems occur with claims to expenses which are not wholly exclusive to the business such as subsistence, hair dressing and clothes. A good example would be Elton John's glasses – normally not allowable, but in the case of an entertainer like Elton John, very much part of his act and not worn for everyday use.

The Inland Revenue accepts that certain expenses have a private element, such as the telephone, car, and light and heat at home. In these cases the costs are apportioned between private and business use.

See Checklist of expenses allowable against tax, below.

CAPITAL ALLOWANCES

You may also claim allowances for capital items such as Hi-fi equipment, guitars, keyboards, videos, televisions, and, of course, the cost of your motor vehicle. You can claim 25% of these costs in the first year, and in subsequent years 25% of their depreciated or 'written down' value.

See checklist below.

CHECKLIST FOR EXPENSES ALLOWABLE AGAINST TAX

Remember to keep all your receipts for the following goods and services. Ideally you should number them consecutively and each receipt should show the vendor, what it is for, the date, the amount and the VAT number. The lists below are not exhaustive and there may be other examples.

DIRECTLY RELATED COSTS

Agent's fees
Hire and leasing of musical equipment
Manager's fees
Recording Studio costs
Record pressing costs

ALLOWABLE OVERHEADS

Accountancy and legal costs
Bank interest and charges on a business account
Gig tickets
Hairdressing and cosmetics
Insurance of equipment and public indemnity
Living expenses whilst touring
Motor vehicle expenses (the business proportion thereof)
Music papers and journals
Postage and stationery
Promotion, publicity and advertising costs
Rent, light and heat (the business proportion thereof)
Records, books and tapes
Repairs and renewals of equipment
Singing and music lessons
Stage clothes and laundry
Subscriptions to professional bodies e.g., MU
TV and video hire
Telephone bills (the business proportion thereof)
Travel from business address (usually your home) to engagements

CHECKLIST OF THINGS TO DO

Register as Self Employed with the Inspector of Taxes local to your business address (which may be your home address)
Register with the local DHSS as Self Employed
Set an accounting year–end date (30th April is a good choice)
Open a business bank account
Start keeping the appropriate books

If your turnover exceeds, or is expected to exceed, £8,000 in any one given quarter you should register for VAT and get a properly qualified accountant to give you some professional advice.

Properly insuring all your equipment – not to mention your lives –
is extremely worthwhile, but easily overlooked. Your musical instruments and backline are the tools of your trade without which you
cannot continue working. If you have spent possibly upwards of
£1,000 on a drum kit, for example, then it makes rather obvious
sense to spend a few pounds insuring against loss, theft or
damage.

WHAT IS THE DIFFERENCE BETWEEN AN INSURANCE COMPANY AND AN INSURANCE BROKER?

THE BROKER

The Insurance Broker looks after your insurance requirements and
the handling and running of a claim. It is the broker's job to sift
through the policies offered by the Insurance companies and get
you the best deal for the best price. The broker is paid for this
service by the Insurance company although sometimes, depending
on the policy and the premium, you might be charged a small
handling fee.

THE INSURANCE COMPANY/UNDERWRITERS

These are the people who take the risk on your claim. It is they and
not the broker who pay out if you make a claim.

Many Insurance companies still regard the music business as an
extremely high risk area and for this reason few companies actually
have policies specifically designed for the music business. They
may be able to offer you a more general equipment insurance
policy, but even a specialist musical equipment policy will probably
not cover you for loss of easily damaged goods like your master
tapes, for example. For this reason it is advisable to go through a
broker who will either have their own specialist policies which are
underwritten by a reputable insurance company – or will be able to
search out the most suitable available policy for you.

Word of mouth is once again the best recommendation. Try and
find someone who has already had to make a claim and been
satisfied in their dealings with their broker/company.

It is worth doing some research to make sure you get the best
deal available and keep in mind that in most cases you will get
what you pay for: cheap insurance is not necessarily the best
insurance. Read the policy thoroughly and pay particular attention
to the small print.

HERE IS A GLOSSARY OF SOME OF THE TERMS YOU ARE LIKELY TO COME ACROSS

(**a**) The Assured: the person taking out insurance, in this case you!

(**b**) Exclusions: are exclusions to the policy. What the policy does NOT cover.

(**c**) Excess: this is the first amount payable by yourself for any claim.

(**d**) Limit of Indemnity: the amount you are insured for. Sometimes more clearly stated as 'Sum Insured'.

(**e**) Clauses: a policy exclusion relating to one particular incident. If that clause is broken and this leads to a claim, the insurance company are not obliged to pay.

(**f**) Premium: the cost of the insurance.

(**g**) Warranty: this is a stipulation and if this is broken the Insurance company are not obliged to pay. Watch out for these because they are nearly always in small print. An example would be a warranty on your equipment policy which says that the equipment is only covered when in the van if there is an alarm fitted. So, even if you have a crash and they discover later that there was no burglar alarm fitted, they can use this as an excuse – and you will not be able to make a claim!

ADVICE AND TIPS

● If at all possible use a specialist Broker/Company. Check our Directory section for some useful numbers.

● Look at your proposal form and make sure that it is designed for the music business. If the policy you use is not a specialist one there will probably be so many restrictive clauses on it that it won't really be worth the paper it is written on.

● Always declare fully the nature of your business or occupation. If you are in the music business you will probably find your premiums are very high – particularly for car insurance – so it will be tempting to call yourself 'Office Manager' if it means paying less than if you put 'Band Manager'. Tempting . . . but risky, because the insurance company will not pay if they find out. This is important even if your music business involvement is part-time because if, for example, equipment is stolen from your car, you may find the insurance company wriggling out of the claim on the grounds that you had not fully informed them of your activities and lifestyle.

If you are ever in doubt about the details on your proposal form ring the Insurance Broker or Company and ask them to explain in writing, if necessary, as much as you need to know. They should agree.

INSURANCE CHECKLIST

This checklist is to show you the various classes of insurance most often used by people in the music business. Along with a brief description of each we have included advice and tips concerning what to look out for in the small print, what to expect in terms of the premium, clauses and warranties, etc. If the class of insurance you need is not here, you should contact a specialist broker.

MUSICAL EQUIPMENT

This is vital at all levels. Use a specialist Broker and do not just add your equipment on to your household insurance policy. A household insurance policy can often be more expensive than a specific policy and it is certain to contain restrictive conditions.

Check all the above points and make sure that your policy also covers the following:

(**a**) Transit Cover/Theft from Vehicles

Most policies will cover equipment damaged in transit (for example in a car crash) but cover against theft from vehicles can be more problematic so you should check carefully any warranties. You may find that the vehicle has to be alarmed (as in the warranty example above) and some policies stipulate that the vehicle has to be immobilised (perhaps by the removal of the rotor arm) when left unattended. Not very convenient if you are on your own in the van and need to go to the loo! An appropriate policy will not carry these warranties.

(**b**) Replacement as New

Always make sure that the Insurance Company undertakes to reimburse you for the full cost of replacing your equipment at the current price. Make sure that they do not try and give you less because your equipment is old or worn.

(**c**) No Claims Bonus

A worthwhile policy is likely to include a benefit such as this, especially if you are paying more than the minimum premium. Bonuses will probably not be transferable between Insurance Companies as in motor insurance.

(**d**) Additional cost of hiring

This is a very useful extension which is included in most specialist policies. It covers you for the extra cost of hiring equipment whilst a claim is being processed.

(**e**) Policy Excess

It is particularly important to check your policy excess when insuring equipment. This is the first amount of any claim which is not accounted for by the insurance company and you should make sure that the figure mentioned is per CLAIM and not per ITEM.

Assuming that it is per claim (any decent policy will be) do not forget to include all your small items such as leads, plugs, and strings.

Be very wary of policies offering excesses as a % of the amount claimed as this could turn out to be a very high figure.

GENERAL NOTES

(1) It is often possible for a band to take out insurance for all their equipment on the same policy proposal form. This can be worth it if you are offered up to £2,000 of cover for a premium of £50 and you only have £1,800 worth of equipment between you. It can also be cheaper because together you will be insuring a higher sum and many Brokers/Insurance Companies have a minimum premium.

(2) When hiring a studio/rehearsal room or storage space, do not assume that the owners of the building will have insurance covering your equipment on their premises. If they tell you they have, always ask for confirmation in writing to avoid problems in the event of a loss.

(3) If you use equipment from a hire company read the small print of their Invoice/Delivery Note. You will almost certainly be held responsible for loss or damage so you should add the hire equipment to your policy for the necessary period. This can often be done over the phone and you will probably be charged a pro rata fee. So, for example, if your insurance policy covers you for £2,000 worth of equipment for an annual premium of £50, and you need to insure hired equipment valued at £2,000 for one month the cost will be one twelfth of the annual payment, which is approximately £4.16p.

TAPES

Generally, you will only be able to insure yourself for the cost of re-recording any tapes that may be lost or damaged and the actual cost of this will vary according to the particular circumstances. As with your equipment do not assume that a studio will have insurance to cover your tapes.

CANCELLATION AND NON APPEARANCE

From the artist's point of view, this policy may be taken out to cover loss of potential earnings (or costs, if higher) should any show(s) be cancelled or re-scheduled due to any reasons beyond your control. Cover should also be considered to protect any 'buy-on' money if no provision has been made for its return in the event of the headlining act cancelling a tour. From the promoter's side, the same type of policy can also cover his or her costs and expenses as well as profit. Always ask the broker about conditions such as:

(1) Illness in the event of no medical
(2) Financial causes/ticket sales
(3) Adverse weather

PUBLIC LIABILITY

This covers you against a member of the audience being injured through the band's negligence. It protects you in the event of legal action being taken but does not constitute an automatic payment.

TRAVEL

To be taken out whenever you travel abroad and should cover you against medical expenses, including flying you home if necessary, personal baggage and personal cash. Always make sure that your insurer is fully aware of your activities, particularly if touring, and do not buy standard holiday insurance.

PERSONAL ACCIDENT

This provides cover in the event of disablement permanently preventing you from continuing your career as a musician. This type of insurance is quite expensive but it is worth considering once you start making money – especially if you are a session musician.

TOUR CASH

Tour cash can only be insured while in your personal possession or in a safe. The premium is calculated on application and is often based on the whole amount carried throughout the tour regardless of how much you will be spending. For example – if you set off with £5,000 to pay for expenses and you earn £5,000, your premium will be calculated on the basis that the Tour Cash amounts to £10,000.

STAGE COSTUMES

If you just have one or two items that you would like to have covered you may be able to include them on your equipment policy for an extra premium. Otherwise, you will need a separate policy form and again the cost will be calculated on application.

THE MUSICIANS' UNION

The Musicians' Union (MU) aims to represent musicians, negotiate on their behalf and improve their standing within the music industry, and help individual members. They are committed to trying to improve the 'status and remuneration of musicians both absolutely and relatively'. Services to their members include general benevolent assistance, sickness or accident benefit, legal advice (contracts advisory service), instrument insurance (free up to £500), assistance in recovering unpaid fees, a Media Rights collection and distribution service, and regular seminars, clinics and workshops on the Music Business. Any musician who is playing for money and is prepared to pay the yearly subscription rate is eligible for membership. If you want to appear on television, or want your video or music to be broadcast, particularly on the BBC, you will have to be a member.

There are about 120 branches of the MU throughout the country and although you may join at your local branch, you are able to contact any of the other branches for advice. Your subscription will be graded according to your earnings from music on a sliding scale which is indicated on the MU membership application form. For example, if your weekly earnings from music are up to £65.00, your subscription for one year (52 weeks) would be £33.80 plus an entrance fee of £1.00. You will be required to sign a declaration agreeing to conform by the rules and constitution of the Union and pledging yourself to promote in all ways the interests of the Union.

The MU have been increasingly criticised over the past ten years for their rather anachronistic and inflexible approach to the rapidly changing nature of the music business. Their drive to 'keep music live' has led to robots being unable to mime to their 'own' records, for example! In the last couple of years, however, the MU has made a renewed attempt to attract young pop and rock musicians to its membership. They have appointed a Music Business Adviser, Mark Melton, and he has been involved in setting up regular seminars and workshops aimed specifically at young bands. If they can substantially increase the number of musicians they represent at this level, they hope that they will be more effectively able to campaign for better pay and conditions on the club and pub circuit.

RECORD COMPANIES

Few record companies actually have offices in Ireland because it constitutes such a small record sales market for them. CBS and WEA have offices in Dublin which also cover Northern Ireland, and EMI has an office in Dublin which covers Eire only. All the other major labels are sub-distributed in Eire and work from London.

An up and coming Irish band should really try and make contacts at one of these Dublin offices because an Irish record company executive could be their introduction to the UK A&R department. CBS is the only record company which has a small (one man) A&R department. Despite this fact, however, some of the major labels in Ireland have reasonably healthy budgets which they can use to take a band a stage further than a 'raw' demo. They can then present them to the UK company, and if the Irish company has a positive attitude towards the band, the A&R department will listen.

CBS records

Unit 2, Carriglea Industrial Estate, Naas Road, Dublin 12.
Represents and sub-distributes Chrysalis (1 staff member), and RCA (BMG, Ariola, Arista – 3 staff members).
Tel: (0001) 553001.

WEA records

130 Slaney Road, Dublin Industrial Estate, Dublin 11.
Represents and sub-distributes Virgin (2 staff members). Also Telstar (1 staff member – TV LPs only).
Tel: (0001) 303700.

EMI Records

130 Slaney Road, Dublin Industrial Estate, Dublin 11.
Represents and sub-distributes Phonogram (8 staff members) and A&M (1 staff member).
Tel: (0001) 309077.

PUBLISHING

It is very unlikely that an Irish publishing company will be able to pay a sizeable advance. However, most major UK publishing companies have Irish agents and operate via the MCPS. Try calling the UK company and asking for the relevant contact company address.

STUDENT UNION GIGS

The National Union of Students in Ireland is known as the Union of Students of Ireland (USI). Although the NUS is a British organisation it is nonetheless known in Ireland as NUS(USI) – whether or not it is in Eire.

For general enquiries on student union venues in the North of Ireland contact: NUS(USI), 34 Botanic Avenue, Belfast BT7 1JQ. Tel: (0232) 244641.

For general enquiries on student union venues in the South of Ireland contact: Trinity College, Dublin. See below.

ATHLONE REGIONAL TECHNICAL COLLEGE (RTC)
Student Union, Athlone.
Capacity: two venues – 400 and 500.
Tel: (010353) 902 74517.

CARLOW REGIONAL TECHNICAL COLLEGE (RTC)
Student Union, Kilkenny Road, Carlow.
Capacity: 200.
Tel: (010353) 503 31324 ext. 207.

CORK REGIONAL TECHNICAL COLLEGE (RTC)
Student Union, Bishopstown, Cork.
Capacity: two venues – 4000 and 500.
Tel: (010353) 21 46106.

DUBLIN INSTITUTE OF TECHNOLOGY
Kevin Street, Dublin 1.
5 campus venues of approximately 500 capacity each.
Tel: (0001) 783154.

DUNDALK REGIONAL TECHNICAL COLLEGE (RTC)
Student Union, Dundalk.
Capacity: 400.
Tel: (010353) 42 34880.

GALWAY REGIONAL TECHNICAL COLLEGE (RTC)
Student Union, Dublin Road, Galway.
Capacity: 400.
Tel: (010353) 91 53161.

LETTERKENNY REGIONAL TECHNICAL COLLEGE (RTC)
Student Union, Letterkenny.
Capacity: 400.
Tel: (010353) 74 21928.

NATIONAL COLLEGE OF ART AND DESIGN (NCAD)
Thomas Street, Dublin 8.
Capacity 100.
Tel: (0001) 711553.

NATIONAL INSTITUTE OF HIGHER EDUCATION (NIHE)
Collins Avenue Extension, Dublin 9.
Capacity: two venues – 180 and 700.
Tel: (0001) 370077 ext. 392.

NATIONAL INSTITUTE OF HIGHER EDUCATION, LIMERICK
Student Union, Castletroy, Limmerick.
Capacity: 4 venues – 1,000, 700, 300 and 180.
Tel: (010353) 61 333644 ext. 2324.

QUEENS UNIVERSITY, BELFAST
Student Union, Belfast.
Capacity: 3 venues – 1,200, 700 and 500. Also book out large concerts in Mandela Hall, Belfast.
Tel: (010353) 84 324803.

ST PATRICK'S COLLEGE, MAYNOOTH
Student Union, Maynooth, Kildare.
Capacity: 650.
Tel: (0001) 286035 ext. 322.

ST PATRICK'S TEACHER TRAINING COLLEGE
Doun Conda, Dublin 9.
Capacity 800.
Tel: (0001) 376191.

SLIGO REGIONAL COLLEGE (RTC)
Student Union, Ballinode, Sligo.
Capacity: 400.
Tel: (010353) 71 63261

TRALEE REGIONAL TECHNICAL COLLEGE (RTC)
Student Union, Clash, Tralee.
Capacity: 400.
Tel: (010353) 66 22310.

TRINITY COLLEGE
Student Union, House 6, Mandela House, Dublin 2.
Capacity: 1,000. Plus six other, smaller potential venues.
Tel: (0001) 776545.

UNIVERSITY COLLEGE, CORK (UCC)
Student Union, College Road, Cork.
Capacity: 230.
Tel: (010353) 21 276871 ext. 2714.

UNIVERSITY COLLEGE DUBLIN (UCD)
Student Union, Belfield, Dublin 4.
Various venues.
Tel: (0001) 691897.

UNIVERSITY COLLEGE, GALWAY (UCG)
Students Union, Galway.
Tel: (010353) 91 24132.

UNIVERSITY OF ULSTER
Student Union, Jordanstown, Newtonabbey, Belfast BT37 0QB.
6 venues.
Tel: (0232) 365121.

WATERFORD REGIONAL TECHNICAL COLLEGE
Students Union, Cork Road, Waterford
Capacity: 400.
Tel: (010353) 51 75934.

The Pogues at the Town & Country Club on St Patrick's night 1988. The Pogues are the only band ever to sell out seven consecutive nights at the T&C – so far! Note the effective backdrop.

VENUES

BACKSTAGE BAR
35–37 East Essex Street, Dublin D2.
Capacity: 200 +
Tel: (0001) 792992.

BAGGOT INN
143 Lower Baggot Street, Dublin D2.
Capacity: 430.
Tel: (0001) 761430.

CATHEDRAL CLUB
Christchurch Centre,
St Michael's Hill, Dublin D8.
Capacity: 600.
Tel: (0001) 795492.

COLNEY RESTAURANT
7 Johnson's Court, Dublin D2.
Capacity: 90.
Tel: (0001) 712276.

DUBLIN RESOURCE CENTRE
6 Crow Street, Dublin D2.
Capacity: 150.
Tel: (0001) 771974.

GAIETY THEATRE
South King Street, Dublin D2.
Capacity: 1,150.
Tel: (0001) 773614.

THE GRATTON
165 Caple Street, Dublin D1.
Capacity: 160.
Tel: (0001) 733049.

HAWKINS
Hawkin Street, Dublin D2.
Capacity: 1,000.
Tel: (0001) 893514.

THE INTERNATIONAL BAR
Wicklow Street, Dublin D2.
Capacity: 50.
Tel: (0001) 779250.

McGONNAGALES
South Anne Street, Dublin D2.
Capacity: 800.
Tel: (0001) 311822.

PROJECT ART CENTRE
39 East Essex Street, Dublin.
Capacity: 200.
Tel: (0001) 719321.

SIDES DANCE CLUB
26 Dame Lane, Dublin D2.
Capacity: 300.
Tel: (0001) 793822.

JJ SMYTH'S
Aungier Street, Dublin D2.
Capacity: 150.
Tel: (0001) 752565.

SPEAKEASY
Temple Lane, Dublin D2.
Capacity: 200.
Tel: (0001) 510825.

THE WATERFRONT
Sir John Rogerson's Quay, Dublin D2.
Capacity: 150.
Contact: Greg Mullen.
Tel: (0001) 605244.

NORTHERN IRELAND

LIMELIGHT CLUB
Ormeau Avenue, Belfast.
Tel: (0232) 248948.

NORTHERN BAR
100 Railway Street, Armagh.
Tel: (0861) 527315.

UNION HALL
42 Ship Quay, Derry.
Tel: (0504) 262890.

AGENTS

MCD – DENNIS DESMOND
Vartry Lodge, Strand Rond, Killiney, Co. Dublin.
Tel: (0001) 826399.

PETER AIKEN
1st. Floor, 49 Malone Road, Belfast BT9 6RY
Tel: (0232) 381047.

LOUIS WALSH
12 Pembroke Road, Dublin 4.
Tel: (0001) 789599.

PROMOTERS

AIKEN PROMOTIONS
1st. Floor, 4a Malone Road, BTG 6RY.
Tel: (0232) 381047.

MCD – DENNIS DESMOND
Vartry Lodge, Strand Rond, Killeney, Co Dublin.
Tel: (0001) 826399.

PAT EGAN SOUND LTD
Merchant's Court, 24 Merchant's Quay, Dublin 8.
Tel: (0001) 997700.

TV STATIONS

RTE I & RTE II
Donnybrook, Dublin 4.
Best Music programmes: 'Late Late Show' and 'Action Station Saturday'.
Tel: (0001) 693111.

UTV (BELFAST)
Havelock House, Ormeau Road, Belfast BT7 1EB.
Tel: (0232) 328122.
BBC (BELFAST)
Ormeau Avenue, Belfast BT2 8HQ.
Tel: (0232) 244400.

RADIO STATIONS

NATIONAL RADIO
RADIO II
Donnybrook, Dublin 4.
Tel: (0001) 693111.

CENTURY RADIO
Tel: (01) 786766
This will be Ireland's only National commercial radio station and has been set up, in part, by Oliver Barry the well known promoter.
　The pirate stations of Ireland were closed down by statute on

December 31st 1988 and it is planned to replace them with legalized commercial radio stations, although the current situation is somewhat confused!

Sunshine Radio, Q102, Kiss FM and Radio Dublin were most notable among the casualties of Government intervention. At time of going to press Sunshine Radio have just failed in a High Court case to preserve their right to broadcast, and Radio Dublin has announced its intention to go as far as the European Court of Human Rights – although it will be a European first if either station wins. The implications of victory are obviously frightening for the Dublin Government and would in theory affect the status of pirate radio stations throughout the EEC.

On a more realistic front there are radio stations at present which have been granted licenses and they are as follows.

DUBLIN

CAPITAL RADIO
Tel: (0001) 698555.
Ex General Manager of Q102, Martin Block, in conjunction with major Irish promoter Jim Aiken head up a large board of directors for this new Dublin station.

RADIO 2,000
Tel: (0001) 760126.
Another Dublin station whose main instigator is Dennis O'Brien.

RADIO TARA (AM only)
No details available at time of going to press.

NORTHERN IRELAND

DOWNTOWN RADIO
Tel: 0247 815555.

A useful publication containing many relevant addresses – the 'Hot Press Yearbook' is available from Glendenning House, 23 Wicklow Street, Dublin D2, Price IR£4.00.

DIRECTORY

In our efforts to provide the most up to date information available we have checked every name, address and telephone number listed – but we cannot take responsibility for any mistakes. If there are any inaccuracies or important omissions – please let us know and we will make corrections for the next edition.

INDEX

ACCOUNTANTS

STEPHEN ABERRY & CO.
56 WIGMORE STREET,
LONDON W1H 9DG.
TEL: 01-935 5133.

ADDIS & CO.
STROLL HOUSE,
681A WILMSLOW ROAD,
DIDSBURY,
MANCHESTER M20 0RB.
TEL: 061-434 8040. FAX: 061 434 4618.
(LONDON OFFICE) TEL: 01-359 1851.

ARTHUR ANDERSON
1 SURVEY STREET,
LONDON WC2R 2PS.
TEL: 01-036 1200. FAX: 01-031 1133.

CASSON BECKMAN
HOBSON HOUSE,
155 GOWER STREET,
LONDON WC1E 6BJ.
TEL: 01-387 2888. FAX: 01-388 0600.

COMINS & CO.
22 ST ANDREW STREET,
LONDON EC4A 3AN.
TEL: 01-353 5691. FAX: 01-583 1296.

DELOITTE HASKINS & SELLS
(MAIN OFFICES):
128 QUEEN VICTORIA STREET,
LONDON EC4P 4JX.
TEL: 01-248 3913. FAX: 01-248 3623.
ALSO AT:
P.O. BOX 198 HILLGATE HOUSE,
26 OLD BAILEY,
LONDON EC4M 7PL.
TEL: 01-248 3913. FAX: 01-236 2367.

GELFAND RENNERT & FELDMAN
82 BROOK STREET,
LONDON W1Y 1YG.
TEL: 01-629 7169.

MARTIN GREENE RAVDEN
55 LOUDOUN ROAD,
ST JOHN'S WOOD,
LONDON NW8 0DL.
TEL: 01-625 4545. FAX: 01-625 5265.

HARTLEY LAWRENCE MARKS & CO.
5 PORTMAN MEWS SOUTH,
LONDON W1H 9AU.
TEL: 01-408 1097.

GEORGE HAY & CO.
170 HIGH ROAD, EAST FINCHLEY,
LONDON N2 9AS.
TEL: 01-444 4136. FAX: 01-883 4248.

HILL VELLACOTT
21 NEW WALK, LEICESTER LE1 6TE.
TEL: 0533 543363. FAX: 0533 542814.

H. W. FISCHER & CO.
ACRE HOUSE, 69–76 LONG ACRE,
LONDON WC2E 9JW.
TEL: 01-379 3461.

IAN SKOLNICK & CO.
TRAFALGAR HOUSE,
GRENVILLE PLACE,
LONDON NW7 3SA.
TEL: 01-959 3611. FAX: 01-906 1700.

IAN SOPHER & CO.
STUDIO HOUSE,
ELSTREE STUDIOS,
SHENLEY ROAD, HERTS, WD6 1JG.
TEL: 01-207 0602.

KEITH EVANS & CO.
56 WIGMORE STREET,
LONDON W1H 9DG.
TEL: 01-935 5133.

LUBBOCK FINE
3–5 BEDFORD ROW,
LONDON WC1R 4DB.
TEL: 01-242 9881. FAX: 01-430 2626.

NEWMAN & CO.
12 THAYER STREET,
LONDON W1M 6AU.
TEL: 01-935 8323. FAX: 01-486 4915.

PEAT MARWICK MCLINTOCK
1 PUDDLE DOCK, BLACKFRIARS,
LONDON EC4V 3PD.
TEL: 01-236 8000. FAX: 01-248 6552.

QUINNEL & CO.
100 BAKER STREET,
LONDON W1M 2BA.
TEL: 01-935 8635. FAX: 01-486 0092.

GUY RIPPON & PARTNERS
17 ST PETERSBURGH MEWS,
LONDON W2 4JT.
TEL: 01-727 2692. FAX: 01-229 8563.

SIDNEY ARNOLD & CO.
FURNIVAL HOUSE,
14–18 HIGH HOLBORN
LONDON WC1V 6DB.
TEL: 01-242 7272. FAX: 01-404 5525.

SLOANE & CO.
112 A AND B WESTBOURNE GROVE,
LONDON W2 5RU.
TEL: 01-221 3292. FAX: 01-229 4810.

STAINTON & SHAFTO
21 WIGMORE STREET,
LONDON W1H 9LA.
TEL: 01-491 7355. FAX: 01-493 7177.

C. R. THOMAS & CO.
11 QUEENS ROAD, WIMBLEDON,
LONDON SW19 8NG.
TEL: 01-879 3404.

TOUCHE ROSS
(HEAD) OFFICE) HILL HOUSE,
1 LITTLE NEW STREET,
LONDON EC4A 3TA.
TEL: 01-936 3000. FAX: 01-583 8517.
ALSO AT: 33–34 CHANCERY LANE,
LONDON WC2A 1EW.
TEL: 01-405 8799. FAX: 01-831 2628.

AGENTS

If you would like more information about the bands on a particular agency's roster – ring and ask them to send you their latest 'representation list'. Unless otherwise indicated all the agencies below deal with a wide variety of contemporary music. Those agents marked with an * are currently the most actively involved in breaking new acts. Again, the most important companies are London Based. Local regional companies may be useful early on – but our advice is, don't sign anything, as only the big London agents can properly book and organize UK-wide and European tours.

THE AGENCY GROUP OF COMPANIES *
370 CITY ROAD,
LONDON EC1V 2QA.
TEL: 01-278 3331. FAX: 01-837 4672.

ALAN ROBINSON AGENCY DEPT. *
100–104 UPPER RICHMOND ROAD,
LONDON SW15 2SP.
TEL: 01-785 4511. FAX: 01-785 9816.

ALLIED AGENCY AND MANAGEMENT *
75 TOTTENHAM COURT ROAD,
LONDON W1P 9PA.
Roots, Folk, World & Indie music.
TEL: 01-636 1174. FAX: 01-436 3207.

ARTIST BOOKING SERVICES
363–365 HARROW ROAD,
LONDON W9 0NA.
Reggae – Rock.
TEL: 01-968 5354. FAX: 01-968 4897.

ASGARD *
125 PARKWAY, LONDON NW1 7PS.
No heavy metal.
TEL: 01-387 5090. FAX: 01-387 8740.

DEREK BLOCK ARTISTS AGENCY
ILFORD HOUSE,
133–135 OXFORD STREET,
LONDON W1R 1TD.
TEL: 01-434 2100. FAX: 01-434 0200.

BARRY COLLINGS ENTERPRISES
49 HIGH STREET,
SOUTHEND-ON-SEA ESSEX FF1 1HZ.
TEL: (0702) 343464/347343.

CAROUSEL ARTISTS AGENCY
AMBER HOUSE,
278 SEVEN SISTERS ROAD,
LONDON N4 2HY.
TEL: 01-272 9122.

CONCORDE ARTISTES *
1 BARB MEWS, BROOK GREEN,
LONDON W6 7PA.
TEL: 01-602 8822. FAX: 01-603 2352.

CROMWELL MANAGEMENT
THE COACH HOUSE,
9A THE BROADWAY, ST IVES,
CAMBRIDGE PE17 4BX.
Jazz, R&B & Folk. Will take on bands without deals.
TEL: (0480) 65695.

C & W ENTERTAINMENTS
9A HIGH STREET, NORMANBY,
CLEVELAND TS6 0NQ.
Any acts suitable for N. England clubland.
TEL: (0642) 455366/455072.

FAIR WARNING AGENCY *
40–42 NEWMAN STREET,
LONDON W1T 3PA.
Must have record deal.
TEL: 01-631 1844. FAX: 01-580 4088.

HENRY SELLERS AGENCY AND PROMOTIONS
P.O. BOX 626, LONDON NW8 0NJ.
USA bands only. 1950s–1960s music.
TEL: 01-586 7963.

INTERNATIONAL TALENT BOOKING (ITB) *
HAMMER HOUSE,
113–117 WARDOUR STREET,
LONDON W1V 3TD.
TEL: 01-439 8041. FAX: 01-434 2577.

JSE
9 ECCLESTON STREET,
BELGRAVIA, LONDON SW1W 9LX.
Variety of music including Irish, New Zealand bands and poets.
TEL: 01-730 9875. FAX: 01-730 2721.

JOHN STEDMAN PRODUCTIONS
112 SUNNY GARDENS ROAD,
LONDON NW4 1RY.
Blues, jazz. Mainly USA bands. Must be estab. with record deals.
TEL: 01-203 1324.

MALCOLM FELD AGENCY
MALINA HOUSE, CAMP ROAD,
GERRARDS'S CROSS,
BUCKS. SL9 7PS.
TEL: (0753) 889414.

THE MIRACLE AGENCY *
5th FLOOR, 5 DEAN STREET,
LONDON W1V 5RN.
Contemp, Gospel, Jumpin Jive, Indies, Rock.
TEL: 01-439 7081.

NOEL GAY ARTISTS
24 DENMARK STREET,
LONDON WC2H 8NJ.
TEL: 01-836 3941. FAX: 01-379 7027.

PERFORMANCE
1 ELIZABETH COURT,
210 SHEPHERDS BUSH ROAD,
LONDON W6 7NL.
TEL: 01-371 1322. FAX: 01-603 8663.

PRESTIGE TALENT *
BUGLE HOUSE, 21A NOEL STREET,
W1V 3PD.
TEL: 01-439 8907. FAX: 01-439 7649.

SERIOUS PRODUCTIONS
42 OLD COMPTON STREET,
LONDON W1V 5PB.
Jazz.
TEL: 01-437 4967.

SOLO *
55 FULHAM HIGH STREET,
LONDON SW6 3JJ.
Chart music. Must have a record deal.
TEL: 01-736 5925. FAX: 01-731 6921.

THE STATION AGENCY *
132 LIVERPOOL ROAD,
LONDON N1 1LA.
TEL: 01-607 9611/9577.
FAX: 01-700 4680.

TERRY KING ASSOCIATES
9–11 MONMOUTH STREET,
LONDON WC2H 9DA.
TEL: 01-836 4761.
FAX: 01-836 7311.

TONY LEWIS ENTERTAINMENTS
235–241 REGENT STREET,
LONDON W1R 8TL.
TEL: 01-734 2285.

VALUE ADDED TALENT *
1–2 PURLEY PLACE,
LONDON N1 1QA.
TEL: 01-704 9720. FAX: 01-226 6135.

**WASTED TALENT ARTISTES
AGENCY** *
321 FULHAM ROAD,
LONDON SW10 9QL.
TEL: 01-351 7421. FAX: 01-351 4769.

**ALAN WHITEHEAD AND
ASSOCIATES** *
2 GREAT MARLBOROUGH STREET,
LONDON W1.
TEL: 01-258 3405.
FAX: 01-0438 715247.

WORLD SERVICE AGENCY *
134 WIGMORE STREET,
LONDON W1H 9FF.
TEL: 01-486 7961. FAX: 01-487 2589.

BACKLINE EQUIPMENT

HIRE AND FACILITIES

Try out your local music shop. If they know and trust you, they might hire you some equipment. You should also check the classified pages in the Melody Maker. Otherwise, as far as we know, you will have to hire from one of the large London companies which have been established for years. They have their own vans and will supply you wherever you are. If you know different – that there is a great backline hire company in Llantwit Major, for example, please let us know!

JOHN HENRY ENTERPRISES
16–24 BREWERY ROAD,
LONDON N7 9NH
TEL: 01-609 9181/607 7315.

KEYBOARD HIRE LTD
UNIT 5,6 ERSKINE ROAD,
LONDON NW3 3AJ.
TEL: 01-586 8586

**LONDON SOUND HIRE (studio
equipment)**
32 LIDDELL ROAD,
LONDON NW6 2EW.
TEL: 01-372 6595.

MAURICE PLAQUET LTD.
69 JEDDO ROAD,
SHEPHERDS BUSH,
LONDON W12 9ED.
TEL: 01-749 3232.

THE MUSIC BANK (touring)
32 LIDDELL ROAD,
LONDON NW6 2EW.
TEL: 01-625 4438.

NOMIS COMPLEX
45–53 SINCLAIR ROAD,
LONDON W14 0NS.
TEL: 01-602 6351.

PETER WEBBER HIRE LTD
110 DISRAELI ROAD, PUTNEY,
LONDON SW15.
TEL: 01-870 1335

SENSIBLE MUSIC LTD.
UNIT 44,
ACORN PRODUCTION CENTRE,
105 BLUNDELL STREET,
LONDON N7 9BN.
TEL: 01-609 4118. FAX: 01-609 9478.

BOOKS

A USER'S GUIDE TO COPYRIGHT
(1989 edition to be published soon).
MICHAEL F. FLINT.
BUTTERWORTHS.

ARTS FESTIVALS IN BRITAIN AND IRELAND
ED. SHEENA BARBOUR.
RHINEGOLD PUBLISHING LTD,
241 SHAFTESBURY AVENUE,
LONDON WC2H 8EH.
Available from some bookshops and from the above address. Price £7.95 incl. p&p.
TEL: 01-240 5749.

BAND'S GUIDE TO THE MUSIC INDUSTRY (1984)
JOHN LEONARD AND DAVE SHANNON,
INTERNATIONAL MUSIC PUBLICATIONS.

BPI YEAR BOOK
BRITISH PHONOGRAPHIC INDUSTRY,
273–287 REGENT STREET,
LONDON W1R 8BN.
TEL: 01-629 8642.

BRITISH THEATRE DIRECTORY
RICHMOND HOUSE PUBLISHING CO LTD,
12–13 RICHMOND BUILDINGS,
DEAN STREET,
LONDON W1V 5AF.
TEL: 01-434 2100.

DIRECTORY OF ARTS CENTRES
Arts Council of GB in association with John Offord (Publications) Ltd. Will tell you of your nearest centre and its facilities. Available from the Information Dept. of the Arts Council. Free.
ARTS COUNCIL OF GREAT BRITAIN,
105 PICCADILLY,
LONDON W1B 0AU.
TEL: 01-629 9495.

EXPENSIVE HABITS:
The Dark Side of the Music Industry (1986)
SIMON GARFIELD
FABER & FABER

INTERNATIONAL MUSIC AND RECORDING INDUSTRY YEARBOOK
THE KEMPS GROUP,
TEL: 01-253 4761.

MAKING 4 TRACK MUSIC
Guide to fourtrack recording.
TRACK RECORD PUBLISHING LTD.,
20 BOWLING GREEN LANE,
LONDON EC1R 0BD.
TEL: 01-251 1900

MAKING MUSIC:
The Guide to writing, performing and recording, (1983)
ED, GEORGE MARTIN,
BARRIE AND JENKINS.

THE MAKING MUSIC HANDBOOK (1988)
Good lists of studios and venues by geographical area. Price £7.95 incl. p&p.
TRACK RECORD PUBLISHING LTD.,
20 BOWLING GREEN LANE,
LONDON EC1R 0BD.
TEL: 01-251 1900.

MUSIC COMPETITIONS AWARDS AND SCHOLARSHIPS,
(Applies mainly to classical musicians – but also includes awards for contemporary and jazz). Free.
ARTS COUNCIL OF GREAT BRITAIN,
105 PICCADILLY,
LONDON W1V 0AU.
TEL: 01-629 9495.

TAX AND FINANCIAL PLANNING FOR SPORTSMEN & ENTERTAINERS (1987)
RICHARD BALDWIN AND RICHARD HARVEY
BUTTERWORTHS & CO.

THE PLATINUM RAINBOW:
How to make it big in the music business, (1987)
BOB MONACO AND JAMES RIORDAN (USA),
OMNIBUS PRESS.

THE MUSIC WEEK DIRECTORY
Music business directory. Price £17.50 for '89 edition.
MUSIC WEEK PUBLICATIONS,
40 LONG ACRE,
LONDON WC2E 9J2.
TEL: 01-387 6611.

THE ROCK YEARBOOK
ED. AL CLARKE, VIRGIN BOOKS.

THE WHITE BOOK
Music business directory. Price £25.00.
BIRDHURST LTD.,
P.O. BOX 55, STAINES,
MIDDLESEX, TW18 4UG.
TEL: (0784) 64441.

THE CARTEL

For a brief explanation of the workings of the Cartel see the Guide
(Releasing your own record).
Key: Dist.   = Distribution
     Whole. = Wholesale

BACKS (East Anglia and East Midlands)
ST MARY'S WORKS,
ST MARY'S PLAIN, NORWICH,
NORFOLK NR3 3AF.
TEL: DIST: (0603) 624290. WHOLE:
(0603) 626221. FAX: 0603 619999.

FAST FORWARD (Scotland)
21A ALVA STREET,
EDINBURGH EH2 4PS.
TEL: DIST: 031-226 3129.
WHOLE: 031-226 4616.
FAX: 031-226 3133.

NINE MILE (Midlands, North Wales & North West)
6 NEW STREET,
WARWICK CV34 4RX.
TEL: DIST: (0926) 499899.
WHOLE: (0926) 496060.
FAX: 0926 497737.

PROBE PLUS (Record label, Distribution)
8–12 RAINFORD GARDENS,
LIVERPOOL 2,
TEL: DIST: 051-236 6591.

REVOLVER (South West & South Wales)
THE OLD MALT HOUSE,
LITTLE ANN STREET,
BRISTOL BS2 9EB.
TEL: DIST: (0272) 540004.
WHOLE: (0272) 541291.
FAX: 0272 540013.

ROUGH TRADE (South East)
61 COLLIER STREET,
LONDON N1 9BE.
TEL: DIST: 01-833 2133.
WHOLE: 01-837 4404.
FAX: 01-833 4624.

Specialist units within Rough Trade

DEMIX: Dance, Soul & Funk
61 COLLIER STREET,
LONDON N1 9BE.
TEL: 01-833 5635. FAX: 01-833 4624.

NEW ROUTES: Folk, Blues & Ethnic
61 COLLIER STREET,
LONDON N1 9BE.
TEL: 01-837 5536. FAX: 01-833 4624.

WORLD SERVICE: Rock, as well as across the board imports
61 COLLIER STREET,
LONDON N1 9BE.
TEL: 01-837 5653. FAX: 01-833 4624.

CATERING

EAT TO THE BEAT
43 BEACON WAY,
RICKMANSWORTH,
HERTS. WD3 2PB.
TEL: (0923) 777779. FAX: 0923 775729.

EAT YOUR HEART OUT
BASEMENT, 108A ELGIN AVENUE,
LONDON W9 2HD.
TEL: 01-289 9446.

ILLUSION
CWM NAN TRHYS, GWERNOGLE,
CARNARVON, DWFED SA32 75E.
TEL: (0267) 89364.

JUST DESERTS
44 MAIDSTONE ROAD, PEMBURY,
KENT TN2 4DE.
TEL. (089) 202 2499.
FAX: (089) 282 5223.

LIVINGSTONE DINING SERVICES
19 SAUNDERS LANE,
MAYFORD, WOKING,
SURREY GU22 0NN.
Mobile Eating Hall/Bus.
TEL: (0932) 563882.

OUT TO LUNCH
18 JUER STREET,
LONDON SW11 4RF.
TEL: 01-288 0414.

RHYTHM & FOOD
RHYTHM & FOOD,
23 CROSS PARK, BRIXHAM,
SOUTH DEVON TQ5 9LZ.
TEL: (08045) 51561.

GASTRONOME
11 HARVARD MANSIONS,
ST JOHNS HILL,
BATTERSEA, LONDON SW11.
TEL:01-941 5411.

SPECIAL FOOD SERVICES
274 QUEENSTOWN ROAD,
BATTERSEA, LONDON SW8.
TEL: 01-627 4001.

CUTTING AND PRESSING

Some of the studios below can provide a fully comprehensive record making service, but others are more specialised. Cutting studios that do not have their own pressing facilities will probably have a good working relationship with a pressing plant in the locality, and vice versa, so they will probably recommend each other. From your point of view, it can be helpful if the companies you use have worked together before and can communicate directly with each other.

Key: (C) = Cutting. (P) = Record Pressing. (C&P) = Both services are provided, although it may be that some of the work is sub-contracted.

ADRENALIN (P)
252–3 ARGYLL AVENUE TRADING ESTATE,
SLOUGH, BERKS. SL1 4HA.
TEL: (0753) 23200.

AUDIO 1 (C)
17 ST ANN'S COURT,
LONDON W1V 5YR.
TEL: 01-734 9901. FAX: 01-734 8833.

ABBEY ROAD STUDIOS (EMI) (C)
3 ABBEY ROAD, ST JOHNS WOOD,
LONDON NW8 9AY.
TEL: 01-286 1161. FAX: 01-289 752.

CAFE STUDIOS (C&P)
71–75 WHITELEY STREET,
MILNESBRIDGE,
HUDDERSFIELD HD3 4LT.
TEL: (0484) 640916.

CBS STUDIOS (C)
31–37 WHITFIELD STREET,
LONDON W1P 5RE.
TEL: 01-636 3434. FAX: 01-580 0543.

CBS RECORDS (P)
RABANS LANE, AYLESBURY,
BUCKS HP19 3BX.

CTS STUDIOS (C)
ENGINEERS WAY, WEMBLEY,
MIDDLESEX HA9 0DR.
TEL: 01-903 4611.

FORESIGHT RECORDS (C&P)
7–9 PAUL STREET,
LIVERPOOL, L3 6DX.
TEL: 051-236 3724.

THE MASTER ROOM CUTTING STUDIOS (C)
59 RIDING HOUSE STREET,
LONDON W1P 7PP.
TEL: 01-637 2223.

MAYKING RECORDS (C&P)
250 YORK ROAD,
LONDON SW11 3SJ.
TEL: 01-924 1661.

THE MUSIC ROOM (C&P)
79 MAYOR'S WALK,
PETERBOROUGH
TEL: (0733) 46901.

NIMBUS RECORDS LTD. (C)
MONMOUTH, GWENT NP5 5SR.
TEL: (0600) 890682.
FAX: 0600 890779.

PORKY'S MASTERING SERVICE (C)
55–59 SHAFTESBURY AVENUE,
LONDON W17 7AA.
TEL: 01-494 3131. FAX: 01-494 1669.

PRT STUDIOS (C)
A.C.C. HOUSE,
40 BRYANSTON STREET,
LONDON W1H 7AW.
TEL: 01-402 8114. FAX: 01-640 2586.

PR RECORDS (P)
HAMILTON HOUSE,
ENDEAVOUR WAY, WIMBLEDON,
LONDON SW19 8UH.
TEL: 01-946 8686.

SRT (C&P)
EDDISON ROAD, ST IVES,
NR HUNTINGDON,
CAMBRIDGESHIRE PE17 4LF.
TEL: (0480) 6188.
ALSO AT: 01-446 3218.

STATE TUNE LTD. (C&P)
GRANT ROAD, WELLINGBOROUGH,
NORTHANTS NN8 1EE.
TEL: (0993) 77442.

TAM STUDIOS (C&P)
13A HAMILTON WAY,
LONDON N3 1AN.
TEL: 01-346 0033. FAX: 01-346 0530.

TAPE ONE STUDIOS
20–30 WINDMILL STREET,
LONDON W1P 1HJ.
TEL: 01-580 0444/5/6.
FAX: 01-580 5455.

THE TOWNHOUSE STUDIOS (C)
150 GOLDHAWK ROAD,
LONDON W12 8HH.
TEL: 01-743 9313.
FAX: 01-740 1180.

UTOPIA RECORDING STUDIOS (C)
UTOPIA VILLAGE,
7 CHALCOT ROAD,
LONDON NW1 8LH.
TEL: 01-586 3434. FAX: 01-586 3438.

DISTRIBUTION COMPANIES

Distributors generally take between 25%–30% of the wholesale price before VAT – although this will depend on the deal you do with them. Get legal advice before you sign anything.

THE CARTEL – see The Cartel.

CHARLEY RECORDS LTD
156–166 ILDERTON ROAD,
SE15 1NT
R&B, Jazz, Blues, Soul, Psychedelic,
Country, Indies, Re-releases.
TEL: 01-639 8603. FAX: 01-639 2532.

Q AND M TAPE AND RECORDS WHOLESALE
308 HIGH STREET, STRATFORD,
LONDON E15 1AJ.
Black music. Indies.
TEL: 01-534 4882. FAX: 01-519 8128.

HR TAYLOR
139 BROMSGROVE STREET,
BIRMINGHAM B5 6RG.
Specialised wholesaler, M.O.R.,
Classical and Jazz. No Indies or Pop.
TEL: (021) 622 2377.

JET-STAR PHONOGRAPHICS LTD
78 CRAVEN PARK ROAD,
LONDON NW10 4AE.
Reggae, Soul, Calypso, Gospel, African,
Indies, Imports.
TEL: 01-961 5818. FAX: 01-965 7008.

JUNGLE RECORDS
24 GASKIN STREET,
LONDON N1 2RY.
All types music (but no Country or
Classical yet). No 7″ singles.
TEL: 01-359 8444. FAX: 01-226 3722.

PINNACLE RECORDS
UNIT 2,
ORPINGTON TRADING ESTATE,
SEVENOAKS WAY, ORPINGTON,
KENT BR5 3SR.
All types of music. Deal mainly with
labels. National.
TEL: (0689) 70622. FAX: 0689 78269.

PRIORITY RECORDS
57 RAMSAY ROAD,
LONDON W3 8AZ.
All types music.
TEL: 01-992 7021. FAX: 01-993 5106.

PRT DISTRIBUTION
105 BOND ROAD, MITCHAM,
SURREY CR4 3UT.
All types music.
TEL: 01-648 7000. FAX: 01-640 2586.

SOUTHERN DISTRIBUTORS
10 MYDDLETON ROAD,
LONDON N22 4NS.
All types music.
TEL: 01-889 6555. FAX: 01-889 6166.

SPARTAN RECORDS
LONDON ROAD, WEMBLEY,
MIDDLESEX HA9 7HQ.
All types music.
TEL: 01-903 4753. FAX: 01-903 7853.

STERNS AFRICAN RECORD CENTRE
116 WHITFIELD STREET,
LONDON W1P 5RW.
African, Salsa, West Indian, Indian
(Third World).
TEL: 01-387 5550.
FAX: 01-387 5324 STERNS.

ENVELOPES FOR RECORDS

WILTON OF LONDON
STANHOPE HOUSE,
4–8 HIGHGATE HIGH STREET,
LONDON N6 5JL.
Main UK supplier of protective
envelopes for records.
TEL: 01-341 7070.

FLIGHT CASES

ABS CASES
CROWS ROAD,
STRATFORD E15 3BX.
TEL: 01-474 0333.

BULLDOG CASES LTD
2–4 CANFIELD PLACE,
LONDON NW6 3BT.
TEL: 01-624 2134.

CP MEGA LTD. (CP Cases)
WORTON HALL INDUSTRIAL
ESTATE, WORTON ROAD,
ISLEWORTH,
MIDDLESEX TW7 6ER.
TEL: 01-568 1881.

CRIPPLECREEK CASE CO. LTD
DEVONSHIRE WORKS,
BARLEY MOW PASSAGE,
CHISWICK, LONDON W4 4PH.
TEL: 01-995 5348.

FRONTLINE CASES
563 HIGH ROAD, CHISWICK,
LONDON W4 3AY.
TEL: 01-994 2689.

PACKHORSE CASE COMPANY LTD
9 STAPLEDON ROAD, ORTON,
SOUTHGATE, PETERBOROUGH,
CAMBS PE2 0TB.
TEL: (0733) 232440.

INDUSTRY ORGANIZATIONS

AIRC (Association of Independent Radio Contractors Ltd.)
46 WESTBOURNE GROVE,
LONDON W2 5SH.
The AIRC is a voluntary, non profit-making organisation which represents radio contractors who have franchises awarded by the Independent Broadcasting Authority (IBA) to provide local community radio services in the UK.
TEL: 01-727 2624.

APRS (Association of Professional Recording Studios)
163A HIGH STREET,
RICKMANSWORTH,
HERTFORDSHIRE WD3 1AY.
Promotes and protects the interests of the professional sound recording industry – including recording studios, record producers, manufacturers and distributors who supply equipment and services.
TEL: (0923) 772907.

ASCAP (American Society of Composers, Authors and Publishers)
SUITE 9, 52 HAYMARKET,
LONDON SW1Y 4RP.
Performing right licensing organisation for the USA.
TEL: 01-930 1121.

BASCA (British Academy of Songwriters, Composers and Authors)
34 HANWAY STREET,
LONDON W1P 9DE.
Aims to assist both established and aspiring British songwriters with advice, guidance and encouragement. Hold regular 'Surgeries' for members which are attended by well-known songwriters who listen to and review tapes and answer questions on many aspects of the music business. BASCA also issues standard contracts between publisher and songwriter (25p each) and circulates BASCA News to members. Subscription costs £11.50 for 12 months.
TEL: 01-436 2261/2.

BFI (British Film Institute)
21 STEPHEN STREET,
LONDON W1P 1PL.
Information department dealing with general enquiries concerning film, TV and video open 10 a.m.–5 p.m. Monday to Friday. Membership on application, cost £15.75. Publish the BFI Film and TV Yearbook and Directions (see Books listing).
TEL: 01-255 1444.

BPI (British Phonographic Industry Ltd.)
ROXBURGHE HOUSE,
273–287 REGENT STREET,
LONSON W1R 7BP.
Industry organisation for record manufacturers and distributors which is funded mainly by members' subscriptions. Jointly funds and administrates the charts with the BBC and Music Week. the BPI Pop Awards are held once a year.
TEL: 01-629 8642.

CAMPAIGN FOR PRESS AND BROADCASTING FREEDOM
9 POLAND STREET,
LONDON W1V 3DG.
A broad-based membership organisation campaigning for more diverse, accessible and accountable media in Britain.
TEL: 01-437 2795.

COMMUNITY RADIO ASSOCIATION

SOUTH BANK HOUSE,
BACK PRINCE ROAD,
LONDON SE1 7SJ.
Advisory service for community radio stations (radio stations which have not been granted a license by the IBA). Produces a training bulletin and a bi-monthly newsletter called 'Airflash'.
TEL: 01-582 7972/01-735 8171.

COUNTRY MUSIC ASSOCIATION INC.

SUITE 3, 52 HAYMARKET,
LONDON SW1Y 4RP.
The professional trade organisation for the Country Music industry. Is the principal advocate for the growth and development of Country Music worldwide.
TEL: 01-930 2445.

FAA (Film Artistes' Association)

61 MARLOES ROAD,
LONDON W8 6LF.
The FAA represents 'extras, doubles, stand-ins and small parts'(!). Under an agreement with the BFTPA, any crowd scenes within 65 miles of Charing Cross Road must use FAA members.
TEL: 01-937 4567.

IBA (The Independent Broadcasting Authority)

70 BROMPTON ROAD,
LONDON SW3 1EY.
The IBA fulfils the wishes of Parliament in providing TV and radio services of information, education and entertainment additional to the BBC. Its four main functions are: a) to select and appoint the ITV and ILR companies, b) to supervise programming, c) to control the advertising and, d) to transmit the programmes.
TEL: 01-584 7011.

ISA (International Songwriters' Association)

22 SULLANE CRESCENT,
RAHEEN HEIGHTS,
LIMERICK, IRELAND.
Founded in 1967, the ISA represents songwriters in more than 40 countries and publishes 'Songwriter' magazine.
TEL: (010 353 61) 28837.

MCPS (Mechanical Copyright Protection Society Ltd.)

ELGAR HOUSE,
41 STREATHAM HIGH ROAD,
LONDON SW16 1ER.
A society of music copyright holders (music publishers, authors and composers) that collects the royalties due when their music is 'mechanically' recorded. (see Guide).
TEL: 01-769 4400.

MFVPA (Music Film and Video Producers' Association)

32 SEKFORDE STREET,
LONDON EC1R 0HH.
Represents the interests of rock promo production companies. It negotiates agreements with bodies such as the BPI and ACTT on behalf of its members. Membership is restricted to companies involved in the making of promos.
TEL: 01-439 0717.

MPA (Music Publishers' Association Ltd.)

7th FLOOR, KINGSWAY HOUSE,
103 KINGSWAY,
LONDON WC2B 6QX.
The only trade association in this country which represents music publishers. List of members available at £2.50.
TEL: 01-831 7591.

THE MUSIC RETAILERS ASSOCIATION

PO BOX 249,
LONDON W4 5EX.
Trade association for music retailers. List of members available free. Over 1,800 retail outlets listed according to geographical area and an indication given of the type of goods they sell.
TEL: 01-994 7592.

MUSICIANS BENEVOLENT FUND

16 OGLE STREET,
LONDON W1P 7LG.
Established to help professional musicians and their dependents when age, illness or accident deprive them of their means of livelihood.
TEL: 01-636 4481.

MUSICIAN'S UNION

60–62 CLAPHAM ROAD,
LONDON SW9 0JJ.
Represents the interests of musicians. (see Guide).
TEL: 01-582 5566.

NATIONAL DISCOGRAPHY LTD

ELGAR HOUSE,
41 STREATHAM HIGH ROAD,
LONDON SW16 1ER.
Music discography collecting and registering information on all music recordings.
TEL: 01-769 4400.

PPL (Phonographic Performance Ltd.)

GANTON HOUSE,
14–22 GANTON STREET,
LONDON W1V 1LB.
Formed by the British recording industry for the collection and distribution of revenue in respect of the UK public performance and broadcasting sound recordings. (see Guide).
TEL: 01-437 0311.

PRS (Performing Rights Society)

29–33 BERNERS STREET,
LONDON W1P 4AA.
The PRS is a non-profit making association of composers, authors and publishers of musical works. It collects and distributes royalties for the use, in public performances, broadcasts and cable programmes, of its members' copyright music and has links with other performing rights societies throughout the world. (see Guide).
TEL: 01-580 5544.

STATIONERS' HALL REGISTRY

AVE MARIA LANE,
LONDON EC4M 7DD.
Registration of lyrics and music for the purpose of establishing proof of their existence on a given date can be made

at Stationers' Hall Registry. A copy of the manuscript of the music and lyrics has to be filed at Stationers' Hall at the time of registration. Registration costs £23.00 (Incl. VAT) and a certified copy of entry (if required) costs a further £11.50. Registrations cannot be made in person: all communications must be made by telephone or writing. TEL: 01-248 2934.

USS (UNION OF SOUND SYNTHESISTS)
C/O THE SOUND HOUSE,
PO BOX 37B EAST MOLESEY,
SURREY KT8 9JB.
TEL: 01-979 9997.

WOMEN IN ENTERTAINMENT
7 THORPE CLOSE,
LADBROKE GROVE,
LONDON W10 5XL.
WIE is a national organisation whose members are committed to creating better opportunities for women in the arts. WIE acts as a support network and resource centre, produces an annual Directory of Women in the Arts, a bi-monthly newsletter and factsheets on womens' bands, cabaret acts and visual artists/designers. Also initiates regular workshops and meetings. TEL: 01-969 2292.

INFORMATION AND TRAVEL

CAPITAL HELPLINE
TEL: 01-388 7575.

NATIONAL ASSOCIATION OF CITIZENS ADVICE BUREAU
TEL: 01-833 2181.

CITY OF LONDON INFORMATION SERVICE
TEL: 01-606 3030.

LONDON TOURIST BOARD
TEL: 01-730 3488.

RESTAURANT SWITCHBOARD
Free information about eating out in London.
TEL: 01-888 8080.

MUSICAL

COMMUNITY MUSIC
INTERCHANGE STUDIOS,
15 WILKIN STREET,
LONDON NW5 3NG.
For administrative and general enquiries:
TEL: 01-485 8553.
For workshops and courses:
90 DE BEAUVOIR ROAD,
LONDON N1 4EN.
TEL: 01-241 2614.

CAPITAL CLASSIFIED
C/O CAPITAL HELPLINE,
Musicians' classifieds broadcast on the Alan Freeman Show, Capital Radio.
TEL: 01-388 7575.

LINKING MUSIC
Services for musicians.
TEL: 01-274 0883.

TRAVEL
AA
HEAD OFFICE. TEL: (0256) 20123.
5 STAR, TRAVEL DEPARTMENT,
MAIN OFFICE,
5 NEW COVENTRY STREET,
LONDON W1.
TEL: 01-891 9100.
INSURANCE: DIAL 100 FREEPHONE AA AUTOQUOTE.

BRITISH TRAVEL CENTRE
12 REGENT STREET,
PICCADILLY CIRCUS,
LONDON SW1.
Provide travel and accomodation information for the whole of Great Britain.
TEL: 01-730 3400.

CAR HIRE
AVIS. TEL: 01-848 8765.
(For UK tariff showing Avis locations in UK contact the Head Office, Marketing Department on the number shown – or your local outlet).
EUROPCAR/GODFREY DAVIS.
TEL: 01-950 4080.
HERTZ: TEL: 01-679 1777.
(The Worldwide Directory of Hertz outlets available free from the Head Office on application).

CARNET: THE EEC CARNET
Can be obtained free of charge from local Customs and Excise offices.

CARNET: THE ATA CARNET
Can be obtained from Chambers of Commerce at: Birmingham, Edinburgh, Glasgow, Leeds, Leicester, Liverpool, Manchester, Nottingham, Northern Ireland, SE Hants, Port of Portsmouth, and Southampton.

Also available from the Head Office in London:

CHAMBER OF COMMERCE AND INDUSTRY
69 CANNON STREET EC4.
TEL: 01-248 4444.

CARNET CONSULTANT
SHARON ASHLEY,
P.O. BOX 410,
LONDON SW17 0QU.
TEL: 01-767 0192.

EUROPEAN RAIL TRAVEL CENTRE
TEL: 01-834 2345.

LONDON TRANSPORT (24 hr)
Information on bus and Underground services in London.
TEL: 01-222 1234.

NATIONAL EXPRESS BUS COMPANY
HEAD OFFICE. TEL: 021-456 1122.

PASSPORTS
Passport application forms are obtainable from all main Post Offices.
PASSPORT OFFICE, LONDON:
CLIVE HOUSE,
70–78 PETTY FRANCE,
LONDON SW1.
(normal office hours: 9 a.m.–4.30 p.m)
TEL: PASSPORT ENQS. 01-279 3434.
RE-ENTRY VISA ENQS. 01-271 8560.

RAC
Continental Motoring Guide available from all RAC shops – price £1.95.
HEAD OFFICE. TEL: 01-452 8000.

SEALINK SERVICES
General Information Service.
TEL: (0233) 47047.

VAN HIRE
SMITHS SELF DRIVE:
9 SPITALFIELDS
(OFF NURSERY STREET),
SHEFFIELD S3.
TEL: (0742) 752222.
ALSO: AT: 31–37 TOWER ROAD
(OPPOSITE STRAWBERRY HILL ST).
TWICKENHAM, MIDDX.
TEL: 01-892 8866.

**BRITISH RAIL
CHARING CROSS**
SOUTHEAST. TEL: 01-928 5100.

EUSTON
NORTHWEST – MIDLANDS,
NORTH WALES,
WEST COAST TO SCOTLAND.
TEL: 01-387 7070.

KINGS CROSS
WEST YORKSHIRE, NORTHEAST,
EAST COAST TO SCOTLAND
TEL: 01-278 2477.

LIVERPOOL STREET
EAST ANGLIA, ESSEX, NORFOLK.
TEL: 01-928 5100.

PADDINGTON
SOUTHWEST – WEST MIDLANDS,
SOUTH WALES.
TEL: 01-262 6767.

ST. PANCRAS
MIDLANDS REGION.
TEL: 01-387 7070.

VICTORIA
SOUTHEAST, SOUTH.
TEL: 01-928 5100.

WATERLOO
SOUTHWEST AND SOUTHEAST.
TEL: 01-928 5100.

INSURANCE SERVICES

ARTHUR DODDSON (BROKERS LTD.)
219 SLADE LANE, LEVENHULME,
MANCHESTER M19 2EX.
TEL: 061-225 9060.

ELKAN & BARRY SIMONS LTD.
31 SHIREHALL PARK, HENDON,
LONDON NW4 2QN
TEL: 01-202 8443.

ENDSLEIGH INSURANCE SERVICES
ENDSLEIGH HOUSE,
AMBROSE STREET, CHELTENHAM,
GLOS. G50 3NR.
(Not professional – student personal property only.)
TEL: (0242) 36151.

GALAXY 7
1ST FLOOR, 21 MARKET PLACE,
ABBEY GATE, NUNEATON, WARKS.
CV11 5VII.
TEL: (0203) 326128.

HERBERT WATSON INSURANCE BROKERS LTD
IRONGATE HOUSE, DUKES PLACE,
BEVIS MARKS, LONDON EC3A 7JE.
TEL: 01-623 4811.

GORDON & CO.
45, LONDON FRUIT EXCHANGE,
BRUSHFIELD STREET,
LONDON E1 6AA.
TEL: 01-247 0841.

HAMILTON BARR INSURANCE BROKERS LTD.
96 GREAT GEORGE STREET,
GODALMING, SURREY GU7 1E.
TEL: (04868) 28111.

HOLYOAKE INSURANCE BROKERS LTD.
NEW CENTURY HOUSE,
MANCHESTER M60 4ES.
TEL: 061-834 6208.

JOHN KEEVIL & CO.
4A RUSSELL HILL ROAD, PURLEY,
SURREY CR2 2LA.
TEL: 01-668 1466.

ROBERTSON TAYLOR INSURANCE BROKERS LTD.
MILLARD HOUSE, CUTLER STREET,
LONDON E1 7DJ.
TEL: 01-283 3951.
Also at: 55 FULHAM STREET,
LONDON SW6.
TEL: 01-731 1454.

LABEL PRINTERS

AUDIOPRINT LTD.
3–4 WOLSELEY COURT,
WOBURN ROAD INDUSTRIAL
ESTATE,
BEDFORD MK42 7AY.
TEL: (0234) 857566.

CMCS
UNIT 1, KENNET ROAD,
OFF THAMES ROAD,
CRAYFORD, KENT DA1 4QN.
TEL: (0322) 59393. FAX: 0322 53741.

CRS (CASSETTE & RECORD SERVICES LTD.)
WOLSELEY ROAD,
WOBURN ROAD INDUSTRIAL
ESTATE,
KEMPSTON, BEDFORD MK42 7RA.
TEL: (0234) 56317. FAX: 0234 857456.

CHORD PRINT & DESIGN
UNIT 13, 25 COWLEAZE ROAD,
KINGSTON UPON THAMES KT2 6DZ.
TEL: 01-549 4807. FAX: 01 549 4807.

D & M PRINT LTD.
188 MANOR ROAD NORTH,
THAMES-DITTON,
SURREY KT7 0BQ.
TEL: 01-942 2496.

GREENAWAY HARRISON LTD.
PRINTING HOUSE LANE, HAYES,
MIDDLESEX UB3 1HQ.
TEL: 01-573 3828. FAX: 01 573 3467.

E HANNIBAL & CO.
PINFOLD ROAD, THURMASTON,
LEICESTER LE4 8AP.
TEL: (0533) 695413. FAX: 0533 601072.

PETER GRAY PRINTERS LTD.
WELLINGTON ROAD, BROMLEY,
KENT BR2 9NG.
TEL: 01-464 0828. FAX: 01 464 4759.

POTTS PRINTERS
WATERVILLE ROAD,
NORTH SHIELDS,
TYNE AND WEAR NE29 6UX.
TEL: 091-257 0817.

SHALFORD PRESS LTD.
85 B BRADFORD STREET,
BRAINTREE, ESSEX CM7 6AU.
TEL: (0376) 21125. FAX: 0376 24535.

TINSLEY ROBOR LABELS LTD.
31 REA STREET SOUTH,
BIRMINGHAM B5 6LB.
TEL: 021-622 6741. FAX: 021 622 1488.

LAWYERS

CAMPBELL HOOPER
35 OLD QUEEN STREET,
LONDON SW1H.
TEL: 01-222 9070. FAX: 01-222 5591.

CLINTONS
WELLINGTON HOUSE,
6–9 UPPER ST. MARTIN'S LANE,
LONDON WC2H 9DF.
TEL: 01-379 6080. FAX: 01-240 9310.

COMPTON CARR
6 DYERS BUILDINGS,
HOLBORN,
LONDON EC1N 2JT.
TEL: 01-831 6981. FAX: 01-831 2069.

DAVENPORT LYONS
KNIGHTWAY HOUSE,
20 SOHO SQUARE,
LONDON W1V 6QJ.
TEL: 01-474 2255. FAX: 01-437 8216.

DENTON HALL BURGIN & WARRENS
DENNING HOUSE,
CHANCERY LANE,
LONDON WC1.
TEL: 01-242 1212. FAX: 01-404 0087.

GENTLE JAYES
26 GROSVENOR STREET,
LONDON W1X 0BD.
TEL: 01-629 3304. FAX: 01-493 0246.

HARBOTTLE AND LEWIS
HANOVER HOUSE,
14 HANOVER SQUARE,
LONDON W1R 0BE.
TEL: 01-629 7633. FAX: 01-491 3799.

HART-JACKSON AND HALL
3A RIDLEY PLACE,
NEWCASTLE-UPON-TYNE NE1 8JQ.
TEL: (091) 232 1987. FAX: 091 232 0429

IAIN ADAM ESQ.
88 VICTORIA ROAD,
LONDON NW6.
TEL: 01-328 2540. FAX: 01-328 2540.

JEFFREY GREEN & RUSSELL
APPOLLO HOUSE,
56 NEW BOND STREET,
LONDON W1Y 9DG.
TEL: 01-499 7020. FAX 01-499 2449.

JOYNSON-HICKS
10 MALTRAVERS STREET,
LONDON WC2R 3BS.
TEL: 01-836 8456. FAX: 01-379 7196.

KANAAR HOLMES
126 WIGMORE STREET,
LONDON W1H 0JJ.
TEL: 01-486 9431. FAX: 01 935 8259.

JOHN KENNEDY & CO.
54A YORK STREET,
LONDON W1H 1FN.
TEL: 01-724 4707. FAX: 01-724 6641.

D. M. LANDSMAN & CO.
4 WIMPOLE STREET,
LONDON W1M 7AB.
TEL: 01-636 6602. FAX: 01-637 1992.

LEE AND THOMSON
GREEN GARDEN HOUSE,
ST. CHRISTOPHERS PLACE,
LONDON W1M 5HD.
TEL: 01-935 4665. FAX: 01 486 2301.

NICHOLAS MORRIS
81 PICCADILLY,
LONDON W1V 0JH.
TEL: 01-493 8811. FAX: 01-491 2094.

SIMON OLSWANG & CO.
1 GREAT CUMBERLAND PLACE,
LONDON W1H 7AL.
TEL: 01-723 9393. FAX: 01-723 6992.

RUSSELS
REGENCY HOUSE,
1–4 WARWICK STREET,
LONDON W1R 5WB.
TEL: 01-439 8692. FAX: 01-734 3648.

SEIFERT SEDLEY WILLIAMS
3 DYERS BUILDINGS, HOLBORN,
LONDON EC1N 2SL.
TEL: 01-831 3030. FAX: 01-831 7197.

SHERIDANS & CO.
14 RED LION SQUARE,
LONDON WC1R 4QL.
TEL: 01-404 0444. FAX: 01-831 1982.

THE SIMKINS PARTNERSHIP
45–51 WHITFIELD STREET,
LONDON W1P 5RJ.
TEL: 01-631 1050. FAX: 01 436 2744.

STEPHEN FISHER & CO.
25–27 OXFORD STREET,
LONDON W1R 1RF.
TEL: 01-437 8427. FAX: 01-434 1726.

WOOLF SEDDON
5 PORTMAN SQUARE,
LONDON W1H 9PS.
TEL. 01-486 9681. FAX. 01-935 5049.

WRIGHT WEBB SYRETT
10 SOHO SQUARE,
LONDON W1V 6EE.
TEL: 01-439 3111. FAX: 01-434 1520.

LIGHTING EQUIPMENT

A good source of information on cheap lighting companies is any small promoter in your area – especially the Social Secretary at the nearest college. Unless otherwise indicated the companies listed below will be able to supply a 38K rig at a budget price. You may find that the larger companies can be persuaded to supply small rigs if they think you are going to become successful.

A. C. LIGHTING LTD.
UNIT 4, SPEARMAST INDUSTRIAL PARK,
HIGH WYCOMBE, BUCKS, HP12 4JG.
(Main supplier of all lighting companies. Sales only).
TEL: (0494) 39076. FAX: (0494) 461024.

AVOLITES PRODUCTION CO. LTD.
184 PARK AVENUE,
LONDON NW10 7XL.
Manufacture and sale.
TEL: 01-965 8522. FAX: 01-965 0290.

MARTIN BRADLEY LIGHTING & SOUND
69A BROAD LANE, HAMPTON,
MIDDLESEX TW12 3AX.
Lights and PA.
TEL: 01-979 0672.

BRITANNIA ROW PRODUCTIONS LTD.
35 BRITANNIA ROW,
LONDON N1 8QH.
Follow spots and PA.
TEL: 01-359 0955. FAX: 01-359 1454.

CELCO LTD,
3 BELLINGHAM ROAD,
LONDON SE6 2PN.
Control Equipment only.
TEL: 01-698 1027. FAX: 01-461 2017.

CENTAUR LIGHTING
123 NELSON AVENUE,
LIVINGSTON, WEST LOTHIAN.
Hire and sale.
TEL: (0506) 34587.

CEREBRUM LIGHTING (SALES) LTD.
168 CHILDERN DRIVE,
SURBITON, SURREY KT5 8LS.
Sales only: mostly disco.
TEL: 01-390 4841/01-390 0051.
FAX: 01-390 4938.

CHAMELEON LIGHTING LTD.
53 NORTHFIELD ROAD,
LONDON W13 9SY.
Mainly big productions.
TEL: 01-579 7279. FAX: 01-840 6482.

ENTEC SOUND & LIGHT
SHEPPERTON STUDIO CENTRE,
STUDIOS ROAD, SHEPPERTON,
MIDDX. TW17 0QD.
Mainly big production. Lights and PA hire.
TEL: (0932) 566777. FAX: 0932 568989.
Warehouse TEL: (0784) 243755.

ESSENTIAL LIGHTING
UNIT 68, ABBEY BUSINESS CENTRE,
INGATE PLACE, LONDON SW8 3NS.
Mainly big productions.
TEL: 01-627 5782.

KEYLIGHT (UK) LTD.
No 4 HORATIUS WAY,
SILVERWING INDUSTRIAL PARK,
CROYDON, SURREY CR0 4RU.
Small to big productions.
TEL: 01-686 4542. FAX: 01-681 5146.

LIGHT & SOUND DESIGN LTD. (L.S.D.)
38–43 OXFORD STREET,
BIRMINGHAM B5 5LT.
Big productions only.
TEL: 021-632 5663. FAX: 021 631 2355.

MOONLIGHTING
37 EDMONSCOTE, ARGYLL ROAD,
EALING W13 0HQ.
Small to big productions.
TEL: 01-991 0934.

PLAYLIGHT HIRE LTD.
15 PARK STREET, SWINTON,
MANCHESTER M27 1UG.
Theatrical and general.
TEL: 061-793 5848. FAX: 061-794 5651.

POWERHOUSE HIRE
247 OAKLEIGH ROAD NORTH,
WHETSTONE, LONDON N20 0TX.
Lights and PA. Mainly big productions.
TEL: 01-361 1143.
FAX: 01-368 6229 (Powerhouse).

R.D.E. PRODUCTION SERVICES LTD.
8A LEATHERMARKET,
WESTON STREET,
LONDON SE1 3ER.
Big productions. Mainly conferences.
TEL: 01-403 1300. FAX: 01-403 0937.

SAMUELSON CONCERT PRODUCTIONS
112, CRICKLEWOOD LANE,
LONDON NW2 2DP.
Mainly big productions. Also now includes Zenith and Vari-lites.
TEL: 01-450 8955. FAX: 01-450 7921.

SEE FACTOR LIGHTING LTD.
74–75 COUNTY STREET,
LONDON SE1 4AD.
Branch of an American Co. aimed at USA acts.
TEL: 01-403 1466. FAX: 01-357 7859.

STAGE LIGHT DESIGN
36A DURHAM ROAD,
LONDON SW20 0TW.
Lighting and set design service. Small to big productions.
TEL: 01-879 3439.

SUPERMICK LIGHTS
119–121 FRESTON ROAD,
LONDON W11 4BD.
Mainly big productions, House lighting
company at the Town & Country Club.
TEL: 01-221 2322. FAX: 01 221 2722.

TASCO
138–140 NATHAN WAY,
LONDON SE28 0AU.
Small to big productions.
TEL: 01-311 8800. FAX: 01-311 5621.

**THEATRE SOUND & LIGHTING
(SERVICES) LTD.**
QUEENS THEATRE,
51 SHAFTESBURY AVENUE,
LONDON W1V 8BA.
Mainly theatrical
TEL: 01-439 2441. FAX: 01-836 7879.

MERCHANDISING COMPANIES

Key (manf.) = manufacturers. (Where a company doesn't manufacture their own products they buy in bulk and concentrate on printing only.) T = T-shirts; B = Badges; P = Posters.

ACME TOTAL MERCHANDISING
ACME HOUSE,
78 BUNTING ROAD,
NORTHAMPTON NN2 6EE.
TEL: (0604) 720805.
LONDON OFFICE:
122 WARDOUR STREET,
LONDON W1V 3LA.
TEL: 01-439 2472. (manf) T B & P etc.

**ADRIAN HOPKINS CONCERT
PROMOTIONS**
126 WIGMORE STREET,
LONDON W1.
TEL: 01-486 9691. (manf.) T B & P etc.
Mainly large bands.

ALEXCO
94 GUILDFORD ROAD,
CROYDON, SURREY CRO 2HJ.
TEL: 01-683 0546. (manf.) T B & P etc.

BADGEMAN LTD.
544 CHISWICK HIGH ROAD,
LONDON W4 5RG.
TEL: 01-994 0826, B.

BADGE SALES
83 BERWICK STREET,
LONDON W1V 3PJ.
TEL: 01-437 5121. B (100 min.)

BETTER BADGES
98 CALEDONIAN ROAD,
LONDON N1 9BT.
TEL: 01-837 0509. B.

B & M TOUR JACKETS
2 LIONEL STREET,
BIRMINGHAM B3 1AG.
TEL: 021-233 1573.
T & B plus Tour Jackets.

**BRAVADO MERCHANDISING
LTD.**
Deer Park Road,
LONDON SW19 3TN.
TEL: 01-540 8211.
(manf.) T, min order 1,000.

**THE CONCERT PUBLISHING
COMPANY**
166–198 LIVERPOOL ROAD,
LONDON N1 1LA.
TEL: 01-609 6131/4. (manf.) T B & P
etc.

CONCESSIONS
513 FULHAM ROAD,
LONDON SW6 1HH.
TEL: 01-381 4777. (manf.) T B & P etc.

CREATIVE PROMOTIONS LTD.
79 WEST REGENT STREET,
GLASGOW G2 2AW.
TEL: 041-332 7471. T B & P etc.

CULTURE SHOCK
UNIT 16,
WIMBLEDON STADIUM BUSINESS
CENTRE,
LONDON SW17 0BA.
TEL: 01-879 3949. T.

DE GRAFF
2 ST. MARK'S PLACE,
LONDON SW19 7ND.
TEL: 01-946 4444. B & P.

DIAL A STYLE
EMBLEM HOUSE,
HILDERS LANE,
EDENBRIDGE, KENT TN8 6JX.
TEL: (0732) 863574. (manf.) B & T.

ENGLISH TEES
94 GUILDFORD ROAD,
CROYDON, SURREY CR0 2HJ.
TEL: 01-683 0546. T B & P.

EVENT MERCHANDISING
199 QUEENS CRESCENT,
LONDON NW5 4DS.
TEL: 01-267 3171/485 3333.
T B & P etc.

FIFTH COLUMN
276 KENTISH TOWN ROAD,
LONDON NW5 2AA.
TEL: 01-267 0981. T & Sweatshirts etc.

FROG MERCHANDISING
FRONT UNIT, 2ND FLOOR,
87 GREAT EASTERN STREET,
LONDON EC2.
TEL: 01-739 1351. T B & P etc.

**THE GREAT BRITISH T-SHIRT
COMPANY**
40 CHELTENHAM PLACE,
BRIGTON BN1 4AB.
TEL: (0273) 609487.
(manf.) T & Sweatshirts.

ICM SWANSWING
64 CHALFRONT ROAD,
LIVERPOOL L18 9UR.
TEL: 051-427 6030. (manf.) T B & P etc.

London Office:
(Visions) ICM SWANSWING,
57 COLLEGE ROAD,
HARROW HA1 1BZ.
TEL: 01-863 8562.

MIRACLE WORKS
5 DEAN STREET,
LONDON W1.
TEL: 01-439 7081. T B & P etc.

**MOBILE MERCHANDISING
COMPANY**
12 OSSORY ROAD,
LONDON SE1 5AN.
TEL: 01-252 0806.

OFFBEAT
UNIT 19,
CAROL STREET WORKSHOPS,
43 CAROL STREET, NW1 0HT.
TEL: 01-482 3983. T B & P etc.

PROMOTION PROVIDERS
THE ROOFING CENTRE,
WORKS ROAD, LETCHWORTH,
HERTS, SG6.
TEL: (0462) 679408. T B & P etc.

RAZAMATAZ
THE WAREHOUSE,
4 DERBY STREET,
COLNE, LANCS.
TEL: (0282) 602101.
T & Sweatshirts & Patches.

RED MOON MERCHANDISING
1ST FLOOR, 21 BERWICK STREET,
LONDON W1.
TEL: 01-439 7420. T B & P etc.

STAGE 3 PROMOTIONS
WHEELWRIGHTS, HOOK NORTON,
BANBURY, OXON. OX15 5NT.
TEL: (0608) 737831. T B & P.

SUNRISE DESIGNS
UNIT 6, SILKSTONE ROAD,
LONDON W10.
TEL: 01-969 5200. T.

**WEST COUNTRY MARKETING &
ADVERTISING (WCM & A)**
13 TRIANGLE SOUTH,
CLIFTON, BRISTOL BS8 1EY.
TEL: (0272) 272757. T B & P etc.

WINTERLAND PRODUCTIONS,
37 SOHO SQUARE,
LONDON W1V 5DG.
TEL: 01-434 4503. Tour merchandising
for bands with record deals.

ZINCPARK,
KAYMAR INDUSTRIAL ESTATE,
TROUT STREET, PRESTON,
LANCS.
TEL: (0772) 562211. T B & P etc.

MOBILES

Prices quoted include the cost of engineers but exclude the cost of tape and VAT. Note that one reel of $1\frac{1}{2}$ in tape will cost £80–90 and you will need six to record $1\frac{1}{2}$ hours of music!

ADVISION LTD.
23 GOSFIELD STREET,
LONDON W1P 7HB.
£750 per day inc. 3 engineers.
TEL: 01-580 5707.

FLEETWOOD MOBILE
41 KINGSWOOD LANE,
WARLINGHAM, SURREY CR3 9AB.
£800 per day inc. 3 man crew.
TEL: 01-651 5108.

MANOR MOBILE
SHIPTON-ON-CHERWELL,
KIDLINGTON, OXFORD OX5 1JL.
£750 for 24 hour day inc. 2 engineers.
Extra charge outside London –
mileage/expenses.
TEL: (08675) 77551/200 1288.

RAK MOBILE
RAK STUDIOS,
42–48 CHARLBERT STREET,
LONDON NW8 7BU.
£750 per day inc. engineers. Extra
charge outside London –
mileages/expenses.
TEL: 01-352 0005/01-586 2012.

THE ZIPPER MOBILE
272 CRICKLEWOOD LANE,
CRICKLEWOOD,
LONDON NW2 2PU.
£450 per day inc. engineers. Mileage
charge if outside London – 35p per
mile.
TEL: 01-450 4130.

PA EQUIPMENT

Most of the PA companies listed below will supply touring PA rigs of 5K and upwards. They generally work the larger venues starting at big clubs and small dance halls and going up to concert halls and stadia. For the smaller, personally owned local PAs that you will need early on, look in the Melody Maker classified section or, better still, go on personal recommendations from other bands that you know.

ANDROMEDA SOUND SYSTEMS
46 DORGAN CRESCENT,
DUNCRUE ROAD,
BELFAST BT3 9JP.
TEL: (0232) 772491.

AUDIOLEASE
UNIT 8, FERRY LANE WHARF,
FERRY LANE,
LONDON N17 9NP.
TEL: 01-808 0920.

BRITANNIA ROW PRODUCTIONS LTD.
35 BRITANNIA ROW,
LONDON N1 8QH.
TEL: 01-359 0955. FAX: 01-359 1454.

CANEGREEN LTD.
UNIT 2, 12–48 NORTHUMBERLAND PARK,
LONDON N17 0TX.
TEL: 01-801 8133. FAX: 01-801 8139.

CONCERT SOUND LTD.
UNIT 4,
SHAKESPEARE INDUSTRIAL ESTATE,
SHAKESPEARE STREET,
WATFORD, HERTS.
TEL: (0923) 240854.

CONCERT SYSTEMS
37 CORKLAND ROAD,
CHORLTON,
MANCHESTER M21 2UX.
TEL: 061-860 7252/061-881 4505.

EFX AUDIO
UNIT 5,
LUTTON COURT BUSINESS CENTRE,
EDINBURGH EH8 9PD.
TEL: 031-667 6127.

ELECTROMUSIC
97 ST. JOHN STREET,
LONDON EC1M 4AB.
TEL: 01-253 9410/01-253 9079/01-253 1549.

ENTEC SOUND & LIGHT
SHEPPERTON STUDIO CENTRE,
STUDIO ROAD,
SHEPPERTON,
MIDDX. TW17 0QD.
TEL: (0932) 566777. FAX: 0932 568989.

E.S.E. AUDIO LTD.
7 MATILDA CLOSE,
GILLINGHAM BUSINESS PARK,
GILLINGHAM,
KENT ME8 0PY.
TEL: (0634) 375421.

HARDWARE HOUSE (SOUND LTD.)
WEST WORKS,
CHALGROVE ROAD,
MORNING LANE,
LONDON E9 6PB.
TEL: 01-986 6111.

HILL AUDIO LTD.
HOLLINGBOURNE HOUSE,
HOLLINGBOURNE,
MAIDSTONE, KENT ME17 1QJ.
TEL: (062) 780555. FAX: 062 780550.

JOHN HENRY ENTERPRISES
16–24 BREWERY ROAD,
LONDON N7 9NH.
TEL: 01-609 9181. FAX: 01-704 7040.

NOVA SOUND SERVICES
369 MIDDLEWICH ROAD,
RUDHEATH, NORWICH,
CHESHIRE CW9 7DX.
TEL: (0606) 49421.

THE PA COMPANY LTD
14–16 COWLEAZE ROAD,
KINGSTON-UPON-THAMES,
SURREY KT2 6DZ.
TEL: 01-549 4450/01-546 6640.

RAPER & WAYMAN LTD.
34 DANBURY STREET,
LONDON N1.
TEL: 01-359 9342. FAX: 01-354 4765.

SAMUELSON CONCERT PRODUCTIONS
112 CRICKLEWOOD LANE,
LONDON NW2 2DP.
TEL: 01-450 8955. FAX: 01-450 7921.

SKAN PA HIRE LTD.
8 HOLMWOOD AVENUE,
READING, BERKS. RG3 3PJ.
TEL: (0734) 575020.

SSE HIRE LTD.
UNIT 5, KENT HOUSE,
GOOCH STREET NORTH,
BIRMINGHAM B5 6QT.
TEL: (021) 622 4572.

STAR HIRE
UNIT 22,
ROMAN WAY INDUSTRIAL PARK,
GODMANCHESTER,
HUNTINGDON PE18 8LN.
TEL: (0480) 411159. FAX: 0480 55677.

TASCO AND TEXSERV LTD.
Both at: 138–140 NATHAN WAY.
LONDON SE28 0AU.
TEL: 01-311 8800. FAX: 01-311 5621.

TOUR TECH
75 KETTERING ROAD,
NORTHAMPTON,
NORTHANTS.
TEL: (0604) 28419.

THE TOWN & COUNTRY CLUB
Uses a 12K Court PA System
Run by Mick Anthony and supplied
through Raper & Wayman Ltd.
TEL: 01-388 4000.

WIGWAM ACOUSTICS LTD.
ST. ANNE'S HOUSE,
RYECROFT AVENUE,
HEYWOOD, LANCS. OL10 1QB.
TEL: (0706) 624547. FAX: 0706 65565.

WILLPOWER PA SYSTEMS
UNIT 4,
ACORN PRODUCTION CENTRE,
105 BLUNDELL ST.,
LONDON N7.
TEL: 01-609 9870/01-607 4343.
FAX: 01-609 9478.

PHOTOGRAPHERS

Most of the photographers who publish in the music press are freelance and you can usually contact them via the publications they work for. Obviously, the more well known they are – the more they are likely to charge you for posed shots. Keep an eye out for new 'names' whose work you like. The photographers listed below are the ones whose pictures illustrate this book.

ANNE COFFEY
TEL: 01-452 7529

FRANK DRAKE
TEL: (0272) 262557

CHRIS HUGHES
TEL: 01-589 3054

TIM JARVIS
TEL: 01-587 1360

ANGUS McCRAE
TEL: 0273 721103/01-704 9023

PENNY SMITH
TEL: 01-560 6206

DAVID WILLIS
TEL: (06284) 2181

PLUGGERS

We give an indication of the kind of services these record plugging and promotion companies offer – but the most effective way of finding out the level at which they work is to ask them about artists they are currently dealing with.

ANGLO IRISH
27 DAVENTRY STREET,
LONDON W1 6TD.
National TV and Radio. Usually only deal with bands via record companies.
TEL: 01-724 5962. FAX: 01-724 0772.

PAUL ANDREWS
Pirate radio stations and clubs – no Radio 1.
TEL: 01-221 4223.

APEERING
61–71 COLLIER STREET,
LONDON N1 9DC.
Independent promotion on local London radio and national TV, Ceefax, satellites. Deal direct with unsigned bands.
TEL: 01-833 2841. FAX: 01-833 4624.

GEOFF ATHERTON PROMOTIONS
19 ELMSTEAD CLOSE,
EWELL COURT,
SURREY KT19 0EA.
Mainly London based radio and TV. Country specialists.
TEL: 01-393 5425.

BEER DAVIES PUBLICITY
363–365 HARROW ROAD,
LONDON W9 3NA.
Mainly regional TV, radio, media tour promotion. All types of music, but via record companies only.
TEL: 01-969 7373. FAX: 01-968 4869.

BULLET
57 RAMSAY ROAD, ACTON,
LONDON W3 8AZ.
Radio & TV promotion services. Essentially a strike force with promotion back-up covering 650 national retail outlets. Mainly deal with record labels and management companies. Not appropriate for beginners.
TEL: 01-992 7725. FAX: 01-993 5106.

BULLET DISCO PROMOTION
6 TOMAY COTTAGES,
MAY STREET,
HERNE BAY, KENT CT6 6TH.
Disco and club promotion services for records, videos, films and other products. (No Radio 1 coverage).
TEL: (0227) 86604.

CHARTGOLD RECORD PROMOTIONS
PO BOX 195, LONDON N14 5DF.
Radio, club and shop promotions. Sales 'strike force', tele-sales and major distribution. (No Radio 1 coverage).
TEL: 01-368 2921.

GARY FARROW
SUITE 3,
15 CLANRICARDE GARDENS,
LONDON W2.
National TV and Radio. All types of music, but via record companies only.
TEL: 01-727 6251. FAX: Call phone number.

THE FERRET 'N' SPANNER PLUGGING CO.
UNIT 1B, 50 LISSON STREET,
LONDON NW1.
National radio and TV promotion. Mainly deal with record labels.
TEL: 01-402 2401. FAX: 01-723 0069.

FLEMMING AND SMALLMAN PARTNERS LTD.
24 BAKER STREET,
LONDON W1M 1DF.
Radio promotion: no commercial radio outside of London, National TV promotion.
TEL: 01-486 1651.

GARY GORDAN MUSIC ENTERPRISES
PO BOX 216, LONDON W4 3XA.
Personal club promotion, DJ mailout service including video clubs plus ILR promotion. Good for dance music and regional coverage, but not Radio 1 as yet.
TEL: 01-994 0955.

GUT REACTION
36 BOSTON PLACE,
LONDON NW1 6ER.
Promotes London area radio and major TV. All types music.
TEL: 01-706 2402. FAX: 01-706 0324.

THE IMPULSE PROMOTION COMPANY
10–12 CHAPLIN ROAD,
WILLESDEN, LONDON NW2 5PN
Regional Radio & TV & Clubs. Salesforce and Strikeforce.
TEL: 01-459 8866. FAX: 01-459 5711.

INTERNATIONAL RADIO PROMOTIONS
112 TALBOT ROAD,
LONDON W11 1JR.
London regional and European club and radio promotion. All types music.
TEL: 01-727 3458. FAX: 01-221 7240.

JUDD LANDER
C/O: LONDON RECORDS,
1 SUSSEX PLACE,
LONDON W6 9SG.
Independent operator with close links to London Records. National radio and TV. Handles anything he likes.
TEL: 01-748 9998.

HOWARD MARKS
70 GLOUCESTER PLACE,
LONDON W1H 4AJ.
National radio and TV. All types music except country and MOR.
TEL: 01-935 4965. FAX: 01-486 0942.

RON McCRAITHE
SHARP END, GRAFTON HOUSE,
2–3 GOLDEN SQUARE,
LONDON W1.
Very successful dance music plugger. Stock Aitken etc.
TEL: 01-439 8442. FAX: 01-439 1814.

TONY MICHAELIDES PROMOTIONS

48 PRINCESS STREET,
MANCHESTER.
Regional promotion Radio & TV of
'Acts' rather than just their records.
Very good regional coverage plus
national TV, but prefers to sign a
contract with an artist.
TEL: 061-228 1029. FAX: 061-228 6948.

MICHAEL PEYTON ASSOCIATES

STUDIO 5, BRIDGE STUDIOS,
318–326 WANDSWORTH BRIDGE,
LONDON SW6 2TZ.
Promotion of artists, records and videos
on national and regional radio and TV.
Especially MOR.
TEL: 01-731 1422. FAX: 01-371 0334.

PLATINUM PROMOTIONS

13 MANCHESTER MEWS,
LONDON W1M 5PJ.
Independent and major label record
sales and promotion company. Sales
'strike-force' only.
TEL: 01-486 4192.

S AND M SERVICES LTD.

APARTMENT 4,
46 INVERNESS TERRACE,
LONDON W2 3JN.
National radio & network TV for major
and indie labels and bands. All types
of music.
TEL: 01-229 2522/5428, 01-968 9956/7.

THE SUNSHINE PLUGGING COMPANY

3 MONMOUTH PLACE,
LONDON W2 5SA.
Promotion of records, bands and
videos. London based radio only and
national TV.
TEL: 01-229 8705/6.

STREETS AHEAD PROMOTIONS

8A GRANVILLE PARK,
LONDON SE13 7EA.
Nationwide to colleges and universities.
Mainly deals with record labels and
promoters. No Radio 1.
TEL: 01-852 8836.

10 TIMES BETTER

83 CLERKENWELL ROAD,
LONDON EC1 R5HP.
Promotes via national TV and regional
radio, Radio 1. Specialise in Indie, rock
bands. Deal direct with unsigned
bands.
TEL: 01-831 2868.

Reggae.
TEL: 01-387 5090. FAX: 01-387 2863.

BANDSTAND PROMOTIONS

HALESMERE HOUSE,
59 ISLINGTON PARK STREET,
LONDON N1 1QB.
Mainly V2, V3.
TEL: 01-354 3414. FAX: 01-704 0213.

BKD

UNIT 4, THE GLASSHOUSE,
49A GOLDHAWK ROAD,
LONDON W10 8QP.
V2. Mainly Soul.
TEL: 01-740 1535. FAX: 01-740 1148.

DEREK BLOCK CONCERT PROMOTIONS

2ND FLOOR, ILFORD HOUSE,
133–135 OXFORD STREET,
LONDON W1R 1TD.
A, V1, 2, 3. Rock and pop music –
increasingly promotes cabaret,
theatrical and sports events.
TEL: 01-434 2100. FAX: 01-434 0200.

MEL BUSH ORGANISATION LTD

5 STRATFIELD SAYE,
20–22 WELLINGTON ROAD,
BOURNEMOUTH BH8 8JN.
V2, 3. Established bands only.
TEL: (0202) 293093.

CAMBRIDGE FESTIVAL, CAMBRIDGE CITY COUNCIL

(AMENITIES AND RECREATION
DEPARTMENT),
MANDELA HOUSE,
REGENT STREET,
CAMBRIDGE CB2 1BY.
Promote at the Corn Exchange.
TEL: (0223) 358977.

CROSSING THE BORDER

ARTS THEATRE,
GREAT NEWPORT STREET,
LONDON WC2H 7JA.
V2, 3. Folk, Jazz and World Music.
TEL: 01-836 4119.

DNA

PO BOX HP2, LEEDS LS6 1LN.
V2, 3. Variety of music – mainly Rock,
Folk and Goth.
TEL: (0532) 310330. FAX: 0532 310229.

PROMOTERS

(For Arts Festivals see 'Arts Festivals in Britain and Ireland' published by Rhinegold Publishing Ltd which lists all relevant contact names and addresses. See Books.)

Key: A = Also booking agents
V1 = 4,000 plus capacity arenas
V2 = 1,000–4,000 capacity concert halls
V3 = 600–1,000 capacity clubs and dancehalls

ALEC LESLIE ENTERTAINMENT

134 LOTS ROAD,
LONDON SW10 0RJ.
V1, 2. Mainly chart acts.
TEL: 01-351 4333. FAX: 01-352 4652.

ALLIED AGENCY AND MANAGEMENT

76 TOTTENHAM COURT ROAD,
LONDON W1P 9PA.
A, V1, 2, 3. Mainly chart acts with
record company backing.
TEL: 01-636 1174. FAX: 01-436 3207.

ASGARD

125 PARKWAY, LONDON NW1 7PS.
A, V2, 3. A lot of R&B, New Country
and some Pop – no Heavy Metal or

DONNINGTON FESTIVAL
See MCP

THEOBALD DICKSON PRODUCTIONS
DOUGLAS HOUSE,
3 RICHMOND BUILDINGS,
LONDON W1V 5AE.
V1, 2. Mainly Jazz and Blues.
TEL: 01-439 6924. FAX: 01-734 2919.

GLASTONBURY FESTIVAL
WORTHY FARM,
PILTON, SHEPTON MALLET,
SOMERSET BA4 4BY.
Contact: Michael Eavis.
TEL: (0749) 89254/470. FAX: 0749 4997.

HARVEY GOLDSMITH ENTERTAINMENTS/ALLIED ENTERTAINMENTS GROUP PLC.
4TH FLOOR, AVON HOUSE,
360 OXFORD STREET,
LONDON W1N 9IIA.
V1, 2. Pop and Rock – mainly bands
with record company backing.
TEL: 01-409 1984. FAX: 01-493 4286.

ADRIAN HOPKINS PROMOTIONS
126 WIGMORE STREET,
LONDON W1H 9FE.
V1, 2, 3. Mainly M.O.R.
TEL: 01-486 9691. FAX: 01-935 8259.

INTERNATIONAL TALENT BOOKING
4TH FLOOR, HAMMER HOUSE,
113–117 WARDOUR STREET,
LONDON W1V 3TD.
A, V1, 2, 3. Wide variety of music –
mainly big chart acts.
TEL: 01-439 8041. 01-434 2577.

JLP
32 HOLMES ROAD, KENTISH TOWN,
LONDON NW5 3AB.
V1, 2, 3. Wide variety of music – from
Punk and Goth to chart hit and AOR
artists.
TEL: 01-482 4535. FAX: 01-284 0493.

KENNEDY STREET ENTERPRISES
KENNEDY HOUSE,
31 STAMFORD STREET,
ALTRINCHAM,
CHESHIRE WA14 1ES.

A, V1, 2. Top-of-the-league and chart
acts only.
TEL: 061-941 5151. FAX: 061-928 9491.

THE KRUGER ORGANISATION
PO BOX 130, HOVE,
EAST SUSSEX BN3 6QU.
V1, 2. Wide variety of music including
Country & Western.
TEL: (0273) 550088. FAX: 0273 540969.

MARQUEE THE CLUB LTD
105 CHARING CROSS ROAD,
LONDON WC2.
Just book Marquee. Variety of music.
TEL: 01-437 6601/2/3.
FAX: 01-434 1651.

MARSHALL ARTS
6 ERSKINE ROAD,
LONDON NW3 3HA.
V1, 2. Mainly chart acts, mostly soul.
TEL: 01-586 3831. FAX: 01-586 1422.

PHIL McINTYRE PROMOTIONS
15 RIVERSWAY,
NAVIGATION WAY,
PRESTON PR2 2YP.
V1, 2, 3. Wide range of music including
chart bands – as well as variety acts.
TEL: (0772) 720205. FAX: 0772 720238.
(London Office)
23 ARUNDEL SQUARE,
LONDON N7 8AS.
TEL: 01-609 4243. FAX: 01-609 4016.

MCP
JAMES HOUSE, NORTHGATE,
ALDRIDGE, WALSALL,
WEST MIDLANDS WS9 8TH.
V1, 2, 3. Wide variety of music –
specialize in Heavy Metal and
Australian bands as well as chart acts.
Also book and organize the annual
Donnington Festival.
TEL: (0922) 58355. FAX: 0922 743632.

METROPOLIS/SOUND ASYLUM
GROUND FLOOR,
603 HOLLOWAY ROAD,
LONDON N19.
V1, 2, 3. Specializes in Indie, Punk and
Goth – as well as chart acts.
TEL: 01-263 4564. FAX: 01-263 2434.

ANDREW MILLER PROMOTIONS
52 MUSARD ROAD,
LONDON W6 8NW.

V1, 2. Mainly big productions – chart
acts.
TEL: 01-381 3971/3972.
FAX: 01-381 6230.

READING FESTIVAL
24–28A HIGH STREET,
HARLESDEN, LONDON NW10.
TEL: 01-963 0797.

REGULAR MUSIC
25 GREENSIDE PLACE,
EDINBURGH EH1 3AA.
V1, 2, 3. All kinds of music. Promote
only within Scotland.
TEL: 031-557 5678. FAX: 031-557 6571.

SERIOUS PRODUCTIONS
42 OLD COMPTON STREET,
LONDON W1V 5PB.
V2, 3. Specialize in Jazz, Blues,
especially from USA.
TEL: 01-439 0807.

SOLO
55 FULHAM STREET,
LONDON SW6 3JJ.
A, V1, 2, 3. All kinds of music – recently
become involved again in working
bands from scratch.
TEL: 01-736 5925. FAX: 01-731 6921.

UNIVERSAL PROMOTIONS
1–2 MUNROE TERRACE,
LONDON SW10 0DL.
V1, 2, 3. Specialize in Punk, Reggae
and Hip hop – but promote all.
TEL: 01-351 3355.

WILF WALKER ENTERTAINMENTS
391 HARROW ROAD,
LONDON W9 3NA.
V2, 3. Wide variety of acts – particularly
Reggae, Jazz and World music.
TEL: 01-229 7483/960 8196.
FAX: 01-968 4897.

WOMAD
MILL LANE, BOX,
WILTSHIRE SN14 9PN.
Presents music and dance from all
corners of the globe together with top
Western artists and UK-based groups
in the UK and abroad – mainly
festivals.
TEL: (0225) 744044.
FAX: (0225) 743481.

PUBLICATIONS
PAPERS AND MAGAZINES
'What's on' magazines: student press:
Fanzines/Music papers from abroad.

ABSTRACT MAGAZINE/LP
32 ELM ROAD,
THORNTON HEATH,
SURREY, CR4 8RH.
TEL: 01-683 1826.

AUDIO VISUAL
PO BOX 109, MACLAREN HOUSE,
SCARBROOK ROAD,
CROYDON, SURREY CR9 1QH.
TEL: 01-688 7788.

THE BEAT
1 LOWER JAMES STREET,
LONDON W1.
TEL: 01-734 5149/8311.

BILLBOARD
71, BEAK STREET,
LONDON W1R 3LF.
TEL: 01-439 9411.

BLACK BEAT INTERNATIONAL
370 COLDHARBOUR LANE,
BRIXTON, LONDON SW9 8PL.
TEL: 01-737 7377.

BLITZ
40–42 NEWMAN STREET,
LONDON W1P 3PA.
TEL: 01-436 5211.

BLUES & RHYTHM
16 BANK STREET, CHEADLE,
CHESHIRE, SK8 2AZ.
TEL: 061-491 2256.

BLUES & SOUL
153 PRAED STREET,
LONDON W2.
TEL: 01-402 6869/6897.

BRIGHT LIGHTS BIG CITY
44 FAIRLIGHT ROAD,
LONDON SW17.
TEL: 01-672 7700.

BRITISH BLUES REVIEW
41 BRAMLEY ROAD,
LONDON W10.
TEL: 01-289 6394.

BRITISH MUSIC YEARBOOK
241 SHAFTESBURY AVENUE,
LONDON WC2H 8EH.
TEL: EDITORIAL 01-836 2385.
TEL: ADVERTISING 01-836 2534.

BROADCAST
100 AVENUE ROAD,
LONDON NW3 3TP.
TEL: 01-935 6611.

DRUMBEAT MUSIC NEWSPAPER
PO BOX, EDGBASTON,
BIRMINGHAM B16 8UT.
TEL: (021) 455 9659.

THE BUZZ
19 ALL SAINTS ROAD,
LONDON W11 1HE.
TEL: 01-727 9680.

'CAPITAL M'
60A LAWRENCE ROAD,
LONDON W5 4XH.
TEL: 01-560 1508.

THE CATALOGUE (THE CARTEL)
61 COLLIER STREET,
LONDON N1 9BE.
TEL: 01-833 2843.

CHARTMAIL
PO BOX 658, ACTON L13 9HS.
TEL: 01-993 7718/747 1986.

COMPACT DISC REVIEW
MEDIA HOUSE, BOXWELL ROAD,
BERKHAMSTED, HERTS HP4 3ET.
TEL: (04427) 76191/2.

COUNTRY MUSIC PEOPLE
225 LEWISHAM WAY,
LONDON SE14 1UY.
TEL: 01-692 1106.

COUNTRY MUSIC ROUND UP
286/287 HIGH STREET
(UPPER PRECINCT),
LINCOLN LN2 1AL.
TEL: 0522 41546.

CUT
1 ST. BERNARD'S ROW,
EDINBURGH EH4 1HW.
TEL: 031-343 6227.

DAILY EXPRESS
EXPRESS NEWSPAPERS,
121 FLEET STREET,
LONDON EC4P 4JT.
TEL: 01-353 8000.

DAILY MAIL
NORTHCLIFFE HOUSE,
NEW CARMELITE STREET,
LONDON EC4Y 0JA.
TEL: 01-353 6000.

DANCE MUSIC LTD.
SPRINGBRIDGE MEWS,
EALING, LONDON W5 2AB.
Also operators of Rumours Hip-Hop
fortnightly tip sheet.
TEL: 01-840 4800.

DISCO & CLUB TRADE INTERNATIONAL
410 ST. JOHN STREET,
LONDON EC1V 4NJ.
TEL: 01-278 3591/6.

DUE SOUTH MAGAZINE
37 MOUNT PLEASANT ROAD,
SOUTHAMPTON,
HAMPSHIRE SO2 0EG.
TEL: (0703) 332233.

ECHOES
ROCOCO HOUSE,
283 CITY ROAD,
LONDON EC1V 1LA.
TEL: 01-253 6663/4.

THE FACE
OLD LAUNDRY,
OSSINGTON BUILDINGS,
MAXON STREET,
LONDON W1.
TEL: 01-935 8252.

FOLK ROOTS
PO BOX 73,
FARNHAM, SURREY GU9 7UN.
TEL: (0252) 724638.

FOR THE RECORD
57–63 BROWNFIELD,
WELLING GARDEN CITY,
HERTFORDSHIRE AL7 1AN.
TEL: (0707) 333716.

THE GUARDIAN
119 FARRINGDON ROAD,
LONDON EC1R 3ER.
TEL: 01-278 2332.

GUITAR INTERNATIONAL
MUSICAL NEW SERVICES,
GUITAR MUSIC PUBLICATIONS,
MANOR ROAD,
MERE, DORSET.
TEL: (0747) 861033.

GUITARIST
ALEXANDER HOUSE,
1 MILTON ROAD,
CAMBRIDGE CB4 1UY.
TEL: (0223) 313722.

HI-FI ANSWERS
38–42 HAMPTON ROAD,
TEDDINGTON,
MIDDLESEX TW11 0JE.
TEL: 01-977 8787.

HI-FI CHOICE
14 RATHBONE PLACE,
LONDON W1P 1DE.
TEL: 01-436 0350.

HI-FI NEWS AND RECORD REVIEW
LINK HOUSE, DINGWALL AVENUE,
CROYDON, SURREY CR9 2TA.
TEL: 01-686 2599.

HI-FI & VIDEO TRADE DIRECTORY
CAUSTON HALL, CROSS ROAD,
CROYDON, SURREY.
TEL: 01-686 9026.

HOME AND STUDIO RECORDING
ALEXANDER HOUSE,
1, MILTON ROAD,
CAMBRIDGE CB4 1UY.
TEL: (0223) 313722.

HOME KEYBOARD REVIEW
ALEXANDER HOUSE,
1 MILTON ROAD,
CAMBRIDGE CB4 1UY.
TEL: (0223) 313722.

i-D MAGAZINE
27—29 MACKLIN STREET,
LONDON WC2B 5LX.
TEL: 01-430 0871.

THE INDEPENDENT
40 CITY ROAD, LONDON EC1Y 2DB.
TEL: 01-253 1222.

INTERNATIONAL MUSICIAN RECORDING WORLD
C/O THE NORTHERN AND SHELL BUILDING,
PO BOX 381, MILLHARBOUR,
LONDON E14 9TW.
TEL: 01 987 5090.

JAZZ JOURNAL INTERNATIONAL
35 GREAT RUSSELL STREET,
LONDON WC1B 3PP.
TEL: 01-580 6976/580 7244.

JOCKS MAGAZINE
SPOTLIGHT PUBLICATIONS,
GREATER LONDON HOUSE,
HAMPSTEAD ROAD,
LONDON NW1 7QZ.

JUKE BLUES
PO BOX 148, LONDON W9 1DY.
TEL: 01-286 2993.

JUST SEVENTEEN
EMAP, 52–55 CARNABY STREET.
LONDON W1V 1PF.
TEL: 01-437 8050.

KERRANG!
SPOTLIGHT PUBLICATIONS,
GREATER LONDON HOUSE,
HAMPSTEAD ROAD,
LONDON NW1 7QZ.
TEL: 01-387 6611.

KEYBOARD PLAYER
18 TILEYARD ROAD, YORK WAY,
LONDON N7 9AN.
TEL: 01-609 5781/2.

THE MAIL ON SUNDAY
NORTHCLIFFE HOUSE,
NEW CARMELITE STREET,
LONDON EC4Y 0JA.
TEL: 01-353 6000.

MAKING MUSIC
20 BOWLING GREEN LANE,
LONDON EC1R 0BD.
TEL: 01-251 1900.

MAXIMUM ROCK 'N' ROLL
PO BOX 59, LONDON N22 4NF.
TEL: 01-888 8949.

MELODY MAKER
IPC MAGAZINES,
HOLBORN PUBLISHING GROUP,
KING'S REACH TOWER,
STAMFORD STREET,
LONDON SE1 9LS.
TEL: 01-261 5000.

METAL HAMMER
59 QUEENS GARDEN,
LONDON W2 3HF.
TEL: 01-258 0206.

THE MIRROR
MIRROR GROUP NEWSPAPERS,
HOLBORN CIRCUS,
LONDON EC1P 1DQ.
TEL: 01-353 0246.

MIX MAG
PO BOX 89, SLOUGH,
BERKSHIRE SL1 8NA.
TEL: (06286) 67276.

MUSIC AND EQUIPMENT MART
CASTLE HOUSE,
97 HIGH STREET, COLCHESTER,
ESSEX CO1 1TH.
TEL: (0206) 860816.

MUSIC MASTER
JOHN HUMPHRIES (PUBLISHING),
DE CHAM AVENUE, HASTINGS,
EAST SUSSEX TN37 6HE.
TEL: (0424) 715181/424376/814286.

MUSIC TECHNOLOGY
ALEXANDER HOUSE,
1 MILTON ROAD,
CAMBRIDGE CB4 1UY.
TEL: (0223) 313722.

MUSIC WEEK
SPOTLIGHT PUBLICATIONS,
GREATER LONDON HOUSE,
HAMPSTEAD ROAD,
LONDON NE1 7QZ.
TEL: 01-387 6611.

THE MUSICAL TIMES
8 LOWER JAMES STREET,
LONDON W1R 4DN.
TEL: 01-734 8080.

NEW HI-FI SOUND
38–42 HAMPTON ROAD,
TEDDINGTON, MIDDLESEX.
TEL: 01-977 8787.

NEW MUSICAL EXPRESS
IPC MAGAZINES,
HOLBURN PUBLISHING GROUP,
KINGS REACH TOWER,
STAMFORD STREET,
LONDON SE1 9SL.
TEL: 01-261 5000.

NO. 1
IPC MAGAZINES,
HOLBURN PUBLISHING GROUP,
KINGS REACH TOWER,
STAMFORD STREET,
LONDON SE1 9SL.
TEL: 01-261 5000.

NOW DIG THIS
TREVOR CASIAO,
69 QUARRY LANE,
SOUTH SHIELDS, TYNE & WEAR,
NE34 7NW.
TEL: 091-262 4006.

THE OBSERVER
CHELSEA BRIDGE HOUSE,
QUEENSTOWN ROAD,
LONDON SW8 4NN.
TEL: 01-627 0700.

ONE TO ONE
LINK HOUSE, DINGWALL AVENUE,
CROYDON, CR9 2TA.
TEL: 01-686 2599.

PATCHES
D. C. THOMSON & CO,
2 ALBERT SQUARE,
DUNDEE DD1 9QJ.
TEL: (0382) 23131.

'Q'
42–48 GREAT PORTLAND STREET,
LONDON W1N 5AH.
TEL: 01-436 5432.

RADIO TIMES
35 MARYLEBONE HIGH STREET,
LONDON W1M 4AA.
TEL: 01-580 4468.

RECORD COLLECTOR
43–45 ST MARY'S ROAD,
EALING, LONDON W5 5RQ.
TEL: 01-579 1082.

**RECORD INFORMATION
SERVICES**
74 BROCKELY RISE,
LONDON SE23 1LN.
TEL: 01-676 0719.

RECORD MIRROR
SPOTLIGHT PUBLICATIONS,
GREATER LONDON HOUSE,
HAMPSTEAD ROAD,
LONDON NW1 7QZ.
TEL: 01-387 6611.

**THE RECORDER AND MUSIC
MAGAZINE**
9 KENTON CLOSE,
BEXHILL-ON-SEA,
EAST SUSSEX TN39 4HF.
TEL: (0424) 216900.

RHYTHM
ALEXANDER HOUSE,
1 MILTON ROAD,
CAMBRIDGE CB4 1UY.
TEL: (0223) 313722.

SMASH HITS
52–55 CARNABY STREET,
LONDON W1V 1PF.
TEL: 01-437 8050.

THE SONGWRITER
INTERNATIONAL SONGWRITERS'
ASSOCIATION LTD,
LIMERICK CITY, IRELAND.
TEL: (010 353) 61 28837.

**SONGWRITING AND COMPOSING
MAGAZINE**
12 TREWARTHA ROAD, PENZANCE,
CORNWALL TR20 9ST.
TEL: (0736) 762826.

SOUL UNDERGROUND
PO BOX 377, LONDON E7 9NV.
TEL: 01-690 3025.

SOULED OUT
PO BOX 65, LONDON.
TEL: 01-767 2189.

SOUNDS
PUNCH PUBLICATIONS LTD
LUDGATE HOUSE,
245 BLACKFRIARS ROAD,
LONDON SE1 9US.
TEL: 01-921 5900.

**THE STAGE AND TELEVISION
TODAY**
47 BERMONDSEY STREET,
LONDON SE1 3XT.
TEL: 01-403 1818.

STUDIO INTERNATIONAL
TOWER HOUSE,
SOUTHAMPTON STREET,
LONDON WC2E 7LS.
TEL: 01-379 6005.

STUDIO SOUND
LINK HOUSE, DINGWALL AVENUE,
CROYDON, SURREY, CR9 2TA.
TEL: 01-686 2599.

SUNDAY MIRROR
MIRROR GROUP NEWSPAPERS,
HOLBORN CIRCUS,
LONDON EC1.
TEL: 01-353 0246.

SUNDAY PEOPLE
MIRROR GROUP NEWSPAPERS,
HOLBORN CIRCUS,
LONDON EC1.
TEL: 01-353 0246.

THE SYNTHESIZER EXPERIENCE
INFORMATION PACKAGE,
THE SOUND HOUSE,
PO BOX 37B, EAST MOLESEY,
SURREY KT8 9JB.
TEL: 01-979 9997.

TODAY
70 VAUXHALL BRIDGE ROAD,
LONDON SW1V 2RP.
TEL: 01-630 1300.

TRACKS
5 PEMBERTON ROW,
LONDON EC4A 3BA.
TEL: 01-255 1476.

TV TIMES
247 TOTTENHAM COURT ROAD,
LONDON W1P 0AV.
TEL: 01-323 3222.

VARIETY
49 ST JAMES'S STREET,
LONDON SW1 A1JX.
TEL: 01-493 4561.

VIDEO WEEK
SPOTLIGHT PUBLICATIONS,
GREATER LONDON HOUSE,
HAMPSTEAD ROAD,
LONDON NW1 7QZ.
TEL: 01-387 6611.

WIRE
UNITS G & H,
115 CLEVELAND STREET,
LONDON W1P 5PN, ENGLAND.
TEL: 01-580 7522.

WHAT HI-FI?
38/42 HAMPTON ROAD,
TEDDINGTON, MIDDLESEX.
TEL: 01-977 8787.

WHERE TO ROCK 'N' ROLL
LONDON ROCK 'N' ROLL
APPRECIATION SOCIETY,
PO BOX 587,
LONDON N21 1LT.
TEL: 01-363 4758.

WHICH COMPACT DISC?
SPOTLIGHT PUBLICATIONS,
GREATER LONDON HOUSE,
HAMPSTEAD ROAD,
LONDON NW1 7QZ.
TEL: 01-387 6611.

'WHAT'S ON' MAGAZINES

The following publications have a significant readership and would be worth advertising in if you are doing a gig in the area. Most do a free listings service.

BIRMINGHAM: WHAT'S ON
212 BROAD STREET,
BIRMINGHAM, B15 1AY.
TEL: 021-643 8921.

BRISTOL: VENUE MAGAZINE
37–39 JAMAICA STREET,
STOKES CROFT,
BRISTOL BS2 8JP.
TEL: (0272) 428491

EDINBURGH/GLASGOW: THE LIST
Incorporates 'The Rock Report' once a year – a good source of information and advice on venues, studios, PA hire, etc., in the area.
14 HIGH STREET,
EDINBURGH EH1 1TE
TEL: 031 558 1191.

LONDON: CITY LIMITS
8–15 AYLESBURY STREET,
LONDON EC1 0LR.
TEL: 01-250 1299.

LONDON: TIME OUT
TOWER HOUSE,
SOUTHAMPTON STREET,
LONDON WC2E 7HD.
TEL: 01-515 0799/485 2555.

MANCHESTER: CITY LIFE
1–3 STEVENSON SQUARE,
MANCHESTER M1 1DN.
TEL: 061-236 2010.

MANCHESTER: WHAT'S ON IN MANCHESTER
21 ROEBUCK LANE, SALE,
CHESHIRE M33 1SY.
TEL: 061-973 4177.

MERSEYSIDE: LOOK ALIVE
PORT OF LIVERPOOL BUILDING,
LIVERPOOL L31 BZ.
TEL: 051-236 5757.

NORTH EAST: COMING NEXT
PRINCESS BUILDINGS,
QUEEN STREET, QUAYSIDE,
NEWCASTLE-UPON-TYNE NE1 3XL.
TEL. 091-232 5545.

STUDENT PRESS

All colleges, polytechnics and universities will have a student paper although the format and content will vary. Circulation will probably reflect the size of the institution and the larger and more active student unions are more likely to support a good music section featuring forthcoming gigs, interviews and reviews etc. If you are playing a student union or even a nearby venue, it is worth contacting the editor with your publicity details.

For further information ring the student union at the relevant college and simply ask to be put through to the editorial section of the student paper.

Two student union publications are distributed on a wider basis and may be worth contacting on a more regular basis:

LONDON STUDENT
UNIVERSITY OF LONDON UNION,
MALET STREET,
LONDON WC1E 7HY.
Distributed to all the NUS affiliated
London student unions.
TEL: 01-580 7369.

NSM (NATIONAL STUDENT MAGAZINE)
NELSON MANDELA HOUSE,
461 HOLLOWAY ROAD,
LONDON N7 6LJ.
Distributed to all the NUS affiliated
student unions in the UK.
TEL: 01-272 8900 (Editorial).
TEL: (04574) 68003. (Advertising
department based in Glossop).

FANZINES/MUSIC PAPERS FROM ABROAD

Fanzines in the UK rarely sell enough copies to be worthwhile using for promotional purposes, so we have not listed them. There are, however, a number of fanzines/magazines published abroad which have a significant readership and welcome records sent for review by UK bands.

BELGIUM: MAD IN BELGIUM
ATTN. ERIC DIDDEN,
JOSEF II STRAAT, 46–9000, GENT,
BELGIUM.

FRANCE: NEW WAVE
ATTN. ALINE RICHARD,
A.P.M.C. NEW WAVE, BP6,
75462 PARIS, FRANCE.

GREECE: SOUND AND HI-FI
ATTN. ANTHONY FRAGOS,
PO BOX 19041, 117 10 ATHENS,
GREECE.
(Anthony Fragos is also the producer
of a weekly national radio show).

HOLLAND: OOR/VINYL
OOR MAGAZINE, POSTBUS 15113,
1001 MC AMSTERDAM, HOLLAND.

ITALY: ROCKERILLA
ATTN. VITTORE BARONI,
VIA RAFFAELLI 2,
55042 FORTE DEI MARMI, ITALY.

SWEDEN: SLITZ
MATS LUNDGREN, BOX 4524,
S-102 65 STOCKHOLM, SWEDEN.

USA: CMJ
ATTN. SCOTT BYRON,
830 WILLIS AVENUE, ALBERTSON,
NY 11507, USA.

USA: FORCED EXPOSURE
ATTN. JIMMY JOHNSON,
PO BOX 1611, WALTHAM,
MA 02254, USA.

USA: OPTION MAGAZINE
ATTN. BILL CHEN,
2345 WESTWOOD BOULEVARD,
SUITE 2, LOS ANGELES, CA 90064.

WEST GERMANY: POP NOISE
Cabeza Cuadra
ATTN. PETER HARTINGER,
HOHE STRASSE, 4100 DUISBURG 1,
WEST GERMANY.

WEST GERMANY: RUN MR DIAMOND
ATTN. MARTIN ENGELHARDT,
RECKENSTRASSE 5, 5880,
LÜDENSCHEID, WEST GERMANY.

PUBLISHING COMPANIES

If you apply to the Music Publisher's Association (see Industry Organisations) they can send you a full list of all their current members for £2.00. This list contains not only the major publishing houses, but also many tiny one person outfits. We decided that there was no point in us reproducing that list here, so we have restricted ourselves to the half-dozen major companies who have the financial clout to pay advances. Beware of the small publishing houses in particular and, as usual, don't sign anything without legal advice.

Send your demos to a contact, where possible, within the Creative Department of the company. It is this department which deals with young bands and new signings. The Professional Department concentrates on song writers who are not necessarily performers and with back catalogue material.

BMG MUSIC
3 CAVENDISH SQUARE,
LONDON W1M 9HA.
Bands signed include the Mission and the Eurythmics.
TEL: 01-580 5566.

EMI MUSIC
127 CHARING CROSS ROAD,
LONDON WC2H 0EA.
Started out as the American arm of EMI and publishes bands like Queen, Kate Bush, Wedding Present and the Style Council. The EMI music catalogue includes Screengems which controls a lot of American material such as Belinda Carlisle.
TEL: 01-434 2131.

MCA MUSIC
139 PICCADILLY ROAD,
LONDON W1V 9FH.
Direct signings include Fairground Attraction and Skin Games as well as an extensive catalogue of Country artists and writers. MCA also own Leeds Music and Valley Music as well as publishing for Andrew Lloyd Webber's Really Useful Company.
TEL: 01-629 7211.

PEER SOUTHERN ORGANISATION
8 DENMARK STREET,
LONDON WC2H 8CT.
Largest privately owned publishing company in the world. Administrates the Buddy Holly catalogue for Paul McCartney.
TEL: 01-836 4524.

POLYGRAM MUSIC
PO BOX 1420, 1 SUSSEX PLACE,
LONDON W6 9XS.
Basically formed to control DJM Music which in turn control all Elton John's old material plus some of Supertramp's songs. They are also associated with Tony McCauley who was enormously successful as a songwriter in the 60s and 70s. Current signings include Blue Mercedes and Roachford.
TEL: 01-846 8515.

SBK MUSIC
3–5 RATHBONE PLACE,
LONDON W1P 1DA.
Large company which includes the highly successful ATV Music. Signings include Go West, A-Ha, and UB40.
(Used to be known as CBS Songs, soon to be bought by EMI).
TEL: 01-637 5831.

VIRGIN MUSIC
101–109 LADBROKE GROVE,
LONDON W11 1PG.
Virgin Music controls the successful 10 Music, whose signings include The Pet Shop Boys. Direct Virgin Music signings include Phil Collins, Brian Ferry and T'Pau.
TEL: 01-727 6660.

WARNERS/CHAPPELL
129 PARK STREET,
LONDON W1Y 3FA
Undeniably the biggest music publisher in Britain. Direct signings include Michael Jackson, Whitney Houston, Run DMC, The Hothouse Flowers and Prince. They also control the Magnet and Intersong catalogues as well and are a hugely successful company.
TEL: 01-629 7600.

RADIO
BBC NETWORK

HEADQUARTERS:
For Radio One, Two, Three and Four.
BROADCASTING HOUSE,
PORTLAND PLACE,
LONDON W1A 1AA.
TEL: 01-580 4468.

BBC SCOTLAND
QUEEN MARGARET DRIVE,
GLASGOW G12 8DG.
TEL: 041-330 2345.

BBC NORTHERN IRELAND
BROADCASTING HOUSE,
ORMEAU AVENUE,
BELFAST BT2 8HQ.
TEL: (0232) 244400.

BBC WALES
LLANTRISANT ROAD, LLANDAFF,
CARDIFF CFS 2YQ
TEL: (0222) 564888.

REGIONAL PRODUCTION CENTRES
(Some of which provide Network inserts)

BANGOR
BRYN MEIRION, BANGOR,
GWYNEDD, NORTH WALES.
TEL: (0248) 362214.

BIRMINGHAM
PEBBLE MILL ROAD,
BIRMINGHAM B5 7QQ.
TEL: 021-472 5353.

BRISTOL
BROADCASTING HOUSE,
WHITELADIES ROAD, CLIFTON,
BRISTOL BS8 2LR.
TEL: (0272) 732211.

EDINBURGH
5 QUEEN STREET, EDINBURGH,
SCOTLAND EH2 1JF.
TEL: 031-225 3131.

MANCHESTER
NEW BROADCASTING HOUSE,
PO BOX 27, OXFORD ROAD,
MANCHESTER M60 1SJ.
TEL: 061-236 8444.

BBC LOCAL RADIO
HEADQUARTERS
BROADCASTING HOUSE,
PORTLAND PLACE,
LONDON W1A 1AA.
TEL: 01-580 4468.

ABERDEEN
BEECHGROVE TERRACE,
ABERDEEN,
AB9 2ZT, SCOTLAND.
TEL: (0224) 635233.

BBC RADIO BEDFORDSHIRE
PO BOX 476, HASTINGS STREET,
LUTON, BEDS, LU1 5BA.
TEL: (0582) 459111.

BBC RADIO BRISTOL
3 TYNDALLS PARK ROAD,
BRISTOL BS8 1PP.
TEL: (0272) 741111/732211.

BBC RADIO CAMBRIDGESHIRE
BROADCASTING HOUSE,
HILLS ROAD,
CAMBRIDGE CB2 1LD.
TEL: (0223) 315970.

BBC RADIO CLEVELAND
PO BOX 1548,
BROADCASTING HOUSE,
NEWPORT ROAD,
MIDDLESBROUGH,
TS1 5DG.
TEL: (0642) 225211.

BBC RADIO CORNWALL
PHOENIX WHARF, TRURO,
CORNWALL TR1 1UA.
TEL: (0872) 75421.

BBC RADIO CUMBRIA
HILLTOP HEIGHTS, LONDON ROAD,
CARLISLE, CUMBRIA CA1 2NA.
TEL: (0228) 31661.

BBC RADIO DERBY
PO BOX 269, DERBY DE1 3HL.
TEL: (0332) 3611111.

BBC RADIO DEVON
PO BOX 100, ST DAVID'S HILL,
EXETER, DEVON EX4 4DB.
TEL: (0392) 215651.

BBC RADIO ESSEX
198 NEW LONDON ROAD,
CHELMSFORD,
ESSEX CM2 9AB.
TEL: (0245) 262393.

RADIO FOYLE
PO BOX 927, LONDONDERRY,
BT48 7NE.
TEL: (0504) 262244.

BBC RADIO GUERNSEY
COMMERCE HOUSE,
LES BANQUES,
ST PETER PORT, GUERNSEY,
CHANNEL ISLANDS.
TEL: (0481) 28977.

BBC RADIO HUMBERSIDE
63 JAMESON STREET,
HULL HU1 3NU.
TEL: (0482) 23232.

BBC RADIO JERSEY
BROADCASTING HOUSE,
ROUGE BOUILLON,
ST HELIER, JERSEY,
CHANNEL ISLANDS.
TEL: (0534) 70000.

BBC RADIO KENT
SUN PIER, CHATHAM,
KENT ME4 4EZ.
TEL: (0634) 830505.

BBC RADIO LANCASHIRE
KING STREET, BLACKBURN,
LANCASHIRE BB2 2EA.
TEL: (0254) 62411.

BBC RADIO LEEDS
BROADCASTING HOUSE,
WOODHOUSE LANE,
LEEDS LS2 9PN.
TEL: (0532) 442131.

BBC RADIO LEICESTER
EPIC HOUSE, CHARLES STREET,
LEICESTER LE1 3SH.
TEL: (0533) 27113.

BBC RADIO LINCOLNSHIRE
PO BOX 219, NEWPORT,
LINCOLN LN1 3XY.
TEL: (0522) 40011.

BBC RADIO LONDON
PO BOX 4LG, 35A
MARYLEBONE HIGH STREET,
LONDON W1A 4LG.
TEL: 01-486 7611.

BBC RADIO MANCHESTER
PO BOX 90,
NEW BROADCASTING HOUSE,
OXFORD ROAD,
MANCHESTER M60 1SJ.
TEL: 061-228 3434.

BBC RADIO MERSEYSIDE
55 PARADISE STREET,
LIVERPOOL L1 3RP.
TEL: 051-708 5500.

BBC RADIO NEWCASTLE
BROADCASTING CENTRE,
BARRACK ROAD, FENHAM,
NEWCASTLE-UPON-TYNE
NE99 1RN.
TEL: 091-2324141.

BBC RADIO NORFOLK
NORFOLK TOWER,
SURREY STREET,
NORWICH NR1 3PA.
TEL: (0603) 617411.

BBC RADIO NORTHAMPTON
PO BOX 1107,
NORTHAMPTON, NN1 2BE.
TEL: (0604) 239100.

BBC NORTHERN IRELAND
BROADCASTING HOUSE,
ORMEAU AVENUE,
BELFAST BT2 8HQ.
TEL: (0232) 44400.

BBC RADIO NOTTINGHAM
YORK HOUSE, MANSFIELD ROAD,
NOTTINGHAM NG1 3JB.
TEL: (0602) 415161.

BBC RADIO ORKNEY
COMMERCIAL UNION HOUSE,
CASTLE STREET,
KIRKWALL KW15 1DF.
TEL: (0856) 3939.

BBC RADIO OXFORD
242–254 BANBURY ROAD,
OXFORD OX2 7DW.
TEL: (0865) 53411.

BBC RADIO SCOTLAND
5 QUEEN STREET,
EDINBURGH EH2 1JF.
TEL: 031-225 3131.

BBC RADIO SHEFFIELD
ASHDELL GROVE,
60 WESTBOURNE ROAD,
SHEFFIELD S10 2QU.
TEL: (0742) 686185.

BBC RADIO SHETLAND
BRENTHAM HOUSE,
HARBOUR STREET,
LERWICK, SHETLAND ZE1 0LR
TEL: (0595) 4747.

BBC RADIO SHROPSHIRE
2–4 BOSCOBEL DRIVE,
SHREWSBURY SY1 3TT.
TEL: (0743) 248484.

BBC RADIO SOLENT
SOUTH WESTERN HOUSE,
CANUTE ROAD,
SOUTHAMPTON SO9 4PJ.
TEL: (0703) 631311.

RADIO SOLWAY
ELM BANK, LOVER'S WALK,
DUMFRIES DG1 1NZ.
TEL: (0387) 68008.

BBC RADIO STOKE-ON-TRENT
CONWAY HOUSE, CHEAPSIDE,
HANLEY, STOKE-ON-TRENT,
STAFFORDSHIRE ST1 1JJ.
TEL: (0782) 208080.

BBC RADIO SUSSEX
MARLBOROUGH PLACE,
BRIGHTON,
EAST SUSSEX BN1 1TU.
TEL: (0273) 680231.

BBC RADIO TWEED
MUNICIPAL BUILDINGS,
HIGH STREET,
SELKIRK TD7 4BU.
TEL: (0750) 21884.

**BBC RADIO WM
(WEST MIDLANDS)**
PO BOX 206, PEBBLE MILL ROAD,
BIRMINGHAM B5 7SD.
TEL: 021-472 5141.

BBC RADIO WALES
BROADCASTING HOUSE,
LLANDAFF,
CARDIFF CF5 2YQ.
TEL: (0222) 564888.

BBC WORLD SERVICE
BUSH HOUSE, LONDON WC2.
TEL: 01-240 3456.
(Popular Music Unit, direct lines:
01-257 2828/2607).

BBC RADIO YORK
20 BOOTHAM ROW, YORK YO3 7BR.
TEL: (0904) 641351.

RADIO – MISCELLANEOUS

**ASSOCIATION OF INDEPENDENT
RADIO CONTRACTORS**
REGINA HOUSE,
259–269 OLD MARYLEBONE ROAD,
LONDON NW1 5RA.
TEL: 01-262 6681.

**BMS
(Broadcast Marketing Services)**
MACINTOSH HOUSE, 4th FLOOR,
SUITE 1, SHAMBLES SQUARE,
MARKET PLACE,
MANCHESTER M4 3AS.
TEL: 061-834 6734.

**INDEPENDENT BROADCASTING
AUTHORITY**
70 BROMPTON ROAD,
LONDON SW3 1EY.
TEL: 01-584 7011.

INDEPENDENT RADIO SALES (IRS)
86–88 EDGWARE ROAD,
LONDON W2 2EA.
TEL: 01-258 0408.

RADIO MARKETING BUREAU
REGINA HOUSE,
259–269 OLD MARYLEBONE ROAD,
LONDON NW1 5RA.
TEL: 01-258 3705.

INDEPENDENT LOCAL RADIO

Headquarters for information on new stations or alterations to addresses and telephone numbers is the I.B.A., 70 Brompton Road, London, SW3 1EY. TEL: 01-584 7011.

RADIO AIRE (Leeds)
PO BOX 362, 51 BURLEY ROAD,
LEEDS LS3 1LR.
TEL: (0532) 452299.

BEACON RADIO (Wolverhampton & Black Country/Shrewsbury & Telford)
267 TETTENHALL ROAD,
WOLVERHAMPTON WV6 0DQ.
TEL: (0902) 757211.

BRMB RADIO (Birmingham)
RADIO HOUSE, PO BOX 555,
ASTON ROAD NORTH,
BIRMINGHAM B6 4BX.
TEL: 021-359 4481/9.

RADIO BROADLAND (Great Yarmouth & Norwich)
COLEGATE, NORWICH NR3 1DB.
TEL: (0603) 630621.

CAPITAL RADIO (LONDON – General & Entertainment)
EUSTON TOWER,
LONDON NW1 3DR.
TEL: 01-388 1288.

CHILTERN RADIO (Luton, Bedford, & Northampton)
CHILTERN ROAD, DUNSTABLE,
BEDFORDSHIRE LU6 1HQ.
TEL: (0582) 666001.
55 GOLDINGTON ROAD,
BEDFORD MK40 3LS.
TEL: (0234) 49266.
PO BOX 1557, ABINGTON STREET,
NORTHAMPTON NN1 2HW.
TEL: (0604) 29811.

RADIO CITY (Liverpool)
PO BOX 194,
LIVERPOOL L69 1LD.
TEL: 051-227 5100.

RADIO CLWYD
THE OLD SCHOOLHOUSE,
GLANRAFON ROAD, MOLD,
CLWYD CH7 1PA.
TEL: (0352) 59111.

RADIO CLYDE (Glasgow)
CLYDEBANK BUSINESS PARK,
CLYDEBANK,
GLASGOW G81 2RX.
TEL: 041-941 1111.

COUNTY SOUND RADIO (Guildford)
THE FRIARY, GUILDFORD,
SURREY, GU1 4YX.
TEL: (0483) 505566.

DEVONAIR RADIO (Exeter & Torbay)
35–37 ST DAVID'S HILL,
EXETER EX4 4DA.
TEL: (0392) 30703.

DOWNTOWN RADIO (Belfast, Londonderry, Enniskillen & Omagh).
PO BOX 96, NEWTOWNARDS,
CO. DOWN,
NORTHERN IRELAND BT23 4ES.
TEL: (0247) 815555.

ESSEX RADIO (Southend & Chelmsford)
RADIO HOUSE,
20 CLIFFTOWN ROAD,
SOUTHEND-ON-SEA,
ESSEX SS1 1SX.
TEL: (0702) 333711.

RADIO FORTH (Edinburgh)
FORTH HOUSE, FORTH STREET,
EDINBURGH EH1 3LF.
TEL: 031-556 9255.

RW RADIO (Bristol, Swindon, West Wiltshire)
PO BOX 2000, BRISTOL BS99 7SN.
TEL: (0272) 279900.
PO BOX 2000 SWINDON SN4 7EX.
TEL: (0793) 853222.

RADIO HALLAM (Sheffield & Rotherham, Barnsley, Doncaster)
PO BOX 194, HARTSHEAD,
SHEFFIELD S1 1GP.
TEL: (0742) 766766.

HEREWARD RADIO (Peterborough)
PO BOX 225,
QUEENSGATE CENTRE,
PETERBOROUGH PE1 1XJ.
TEL: (0733) 46225.

INVICTA RADIO (Maidstone & Medway, East Kent)
15 STATION ROAD EAST,
CANTERBURY, KENT CT1 2RB.
TEL: (0227) 67661.
37 EARL STREET,
MAIDSTONE ME14 1PS.
TEL: (0622) 679061.

LBC (London Broadcasting Company), (London – News & Information)
COMMUNICATIONS HOUSE,
GOUGH SQUARE,
LONDON EC4P 4LP.
TEL: 01-353 1010.

LEICESTER SOUND (Leicester)
GRANVILLE HOUSE,
GRANVILLE ROAD,
LEICESTER LE1 7RW.
TEL: (0533) 551616.

MARCHER SOUND (Wrexham & Deeside)
THE STUDIOS, MOLD ROAD,
GWERSYLLT, WREXHAM,
CLYWD LL11 4AF.
TEL: (0978) 752202.

MERCIA SOUND (Coventry)
HERTFORD PLACE,
COVENTRY CV1 3TT.
TEL: (0203) 28451.

RADIO MERCURY (Reigate & Crawley)
BROADFIELD HOUSE,
BRIGHTON ROAD, CRAWLEY,
SUSSEX RH11 9TT.
TEL: (0293) 519161.

METRO RADIO (Tyne & Wear)
RADIO HOUSE, LONG RIGG,
SWALWELL,
NEWCASTLE-UPON-TYNE
NE99 1BB.
TEL: 091-488 3131.

MORAY FIRTH RADIO (Inverness)
PO BOX 271,
SCORGUIE PLACE,
INVERNESS, IV3 6SF.
TEL: (0463) 224433.

NORTHANTS 96
71B ABINGTON STREET,
NORTHAMPTON, NN1 2HW.
TEL: (0604) 29811.

NORTHSOUND RADIO (Aberdeen)
45 KING'S GATE,
ABERDEEN AB2 6BL.
TEL: (0224) 632234.

OCEAN SOUND
(Portsmouth & Southampton)
PO BOX 99, FAREHAM,
HANTS PO15 5TA.
TEL: (0489) 589911.

RADIO ORWELL (Ipswich)
ELECTRIC HOUSE,
LLOYDS AVENUE,
IPSWICH IP1 3HZ.
TEL: (0473) 216971.

PENNINE RADIO
(Bradford, Huddersfield & Halifax).
P.O. BOX 235, PENNINE HOUSE,
FORSTER SQUARE,
BRADFORD BD1 5NP.
TEL: (0274) 731521.

PICCADILLY RADIO (Manchester)
127–131 THE PIAZZA,
PICCADILLY PLAZA,
MANCHESTER M1 4AW.
TEL: 061-236 9913.

PLYMOUTH SOUND (Plymouth)
EARLS ACRE, ALMA ROAD,
PLYMOUTH PL3 4HX.
TEL: (0752) 27272.

RED DRAGON RADIO
(Cardiff & Newport)
PO BOX 221, CARDIFF, CF1 5XJ.
TEL: (0222) 384041.

RED ROSE RADIO
(Preston & Blackpool)
PO BOX 301, ST PAUL'S SQUARE,
PRESTON, LANCS. PR1 1YE.
TEL: (0772) 556301.

SAXON RADIO
(Bury St Edmunds)
LONG BRACKLAND,
BURY ST EDMUNDS,
SUFFOLK IP33 1JY.
TEL: (0284) 701511.

SEVERN SOUND
(Gloucester & Cheltenham)
PO BOX 388,
67 SOUTHGATE STREET,
GLOUCESTER GL1 2DQ.
TEL: (0452) 423791.

SIGNAL RADIO (Stoke-on-Trent)
STOKE ROAD, STOKE-ON-TRENT,
STAFFS, ST4 2SR.
TEL: (0782) 747047.

SOUTHERN SOUND RADIO
(Brighton)
PO BOX 1323, RADIO HOUSE,
BRIGHTON, BN4 2SS.
TEL: (0273) 422288.

SWANSEA SOUND (Swansea)
VICTORIA ROAD, GOWERTON,
SWANSEA SA4 3AB.
TEL: (0792) 893751/6.

RADIO TAY (Dundee/Perth)
PO BOX 123, DUNDEE SS1 9UF.
TEL: (0382) 200800.

RADIO TEES (Teeside)
74 DOVECOT STREET,
STOCKTON ON TEES,
CLEVELAND TS18 1HB.
TEL: (0642) 615111.

RADIO TRENT
(Nottingham & Derby)
29–31 CASTLE GATE,
NOTTINGHAM NG1 7AP.
TEL: (0602) 581731.
MARKET PLACE, DERBY DE1 3AA.
TEL: (0332) 29245.

TWO COUNTIES RADIO 2CR
(Bournemouth)
5–7 SOUTHCOTE ROAD,
BOURNEMOUTH, BH1 3LR.
TEL: (0202) 294881.

RADIO 210
(Reading, Basingstoke & Andover)
PO BOX 210, READING,
BERKSHIRE RG3 5RZ.
TEL: (0734) 413131.

VIKING RADIO (Humberside)
COMMERCIAL ROAD, HULL,
NORTH HUMBERSIDE HU1 2SG.
TEL: (0482) 25141.

WEST SOUND (Ayr)
RADIO HOUSE,
54 HOLMSTON ROAD, AYR KA7 3BE.
TEL: (0292) 283662.

RADIO WYVERN
(Hereford/Worcester)
PO BOX 22,
5–6 BARBOURNE TERRACE,
WORCESTER WR1 3JS.
TEL: (0905) 612212.

RADIO – OTHERS

BRITISH FORCES
BROADCASTING SERVICE
(a division of the Services Sound &
Vision Corporation)
BRIDGE HOUSE,
NORTH WHARF ROAD,
LONDON W2 1LA.
TEL: 01-724 1234.

MANX RADIO
PO BOX 219, DOUGLAS,
ISLE OF MAN.
TEL: (0624) 73277.

NORMANDIE SOUND
PO BOX 509, ST HELIER,
JERSEY, CHANNEL ISLANDS.
TEL: (0534) 23322/44971.

RADIO LUXEMBOURG
38 HERTFORD STREET,
LONDON W1Y 8BA.
TEL: 01-493 5961.

RTE RADIO
RADIO CENTRE,
RADIO TELEFIS EIREANN,
DONNYBROOK, DUBLIN 4, EIRE.
TEL: (0001) 693111.

RECORD COMPANIES

Where a record company has its own publishing division we have listed it.

A&M RECORDS
136–144 NEW KING'S ROAD,
LONDON SW6 4LZ.
Contracted artists include: Bryan
Adams, Joan Armatrading, Captain
Sensible, Chris De Burgh, Joe Jackson,
The Police, Squeeze, Suzanne Vega,
Thrashing Doves, David & David, Janet
Jackson, Iggy Pop, Black.
Distribution: PolyGram. Publishing:
Rondor Music.
TEL: 01-736 3311. TELEX 916/342
ALMOSS G. FAX: 01-731 4606.

ABSTRACT SOUNDS
10 TIVERTON ROAD,
LONDON NW10 3HL.
Labels: Abstract Records, T.I.M.
Records. Contracted artists include: The
Three Johns, The Janitors. Distribution:
Abstract Records, Pinnacle. Publishing:
Abstract Sound.
TEL: 01-969 4018.

ANAGRAM RECORDS
(division of Cherry Red)
53 KENSINGTON GARDENS
SQUARE, LONDON W2 4BA.
Contracted artists include: Alien Sex
Fiend, Meteors. Distribution: Pinnacle.
Publishing: see Cherry Red.
TEL: 01-229 8854/5. TELEX: 943763
CROCOM G REF CHR.
FAX: 01-229 8753.

APT (formerly Red Rhino Records)
THE GRAIN STORE,
74 ELDON STREET, YORK, YO3 7NE.
Licensed or subsid, labels: Red Rhino
Europe, Technical Ediesta. Contracted
artists include: Red Lorry Yellow Lorry,
Hula, Front 242, Tony Kay. Distribution:
Self. Publishing: Screaming Red Music.
TEL: (0904) 611656. FAX: 0904 644190.

ARIOLA/ARISTA
(division of BMG Records)
3 CAVENDISH SQUARE,
LONDON W1M 9HA.
Contracted artists include: Hurrah!,
Whitney Houston, Scarlet Fantastic, Hall
and Oates, Bow Wow. Distribution:
RCA. Publishing: see BMG.
TEL: 01-580 5566. FAX: 01-631 5126.

AURA RECORDS
1 LIVERPOOL ROAD, EALING,
LONDON W5 5NZ.
Contracted artists include: RAF, Steve
Marriott, Freakshow, Barbarian Lovers.
Distribution: Pinnacle. Publishing: Aura
Music.
TEL: 01-579 4333. TELEX: 24224 Aura.
FAX: 01-831 9489.

BACKS RECORDING COMPANY
ST MARY'S WORKS,
ST MARY'S ROAD,
NORWICH NR3 3AF.
Labels: Derek Chapman. Contracted
artists include: Venus in Furs, Jack the
Bear, The Fruit Bats. Distribution:
Cartel. Publishing: Back's Music.
TEL: (0603) 626221. FAX: 0603 619999.

BEGGARS BANQUET RECORDS
17–19 ALMA ROAD,
LONDON SW18 1AA.
Licensed or subsidiary labels: Situation
2, Coda, 4AD. Contracted artists
include: The Cult, Icicle Works, The
Fall, Love and Rockets, Peter Murphy,
Gene Loves Jezebel, The Bolshoi, Adult
Net. Distribution: WEA.
TEL: 01-870 9912. TELEX: 915733.
FAX: 01-871 1766.

BLANCO Y NEGRO RECORDS
61 COLLIER STREET,
LONDON N1 9BE.
Contracted artists include: The Jesus &
Mary Chain, Everything But The Girl,
Dream Academy. Distribution: WEA
Records.
TEL: 01-837 6747.

BMG RECORDS (UK) LTD.
1 BEDFORD AVENUE,
LONDON WC1B 3DT.
Labels owned: RCA, RCA Victor, RCA
Victrola, RCA Camden, Jazz Tribune,
Bluebird, RCA Gold Seal, RCA
International, RCA Red Seal, UK-RCA.
Licensed labels: Arista, RCA, Motown,
Ariola, Telstar, Jive, Filmtrax, FM
Revolver, Champion, Priority.
Distribution: Self. Publishing: BMG
Music.
TEL: 01-636 8311. TELEX: 21349.
FAX: 01-631 1244/01-631 5089.

BROADSIDE
STUDLEY HOUSE, 68 LIMES ROAD,
TETTENHALL,
WOLVERHAMPTON WV6 8RB.
Licensed or subsidiary labels:
Beeswing, Jesters Court, Shooting Star.
Contracted artists include: John Raven,
The Furies. Distribution: H. R. Taylor,
Projection, Folk Roots, Celtic Music.
Publishing: Broadside.
TEL: (0902) 753047.

CARRERE RECORDS
PARK LORN, 111 PARK ROAD,
LONDON NW8 7JL.
Contracted artists include: Stephanie,
Rose Royce, Amanda Lear. Distribution:
PRT. Publishing: Carrere Music.
TEL: 01-262 1263. TELEX: 8953657.

CBS RECORDS
17–19 SOHO SQUARE,
LONDON W1V 6HE.
Labels owned: CBS, Epic, Portrait.
Labels licensed: Tabu, Portrait, Def
Jam. Contracted artists include: George
Michael, Michael Jackson, Bruce
Springsteen, Bangles, Bros., Prefab
Sprout, Luther Vandross. Distribution:
CBS. Publishing: CBS Music Publishing.
TEL: 01-734 8181. TELEX: 24203 CBS
REC G. FAX: 01-734 4321.

CELTIC MUSIC
2 HIGH STREET, STARBECK,
HARROGATE, NORTH YORKSHIRE.
Labels owned: Celtic Music, Dambuster,
Black Crow, Alba, Spindrift. Labels
licensed: Folk Freak, Larrakin, Stoney
Plain, Hagdown Music. Contracted
artists include: Freddy Alva Band,
Kipper Family, The Albion Band.
Distribution: Celtic Music, Kieran Haltin.
Publishing: Celtic.
TEL: (0423) 888979. TELEX: 57978 CM
Dist. FAX: 0423 885 761.

CHERRY RED RECORDS
3rd FLOOR, BISHOP'S PARK HOUSE,
25–29 FULHAM HIGH STREET,
LONDON SW6 3JH.
Licensed or subsidiary labels:
Africagram, Anagram, No Future, Time
Stood Still, Zebra, El Records, Mad Pig,
Latymer. Contracted artists include:
Alien Sex Fiend, Yeah Jazz, The
Meteors. Distribution: Pinnacle.
Publishing: Complete Music.
TEL: 01-371 5844. FAX: 01-384 1854.

CHINA RECORDS
27 QUEENSDALE PLACE,
LONDON W11 4SQ.
Contracted artists include: The
Fountainhead, the Art of Noise, The
Name, Labi Siffre. Distribution:
Chrysalis (PolyGram). Publishing:
Empire Music Ltd.
TEL: 01-602 5031. TELEX: 265871.
Attn. DGS1657.

CHRYSALIS RECORDS
12 STRATFORD PLACE,
LONDON W1N 9AF.
Licensed or subsidiary labels: China,
Cooltempo, Blue Guitars. Contracted
artists include: Go West!, Billy Idol,
Huey Lewis, Ice House, Debbie Harry,
Housemartins. Distribution: PolyGram.
Publishing: Chrysalis Music.
TEL: 01-408 2355. TELEX: 21753.
FAX: 01-409 0858.

CIRCA RECORDS
60–66 WARDOUR STREET,
LONDON W1V 3HP.
Contracted artists include: Hindsight,
Hue and Cry, Julia Fordham.
Distribution: Virgin/EMI. Publishing:
Circa Music Ltd.
TEL: 01-491 8527. TELEX: 21758.
FAX: 01-439 2028.

CLADDAGH RECORDS
DAME HOUSE, DAME STREET,
DUBLIN 2, IRELAND
Licensed or subsidiary labels:
Claddagh, Phaetain. Contracted artists
include: The Chieftains, Mat Molloy.
Distribution: Topic, Impetus (UK),
Claddagh (Ireland). Publishing:
Woodtown Music.
TEL: (0001) 793664.

COOKING VINYL
P.O. BOX 1741, LONDON W9 3LA.
Licensed or subsidiary labels: Sinn,
Forward Sounds International.
Contracted artists include: The Oyster
Band, Michelle Shocked, Clive Gregson
and Christine Collister, The Real
Sounds of Africa, (Licensed artists:
Davy Spillane, Sweet Honey In The
Rock, S E Rogie, The Mekons).
Distribution: Nine Mile/Cartel.
Publishing: Cooking Vinyl Music
Publishing.
TEL: 01-960 6000. FAX: 01-960 1120.

CRASHED RECORDS
130 SLANEY ROAD, DUBLIN
INDUSTRIAL ESTATE, FINGLAS,
DUBLIN 11.
Licensed or subsidiary labels: Plasmas,
Smashed. Contracted artists include:
Spyder Sympson, Barney O'Shamrock.
Distribution: EMI (Ireland)/Prism
Leisure (UK). Publishing: Crashed
Music.
TEL: (0001) 729714/474899/309077.
TELEX: 24535. FAX: via EMI.

CREATION RECORDS
83 CLERKENWELL ROAD,
LONDON EC1.
'Trusted' artists include: Biff Bang Pow!,
Blow Up, Felt, Jasmine Minks, Phil
Wilson, House of Love, Jazz Butcher,
Mamus, My Bloody Valentine, Emily.
Distribution: Cartel.
TEL: 01-986 7167.

DEMON RECORDS
CANAL HOUSE, STARS ESTATE,
TRANSPORT AVENUE,
BRENTFORD, MIDDX. TW8 0QP.
Subsidiary labels: Rounder Europa,
Hi Records, HDH Records, Zippo
Records, Demon Verbal. License
from other companies via Edsel
Label. Most recent signings – Head
and Pink Fairies. Distribution:
Pinnacle. Publishing: Demon Music.
TEL: 01-847 2481.
TELEX: 894666.

EG RECORDS AND EDITIONS EG
63A KING'S ROAD,
LONDON SW3 4NT.
Contracted artists include: Robert Fripp,
King Crimson, Bill Bruford Quartet,
Earthworks, Man Jumping, Killing Joke,
Penguin Cafe Orchestra, Toyah, Booo.
Distribution: Virgin. Publishing: Eg
Music.
TEL: 01-730 2162. TELEX: 919205.
FAX: 01-730 1330.

EMI RECORDS (UK)
EMI HOUSE,
20 MANCHESTER SQUARE,
LONDON W1A 1ES.
Licensed labels: RAK. Labels owned:
Blue Note, Capitol, Columbia, EMI,
EMI-America, Harvest, Manhattan
Parlophone, Zonophone, HMV.
Contracted artists include Queen, David
Bowie, Tina Turner, Kate Bush, Cliff
Richard. Distribution: EMI. Publishing:
EMI Music Publishing.
TEL: 01-486. TELEX: 22643.
FAX: 01-935 3852.

ENSIGN RECORDS
3 MONMOUTH PLACE,
OFF MONMOUTH ROAD,
LONDON W2 5SH.
Contracted artists include: Phil Fearon,
Sinead O'Connor, The Waterboys,
Stump. Distribution: Chrysalis via CBS.
Publishing: Dizzy Heights Music
Publishing.
TEL: 01-727 0527.

FACTORY COMMUNICATIONS (Records)
86 PALATINE ROAD,
WEST DIDSBURY,
MANCHESTER 20.
Contracted artists include: A Certain Ratio, Happy Mondays, Joy Division, New Order, Section 25, Stockholm Monsters, Durutti Column, The Railway Children. Distribution: Pinnacle.
TEL: (061) 434 3876. TELEX: 669009 (Facman). FAX: 061 434 6059.

53rd & 3rd
21A ALVA STREET,
EDINBURGH, EH2 4PS.
Contracted artists include: BMX Bandits, Tallulah Gosh, Househunters. Distribution: Fast Forward/Cartel.
TEL: (031) 226 3129.
FAX: 031 226 3133.

FLICKNIFE RECORDS
2nd FLOOR, THE METROSTORE, 5–10 EASTMAN ROAD, THE VALE, LONDON W3 7YG.
Labels: Tuff Enuff, Soho Girl. Contracted artists include: Flicknife, Hawkwind, Mournblade, Diskord Datkord. Distribution: Spartan (except for Soho through Virgin.)
TEL: 01-993 6524.

4AD
17–19 ALMA ROAD,
LONDON SW18 1AA.
Contracted artists include: Cocteau Twins, Colourbox, Dead Can Dance, The Wolfgang Press, This Mortal Coil, Xymox, The Pixies. Distribution: Cartel, Rough Trade.
TEL: 01-870 9724.
TELEX: 915733 BEGBAN G.

FUTURE EARTH RECORDS
59 FITZWILLIAM STREET,
WATH UPON DEARNE,
ROTHERHAM,
SOUTH YORKSHIRE S63 7HG.
Licensed or subsid, labels: Ambush, Rival, Ultraprime, Konexion. Combat (USA). Contracted artists include: The Exploited, Limelight, UV Pop. Distribution: Pinnacle, PRT, Red

Rhino/Cartel. Publishing: Future Earth Music.
TEL: (0709) 872875.

GLASS RECORDS
LINBURN HOUSE,
342 KILBURN HIGH ROAD,
LONDON NW6 2QJ.
Contracted artists include: The Pastels, In Embrace, Spacemen 3, The Membranes, The Apartments. Distribution: Nine Mile/The Cartel.
TEL: 01-624 0060/328 9521.
TELEX: 892843 Offlet G.

GO! DISCS
SON OF GO! MANSIONS,
320–322 KING STREET,
LONDON W6 0RR.
Contracted artists include: Billy Bragg, Butterfield 8, The Housemartins, The La's, No Man's Land, Blue Ox Babes. Distribution: Chrysalis. Publishing: Go Discs Music.
TEL: 01-748 7973. TELEX: 929340 GODISCS G. FAX: 01-741 5936.

GWR RECORDS
15 GREAT WESTERN ROAD,
LONDON W9 3NW.
Licensed or subsid, labels: Aaargh. Contracted artists include: Girlschool, Hawkwind, The Anti-Nowhere League, Motorhead. Distribution: PRT. Publishing: Leosong.
TEL: 01-286 300. TELEX: 299611 UNIQUE G. FAX: 01-286 7093.

HEAVY METAL RECORDS
152 GOLDTHORN HILL, PENN, WOLVERHAMPTON WV2 3JA.
Labels Owned: Heavy Metal America, Heavy Metal Worldwide, FM (commercial), Black (grass roots/Indie), Revolver, (alternative). Contracted artists include: Ansgang, Babysitters, Briar, Jim Dandy and Black Oak Arkansas, The Vibrators, UFO, Tobruk, Torino, Bruce Cockburn. Distribution: RCA. (Black – Cartel). (90% HM and hard rock). Publishing: Rocksong Publications.
TEL: (0902) 345345 (5 lines).
TELEX: 335419 ROKSONG G.

ID RECORDS
1–2 MUNRO TERRACE,
LONDON SW10 0DL.
Labels: Lifeline Records. Contracted artists include: Guana Batz, The Blubbery Hellbellies, The Deltas, Demented Are Go, Frenzy. Distribution: Revolver/Cartel.
TEL: 01-351 3355. TELEX: 8954921.

IRS RECORDS
BUGLE HOUSE, 21A NOEL STREET, LONDON W1V 3PD.
Licensed or subsid. labels: Illegal Records. Contracted artists include: The Alarm, Doctor and the Medics, REM, The Truth, Belinda Carlisle, Let's Active, Stage. Distribution: IRS through MCA, Illegal through Pinnacle. Publishing: Bugel Song.
TEL: 01-439 2282. TELEX: 268152 IRS LON/2 G.

ISLAND RECORDS
22 ST PETER'S SQUARE,
LONDON W6.
Owned labels: Fourth & Broadway, Mango, Antilles. Licensed labels: Mother, Taxi (Inc). Contracted artists include: Aswad, Robert Palmer, John Martyn, The Christians, Julian Cope, Courtney Pine, Anthrax, Salif Keita, Mica Paris, The Triffids. Distribution: EMI. Publishing: Island Music Ltd.
TEL: 01-741 1511. TELEX: 934541.
FAX: 01-748 1998.

JIVE RECORDS
ZOMBA HOUSE,
165–167 WILLESDEN HIGH ROAD, LONDON NW10 2SG.
Subsid Labels: Jive Afrika, Jive Electro, Lifestyle. Contracted artists include: Billy Ocean, Samantha Fox, Jonathan Butler, Mama's Boys, Whodini, Ruby Turner, Millie Jackson, Steady B, The Skinny Boys. Distribution: RCA, NB. Jive is the record company of Zomba Productions. Publishing: Zomba Publishers.
TEL: 01-459 8899. TELEX: 919884.
FAX: 01-451 3900.

LONDON RECORDS (UK)

P.O. BOX 1422,
CHANCELLORS HOUSE,
CHANCELLORS ROAD,
HAMMERSMITH,
LONDON W6 9SG.
Licensed labels: Slash, Yes No.
Contracted artists include:
Bananarama, Carmel, Martin
Stephenson and the Daintees, The
Kane Gang, The Communards, Then
Jerico, John Parr, The Hot House
Flowers, Hard Rain, Run DMC, Voice
of the Beehive. Distribution: PolyGram.
Publishing: Polygram Music Publishing.
TEL: 01-741 1234. TELEX: 263828
POLY GM G. FAX: Marketing, legal,
accounting: 01-741 2600.
A & R: 01-741 1656

MAGNET RECORDS (Subsid, WEA)

MAGNET HOUSE, 22 YORK STREET,
LONDON W1H 1FD.
Contracted artists include: Chris Rea,
Simon Darlow, Ochi Brown.
Distribution: EMI. Publishing: see WEA.
TEL: 01-486 8151. TELEX: 25537
MAGNET G. FAX: 01-487 5766.

MCA RECORDS

72–74 BREWER STREET,
LONDON W1R 3PH.
Licensed or subsid. labels: Impulse,
I.R.S., Solar. Contracted artists include:
Nik Kershaw, Kim Wilde, Paul Barry,
Blue Mercedes, CCP, Transvision
Vamp. Distribution: PolyGram.
Publishing: MCA Music.
TEL: 01-437 9797.
TELEX: MCAREC 299338.
FAX: 01-437 3121.

MIDNIGHT MUSIC (RECORDS)

P.O. BOX 333, BUSHEY,
WATFORD WD2 3UN.
Contracted artists include: Hackney
Five-O, Robyn Hitchcock, The Beyond,
Sad Lovers & Giants. Distribution:
Rough Trade, Cartel. Publishing:
Midnight Publishing.
TEL: 01-950 9507. TELEX: 941 9501
MIDMUS G.

MOKSHA

P.O. BOX 102, LONDON E15 2HH.
Contracted artists include: The Shamen.
Distribution: Nine Mile, The Cartel.
Publishing: Amoksha Song.
TEL: 01-555 5423.

MOTOWN RECORDS

TUDOR HOUSE,
35 GRESSE STREET,
LONDON W1P 1PN.
Labels Owned: Gordy, Mowest, Tamla
Motown. Contracted artists include:
Stevie Wonder, Smokey Robinson,
Lionel Richie, Chico Debarbe.
Distribution: BMG.
TEL: 01-631 8311.
FAX: 01-631 1244/5089.

MUTE RECORDS

429 HARROW ROAD,
LONDON W10 4RE.
Licensed or subsid. labels: Blast First,
Rhythm King, Product Inc. Contracted
artists include: Depeche Mode, Nick
Cave and the Badseeds, Erasure,
These Mortal Souls, Frank Tovey, Nitzer
Ebb, Wire. Distribution: Spartan, Cartel.
'Don't want to be sent tapes – no A&R
– not actively signing' – so they say!
Publishing: Dying Art.
TEL: 01-969 8866. TELEX: 268623
MUTE G. FAX: 01-968 4977.

NIGHTSHIFT

C/O FAST FORWARD/CARTEL,
21A ALVA STREET,
EDINBURGH EH2 4PS.
Labels: Sharko 2, partnership with
D.D.T. Records. Contracted artists
include: Lowlife, Pioneer Corp., The
Scarlet Train, Kid Congo & Co., Two
Helens. Distribution: Fast Forward/The
Cartel.
TEL: 031-226 3129/4616.
FAX: 031 226 3133.

OI! RECORDS

3 MACHEN STREET,
CARDIFF CF1 7NT.
Licensed or subsid. Labels: Ska
Records. Contracted artists include:
(one off deals): Section 5, Condemned
'84, Vicious Rumours. Distribution:
Revolver/Cartel.
TEL: (0222) 221825.

PHONOGRAM RECORDS

P.O. BOX 1422,
CHANCELLORS HOUSE,
CHANCELLORS ROAD,
HAMMERSMITH,
LONDON W6 9SG.
Licensed or subsid. labels:
Casablanca, Club, De-Lite, Mercury,
Neutron, Riva, Rocket, Vertigo,
Contracted artists include: Tears For
Fears, Dire Straits, Curiosity Killed the
Cat, Wet Wet Wet, Swing Out Sister,
The Mission. Distribution: PolyGram.
Publishing: Polygram Music Publishing.
TEL: 01-741 1212.
FAX: A&R: 01-741 1566.
LEGAL/ACCOUNTS 01-741 1616

POLYDOR RECORDS

1 SUSSEX PLACE,
LONDON W6 9XT.
Labels: Vorvo, Fiction (**Int.**),
Wonderland, Urban, Dreyfus.
Contracted artists include: Lloyd
Cole & The Commotions, The
Creatures, The Cure, Level 42,
Siouxsie & The Banshees, The Style
Council. Distribution: PolyGram.
Publishing: Polygram Music
Publishing.
TEL: 01-846 8090.
TELEX: 263828 POLYGM G.
FAX: 01-741 4901.

PRODUCT INC.

LAWFORD HOUSE,
429 HARROW ROAD,
LONDON W10 4RE.
Contracted artists include: Swans,
World Domination Enterprises, Pussy
Galore. Distribution: Cartel.
TEL: 01-969 8866. TELEX: 268623.

RCA RECORDS
(DIVISION OF BMG)

1 BEDFORD AVENUE,
LONDON WC1B 3DT.
Contracted artists include: Glen
Goldsmith, Fairground Attraction, Ellis
Beggs and Howard, Hot House, Five
Star, The Primitives. Distribution: RCA
Publishing: BMG Publishing.
TEL: 01-636 8311. FAX: 01-631 1244.

RED BUS RECORDS (INTERNATIONAL)
RED BUS HOUSE,
48 BROADLEY TERRACE,
LONDON NW1 6UL.
Licensed or Subsid. Labels: Excaliber Records, R&B Records, Telestories, War Records. Contracted artists include: Imagination, Phil Radford. Distribution: PRT, Publishing: Red Bus Music.
TEL: 01-258 0324/5/6/7.
TELEX: 25873 RED BUS G.

RED FLAME
PO BOX 927, LONDON W3 6YB.
Subsid labels: Ink Records. Contracted artists include: C Cat Trance.
Distribution: Nine Mile, The Cartel.
Publishing: Red Flame Music Ltd.
TEL: 01-993 8634. FAX: 01-724 2163.

RED LIGHTNIN' LTD
THE WHITE HOUSE,
THE STREET, NORTH LOPHAM,
DISS, NORFOLK IP22 2LU.
Licensed or subsid labels: Union Pacific, Syndicate Chapter, Daddy Kool.
Owned label: Red Lightnin'. Contracted artists include: Billy Boy Arnold, Mighty Flyers, The Enemy Within, Blues Burglars. Distribution: Self, Swift, Hot Shot, Cadillac, R'n'B music policy.
Publishing: Red Lightnin' Music Publishing.
TEL: (0379) 88693.
TELEX: 97203 Blues G.

RHYTHM KING RECORDS
(see Mute Records)
429 HARROW ROAD,
LONDON W10 4RE.
Labels: Flame Records, Transglobal, Soulmasters. Distribution: Mute.
Publishing: Rhythm King Music.
TEL: 01-969 8866.
TELEX: 268623 Mute G.

ROUGH TRADE RECORDS
61 COLLIER STREET,
LONDON N1 9BE.
Licensed or subsid, labels: Blue Guitar, Blanco y Negro, Big Star. Contracted artists include: The Wooden Tops, Easterhouse, Camper Van Beethoven, Ivor Cutler, Robert Wyatt, The Seers,

Bambi Slam, David Thomas, Pere Ubu, The Cradle, Sandie Shaw. Distribution: Rough Trade, Cartel. Publishing: Rough Trade Music.
TEL: 01-837 6747. TELEX: 929555 RTRECS. FAX: 01-833 1046.

SAIN (RECORDIAU)
CYF, LLANDWROG, CAERNARFON, GWYNEDD LL54 5TG.
Licensed or subsid labels: Cambrian, Sain, Sain-Cambrian, Tryfan, Ty ar y Graig, Welsh Teldisc. Contracted artists include: Pendyrus & Rhos Male Choirs, Margaret Williams, Geraint Griffiths, Aberjaber, Trebor Edwards.
Distribution: Sain, Taylors of Birmingham, D Sharp, Celtic Music, Projection, Record Merchandiser, Harmonia Mundy. Publishing: Cyhoeddiadau Sain.
TEL: (0286) 831111. FAX: 0286 831497.

SIREN /10 RECORDS
61/63 PORTOBELLO ROAD,
LONDON W11 3DD.
Licensed or subsid, labels: Essential Records, Siren's contracted artists include: Fruits of Passion, T'Pau, Delta, Che, Cutting Crew, Light A Big Fire, KCD, Jermaine Stewart, Trouble, Pete Wylie. Artists contracted to 10 include: Billy Connolly, Anne Clarke, Animal Nightlife, Black Britain, 52nd Street, Mantronix, Maxi Priest, Edwin Starr, Two Nations, When in Rome, Blow.
Distribution: EMI via Virgin. Publishing: Virgin Music.
TEL: 01-221 7535. TELEX: 295417 SIREN G. FAX: 01-221 0957.

STERN'S AFRICAN RECORD CENTRE
116 WHITFIELD STREET,
LONDON W1P 5RW.
Contracted artists include: Hi-Life International, Somo Somo, Kintone, Mbelia Bel. Distribution: Self.
TEL: 01-387 5550/388 5533.
TELEX: 8951182 GECOMS G.

SUPREME RECORDS
1A WATERLOW ROAD,
LONDON N19 5JN.
Licensed label: De-construction.

Contracted artists include: Cousin Rachel. Distribution: PRT. Publishing: Supreme Song.
TEL: 01-281 6292.

SURVIVAL RECORDS
PO BOX 337, LONDON W5 4XG.
Label: Premonition. Contracted artists include: Jeanette, James McCormack, The Crows, The Quireboys. Distribution: Cartel. Publishing: Survival Publishing Ltd.
TEL: 01-847 2625/7. FAX: 01-568 6154.

TRIPLE EARTH RECORDS
1–8 WHITFIELD PLACE,
LONDON W1P 5RW.
Contracted artists include: Najma Akhtar, Cheb Khaleb, The Master Musicians of Tanzania. Distribution: Sterns, Triple Earth.
TEL: 01-388 5533.

UNAMERICAN ACTIVITIES
29 ST. MICHAELS ROAD,
LEEDS LS6 3BG.
Owned label: American Activities.
Contracted artists include: Ted Hawkins, Steve Phillips, The Prowlers, Pier La Rue. Distribution: Southern and MMG. Publishing: Endomorph Music Publishing.
TEL: (0532) 742106.

VINYL SOLUTION
39 HEREFORD ROAD, LONDON W2.
Contracted artists include: Sound Asleep, The Stupids, The Milk Monitors, The Hard-Ons. Distribution: Pinnacle.
Publishing: Schnozza Music.
TEL: 01-229 8010. FAX: see tel. no.

VIRGIN RECORDS
553–579 HARROW ROAD,
LONDON W10 4RH.
Owned Labels: Siren /10. Licensed or subsid. labels: Charisma Records, Siren Records, 10 Records, EG Records, MDM, Circa. Contracted artists include: Phil Collins, Balaam & The Angel, Captain Beefheart, China Crisis, Peter Gabriel, General Public, Heaven 17, Human League, It Bites, The Madness, Scritti Politti, Feargal Sharkey, Simple Minds, Well Red,

Working Week. Distribution: EMI.
Publishing: Virgin Music.
TEL: 01-968 6688. TELEX: 22542.
FAX: 01-968 6533.

WATERFRONT RECORDS
1 LEIGH HILL, LEIGH ON SEA,
ESSEX SS9 2EP.
Contracted artists include: Flaco
Jimenez, Rent Party, The Shakers,
Eddie & The Hot Rods, Wilko Johnson,
The Famous Potatoes, Peter Rowan,
Earl Okin, Dave Peabody. Distribution:
Cartel, Blacks. Publishing: Waterfront
Publishing.
TEL: (0702) 714025.

WEA RECORDS
THE ELECTRIC LIGHTING STATION,
46 KENSINGTON COURT,
LONDON W8 5DP.
Licensed or subsid. labels: Atlantic,
Asylum, Atco, Blanco y Negro, Elektra,
Magnet Records, Nonsuch, Geffen,
Qwest, Valentino, Warner Brothers,
WEA UK, Sire, WEA International.
Labels owned: Elevatikon, Oval.
Contracted artists include: Echo and the
Bunnymen, Aztec Camera, Billy
McKenzie, Matt Bianco, Everything But
The Girl, Chiefs of Relief, Primal
Scream, Bhundu Boys, A House, The
Pretenders, Sisters of Mercy, Red Box,
Perils of Plastic, The Jesus and Mary
Chain, Screaming Blue Messiahs,
Simply Red, Gail Ann Dorsey.
Distribution: Self.
TEL: 01-938 2181. TELEX: 261425.
FAX: 01-937 6645.

ZOMBA PRODUCTIONS
(See Jive Records)
ZOMBA HOUSE,
165–167 WILLESDEN HIGH ROAD,
LONDON NW10 2SG.
Subsid Labels: Jive, Jive Electro, Jive
Afrika, Lifestyle. Distribution: RCA
Publishing: Zomba Publication.
TEL: 01-459 8899. TELEX: 919884.
FAX: 01-451 3900.

REHEARSAL STUDIOS

Most rehearsal rooms include the cost of basic backline in their price and supplementary amps, guitars, effects etc. can usually be hired for a small fee. Facilities provided by the Arts Council in your area will be listed in the Arts Council Directory (see book list).

THE ACADEMY, BRIXTON (T/A) ANGEL CRYSTAL
211 STOCKWELL ROAD,
LONDON SW9.
TEL: 01-274 1525.

BACKSTAGE PROJECT
276 RAGLAN STREET, LOWESTOFT,
SUFFOLK NR32 2LB.
TEL: (0502) 512850.

BACKSTREET REHEARSAL STUDIOS
(Rear of) 137 UPPER STREET
LONDON N1 1QP.
TEL: 01-226 8994.

BARRINGTON SOUNDS
HEAD OFFICE,
320A COLDHARBOUR LANE,
LONDON SW9 8SE.
TEL: 01-326 5004.

BLACK BARN STUDIOS
3 THE GREEN,
DUNSBOROUGH COTTAGES,
RIPLEY, SURREY GU23 6AL.
TEL: (0483) 222600.

BLACKBOARD
8 THE LEATHER MARKET,
OFF WESTON STREET,
LONDON SE1 3ER.
TEL: 01-378 7835/6.

BRENT BLACK MUSIC COOP
283 HIGH ROAD, WILLESDEN,
LONDON NW10.
TEL: 01-451 4545.

CMS
PARK HOUSE, LLANGENNECH,
DYFED SA14 8YA.
TEL: (0554) 821147.

CENTRE CITY SOUND
571 SAUCHIEHALL STREET,
GLASGOW G3 7PQ.
TEL: 041-221 5058.

CLINK STUDIOS
1 CLINK STREET, SOHO WHARF,
LONDON BRIDGE, LONDON SE1.
TEL: 01-403 6515/407 1363.

CLOCK
UNIT 6, 13–17 CAROLINE PLACE,
HULL HU2 8DR.
TEL: (0482) 227850.

CRASH
11 DAVIES STREET,
IMPERIAL WAREHOUSE,
LIVERPOOL L1.
TEL: 051-236 0989.

ELECTRIC AVENUE
14A ELECTRIC AVENUE,
LONDON SW9.
TEL: 01-737 4595.

GOLDIGGERS
TIMBER STREET, CHIPPENHAM,
WILTSHIRE SN15 3BP.
TEL: (0249) 656444.

GRAPEVINE
VINE STREET, BRIGHTON,
WEST SUSSEX.
TEL: (0273) 698555.

HAMMERSMITH STUDIOS
55A YELDHAM ROAD,
HAMMERSMITH, LONDON W6.
TEL: 01-748 2768.

HOTHOUSE
WATERLOO WORKS,
GORSEY MT STREET, STOCKPORT,
CHESHIRE.
TEL: (061) 477 6531.

JOE'S GARAGE
6 NORTH ISLA STREET,
DUNDEE DD3 7QJ.
TEL: (0382) 832049.

JOHN HENRY ENTERPRISES
16/24 BREWERY ROAD, ISLINGTON,
LONDON N7 9NH.
TEL: 01-609 9181.

JOHN SAVAGE MUSIC CENTRE
71–72 NORFOLK STREET,
KING'S LYNN, NORFOLK
TEL: (0553) 774026.

JUMBO STUDIOS
387 CHAPTER ROAD,
LONDON NW2 5NQ.
TEL: 01-459 7256.

LE-CAZ CHEOPS STUDIOS
'AVALON', 1 CYPRUS ROAD,
CAMBRIDGE.
TEL: (0223) 249889.

LOWER WHOPPING CONKER CO.
THE STUDIO COMPLEX,
45 VICTORIA ROAD, ROMFORD,
ESSEX RM1 2JH.
TEL: (0708) 44334.

MAINLINE STUDIOS
57 CARDIGAN LANE,
STANMORE HILL, LEEDS LS4 2LE.
TEL: (0532) 304008.

MAKKA
4A RUSSELL STREET,
CAMBRIDGE CB2.
TEL: (0223) 358644.

THE MILL
CASTLEGATE MILL,
CASTLEGATE QUAY,
STOCKTON-ON-TEES,
CLEVELAND TS18 1BZ.
TEL: (0642) 679189.

MIRAGE
225 RIPPONDEN ROAD,
LITTLEMORE, OLDHAM,
LANCASHIRE OL1 4HR.
TEL: 061-665 2278.

MUSIC BOX
98 VICTORIA ROAD, ACTON,
LONDON NW10 6NB.
TEL: 01-965 0155.

THE MUSIC CORPORATION
WATERLOO WORKS,
GORSEY MOUNT STREET,
STOCKPORT, CHESHIRE SK1 3BV.
TEL: (061) 477 6531.

NETWORK STUDIOS
46 AUSTER ROAD,
NORTH YORK TRADING ESTATE,
CLIFTON, YORK YO3 8XA.
TEL: (0904) 691761.

THE NOMIS COMPLEX
45–53 SINCLAIR ROAD,
LONDON W14 0NS.
TEL: 01-602 6351.

**NORTH PADDINGTON
REHEARSAL ROOMS**
235 LANARK ROAD, LONDON W9.
TEL: 01-624 4089.

ORION REHEARSAL STUDIOS
IVER LANE, UXBRIDGE,
MIDDLESEX.
TEL: (0895) 32579.

OUT OF THE BLUE
33 BLOSSOM STREET, ANCOATS,
MANCHESTER M4 6AJ.
TEL: 061-236 7530.

QUAY SOUND STUDIOS
11–15 HIGHBRIDGE WHARF,
EASTNEY STREET,
LONDON SE10 8PB.
TEL: 01-853 2950.

READING
110 MOUNT STREET,
READING RG2 0AB.
TEL: (0734) 876044.

REDAN RECORDERS
23 REDAN PLACE, QUEENSWAY,
LONDON W2 4SA.
TEL: 01-229 9311.

RICH BITCH STUDIOS
505 BRISTOL ROAD, SELLY OAK,
BIRMINGHAM B29 6AU.
TEL: 021-471 1339.

RIVERSIDE STUDIOS
57 MELBOURNE STREET,
NEWCASTLE UPON TYNE, NE1 2JQ.
TEL: 091-261 9585.

SAM
THE MOON CLUB,
6 UPPER YORK STREET,
STOKESCROFT, BRISTOL BS2 8QE.
TEL: (0272) 47147.

SCOTIA
29 NIDDRY STREET,
EDINBURGH EH1.
TEL: 031-226 6620.

SESSION MUSIC
YORK STREET, BELFAST.
TEL: (0232) 238998.

SHOW ME STUDIOS
BLOCK C, IMPERIAL WORKS,
PERREN STREET,
OFF RYLAND ROAD,
LONDON NW5.
TEL: 01-267 5011.

SIMPLEX
43–45 BAILEY STREET,
SHEFFIELD S1 4EH.
TEL: (0742) 754914.

SOLID LIGHT
UNIT J, 44 ST. PAULS CRESCENT,
LONDON NW1.
TEL: 01-485 7412.

SOUND ADVICE
UNIT 9, HOLT ESTATES,
WALKER ROAD, NEWCASTLE.
TEL: 091-276 2511.

SOUND SPACE STUDIO
WEST WHARF ROAD,
CARDIFF CF1 5DD.
TEL: (0222) 373707.

SOUTH LONDON STUDIOS
REAR OF 5B, BRIDGE PARADE,
WADDON, CROYDON CR0 4JH.
TEL: (0883) 44114.

SPIRIT STUDIOS
10 TARIFF STREET,
MANCHESTER, M1 2SS.

STATION HOUSE
ATHERTON STREET,
NEW BRIGHTON,
LIVERPOOL L45 2NY.
TEL: 051-638 5493.

STUDIO DRIVE TWO
1 CLINK STREET, SOHO WHARF,
LONDON BRIDGE,
LONDON WE1 9DG.
TEL: 01-403 1977/407 1598.

SUMMERTIME STUDIOS
UNIT 9,
ACORN PRODUCTION CENTRE,
105 BLUNDELL STREET,
LONDON N7 9BN.
(Linked to Sensible Music Ltd.)
TEL: 01-609 9415.

TERMINAL STUDIOS
29A AMELIA STREET,
LONDON SE17 3PY.
TEL: 01-703 0347.

THUNDER DOME STUDIOS
163 MIDLAND ROAD,
LONDON E10 6JJ.
TEL: 01-539 6996.

UNIVERSITY OF LONDON UNION
MALET STREET, LONDON WC1.
(Students only).
TEL: 01-580 9551.

WAREHOUSE STUDIO
60 SANDFORD LANE,
KENNINGTON, OXFORD.
TEL: (0865) 736411.

WESTAR STUDIOS
1 PRIORY WAY, SOUTHALL,
MIDDLESEX UB2 5EB.
TEL: 01-571 4679.

**WOOD WHARF REHEARSAL
STUDIOS**
28–30 HORSEFERRY PLACE,
LONDON SE10 9BT.
TEL: 01-853 4766.

SECURITY

CP LEVEL ONE LTD
RUSSELL HOUSE,
RUSSELL STREET,
SWANSEA, WEST GLAMORGAN.
TEL: (0792) 702018.

ROCK STEADY SECURITY
25 GREENSIDE PLACE,
EDINBURGH EH1 3AA.
TEL: 031-557 2040.

SHOWSEC INTERNATIONAL
23A BENWELL ROAD,
LONDON N7 7BL.
TEL: 01-609 9411.

**SHOWSEC INTERNATIONAL
(LEEDS)**
BAKER HOUSE, 9 NEW YORK
ROAD, LEEDS LS2 9PF.
TEL: (0532) 424285.

SLEEVE PRINTERS

CMCS
UNIT 1, KENNET ROAD,
OFF THAMES ROAD, CRAYFORD,
KENT, DA1 4QN.
TEL: (0322) 59393. FAX: 0322 53741.

COPS
THE STUDIO, KENT HOUSE,
BARNMEAD ROAD, BECKENHAM,
KENT BR3 1JD.
TEL: 01-778 8556. FAX: 01-676 9716.

DELGA PRESS LTD
DINGWALL HOUSE,
18 MARLBOROUGH ROAD,
BROMLEY, KENT BR2 9NH.
TEL: 01-460 0112. FAX: 01-466 1691.

E. HANNIBAL & CO.
PINFOLD ROAD, THURMASTON,
LEICESTER LE4 8AP.
TEL: (0533) 695413. FAX: 0533 601072.

GOTHIC PRINT & FINISHERS
UNIT 3,
BIGGIN HILL INDUSTRIAL ESTATE,
BIGGIN HILL, KENT TN16 3BX.
TEL: (0959) 71316.

**HOWARD PRINTERS (SLOUGH)
LTD.**
MILL STREET, SLOUGH,
BERKS SL2 5DJ.
TEL: (0753) 32271. FAX: 0753 694667.

JAMES UPTON LTD.
98–138 BARFORD STREET,
BIRMINGHAM B5 6AP.
TEL: 021-692 1171. FAX: 021-622 1488.

ROBERT STAGE & CO. LTD.
CHALKIN WORKS,
LONGFIELD ROAD,
TUNBRIDGE WELLS, KENT TN2 3ET.
TEL: (0892) 24225. FAX: 0892 47334.

SENOL PRINTING
6 SANDIFORD ROAD,
KIMPTON ROAD ESTATE,
SUTTON, SURREY SM3 9RD.
TEL: 01-641 3890.

SLEEVEPRINT
100 CLAPHAM ROAD,
BEDFORD MK4 17PL.
TEL: (0234) 213535. FAX: 0234 64780.

TINSLEY ROBOR LTD.
TINSLEY HOUSE,
67 ROSOMAN STREET,
LONDON EC1R 0HY.
TEL: 01-278 2916. FAX: 01-837 2626.

SOUND RECORDING EQUIPMENT
HIRE AND FACILITIES

AUDIO RENTS LTD.
THE COURTYARD,
44 GLOUCESTER AVENUE,
LONDON NW1 8HT.
TEL: 01-586 7587

DREAMHIRE
18 CHAPLIN ROAD,
LONDON NW2 5PN.
TEL: 01-451 6161. FAX: 01-451 3900.

FELDON AUDIO LTD.
126 GREAT PORTLAND STREET,
LONDON W1N 5PH.
TEL: 01-580 4314. FAX: 01-631 1457.

F.W.O. BAUCH LTD.
49 THEOBALD STREET,
BOREHAMWOOD, HERTS WD6 4RZ.
TEL: 01-953 0091. FAX: 01-207 5970.

HARDWARE HOUSE (SOUND) LTD.
WEST WORKS, CHALGROVE ROAD,
LONDON E9 6PB.
TEL: 01-986 6111.

HHB HIRE & SALES
73–75 SCRUBS LANE,
LONDON NW10 6QU.
TEL: 01-960 2144. FAX: 01-960 1160.

HILTON SOUND
10 STEEDMAN STREET,
LONDON SE17 3 AF.
TEL: 01-708 0483. FAX: 01-703 0744.

LONDON SOUND HIRE
32 LIDDELL ROAD,
LONDON NW6 2EW.
TEL: 01-372 6595.

MUSIC LAB HIRE
76 EVERSHOLT STREET,
LONDON NW1 1BY.
TEL: 01-387 9356. FAX: 01-388 1953.

PAUL FARRAH SOUND LTD
UNIT 7,
ST. GEORGES INDUSTRIAL ESTATE,
RICHMOND ROAD,
KINGSTON KT2 5BQ.
TEL: 01-549 1787. FAX: 01-549 6204.

RAPER & WAYMAN LTD.
34 DANBURY STREET,
LONDON N1.
TEL: 01-359 9342.

STUDENT UNIONS

STUDENT UNIONS: UNIVERSITIES, POLYTECHNICS, COLLEGES OF HIGHER EDUCATION AND COLLEGES OF EDUCATION AND ART COLLEGES

UNIVERSITIES

ABERDEEN UNIVERSITY
50/52 COLLEGE BOUNDS,
ABERDEEN DB2 3DS.
TEL: (0224) 647751.

ABERYSTWYTH UNIVERSITY
GUILD OF STUDENTS, PENGLAIS,
ABERYSTWYTH SY23 3DX.
TEL: (0970) 4242.

BATH UNIVERSITY
CLAVERTON DOWN, BATH,
AVON BA2 7AY.
TEL: (0225) 826826.

BANGOR: UNIVERSITY COLLEGE OF NORTH WALES
DEINIOL ROAD, BANGOR,
GWYNEDD LL57 2TH.
TEL: (0248) 362075.

BELFAST: QUEEN'S UNIVERSITY
UNIVERSITY ROAD,
BELFAST BT17 1PR.
TEL: (0232) 224803.

BELFAST: UNIVERSITY OF ULSTER
JORDANSTOWN CAMPUS,
JORDANSTOWN, CO. ANTRIM,
NORTHERN IRELAND.
TEL: (0231) 67121.

BIRMINGHAM: UNIVERSITY OF ASTON IN BIRMINGHAM
ASTON STREET, GOSTA GREEN,
BIRMINGHAM B4 7ES.
TEL: 021-359 6531.

BIRMINGHAM UNIVERSITY
GUILD OF STUDENTS, THE UNION,
EDGBASTON PARK ROAD,
BIRMINGHAM B15 2TU.
TEL: 021-472 1841.

BRADFORD UNIVERSITY
RICHMOND ROAD,
BRADFORD BD7 1DP.
TEL: (0274) 734135.

BRISTOL UNIVERSITY
QUEEN'S ROAD, CLIFTON,
BRISTOL B58 1LN.
TEL: (0272) 735035.

BRUNEL UNIVERSITY
KINGSTON LANE, UXBRIDGE,
MIDDLESEX UB8 3PH.
TEL: (0895) 39125/6.

BRIGHTON: UNIVERSITY OF SUSSEX
FALMER HOUSE, FALMER,
BRIGHTON.
TEL: (0273) 698111/4.

CAMBRIDGE UNIVERSITY
4 ROUND CHURCH STREET,
CAMBRIDGE CB5 8AD.
TEL: (0223) 44836.

CANTERBURY: UNIVERSITY OF KENT
CANTERBURY, KENT CT2 7NW.
TEL: (0227) 450285.

CARDIFF: UNIVERSITY COLLEGE OF CARDIFF
PARK PLACE, CARDIFF CF1 3QN.
TEL: (0222) 396421/8.

COLCHESTER: UNIVERSITY OF ESSEX
WIVENHOE PARK, COLCHESTER,
ESSEX CO4 3SQ.
TEL: (0206) 863211.

COVENTRY: UNIVERSITY OF WARWICK
COVENTRY,
WARWICKSHIRE CV4 7AL.
TEL: (0203) 417220.

CRANFIELD INSTITUTE OF TECHNOLOGY
4 THE DRIVE, WHARLEY END,
CRANFIELD,
BEDFORDSHIRE MK43 0AL.
TEL: (0234) 750111 ext 3606.

DUNDEE UNIVERSITY
1 AIRLIE PLACE, DUNDEE DD1 4HN.
TEL: (0382) 21841.

DURHAM UNIVERSITY
DUNELM HOUSE, NEW ELVET,
DURHAM DH1 1AA.
TEL: 091-374 3310.

EDINBURGH UNIVERSITY
13 TEVIOT ROW,
EDINBURGH EH8 9AJ.
TEL: 031-667 2091.

EXETER UNIVERSITY
GUILD OF STUDENTS,
DEVONSHIRE HOUSE,
STOCKER ROAD, EXETER,
DEVON EX4 4PZ.
TEL: (0392) 263528.

GLASGOW UNIVERSITY
32 UNIVERSITY AVENUE,
GLASGOW G12.
TEL: 041-339 8697.

GLASGOW: UNIVERSITY OF STRATHCLYDE
90 JOHN STREET,
GLASGOW G1 1JH.
TEL: 041-552 1895.

GUILDFORD: SURREY UNIVERSITY
SURREY UNIVERSITY, GUILDFORD,
SURREY GU2 5XH.
TEL: (0483) 65017.

HULL UNIVERSITY
TOIVO HOUSE, CUTTINGHAM
ROAD, HULL.
TEL: (0482) 445361.

LAMPETER:
ST. DAVID'S UNIVERSITY COLLEGE
LAMPETER, DYFED SA48 7ED.
TEL: (0570) 422619.

LANCASTER UNIVERSITY
BOWLAND ANNEXE, BAILRIGG,
LANCASTER LA1 4YT.
TEL: (0524) 65201 ext. 259/267.

LEEDS UNIVERSITY
PO BOX 157, LEEDS LS1 1UH.
TEL: (0532) 439071.

LEICESTER UNIVERSITY
UNIVERSITY ROAD,
LEICESTER LE1 7RH.
TEL: (0533) 556282.

LIVERPOOL UNIVERSITY
GUILD OF UNDERGRADUATES,
2 BEDFORD STREET NORTH,
LIVERPOOL L7 7BD.
TEL: 051-709 4744.

LONDON: CITY UNIVERSITY
NORTHAMPTON SQUARE,
LONDON EC1V 0HB.
TEL: 01-250 0955.

LONDON:
GOLDSMITH'S COLLEGE
LEWISHAM WAY, NEW CROSS,
LONDON SE14 6NW.
TEL: 01-692 1406.

LONDON: KINGS COLLEGE/
QUEEN ELIZABETH COLLEGE/
CHELSEA COLLEGE
STUDENTS UNION (STRAND SITE),
MACADAM BUILDING,
SURREY STREET, LONDON WC2.
TEL: 01-937 9714.

LONDON: SCHOOL OF
ECONOMICS AND POLITICAL
SCIENCE
PAGE BUILDING,
HOUGHTON STREET,
LONDON WC2A 2AE.
TEL: 01-405 8594.

LONDON:
UNIVERSITY OF LONDON UNION
MALET STREET,
LONDON WC1E 7HY.
TEL: 01-580 9551.

LONDON: QUEEN MARY COLLEGE
432 BANCROFT ROAD,
LONDON E1 4DM.
TEL: 01-980 4811 ext. 3340.

LONDON: SCHOOL OF
ORIENTAL & AFRICAN STUDIES
MALET STREET,
LONDON WC1E 7HP.
TEL: 01-580 0916.

LONDON: UNIVERSITY COLLEGE
25 GOODGE STREET,
LONDON WC1H 0AD.
TEL: 01-387 3611.

LONDON: WESTFIELD COLLEGE
KEDDERPORE AVENUE,
HAMPSTEAD, LONDON NW3 7ST.
TEL: 01-435 6593 ext. 528.

LOUGHBOROUGH UNIVERSITY
ASHBY ROAD, LOUGHBOROUGH,
LEICESTERSHIRE LE11 5TU.
TEL: (0509) 217766.

MANCHESTER UNIVERSITY
OXFORD ROAD,
MANCHESTER M13 9PR.
TEL: 061-273 5111.

NEWCASTLE UPON TYNE
UNIVERSITY
KINGS WALK,
NEWCASTLE UPON TYNE NE1 8QB.
TEL: (0632) 328402.

NORWICH:
UNIVERSITY OF EAST ANGLIA
UNION HOUSE, UNIVERSITY PLAIN,
NORWICH NR4 7TJ.
TEL: (0603) 503711.

NOTTINGHAM UNIVERSITY
PORTLAND BUILDING,
UNIVERSITY PARK,
NOTTINGHAM NG7 2RD.
TEL: (0602) 505912.

OXFORD UNIVERSITY
NEW BARNET HOUSE,
LITTLE CLARENDON STREET,
OXFORD OX1 2HU.
TEL: (0865) 511732.

READING UNIVERSITY
WHITEKNIGHTS PARK, READING,
BERKSHIRE RG6 2AZ.
TEL: (0734) 860222.

SALFORD UNIVERSITY
THE CRESCENT, SALFORD M5 4WT.
TEL: 061-736 7811.

SHEFFIELD UNIVERSITY
WESTERN BANK,
SHEFFIELD S10 2TG.
TEL: (0742) 24076.

SOUTHAMPTON UNIVERSITY
HIGHFIELD,
SOUTHAMPTON SO9 5NH.
TEL: (0703) 586122.

ST. ANDREWS UNIVERSITY
ST. MARY'S PLACE, ST. ANDREWS.
TEL: (0334) 77000.

STIRLING UNIVERSITY
STUDENTS ASSOCIATION,
CSA OFFICE, STIRLING FK9 4LA.
TEL: (0786) 61189/70064.

STOKE ON TRENT:
UNIVERSITY OF KEELE
KEELE, STAFFORDSHIRE ST5 5BJ.
TEL: (0782) 711411.

SWANSEA:
UNIVERSITY COLLEGE OF
SWANSEA
UNION HOUSE, SWANSEA SA2 8PP.
TEL: (0792) 205678.

UMIST
BARNES WALLIS BUILDING,
PO BOX 89, SACKVILLE STREET,
MANCHESTER M60 1QD.
TEL: 061-236 9114/8.

UWIST
JOINT STUDENTS UNION,
PARK PLACE, CARDIFF CF1 3QN.
TEL: (0222) 396421.

YORK UNIVERSITY
GOODRICKE COLLEGE,
HESLINGTON, YORK YO1 5DD.
TEL: (0904) 412328.

POLYTECHNICS

BIRMINGHAM POLYTECHNIC
EDGBASTON CENTRE,
9 WESTBOURNE GROVE
EDGBASTON,
BIRMINGHAM B15 3RT.
TEL: 021-454 5184.

BRIGHTON POLYTECHNIC
(Faculty of Art and Design)
GRAND PARADE, BRIGHTON,
EAST SUSSEX.
TEL: (0273) 683585.

BRISTOL POLYTECHNIC
STUDENTS UNION,
COLDHARBOUR LANE,
BRISTOL B51 5PH.
TEL: (0272) 656261 ext. 257.

**POLYTECHNIC OF
CENTRAL LONDON**
STAFF AND STUDENT CENTRE,
104/108 BOLSOVER STREET,
LONDON W1.
TEL: 01-636 6271/4.

CITY OF LONDON POLYTECHNIC
FAIRHOLDT HOUSE,
102/105 WHITECHAPEL
HIGH STREET, LONDON E1.
TEL: 01-247 1441.

**COVENTRY LANCASTER
POLYTECHNIC**
PRIORY STREET,
COVENTRY CV1 5F.
TEL: (0203) 21167.

HATFIELD POLYTECHNIC
PO BOX 109, HATFIELD,
HERTS AL10 9AB.
TEL: (07072) 68343.

HUDDERSFIELD POLYTECHNIC
QUEENSGATE,
HUDDERSFIELD HD1 3DH.
TEL: (0484) 538156.

KINGSTON POLYTECHNIC
PENRHYN ROAD,
KINGSTON-UPON-THAMES,
SURREY KT1 2EE.
TEL: 01-549 9961.

LANCASHIRE POLYTECHNIC
FYLDE ROAD, PRESTON PR1 2XQ.
TEL: (0772) 58382/57449.

LEEDS POLYTECHNIC
CALVERLEY STREET,
LEEDS LS1 3HE.
TEL: (0532) 430171.

LEICESTER POLYTECHNIC
4 NEWARKE CLOSE,
LEICESTER LE2 7BJ.
TEL: (0533) 555576.

LIVERPOOL POLYTECHNIC
THE HAIGH BUILDING,
MARYLAND STREET,
LIVERPOOL L1 9DE.
TEL: 051-709 4047.

MANCHESTER POLYTECHNIC
MANDELA BUILDING,
OXFORD ROAD,
MANCHESTER M1 7EL.
TEL: 061-273 1162/5.

MIDDLESEX POLYTECHNIC
ALL SAINTS SITE,
WHITE HART LANE, TOTTENHAM,
LONDON N17 8HR.
TEL: 01-808 1533.

NEWCASTLE POLYTECHNIC
2 SANDY FORD ROAD,
NEWCASTLE UPON TYNE NE1 8SB.
TEL: (0632) 328761.

**NORTH EAST LONDON
POLYTECHNIC**
MANBEY PARK ROAD,
STRATFORD,
LONDON E15.
TEL: 01-555 8447.

**POLYTECHNIC OF NORTH
LONDON**
HOLLOWAY ROAD,
LONDON N7 8DB.
TEL: (607) 2789 ext. 2291/3.

OXFORD POLYTECHNIC
GYPSEYS LANE, HEADINGTON,
OXFORD OX3 0BP.
TEL: (0865) 64777/61998.

PLYMOUTH POLYTECHNIC
DRAKE CIRCUS,
PLYMOUTH PL4 8AA.
TEL: (0752) 663337.

PORTSMOUTH POLYTECHNIC
ALEXANDRA HOUSE,
MUSEUM ROAD,
PORTSMOUTH PO1 2QH.
TEL: (0705) 819141.

SHEFFIELD CITY POLYTECHNIC
PHOENIX BUILDING,
POND STREET,
SHEFFIELD S1 2BW.
TEL: (0742) 738934/7.

**NORTH STAFFORDSHIRE
POLYTECHNIC**
BECONSIDE, STAFFORD,
STAFFORDSHIRE ST18 0AD.
TEL: (0785) 211738.

**NORTH STAFFORDSHIRE
POLYTECHNIC**
STOKE SITE, COLLEGE ROAD,
STOKE UPON TRENT,
STAFFORDSHIRE ST4 2DE.
TEL: (0782) 744416.

**POLYTECHNIC OF THE
SOUTH BANK**
ROTARY STREET,
ELEPHANT AND CASTLE,
LONDON SE1.
TEL: 01-261 1525.

SUNDERLAND POLYTECHNIC
WEARMOUTH HALL,
CHESTER ROAD, SUNDERLAND,
TYNE & WEAR SR1 3SD.
TEL: (0915) 145512.

TEESIDE POLYTECHNIC
BOROUGH ROAD,
MIDDLESBROUGH,
CLEVELAND TS1 3BA.
TEL: (0642) 210423.

THAMES POLYTECHNIC
THOMAS STREET, WOOLWICH,
LONDON SE18 6HU.
TEL: 01-855 0618.

TRENT POLYTECHNIC
BYRON BUILDING,

SHAKESPEARE STREET,
NOTTINGHAM NG1 4BU.
TEL: (0602) 476725/6/7/8.

POLYTECHNIC OF WALES
FOREST GROVE, TREFOREST,
MID-GLAMORGAN CF37 1UF.
TEL: (0443) 408227.

**WOLVERHAMPTON
POLYTECHNIC**
ST. PETER'S SQUARE SITE,
WULFRUNA STREET,
WOLVERHAMPTON,
WEST MIDLANDS WV1 1LY.
TEL: (0902) 712901.

COLLEGES AND INSTITUTIONS OF HIGHER EDUCATION:

Listed by title

**BATH COLLEGE OF HIGHER
EDUCATION**
WINIFRED'S LANE, BATH BA1 5SE.
TEL: (0225) 20277.

**BEDFORD COLLEGE OF HIGHER
EDUCATION**
POLIHULL AVENUE SITE,
BEDFORD MK41 9EA.
TEL: (0234) 59503.

BOLTON INSTITUTE OF HE
DEANE ROAD, BOLTON BL3 5AB.
TEL: (0204) 389024.

**BUCKINGHAMSHIRE COLLEGE
OF HE**
QUEEN ALEXANDER ROAD,
HIGH WYCOMBE,
BUCKINGHAMSHIRE HP11 2JZ.
TEL: (0494) 446330.

BULMERSCHE COLLEGE OF HE
BULMERSCHE COURT,
WOODLANDS AVENUE, EARLEY,
BERKSHIRE RG6 1HY.
TEL: (0734) 666506.

CHELMER INSTITUTE OF HE
SAWYERS HALL LANE,
BRETWOOD,
ESSEX CM15 9BT.
TEL: (0277) 217421.

CHELMER INSTITUTE OF HE
VICTORIA ROAD SOUTH,
CHELMSFORD, ESSEX CM1 1LL.
TEL: (0245) 58178.

CHESTER COLLEGE OF HE
THE COLLEGE, CHENEY ROAD,
CHESTER CH1 4BJ.
TEL: (0224) 375093.

COLCHESTER INSTITUTE OF HE
ENDSLEIGH ANNEXE,
LEYDEN ROAD, COLCHESTER,
ESSEX.
TEL: (0206) 572462.

**COLLEGE OF RIPON AND ST
JOHN**
LORD MAYOR'S WALK,
YORK YO3 7EX.
TEL: (0904) 29816.

**COLLEGE OF RIPON AND ST
JOHN**
COLLEGE ROAD, RIPON HG4 2QX.
TEL: (0765) 3221.

**CREW AND ALSAGER COLLEGE
OF HE**
ALSAGER SITE, HASSALL ROAD,
ALSAGER, STOKE ON TRENT
ST7 2HL.
TEL: (09363) 3412.

**CREW AND ALSAGER COLLEGE
OF HE**
CREWE ROAD, CREWE,
CHESHIRE CW1 1DU.
TEL: (0270) 583690.

DERBYSHIRE COLLEGE OF HE
DERBY LONSDALE COLLEGE
OF HE,
KEDLESTON ROAD,
DERBY DE3 1GB.
TEL: (0332) 48846.

DIGBY STUART COLLEGE
ROEHAMPTON LANE,
LONDON SW15.
TEL: 01-876 8273.

DORSET INSTITUTE OF HE
WALLISDOWN ROAD,
WALLISDOWN, POOLE,

DORSET BH12 5BB.
TEL: (0202) 523755 ext. 297.

EALING COLLEGE OF HE
ST MARY'S ROAD, EALING,
LONDON W5 5RF.
TEL: 01-579 5000/4111 ext. 261.

EDGE HILL COLLEGE OF HE
ST HELEN'S ROAD, ORMSKIRK,
LANCASHIRE L39 4QP.
TEL: (0695) 75457/75171 ext. 255.

**FROEBEL EDUCATIONAL
INSTITUTE**
GROVE HOUSE,
ROEHAMPTON LANE,
LONDON SW15.
TEL: 01-878 1947.

**GLOUCESTER COLLEGE OF ARTS
AND TECHNOLOGY**
OXSTALLS CAMPUS,
OXSTALLS LANE,
GLOUCESTER GL2 9HW.
TEL: (0452) 26321.

GWENT COLLEGE OF HE
EMYLN STREET, NEWPORT,
GWENT NPT 1EU.
TEL: (0603) 63876.

HARROW COLLEGE OF HE
WATFORD ROAD,
NORTHWICK PARK, HARROW,
MIDDLESEX HA1 3TP.
TEL: 01-422 5206.

**HERTFORDSHIRE COLLEGE OF
HE**
WALL HALL, ALDENHAM,
NR WATFORD, HERTS WD2 8AT.
TEL: (092) 764158.

HUMBERSIDE COLLEGE OF HE
TIJA HOUSE, COTTINGHAM ROAD,
HULL, HUMBERSIDE HU6 9QG.
TEL: (0482) 43007.

KING ALFRED'S COLLEGE
SPARKFORD ROAD, WINCHESTER,
HAMPSHIRE, SO22 4NR.
TEL: (0962) 64507/53114.

LUTON COLLEGE OF HE
EUROPA HOUSE,
VICARAGE STREET,

LUTON, BEDFORDSHIRE LU1 3HZ.
TEL: (0582) 30035.

NENE COLLEGE OF HE
MOULTON PARK,
BOUGHTON GREEN ROAD,
NORTHAMPTON NN2 7AL.
TEL: (0604) 711697.

NEW COLLEGE DURHAM
NEW COLLEGE,
NEVILLES CROSS SITE,
NEVILLES CROSS,
DURHAM DH1 4SY.
TEL: (0385) 63272.

NORTH CHESHIRE COLLEGE
PADGATE CAMPUS, FEARNHEAD,
WARRINGTON, CHESHIRE
TEL: (0925) 821336.

**NORTH EAST WALES INSTITUTE
OF HE**
ASTON COLLEGE, MOLD ROAD,
WREXHAM, CLWYD.
TEL: (0978) 357319.

SLOUGH COLLEGE OF HE
WELLINGTON STREET,
SLOUGH SL1 1YG.
TEL: (0753) 22338.

**SOUTH GLAMORGAN INSTITUTE
OF HE**
HOWARD GARDENS SITE,
HOWARD GARDENS,
CARDIFF CF2 1SP.
TEL: (0222) 44291.

**TRINITY AND ALL SAINTS
COLLEGES**
BROWNBERRIE LANE,
HORSFORTH,
LEEDS LS13 5HD.
TEL: (0532) 585793.

**WEST LONDON INSTITUTE OF
HE**
BOROUGH ROAD SITE,
COLLEGE ROAD, ISLEWORTH,
MIDDLESEX.
TEL: 01-560 2984.

**WEST LONDON INSTITUTE OF
HE**
MARIA GREEN SITE,

300 ST MARGARET'S ROAD,
TWICKENHAM, MIDDLESEX.
TEL: 01-892 6085.

**WEST MIDLANDS COLLEGE OF
HE**
GORWAY ROAD, GORWAY,
WALSALL,
WEST MIDLANDS WS1 3BD.
TEL: (0922) 720781.

WHITELANDS COLLEGE
127 SUTHERLAND GROVE,
LONDON SW18.
TEL: 01-788 8268 ext. 5223.

WORCESTER COLLEGE OF HE
HENWICK GROVE, ST JOHNS,
WORCESTER WR2 6AJ.
TEL: (0905) 424788/427672/428080
ext. 272.

COLLEGES OF EDUCATION

**BRETTON HALL COLLEGE OF
EDUCATION**
WEST BRETTON, NR WAKEFIELD,
YORKSHIRE WF4 4LG.
TEL: (092) 485261.

CHRIST CHURCH COLLEGE
NORTH HOMES ROAD,
CANTERBURY, KENT CT1 1QU.
TEL: (0227) 52551.

**CRAIGIE COLLEGE OF
EDUCATION**
BREECH GROVE, AYR, SCOTLAND.
TEL: (0292) 68392.

**DE LA SALLE COLLEGE OF
EDUCATION**
HOPWOOD HALL, MIDDLETON,
MANCHESTER M24 3XH.
TEL: 061-6533679.

GARNET COLLEGE
MANRESA HOUSE,
HOLYBOURNE AVENUE,
ROEHAMPTON, LONDON SW15 4JF.
TEL: 01-788 2384.

ILKLEY COLLEGE
WELLS ROAD, ILKLEY,
WEST YORKSHIRE LS29 9RD.
TEL: (0943) 607768.

**LA SAINTE UNION COLLEGE OF
HE**
8 ARCHERS ROAD, SOUTHAMPTON
TEL: (0703) 226379.

**NORTH RIDING COLLEGE OF
EDUCATION**
FILEY ROAD, SCARBOROUGH,
NORTH YORKSHIRE YO11 3AZ.
TEL: (0723) 373864.

**SAINT MARTIN'S COLLEGE OF
HIGHER EDUCATION**
BOWEHAM ROAD, LANCASTER,
LANCASHIRE LA1 3JD.
TEL: (0524) 63446/65827 ext. 21.

SAINT MARY'S COLLEGE
STRAWBERRY HILL, TWICKENHAM,
MIDDLESEX TW1 4SX.
TEL: 01-892 0092.

WESTHILL COLLEGE
MELVILLE HALL,
14–16 WEDLEY PARK ROAD,
BIRMINGHAM, B29 6LT.
TEL: 021-472 7245 ext. 206.

ART COLLEGES

**BOURNEMOUTH AND POOLE
COLLEGE OF ART AND DESIGN**
WALLISDOWN ROAD,
WALLISDOWN, POOLE,
DORSET BH12 5BB.
TEL: (0202) 532873.

CANTERBURY COLLEGE OF ART
NEW DOVER ROAD,
CANTERBURY, KENT
TEL: (0227) 60463.

**PLYMOUTH COLLEGE OF ART
AND DESIGN**
STUDENTS ASSOCIATION,
TAVISTOCK PLACE,
PLYMOUTH PL4 8AT.
TEL: (0752) 264774.

WINCHESTER SCHOOL OF ART
PARK AVENUE, WINCHESTER,
HAMPSHIRE SO23 8DL.
TEL: (0962) 67028.

TAPE DUPLICATION

Most recording studios will duplicate. If not, ask them who they recommend in their area.

'COPY 2' TAPES
15 STOCKWELL STREET,
GLASGOW G1 4LR.
TEL: 041-552 0969.

GRAMPIAN RECORDS
AIRPORT INDUSTRIAL ESTATE,
WICK, CAITHNESS KW1 4QS.
TEL: (0955) 2787.

JAMES YORK LTD.
YORK HOUSE, CORPUS STREET,
CHELTENHAM,
GLOUCESTERSHIRE.
TEL: (0242) 584222.

LE-CAZ CHEOPS STUDIOS
'AVALON', 1 CYPRUS ROAD,
CAMBRIDGE.
TEL: (0223) 239889.

P.R.E. COMPLEX
ROPER STREET,
PAILLION INDUSTRIAL ESTATE,
SUNDERLAND.
TEL: 091-510 9292.

RAINHILL TAPE SPECIALISTS
MUSIC HOUSE,
369 WARRINGTON ROAD,
RAINHILL,
PRESCOT, MERSEYSIDE.
TEL: 051-430 9001.

SOLID BOND STUDIOS
GARDEN ENTRANCE,
STANHOPE HOUSE,
STANHOPE PLACE, LONDON W2.
TEL: 01-402 6121.

SOUND BASEMENT
10 AMWELL STREET,
LONDON EC1 R1UQ.
TEL: 01-278 4916.

TAPE DUPLICATING COMPANY
4–10 NORTH ROAD, ISLINGTON,
LONDON N7 9HN.
TEL: 01-609 0087.

TAPE ONE STUDIOS
29–30 WINDMILL STREET,
LONDON W1P 1HG.
TEL: 01-580 044.

THE DUPLICATION PLANT
14–16 TOWER CRESCENT,
NEATH HILL, MILTON KEYNES,
BUCKS. MK14 6HX.
TEL: (0908) 678712.

TELEVISION

We have not listed individual television programmes under this section because they change so regularly. If you are trying to contact the producers or researchers of a particular programme, then you should look in the TV Times or Radio Times to discover which television company is responsible. All the BBC and independent television companies are listed below. However, it is increasingly common to find that the conception and production of television shows is put out to tender, and there are a lot of independent programme makers who supply the programmes broadcast by the television networks. Their addresses are too numerous to list here – you will have to get this information from the TV stations.

BBC TELEVISION

BBC TELEVISION CENTRE
WOOD LANE, LONDON W12 7RJ.
TEL: 01-743 8000. FAX: 01-749 7520.

BBC NORTHERN IRELAND
BROADCASTING HOUSE,
25–27 ORMEAU AVENUE,
BELFAST BT2 BHQ.
TEL: (0232) 244400. FAX: 0232 322246.

BBC WALES
BROADCASTING HOUSE,
LLANTRISANT ROAD, LLANDAFF,
CARDIFF CF5 2YQ.
TEL: (0222) 564888. FAX: 0222 552973.

BBC SCOTLAND
BROADCASTING HOUSE,
QUEEN MARGARET DRIVE,
GLASGOW G12 8DG.
TEL: 041-339 8844. FAX: 041 3340614.

BBC ABERDEEN
BROADCASTING HOUSE,
BEECHGROVE TERRACE,
ABERDEEN AB9 2ZT.
TEL: (0224) 62533. FAX: 0224 642931.

BBC BANGOR
BROADCASTING HOUSE,
BRYN MEIRION ROAD, BANGOR
GWYNEDD LL57 2BY.
TEL: (0248) 362214. FAX: 0248 352784.

BBC BREAKFAST TIME
BBC TV CENTRE, WOOD LANE,
LONDON W17 7RJ.
TEL: 01-743 8000. FAX. 01-749 7872.

BBC DUNDEE
12–13 DOCK STREET,
DUNDEE DD1 4BT.
TEL: (0382) 25025.

BBC EDINBURGH
BROADCASTING HOUSE,
27–35 THISTLE STREET,
EDINBURGH EH2 1DH.
TEL: 031-225 3131. FAX: 031-225 7708.

BBC EAST MIDLANDS
WILSON HOUSE, 25 DERBY ROAD,
NOTTINGHAM NG1 5AX.
TEL: (0602) 472395.

BBC MIDLANDS
BROADCASTING CENTRE,
PEBBLE MILL ROAD,
BIRMINGHAM B5 7QQ.
TEL: 021-472 5353. FAX: 021-471 2814.

BBC NORTH
BROADCASTING CENTRE,
WOODHOUSE LANE, LEEDS
LS2 9PX.
TEL: (0532) 441188. FAX: 0532 439387.

BBC NORTH EAST
BROADCASTING HOUSE,
54 NEW BRIDGE STREET,
NEWCASTLE-UPON-TYNE NE1 8AA.
TEL: 091 232 1313. FAX: 091-232 5082.

BBC NORTH WEST
NEW BROADCASTING HOUSE,
OXFORD ROAD,
MANCHESTER M60 1SJ.
TEL: 061-236 8444. FAX: 061-236 1005.

BBC SOUTH
SOUTH WESTERN HOUSE,
CANUTE ROAD,
SOUTHAMPTON SO9 1PF.
TEL: (0703) 226201. FAX: 0703 330931.

BBC SOUTH WEST
BROADCASTING HOUSE,
SEYMOUR ROAD, MANNAMEAD,
PLYMOUTH PL3 5BD.
TEL: (0752) 229201. FAX: 0752 222058.

BBC SWANSEA
32 ALEXANDRA ROAD,
SWANSEA SA1 5DZ.
TEL: (0792) 54986. FAX: 0792 468194.

BBC WEST
BROADCASTING HOUSE,
21–33 WHITELADIES ROAD,
CLIFTON, BRISTOL BS8 2LR.
TEL: (0272) 732211. FAX: 0272 744114.

THE INDEPENDENT TELEVISION PROGRAMME COMPANIES

ANGLIA TELEVISION
ANGLIA HOUSE,
NORWICH NR1 3JG.
TEL: (0603) 615151. FAX: 0603 63132.

REGIONAL NEWS CENTRES:
Chelmsford (0245) 357676; Ipswich
(0473) 226157; Luton (0582) 29666;
Peterborough (0733) 46677 and
Northampton (0604) 24343.

BORDER TELEVISION
TELEVISION CENTRE,
CARLISLE CA1 3NT.
TEL: (0228) 25101.
18 CLERKENWELL CLOSE,
LONDON EC1R 0AA.
TEL: 01-253 3737. FAX: 01-490 0717.

CENTRAL INDEPENDENT TELEVISION
WEST MIDLANDS:
CENTRAL HOUSE, BROAD STREET,
BIRMINGHAM B1 2JP.
TEL: 021-643 9898.
EAST MIDLANDS TELEVISION
CENTRE, LENTON LANE,
NOTTINGHAM NG7 2NA.
TEL: (0602) 863322.

CHANNEL 4
CHANNEL 4 TELEVISION COMPANY
LIMITED,
60 CHARLOTTE STREET,
LONDON W1P 2AX.
TEL: 01-631 4444. FAX: 01-637 4872.
The IBA's wholly-owned subsidiary
provides the Fourth Channels
programme service throughout the UK
(except Wales).
TEL: 01-631 444.
In Wales the IBA transmits the S4C
programme service (Sianel Tedwar
Cymru) provided by the
WELSH FOURTH CHANNEL
AUTHORITY,
CLOS SOPHIA, CAERDYDD
(CARDIFF) CF1 9XY.
TEL: (0222) 43421.

CHANNEL TELEVISION
THE TELEVISION CENTRE,
ST. HELIER, JERSEY,
CHANNEL ISLANDS.
TEL: (0534) 73999. FAX: 0534 59446.
THE TELEVISION CENTRE,
ST. GEORGE'S PLACE,
ST. PETER PORT, GUERNSEY,
CHANNEL ISLANDS.
TEL: (0481) 23451.

GRAMPIAN TELEVISON
QUEEN'S CROSS,
ABERDEEN AB9 2XJ.
TEL: (0224) 646464. FAX: 0224 635127.
ALBANY HOUSE,
68 ALBANY ROAD,
WEST FERRY, DUNDEE DD5 1NW.
TEL: (0382) 739363.
23/25 HUNTLY STREET
INVERNESS IV3 5PR.
TEL: (0463) 242624. FAX: 0463 223637.

GRANADA TELEVISION
GRANADA TV LTD.,
MANCHESTER M60 9EA.
TEL: 061-832 7211. Ring for FAX
details.
ALBERT DOCK (GRANADA
REPORTS), LIVERPOOL L3 4BA.
TEL: 051-709 9393. FAX: 051 709 9393.
36 GOLDEN SQUARE,
LONDON W1R 4AH.
TEL: 01-734 8080.
WHITE CROSS,
LANCASTER LA1 4XQ.
TEL: (0524) 60688.
5 BRIDGE PLACE,
LOWER BRIDGE STREET,
CHESTER CH1 15A.
TEL: (0244) 313966.

HTV
HTV WALES, TELEVISION CENTRE,
CULVERHOUSE CROSS,
CARDIFF CF5 6XJ.
TEL: (0222) 590590. FAX: 0222 590325.
HTV WEST, TELEVISION CENTRE,
BATH ROAD, BRISTOL BS4 3HG.
TEL: (0272) 778366.
FAX: 0272 723122.

LONDON WEEKEND TELEVISION
SOUTH BANK TELEVISION CENTRE,
KENT HOUSE, UPPER GROUND,
LONDON SE1 9LT.
TEL: 01-261 3434. FAX: 01-928 6941.

SCOTTISH TELEVISION
COWCADDENS, GLASGOW G2 3PR.
TEL: 041-332 9999. FAX: 041 332 6982.
THE GATEWAY, ELM ROW,
EDINBURGH EH7 4AH.
TEL: 031-557 4554.

THAMES TELEVISION
THAMES TELEVISION HOUSE,
306–316 EUSTON ROAD,
LONDON NW1 3BB.
TEL: 01-387 9494. FAX: 01-388 7253.
149 TOTTENHAM COURT ROAD,
LONDON W1P 9LL.
TEL: 01-387 9494.

TV-AM
BREAKFAST TELEVISION CENTRE,
HAWLEY CRESCENT,
CAMDEN LOCK, LONDON NW1 8EF.
TV-AM provides ITV's breakfast-time
television service, primarily of news
information and current affairs.
TEL: 01-267 4300. FAX: 01-267 6513.

TSW TELEVISION SOUTH WEST
DERRY'S CROSS,
PLYMOUTH PL1 2SP.
TEL: (0752) 663322. FAX: 0752 671970.

TVS TELEVISION SOUTH
TELEVISION CENTRE,
SOUTHAMPTON SO9 5HZ.
TEL: (0703) 634211. FAX: 0703 83409.
TELEVISION CENTRE,
VINTERS PARK,
MAIDSTONE, KENT ME14 5NZ.
TEL: (0622) 54945. FAX: 0622 684446.

TYNE TEES TELEVISION
THE TELEVISION CENTRE,
CITY ROAD,
NEWCASTLE-UPON-TYNE NE1 2AL.
TEL: 091-261 0181. FAX: 091-261 2302.
CORPORATION HOUSE,
CORPORATION ROAD,
MIDDLESBROUGH TS1 2RX.
TEL: (0642) 219181. FAX: 0642 249961.
UNITED HOUSE,
PICCADILLY, YORK YO1 1PQ.
TEL: (0904) 647012. FAX: 0904 610236.

ULSTER TELEVISION
HAVELOCK HOUSE,
ORMEAU ROAD,
BELFAST BT7 1EB.
TEL: (0232) 328122. FAX: 0232 246695.

YORKSHIRE TELEVISION
THE TELEVISION CENTRE,
LEEDS LS3 1JS.
TEL: (0532) 438283. FAX: 0532 445107.

INDEPENDENT TELEVISION NEWS
ITN HOUSE, 48 WELLS STREET,
LONDON W1P 4DE.
Provides the national and international
news programmes for all ITV areas.
TEL: 01-637 2424. FAX: 01-636 0399.

INDEPENDENT TELEVISION COMPANIES ASSOCIATION LIMITED
KNIGHTON HOUSE,
56 MORTIMER STREET,
LONDON W1N 8AN.
The trade association of the ITV
companies.
TEL: 01-636 6866.

INDEPENDENT TELEVISION PUBLICATIONS LTD
247 TOTTENHAM COURT ROAD,
LONDON W1P 0AU.
Owned jointly by the fifteen ITV
companies operating in Great Britain
and Northern Ireland. It publishes TV
Times and Look-In.
TEL: 01-323 3222.

ORACLE TELETEXT LTD.
CRAVEN HOUSE,
25–32 MARSHALL STREET,
LONDON W1V 1LL.
Oracle provides the teletext service for
ITV and Channel 4 and is owned jointly
by all the ITV companies operating in
Britain. Oracle broadcasts weather
information, TV guides and a What's On
guide for each ITV area.
TEL: 01-434 3121. FAX: 01-439 8974.

OTHER

MUSIC BOX
19–21 RATHBONE PLACE,
LONDON W1P 1DF.
TEL: 01-636 7888. FAX: 01-323 1549.

SKY CHANNEL
31–36 FOLEY STREET,
LONDON W1P 7LB.
TEL: 01-636 4077. FAX: 01-499 1656.

VENUES

We compiled this list with the help of a well known agent. Where we came across venues that we know to be run by particularly unreliable or unpleasant people, we have left them out. At the same time, however, there are probably a lot of excellent small pub and club venues of which we are unaware.

We have listed the London venues separately. Again, this is not a comprehensive list and there may be a number of pubs and small club gigs which we have overlooked. In common with the other major cities, London has 'What's On' magazines which include lists of venue addresses and telephone numbers in their gig listings every week.

Please let us know of any good small venues you come across and tell us of any bad experiences.

Key: To help you avoid approaching totally inappropriate venues we have given a rough guide as to their capacity. **V1** = mega size venue of 4,000 capacity upwards, **V2** = Concert Hall size venues which can be from 1,000 capacity upwards. **V3** = the kind of venue you may be able to approach without an agent. V3 venues range in capacity from 100 to 1,000 and are usually pubs and clubs.

LONDON

AFRICA CENTRE (V3)
38 KING STREET, LONDON WC2,
TEL: 01-836 1973.

ALBANY EMPIRE (V2)
DOUGLAS WAY,
LONDON SE8 4AG,
TEL: 01-691 8016.

ARCHWAY TAVERN (V3)
1 ARCHWAY CLOSE, LONDON N19,
TEL: 01-272 2840.

BASS CLEF (V3)
35 CORONET STREET,
HOXTON SQUARE, LONDON N1,
TEL: 01-729 2476.

BOSTON ARMS (V3)
178 JUNCTION ROAD, LONDON N19.
TEL: 01-272 3411.

BRAHMS & LISZT (V3)
19 RUSSELL STREET,
LONDON WC2.
TEL: 01-240 3661.

BREAK FOR THE BORDER (V3)
GOSLETT YARD,
127 CHARING CROSS ROAD,
LONDON WC2.
TEL: 01-437 8595.

BRIXTON ACADEMY (V1)
221 STOCKWELL ROAD,
LONDON SW9.
TEL: 01-274 1525.

BULL & GATE (V3)
389 KENTISH TOWN ROAD,
LONDON NW5.
TEL: 01-485 5358.

BUSBY'S (V3)
157 TOTTENHAM COURT ROAD,
LONDON W1.
TEL: 01-734 6963.

CAMDEN PALACE (V2)
1a CAMDEN HIGH STREET,
LONDON NW1.
TEL: 01-387 0428.

CORONET (V3)
LAVENDER GARDENS,
LONDON SW11.
TEL: 01-228 3744.

CRICKETERS (V3)
THE OVAL, LONDON SE11.
TEL: 01-735 3059.

CRYPT (V3)
ST PAUL'S CHURCH,
DEPTFORD HIGH STREET,
LONDON SE8.
TEL: 01-302 0815.

DINGWALLS (V3)
CAMDEN LOCK,
CHALK FARM ROAD,
CAMDEN TOWN,
LONDON NW1.
TEL: 01-267 4967.

DOMINION (V2)
TOTTENHAM COURT ROAD,
LONDON W1P 0AG.
TEL: 01-636 2295.

DUBLIN CASTLE (V3)
94 PARKWAY, CAMDEN TOWN,
LONDON NW1.
TEL: 01-485 1773.

EARLS COURT (V1)
WARWICK ROAD,
LONDON SW5 9TA.
TEL: 01-381 4255.

ELECTRIC BALLROOM (V2)
184 CAMDEN HIGH STREET,
LONDON NW1.
TEL: 01-485 9006.

EMPIRE BALLROOM (V2)
LEICESTER SQUARE,
LONDON WC2.
TEL: 01-437 1446.

EMPIRE SUITE (V3)
161 TOTTENHAM COURT ROAD,
LONDON W1.
TEL: 01-380 0731.

FRIDGE (V2)
TOWN HALL PARADE,
BRIXTON HILL,
LONDON SW2.
TEL: 01-326 5100.

GOSSIPS (V3)
69 DEAN STREET,
LONDON W1.
TEL: 01-434 4480.

GREYHOUND (V3)
175 FULHAM PALACE ROAD,
LONDON W6 8QT.
TEL: 01-385 0526..

HACKNEY EMPIRE (V2)
291 MARE STREET,
LONDON E8.
TEL: 01-985 2424.

HALF MOON (V3)
19 HALF MOON LANE,
HERNE HILL, LONDON SE24.
TEL: 01-274 2733.

HALF MOON (V3)
93 LOWER RICHMOND ROAD,
PUTNEY, LONDON SW15.
TEL: 01-788 2387.

HAMMERSMITH ODEON (V2)
QUEEN CAROLINE STREET,
HAMMERSMITH, LONDON W6 2PU.
TEL: 01-748 4081.

HAMMERSMITH PALAIS (V2)
242 SHEPHERD'S BUSH ROAD,
LONDON W6.
TEL: 01-748 2812.

HAMMERSMITH TOWN HALL (V2)
KING STREET,
HAMMERSMITH, LONDON W6.
TEL: 01-748 3020.

HEAVEN (V3)
UNDER THE ARCHES,
VILLIERS ROAD,
CHARING CROSS, LONDON WC1.
TEL: 01-839 3852.

HIPPODROME (V2)
LEICESTER SQUARE,
LONDON WC2.
TEL: 01-437 4311.

ICA (V3)
NASH HOUSE,
CARLTON TERRACE, THE MALL,
LONDON SW1.
TEL: 01-930 0493.

David McComb of the Australian band the Triffids at the ICA, London 1986.

KING'S HEAD (V3)
4 FULHAM HIGH STREET,
LONDON SW6.
TEL: 01-736 1413.

**LE PALAIS –
SEE HAMMERSMITH PALAIS.**

LIMELIGHT (V3)
136 SHAFTESBURY AVENUE,
LONDON W1.
TEL: 01-434 1761.

MARQUEE (V3)
105 CHARING CROSS ROAD,
LONDON W1.
TEL: 01-437 6603.

MEAN FIDDLER (V3)
28a HARLESDEN HIGH STREET,
LONDON NW10.
TEL: 01-961 5490.

100 CLUB (V3)
100 OXFORD STREET, LONDON W1.
TEL: 01-636 0933.

PIZZA EXPRESS (V3)
10 DEAN STREET, LONDON W1.
TEL: 01-439 8722.

POWERHAUS (V3)
1 LIVERPOOL ROAD, ISLINGTON,
LONDON N1
TEL: 01-961 5490.

QUEEN ELIZABETH HALL (V2)
SOUTH BANK, LONDON SE1.
TEL: 01-928 3191.

RIVERSIDE STUDIOS (V3)
CRISP ROAD, HAMMERSMITH,
LONDON.
TEL: 01-741 2251.

ROCK GARDEN (V3)
THE PIAZZA, COVENT GARDEN,
LONDON WC2.
TEL: 01-240 3961.

RONNIE SCOTTS (V3)
47 FRITH STREET, LONDON W1.
TEL: 01-439 0747.

ROYAL ALBERT HALL (V2)
KENSINGTON GORE, LONDON SW7.
TEL: 01-589 8212.

ROYAL FESTIVAL HALL (V2)
SOUTH BANK, LONDON SE1.
TEL: 01-928 3002.

SADLERS WELLS (V2)
ROSEBERY AVENUE, LONDON EC1.
TEL: 01-278 8916.

SIR GEORGE ROBEY (V3)
240 SEVEN SISTERS ROAD,
LONDON N4.
TEL: 01-263 1226.

SUBTERANIA (V3)
12 ACKLAND ROAD, LONDON W10.
TEL: 01-961 5490.

TABERNACLE (V3)
POWIS SQUARE, LONDON W11 2AY.
TEL: 01-221 5172.

TOWN & COUNTRY CLUB (V2)
9-17 HIGHGATE ROAD,
KENTISH TOWN, LONDON NW5 1JY.
TEL: BOX OFFICE 01-284 0303,
CREDIT CARD BOOKINGS 01-284 1221
MANAGEMENT 01-485 5256.

T&C 2 (V3)
20-22 HIGHBURY CORNER,
ISLINGTON, LONDON N7.
TEL: 01-700 5716.
MANAGEMENT (AS T&C 1) 01-485 5256

TRAMSHED (V3)
51 WOOLWICH NEW ROAD,
LONDON SE18.
TEL: 01-855 3371.

TUNNEL CLUB (V3)
THE MITRE, 338 TUNNEL AVENUE,
GREENWICH, LONDON SE10.
TEL: 01-858 0895.

WAG CLUB (V3)
35–37 WARDOUR STREET,
LONDON W1.
TEL: 01-437 5534.

**WALTHAMSTOW ASSEMBLY
HALL (V2)**
TOWN HALL COMPLEX,
FOREST ROAD, LONDON E17.
TEL: 01-521 7111.

The Pixies

Stage diving for beginners

REGIONAL VENUES

ADELPHI CLUB (V3)
89 DE GREY STREET,
HULL HU5 2RY.
TEL: (0482) 48216.

ARCHERY (V3)
346 SEASIDE, EASTBOURNE,
EAST SUSSEX BN21.
TEL: (0323) 22069.

ASSEMBLY ROOMS (V2)
MARKET SQUARE, DERBY DE1 3AH.
TEL: (0332) 31111.

ASTORIA (V3 - TWO VENUES)
339 ROUNDHAY ROAD,
LEEDS LS8 4HT.
TEL: (0532) 490362.

BAND ON THE WALL (V3)
25 SWAN STREET,
MANCHESTER M4 5JQ.
TEL: 061-832 6625.

BAR LUXEMBOURG (V3)
197 PITT STREET, GLASGOW.
TEL: 041-332 1111.

BARREL ORGAN (V3)
57 DIGBETH, BIRMINGHAM B5.
TEL: 021-622 1353.

BARROWLAND BALLROOM (V2)
266 GALLOWGATE, GLASGOW.
TEL: 041-522 4601.

**BISHOP GROSSETESTE
COLLEGE (V3)**
NEWPORT, LINCOLN.
TEL: (0522) 27347.

BLACKFRIARS (V3)
36 BELL STREET, GLASGOW.
TEL: 041-552 5924.

BOARDWALK (V3)
LITTLE PETER STREET,
MANCHESTER M15.
TEL: 061-228 3555.

BOWES LYON HOUSE (V3)
ST GEORGE'S WAY, STEVENAGE,
HERTFORDSHIRE.
TEL: (0438) 353175.

BRIGHTON CENTRE (V2)
KING'S ROAD, BRIGHTON,
SUSSEX BN1 2GR.
TEL: (0273) 203131.

BRISTOL STUDIO (V2)
MECCA LEISURE,
FROGMORE STREET,
BRISTOL BS1 5NA.
TEL: (0272) 276193.

**BROKEN DOLL (V3 – TWO
VENUES)**
85 BLENHEIM STREET,
NEWCASTLE-UPON-TYNE.
TEL: 091-232 1047.

BRUNEL ROOMS (V3)
HAVELOCK SQUARE, SWINDON,
WILTS.
TEL: (0793) 31384.

BURBERRIES (V3)
BROAD STREET, BIRMINGHAM B15.
TEL: 021-643 1500.

BUTTERMARKET (V3)
HOWARD STREET,
SHREWSBURY SY1 2LF.
TEL: (0743) 241455.

CALTON STUDIOS (V2)
22–26 CALTON ROAD, EDINBURGH.
TEL: 031-556 7066.

CANNY MAN'S (V3)
237 MORNINGSIDE ROAD,
EDINBURGH.
TEL: 031-447 1484.

The Proclaimers Exeter University, 1987.

An early Julia Fordham gig at Ronnie Scott's, London in April 1988.

The Stray Cats reunited at the Town & Country Club, March 1989. Slim Jim Phantom, Brian Setzer and Lee Rocker at the end of the second sold out show.

CARNEGIE HALL (V3)
FINKLE STREET, WORKINGTON,
CUMBRIA.
TEL: (0900) 2122.

CARTOON (V3)
179/181 LONDON ROAD, CROYDON.
TEL: 01-688 4500.

CAVERN (V3)
COWGATE, EDINBURGH.
TEL: 031-229 5661.

CHAMPAGNES (V3)
CARFAX, HORSHAM, SUSSEX.
TEL: (0403) 66914.

CHERRY TREE (V3)
LINK WAY, RUNCORN, CHESHIRE.
TEL: (09285) 74171.

**CINDERELLA ROCKERFELLA'S
(V3)**
BRUTON WAY, GLOUCESTER GL1.
TEL: (0452) 305203.

CITY HALL (V2)
BARKERS PEEL,
SHEFFIELD S1 2HB.
TEL: (0742) 734550.

CIVIC HALL (V2)
DIGBETH, BIRMINGHAM B5 6DY.
TEL: 021-235 2434.

CIVIC HALL (V2)
MILLMEAD HOUSE, MILLMEAD,
GUILDFORD, SURREY GU15 3SY.
TEL: (0483) 505050.

COASTERS (V3 AND V2)
3 WEST TOLL CROSS, EDINBURGH.
TEL: 031-228 3252.

COLISSEUM (V2)
CARLYON BAY, ST AUSTELL,
CORNWALL PL25 3RG.
TEL: (072681) 4261.

COLSTON HALL (V2)
COLSTON AVENUE,
BRISTOL BS1 5AR.
TEL: (0272) 291768.

CONFETTI'S (V2)
BABBINGTON LANE,
DERBY DE1 1TD.
TEL: (0332) 41441.

CORN DOLLY (V3)
CORNMARKET STREET, OXFORD.
TEL: (0865) 44761.

CORN EXCHANGE (V2)
WHEELER STREET,
CAMBRIDGE CB2 3QB.
TEL: (0223) 358977.

THE COTTON CLUB (V3)
5–7 SCOTT STREET, GLASGOW.
TEL: 041-332 0712.

CRYPT (V3)
CAMBRIDGE ROAD, HASTINGS,
EAST SUSSEX:
TEL: (0424) 444675.

DARLINGTON ARTS CENTRE (V3)
VANE TERRACE,
DARLINGTON DL3 7AX.
TEL: (0325) 483271.

DE MONTFORT HALL (V2)
GRANVILLE ROAD, LEICESTER.
TEL: (0533) 549922.

DIVISION ONE (V3)
WELLHEAD INN, HAYLE ROAD,
WENDOVER, BUCKS.
TEL: (0296) 622733.

DOG & TRUMPET (V3)
HERTFORD STREET,
COVENTRY CV1 5FJ.
TEL: (0303) 216778.

DOME (V2)
29 NEW ROAD, BRIGHTON,
SUSSEX BN1 1UG.
TEL: (0273) 685097.

DOVECOT ARTS CENTRE (V3)
DOVECOT STREET,
STOCKTON-ON-TEES,
CLEVELAND TS18 1LL.
TEL: (0642) 611625.

DUCHESS OF YORK (V3)
VICAR LANE, LEEDS LS1.
TEL: (0532) 453929.

EDEN (V3)
19 GREYHOUND STREET,
NOTTINGHAM.
TEL: (0602) 501251.

FAIRFIELD HALLS (V3)
PARK LANE, CROYDON, SURREY.
TEL: 01-681 0821.

FAT SAM'S (V3)
31 SOUTHWARD ROAD,
DUNDEE DD1 1PY.
TEL: (0382) 28181.

THE FIXX (V3)
86 MILLER STREET, GLASGOW.
TEL: 041-248 2859.

THE FLAG (V3)
86 EAST LANE, NORTH WEMBLEY,
MIDDLESEX HA0 3NJ.
TEL: 01-450 4506.

FLEECE AND FIRKIN (V3)
12 ST THOMAS STREET, BRISTOL.
TEL: (0272) 277150.

FROG AND BUCKET (V3)
COOPER'S CORNER, IDE HILL,
KENT.
TEL: (0732) 75219.

FRONT PAGE CLUB (V3)
4-8 FISHER STREET, CARLISLE.
TEL: (0228) 34168.

FURY MURRY'S (V3)
96 MAXWELL STREET,
GLASGOW G1.
TEL: 041-221 6511

GARDNER ARTS CENTRE (V3)
FALMER, SUSSEX BN1,
(PART OF UNIV. OF SUSSEX)
TEL: (0273) 685447.

GENERAL WOLF (V3)
551 FOLESHILL ROAD,
COVENTRY CV6.
TEL: (0203) 688402.

GOLDIGGERS (V2)
TIMBER STREET,
CHIPPENHAM,
WILTSHIRE SN15 3BP.
TEL: (0249) 656444.

GREY HORSE (V3)
46 RICHMOND ROAD,
KINGSTON,
SURREY KT2.
TEL: 01-546 4818.

GUILDHALL (V3)
GUILDHALL SQUARE,
PORTSMOUTH.
TEL: (0705) 834146.

GUILDHALL (V2)
CIVIC CENTRE,
SOUTHAMPTON SD1 4XF.
TEL: (0703) 223855.

HACIENDA (V2)
11–13 WHITWORTH STREET WEST,
MANCHESTER.
TEL: 061-236 5051.

THE HALT BAR (V3)
160 WOODLANDS ROAD,
GLASGOW.
TEL: 041-332 1210.

**HAYMARKET STUDIO THEATRE
(V3)**
BELGRAVE GATE,
LEICESTER LE1 3YD.
TEL: (0533) 530021.

HEATH INN (V3)
FOLESHILL ROAD,
COVENTRY CV6.
TEL: 021-550 8601.

HIPPODROME (V2)
HURST STREET,
BIRMINGHAM B5 4TB.
TEL: 021-622 7437.

HIPPODROME (V2)
ST AUGUSTINE'S PARADE,
BRISTOL BS1 4UZ.
TEL: (0272) 265524.

HUMMINGBIRD (V2)
DALE END,
BIRMINGHAM B4 7LS.
TEL: 021-236 4236.

Mike Scott from the Waterboys at Portsmouth Guildhall, February 1989.

IMAGES ON GLASS (V3)
THE BUTTS, WORCESTER.
TEL: (0905) 21005.

INTERNATIONAL ONE (V3)
47 ANSON ROAD, RUSHOLME,
MANCHESTER M14.
TEL: 061-224 5050.

INTERNATIONAL TWO (V3)
210 PLYMOUTH GROVE,
LONGSIGHT, MANCHESTER.
TEL: 061-224 2655.

IRISH CENTRE (V2)
YORK ROAD,
LEEDS LS9.
TEL: (0532) 480613.

**IRISH CENTRE – DIAMOND
SUITE (V3)**
12–14 HIGH STREET, DERRIT END,
BIRMINGHAM B12 0LM.
TEL: 021-622 2314.

**JAMES BURTON FREEHOUSE
(V3)**
42 MARINA,
ST. LEONARDS-ON-SEA,
SUSSEX TN38.
TEL: (0424) 422705.

JB'S (V3)
KING STREET, DUDLEY,
BIRMINGHAM.
TEL: (0384) 53597.

JOINER'S ARMS (V3)
141 ST MARY STREET,
SOUTHAMPTON SO1 1NS.
TEL: (0703) 225612.

KALEIDOSCOPE (V3)
HILL STREET, BIRMINGHAM B5.
TEL: 021-550 8601.

KOOL KAT (V3)
41 ST MARY'S GATE,
LACEMARKET,
NOTTINGHAM.
TEL: (0602) 474290.

LA TANIERE (V3)
15 FOX STREET, GLASGOW.
TEL: 041-221 4844.

LEADMILL (V3)
6–7 LEADMILL ROAD,
SHEFFIELD S1 4FF.
TEL: (0742) 754500.

LEAS CLIFF HALL (V2)
THE LEAS, FOLKESTONE,
KENT CT20 2QZ.
TEL: (0303) 54695.

LEGENDS (V2)
PRIORY STREET,
WARRINGTON WA4 6PZ.
TEL: (0925) 36658.

LIMIT (V3)
70–82 WEST STREET,
SHEFFIELD S1.
TEL: (0742) 730940.

LORD DARNLEY (V3)
WEST PORT, EDINBURGH
TEL: 031-229 4341.

MAJESTIC (V2)
59 CAVERSHAM ROAD, READING,
BERKSHIRE.
TEL: (0734) 586093.

MARDI GRAS (V3)
REGINA HOUSE,
QUEENS BRIDGE ROAD,
NOTTINGHAM NG2 1NB.
TEL: (0602) 862 368.

MAYFAIR (V3)
490 SAUCHIEHALL STREET,
GLASGOW G1 4EK.
TEL: 041-332 3872.

MAYFAIR (V2)
COURT ROAD,
SOUTHAMPTON SO1 2JR.
TEL: (0703) 226080.

MECHANICS (V3)
MANCHESTER ROAD, BURNLEY,
LANCASHIRE BBL 1JA.
TEL: (0282) 30005.

MOLES CLUB (V3)
14 GEORGE STREET,
BATH BA1 2EN.
TEL: (0225) 333448.

MOON CLUB (V3)
6 UPPER YORK STREET,
BRISTOL BS2 8QE.
TEL: (0272) 427727.

MOSELEY DANCE CENTRE (V2)
MOSELEY ROAD,
BIRMINGHAM B12.
TEL: 021-449 0779.

**NEC (NATIONAL EXHIBITION
CENTRE, BIRMINGHAM) (V1)**
BIRMINGHAM B40 1PP.
TEL: 021-780 4141.

NEGOCIANTS (V3)
45–47 LOTHIAN STREET,
EDINBURGH EH1 1HB.
TEL: 031-225 6313.

NEW THEATRE ROYAL (V3)
GUILDHALL ROAD,
PORTSMOUTH PO1 2DD.
TEL: (0705) 823729.

ODDFELLOWS (V3)
14 FORREST ROAD, EDINBURGH.
TEL: 031-220 1816.

OLD VIC (V3)
SHIP STREET, BRIGHTON.
TEL: (0273) 24744.

PARR HALL (V2)
PALMYRA SQUARE SOUTH,
WARRINGTON, CHESHIRE WA1 1BL.
TEL: (0925) 34958.

PIER PAVILION
PIER, HASTINGS, EAST SUSSEX.
TEL: (0424) 424912.

PINK TOOTHBRUSH (V3)
19–23 HIGH STREET, RAYLEIGH,
ESSEX.
TEL: (0268) 770003.

PLAYHOUSE (V1)
GREENSIDE PLACE,
EDINBURGH EH1 3JD.
TEL: 031-557 2590.

PLEASURE DOME (V2)
HENRY STREET, BIRKENHEAD,
MERSEYSIDE L41 5SW.
TEL: 051-647 6631.

PORTERHOUSE (V3)
20 CAROLGATE, RETFORD, NOTTS.
TEL: (0777) 704981.

PORTLAND (V3)
100 ICKFIELD PORT ROAD,
EDGBASTON, BIRMINGHAM.
TEL: 021-454 8960.

PRESERVATION HALL (V3)
9 VICTORIA STREET, EDINBURGH.
TEL: 031-226 3816.

PRINCESS CHARLOTTE (V3)
8 OXFORD STREET, LEICESTER.
TEL: (0533) 553956.

POWERHOUSE (V2)
HURST STREET,
BIRMINGHAM B5 4HE.
TEL: 021-643 4715.

QUEENS HALL (V2)
CLERK STREET,
EDINBURGH EH8 97G.
TEL: 031-668 2019.

RED LION (V3)
CRETE HALL ROAD, NORTHFLEET,
KENT DA11 9AA.
TEL: (0474) 66127.

RED LION (V3)
318 HIGH STREET, BRENTFORD,
MIDDLESEX.
TEL: 01-560 6181.

THE REVUE (V3)
244 GALLOWGATE,
GLASGOW G4 0TS.
TEL: 041-552 4601.

THE RICHMOND (V3)
33 RICHMOND PLACE, BRIGHTON.
TEL: (0273) 603974.

RIVERSIDE (V3)
57–59 MELBOURNE STREET,
NEWCASTLE-UPON-TYNE NE1 2JQ.
TEL: 091-261 4386.

ROCK CITY (V2)
8 TALBOT STREET,
NOTTINGHAM NG1 5GG.
TEL: (0602) 412544.

ROCK HOUSE (V3)
BABBINGTON LANE, DERBY.
TEL: (0332) 41154.

ROOFTOPS (V3)
92 SAUCHIEHALL STREET,
GLASGOW G1.
TEL: 041-332 5883.

ROYAL COURT (V2)
1 ROE STREET, LIVERPOOL.
TEL: 051-709 4321.

ROYAL STANDARD (V3)
COLDHARBOUR LANE, HAYES,
MIDDLESEX.
TEL: 01-573 0240.

SALISBURY ARTS CENTRE (V3)
BEDWIN STREET, SALISBURY,
WILTSHIRE SP1 3UT.
TEL: (0722) 21744.

**SCOTTISH EXHIBITION CENTRE
(V1)**
46 FINNIESTON, GLASGOW G3 8YW.
TEL: 041-248 3000.

SHELLEY'S (V3)
EDENSOR ROAD, LONGTON,
STOKE-ON-TRENT.
TEL: (0782) 322209.

SHELLEY ARMS (V3)
NUTLEY, SUSSEX
TEL: (0825) 713121

SOUTHAMPTON GUILDHALL (V2)
CIVIC CENTRE,
WEST MARLANDS ROAD,
SOUTHAMPTON.
TEL: (0703) 832453.

THE SQUARE (V3)
FOURTH AVENUE, HARLOW,
ESSEX.
TEL: (0279) 25594.

STAIRWAY CLUB (V3)
28 OLIVER STREET EAST,
BIRKENHEAD, MERSEYSIDE.
TEL: 051-647 6544.

STARS & STRIPES (V3)
143 BOTCHER GATE,
CARLISLE CK1 1RZ.
TEL: (0228) 46361.